EATCS
Monographs on Theoretical Computer Science

Editors: W. Brauer G. Rozenberg A. Salomaa

Kurt Mehlhorn

Data Structures and Algorithms 1:
Sorting and Searching

With 87 Figures

Springer-Verlag
Berlin Heidelberg New York Tokyo 1984

Editors

Prof. Dr. Wilfried Brauer
FB Informatik der Universität
Rothenbaum-Chausee 67–69, 2000 Hamburg 13, Germany

Prof. Dr. Grzegorz Rozenberg
Institut of Applied Mathematics and Computer Science
University of Leiden, Wassenaarseweg 80, P. O. Box 9512
2300 RA Leiden, The Netherlands

Prof. Dr. Arto Salomaa
Department of Mathematics, University of Turku
20500 Turku 50, Finland

Author

Prof. Dr. Kurt Mehlhorn
FB 10, Angewandte Mathematik und Informatik
Universität des Saarlandes, 6600 Saarbrücken, Germany

With the permission of B. G. Teubner publishers, Stuttgart,
arranged, solely authorized and revised English translation of the original
German edition: Effiziente Allgorithmen (1977)

ISBN-13:978-3-642-69674-9   e-ISBN-13:978-3-642-69672-5
DOI: 10.1007/978-3-642-69672-5

2145/3140-543210

For Ena, Uli, Steffi, and Tim

Preface

The design and analysis of data structures and efficient algorithms has gained considerable importance in recent years. The concept of "algorithm" is central in computer science, and "efficiency" is central in the world of money.

I have organized the material in three volumes and nine chapters.

Vol. 1: Sorting and Searching (chapters I to III)

Vol. 2: Graph Algorithms and NP-completeness (chapters IV to VI)

Vol. 3: Multi-dimensional Searching and Computational Geometry (chapters VII and VIII)

Volumes 2 and 3 have volume 1 as a common basis but are independent from each other. Most of volumes 2 and 3 can be understood without knowing volume 1 in detail. A general kowledge of algorithmic principles as laid out in chapter 1 or in many other books on algorithms and data structures suffices for most parts of volumes 2 and 3. The specific prerequisites for volumes 2 and 3 are listed in the prefaces to these volumes. In all three volumes we present and analyse many important efficient algorithms for the fundamental computational problems in the area. Efficiency is measured by the running time on a realistic model of a computing machine which we present in chapter I. Most of the algorithms presented are very recent inventions; after all computer science is a very young field. There are hardly any theorems in this book which are older than 20 years and at least fifty percent of the material is younger than 10 years. Moreover, I have always tried to lead the reader all the way to current research.

We did not just want to present a collection of algorithms; rather we also wanted to develop the fundamental principles underlying efficient algorithms and their analysis. Therefore, the algorithms are usually developed starting from a high-level idea and are not presented as detailed programs. I have always attempted to uncover the principle underlying the solution. At various occasions several solutions to the same problem are presented and the merits of the various solutions are compared (e. g. II. 1.5, III. 7 and V. 4). Also, the main algorithmic paradigms are collected in chapter IX, and an orthogonal view of the book is developed there. This allows the reader to see where various paradigms are used to develop algorithms and data structures. Chapter IX is included in all three volumes.

Developing an efficient algorithm also implies to ask for the optimum. Techniques for proving lower bounds are dealt with in sections II. 1.6,

II.3, V.7, VII.1.1, VII.2.3; most of chapter VI on NP-completeness also deals in some sense with lower bounds.

The organization of the book is quite simple. There are nine chapters which are numbered using roman numerals. Sections and subsections of chapters are numbered using arabic numerals. Within each section, theorems and lemmas are numbered consecutively. Cross references are made by giving the identifier of the section (or subsection) and the number of the theorem. The common prefix of the identifiers of origin and destination of a cross reference may be suppressed, i.e., a cross reference to section VII.1.2 in section VII.2 can be made by either referring to section VII.1.2 or to section 1.2.

Each Chapter has an extensive list of exercises and a section on bibliographic remarks. The exercises are of varying degrees of difficulty. In many cases hints are given or a reference is provided in the section on bibliographic remarks.

Most parts of this book were used as course notes either by myself or by my colleagues N. Blum, Th. Lengauer, and A. Tsakalidis. Their comments were a big help. I also want to thank H. Alt, O. Fries, St. Hertel, B. Schmidt, and K. Simon who collaborated with me on several sections, and I want to thank the many students who helped to improve the presentation by their criticism. Discussions with many colleagues helped to shape my ideas: B. Becker, J. Berstel, B. Commentz-Walter, H. Edelsbrunner, B. Eisenbarth, Ph. Flajolet, M. Fontet, G. Gonnet, R. Güttler, G. Hotz, S. Huddleston, I. Munro, J. Nievergelt, Th. Ottmann, M. Overmars, M. Paterson, F. Preparata, A. Rozenberg, M. Stadel, R. E. Tarjan, J. van Leeuwen, D. Wood, and N. Ziviani.

The drawings and the proof reading was done by my student Hans Rohnert. He did a fantastic job. Of course, all remaining errors are my sole responsibility. Thanks to him, there should not be too many left. The typescript was prepared by Christel Korten-Michels, Martina Horn, Marianne Weis and Doris Schindler under sometimes hectic conditions. I thank them all.

Saarbrücken, April 1984   Kurt Mehlhorn

Preface to Volume 1

Volume 1 deals with sorting and searching. In addition, there is a chapter on fundamentals. Sorting and searching are the oldest topics in the area of data structures and efficient algorithms. They are still very lively and significant progress has been made in the last 10 years. I want to mention just a few recent inventions here; they and many others are covered extensively in the book: randomized algorithms, new methods for proving lower bounds, new hashing methods, new data structures for weighted and/or dynamic data, amortized analysis of data structures, ... Many of these new techniques have never appeared in book form before. I have tried to combine them with the classical knowledge about sorting and searching so as to lead the reader from the basics to current research.

Chapter I (Fundamentals) covers the basics of computer algorithms. First, a realistic model of computation (deterministic or probabilistic random access stored program machine) is defined, and the concepts of running time and storage space are introduced. Then a high level programming language and its connection with the machine model is discussed. Finally, some basic data structures such as queues, stacks, linked lists, and static trees are introduced, and some of their properties are derived. The material covered in this chapter lays the ground for all other chapters; the material (except for the section on randomized algorithms) is usually covered in introductory computer science courses.

In Chapter II (Sorting) we deal with sorting, selection, and lower bounds. We start with a detailed discussion of several general sorting methods, most notably heapsort, quicksort, and mergesort. The section on quicksort also contains a treatment of recurrence equations which arise frequently in the analysis of recursive programs. In section 2 we deal with sorting by distribution (bucketsort). We apply it to sorting words and sorting reals. The last section, finally, discusses fast algorithms for the selection problem. The sections on efficient algorithms are contrasted with methods for proving lower bounds. We first discuss methods for proving lower bounds in various decision tree models and then show how to lift some of these lower bounds to (restricted) RAM models.

Chapter III (Sets) is an in depth treatment of (one-dimensional) searching problems; multi-dimensional searching is discussed in chapter VII. We cover digital search trees, hashing, weighted trees, balanced trees, and dynamic weighted trees as methods for representing subsets of an infinite (or at least very large) universe. In section 7 we compare the data structures introduced in the first six sections. The last section covers data structures for subsets of a small universe where direct access using arrays becomes feasible. In the course of chapter III we also deal with important algorithmic paradigms, e. g. dynamic programming, balancing, and amortization.

There are no special prerequisites for volume 1. However, a certain mathematical maturity and previous exposure to programming and computer science in general is required. The Vordiplom (= examination at the end of the second year within the German university system) in Computer Science certainly suffices.

Saarbrücken, April 84   Kurt Mehlhorn

Contents Vol. 1: Sorting and Searching

Contents Vol. 2: Graph Algorithms and NP-Completeness

Contents Vol. 3: Multidimensional Searching and Computational Geometry

I. Foundations

We use computer algorithms to solve problems, e.g. to compute the maximum of a set of real numbers or to compute the product of two integers.
A problem P consists of infinitely problem instances. An instance of
the maximum problem is e.g. to compute the maximum of the following
set of 5 numbers 2,7,3,9,8. An instance of the multiplication problem
is e.g. to compute the product of 257 and 123. We associate with every
problem instance $p \in P$ a natural number $g(p)$, its size. Sometimes, size
will be a tuple of natural numbers; e.g. we measure the size of a graph
by a pair consisting of the number of nodes and the number of edges. In the
maximum problem we can define size as the cardinality of the input set
(5 in our example), in the multiplication problem we can define size
as the sum of the lengths of the decimal representations of the factors
(6 in our example). Although the definition of size is arbitrary, there
is usually a natural choice.

Execution of a program on a machine requires resources, e.g. time and
space. Resource requirements depend on the input. We use $T_A(p)$ to denote the run time of algorithm A on problem instance p. We can determine $T_A(p)$ by experiment and measure it in milliseconds.

Global information about the resource requirements of an algorithm is
in general more informative than information about resource requirements on particular instances. Global information such as maximal run
time on an input of size n cannot be determined by experiment. Two
abstractions are generally used: worst case and average case behaviour.

Worst case behaviour is maximal run time on any input of a particular
size. We use $T_A(n)$ to denote the

$$T_A(n) = \sup\{T_A(p); \ p \in P \text{ and } g(p) = n\}$$

(worst case) run time of algorithm A on an input of size n. Worst case
behaviour takes a pessimistic look at algorithms. For every n we single
out the input with maximal run time.

Sometimes, we are given a probability distribution on the set of problem instances. We can then talk about average (expected) case behaviour;

it is defined as the expectation of the run time on problems of a particular size

$$T_A^{av} (n) = E(\{T_A(p); p \in P \text{ and } g(p) = n\})$$

In this book (chapters II and III) computing expectations always reduces to computing finite sums. Of course, average case run time is never larger than worst case run time and sometimes much smaller. However, there is always a problem with average case analysis: does the actual usage of the algorithm conform with the probability distribution on which our analysis is based?

We can now formulaize one goal of this book. Determine $T_A(n)$ for important algorithms A. More generally, develop methods for determining $T_A(n)$. Unfortunately, this goal is beyond our reach for many algorithms in the moment. We have to confine ourselves to determine upper and lower bounds for $T_A(n)$, i.e. to asymptotic analysis. A typical claim will be: T(n) is bounded above by some quadratic function. We write $T(n) = O(n^2)$ and mean that $T(n) \leq cn^2$ for some $c > 0$, n_0 and all $n \geq n_0$. Or we claim that T(n) grows at least as fast as n log n. We write $T(n) = \Omega(n \log n)$ and mean that there are constants $c > 0$ and n_0 such that $T(n) \geq c\, n \log n$ for all $n \geq n_0$. We come back to this notation in section I.6.

We can also compare two algorithms A_1 and A_2 for the same problem. We say, that A_1 is faster than A_2 if $T_{A_1}(n) \leq T_{A_2}(n)$ for all n and that A_1 is asymptotically faster than A_2 if $\lim_{n \to \infty} T_{A_1}(n)/T_{A_2}(n) = 0$. Of course, if A_1 is asymptotically faster than A_2 then A_2 may still be more efficient than A_1 on instances of small size. This trivial observation is worth being exemplified.

Let us assume that we have 4 algorithms A,B,C,D for solving problem P with run times $T_A(n) = 1000\, n$, $T_B(n) = 200\, n \log n$, $T_C(n) = 10\, n^2$ and $T_D = 2^n$ milliseconds (log denotes log to base two throughout this book). Then D is fastest for $0 \leq n \leq 9$, C is fastest for $10 \leq n \leq 100$ and A is fastest for $n \geq 101$. Algorithm B is never the most efficient.

How large a problem instance can we solve in one hour of computing time? The answer is 3600 (1500, 600, 22) for algorithm A(B,C,D). If maximal solvable problem size is too small we can do either one of two things. Buy a larger machine or switch to a more efficient algorithm.

Assume first that we buy a machine which is ten times as fast as the
present one, or alternatively that we are willing to spend 10 hours of
computing time. Then maximal solvable problem size goes up to 36000
(13500, 1900, 25) for algorithms A(B,C,D). We infer from this example,
that buying a faster machine hardly helps if we use a very inefficient
algorithm (algorithm D) and that switching to a faster algorithm has a
more drastic effect on maximally solvable problem size. More generally,
we infer from this example that asymptotic analysis is a useful concept
and that special considerations are required for small instances. (cf.
sections II.1.5 and V.4)

So far, we discussed the complexity of algorithms, sometimes, we will
also talk about the complexity of problems. An upper bound on the complexity of a problem is established by devising and analysing an algorithm;
i.e. a problem P has complexity $O(n^2)$ if there is an algorithm for P
whose run time is bounded by a quadratic function. Lower bounds are
harder to obtain. A problem P has complexity $\Omega(n^2)$ if _every_ algorithm
for P has run time at least $\Omega(n^2)$. Lower bound proofs require us to
argue about an entire class of algorithms and are usually very difficult. Lower bounds are available only in very rare circumstances (cf.
II.1.6.,II.3.,III.4. and V.7.).

We will next define run time and storage space in precise terms. To do
so we have to introduce a machine model. We want this machine model to
abstract the most important features of existing computers, so as to
make our analysis meaningful for every-day computing, and to make it
simple enough, to make analysis possible.

I. 1. Machine Models: RAM and RASP

A random access machine (RAM) consists of 4 registers, the accumulator
α and index registers $\gamma_1, \gamma_2, \gamma_3$ (the choice of three index registers is
arbitrary), and an infinite set of storage locations numbered $0,1,2,\ldots$.
(see figure next page).

The instruction set of a RAM consists of the following list of one
address instructions. We use reg to denote an arbitrary element of α,
$\gamma_1, \gamma_2, \gamma_3$, i to denote a non-negative integer, op to denote an operand
of the form i, $\rho(i)$ or reg, and mop to denote a modified operand of the
form $\rho(i + \gamma_j)$. In applied position operand i evaluates to number i,
$\rho(i)$ evaluates to the content of location i, reg evaluates to the content of reg and $\rho(i + \gamma_j)$ evaluates to the content of locaction numbered (i + content of γ_j). Modified operands are the only means of
address calculation in RAMs. We discuss other possibilities at the end
of the section. The instruction set consists of four groups:

Load and store instructions

$$\text{reg} \leftarrow \text{op} \quad , \text{ e.g. } \gamma_1 \leftarrow \rho(2)$$
$$\alpha \leftarrow \text{mop} \quad , \text{ e.g. } \alpha \leftarrow \rho(\gamma_2 + 3)$$
$$\text{op} \leftarrow \text{reg} \quad , \text{ e.g. } \rho(3) \leftarrow \alpha$$
$$\text{mop} \leftarrow \alpha \quad , \text{ e.g. } \rho(\gamma_2 + 3) \leftarrow \alpha$$

Jump instructions

goto   k   , $k \in \mathbb{N}_0$
if reg π then goto k   , $k \in \mathbb{N}_0$

where $\pi \in \{ =, \neq, <, \leq, >, \geq \}$ is a comparison operator.

Arithmetic instructions

$$\alpha \leftarrow \alpha \ \pi \ \text{mop}$$

where $\pi \in \{ +, -, \times, \text{div}, \text{mod}\}$ is an arithmetic operator.

Index register instructions

$$Y_j \leftarrow Y_j \pm i \qquad 1 \le j \le 3, \; i \in \mathbb{N}_0$$

A RAM program is a sequence of instructions numbered $0,1,2,\dots$. Integer k in jump instructions refers to this numbering. Flow of control runs through the program from top to bottom except for jump instructions.

Example: A RAM program for computing 2^n: We assume that n is initially stored in location 0. The output is stored in location 1.

```
0: Y₁ ← ρ(0)                    1
1: α ← 1                        1
2: if Y₁ = 0 then goto 6        n+1
3: α ← α x 2                    n
4: Y₁ ← Y₁ - 1                  n
5: goto 2                       n
6: ρ(1) ← α                     1
```

The right column shows the number of executions of each instruction on input n. □

In our RAMs there is only one data type: integer. It is straightforward to extend RAMs to other data types such as boolean and reals; but no additional insights are gained by doing so. Registers and locations can store arbitrary integers, an unrealistic assumption. We balance this unrealistic assumption by a careful definition of execution time. Execution time of an instruction consists of two parts: storage access time and execution time of the instruction proper. We distinguish two cost measures: unit cost and logarithmic cost. In the unit cost measure we abstract from the size of the operands and charge one time unit for each storage access and instruction execution. The unit cost measure is reasonable whenever algorithms use only numbers which fit into single locations of real computers. All agorithms in this book (except chapter VI) are of this kind for practical problem sizes and we will therefore always use unit cost measure outside chapter VI. However, the reader should be warned. Whenever, he analyses an algorithm in the unit cost measure, he should give careful thought to the size of the operands involved. In the <u>logarithmic cost measure</u> we explicitely account for the size of the operands and charge according to their lenght L(   ). If binary representation is used then

$$L(n) = \begin{cases} 1 & \text{if } n = 0 \\ \lfloor \log n \rfloor + 1 & \text{otherwise} \end{cases}$$

and this explains the name logarithmic cost measure. The logarithmic cost measure has to be used if the numbers involved do not fit into single storage locations anymore. It is used exclusively in chapter VI. In the following table we use m to denote the number moved in load and store instructions, and m_1 and m_2 to denote the numbers operated on in an arithmetic instruction. The meaning of all other quantities is immediate from the instruction format.

Cost for Storage Access

Operand	Unit Cost	Logarithmic Cost
i	O	O
reg	O	O
$\rho(i)$	1	$L(i)$
$\rho(i + \gamma_j)$	1	$L(i) + L(\gamma_j)$

Cost for Executing the Instruction Proper

Load and Stores	1	$1 + L(m)$
Jumps	1	$1 + L(k)$
Arithmetic	1	$1 + L(m_1) + L(m_2)$
Index	1	$1 + L(\gamma_j) + L(i)$

The cost of a conditional jump <u>if</u> reg π O <u>then</u> <u>goto</u> k is independent of the content of reg because all comparison operators require only to check a single bit of the binary representation of reg.

Under the unit cost measure the cost of an instruction is 1 + # of storage accesses, under the logarithmic cost measure it is 1 + # of storage accesses + sum of the lengths of the numbers involved. Thus the execution time of an instruction is independent of the data in the unit cost measure, and it depends on the data in the logarithmic cost measure.

Example continued: In our example program the instructions have the following costs

Instruction	Unit Cost	Logarithmic Cost
0	2	$L(0) + 1 + L(\rho(0))$
1	1	$1 + L(1)$
2	1	$1 + L(6)$
3	1	$1 + L(\alpha) + L(2)$
4	1	$1 + L(\gamma_1) + L(1)$
5	1	$1 + L(2)$
6	2	$L(1) + 1 + L(\alpha)$

We thus have total cost $4n + 6$ under the unit cost measure and $\Theta(n^2)$ under the logarithmic cost measure (compare I.6. for a definition of Θ). Note that a cost of $\sum_{i=0}^{n-1} (1 + L(2^i) + L(2)) = \Theta(n^2)$ arises in line 3. Note however, that one can improve the cost of computing 2^n to $\Theta(\log n)$ under the unit cost measure and $\Theta(n)$ under the logarithmic cost measure. (cf. exercise 1). □

We infer from this example that the cost of a program can differ drastically under the two measures. It is therefore important to always check whether the unit cost measure can be reasonably used. This will be the case in chapters II to V, VII, and VIII.

Analogously, we use unit and logarithmic cost measure for storage space also. In the unit cost measure we count the number of storage locations and registers which are used in the computation and forget about the actual contents, in the logarithmic cost measure we sum the lengths of the binary representations of the contents of registers and storage locations and maximize over time.

Example continued: Our example program uses registers α and γ_1 and locations 0 and 1. Hence its space complexity is 4 under the unit cost measure. The content of all 4 cells is bounded by 2^n, two of them actually achieve that value. Hence space complexity is $\Theta(L(2^n)) = \Theta(n)$ under the logarithmic cost measure. □

Address modification by index register is the only means of address modification in RAMs. Most realistic computers allow two other techniques for address modification: general address substitution and direct address calculation. General address substitution allows us to use any location as an index register, i.e. modified operands of the form $\rho(i+\rho(j))$ can be used also. The cost of fetching such an operand is 2 in the unit cost and $L(i) + L(j) + L(\rho(j))$ in the logarithmic cost measure. It is not too hard to simulate the enlarged instruction set by our original instruction set with only a constant increase in cost. Let us for example consider instruction $\alpha \leftarrow \rho(i + \rho(j))$. It is simulated by

$$\gamma_1 \leftarrow \rho(j)$$
$$\alpha \leftarrow \rho(i + \gamma_1)$$

However, the content of γ_1 is destroyed by this piece of code. We therefore have to save the content of γ_1 before executing it. Let us assume that location 0 is not used (exercise 2 discusses this assumption in detail) in the program to be simulated. Then we only have to bracket the above piece of code by $\rho(0) \leftarrow \gamma_1$ and $\gamma_1 \leftarrow \rho(0)$. We obtain

New Instruction	Unit Cost	Logarithmic Cost
$\alpha \leftarrow \rho(i+\rho(j)$	3	$1 + L(i) + L(j) +$ $L(\rho(j)) + L(\rho(i+\rho(j)))$

Simulating Program		
$\rho(0) \leftarrow \gamma_1$	8	$6 + L(i) + L(j) +$
$\gamma_1 \leftarrow \rho(j)$		$2 L(\rho(j)) + L(\rho(i+\rho(j)))$
$\alpha \leftarrow \rho(i+\gamma_1)$		$+ 2 L(\gamma_1)$
$\gamma_1 \leftarrow \rho(0)$		

The cost of the simulating program is only larger by a constant factor under the unit cost measure. We thus have

Lemma 1: General address substitution reduces the cost of RAM-programs by only a constant factor under the unit cost measure.

The situtation is slightly more complicated for the logarithmic cost measure. Factor $L(\gamma_1)$ cannot be estimated in a simple way. We therefore change the simulation method and obtain a simple connection between the cost of the original program and the cost of the simulating program. We want that location O always contains the content of γ_1. We achieve this goal by inserting $\rho(0) \leftarrow \gamma_1$ after every instruction which modifies γ_1 and by inserting $\gamma_1 \leftarrow \rho(0)$ before every instruction which uses γ_1. For example, we replace $\alpha \leftarrow \rho(i + \gamma_1)$ by $\gamma_1 \leftarrow \rho(0)$; $\alpha \leftarrow \rho(i + \gamma_1)$ and $\gamma_1 \leftarrow \rho(i)$ by $\gamma_1 \leftarrow \rho(i)$; $\rho(0) \leftarrow \gamma_1$. This modification increases the cost only by a constant factor under both measures. Finally, we replace the instructions using general address substitution as described above, i.e. we replace e.g. $\alpha \leftarrow \rho(i + \rho(j))$ by $\gamma_1 \leftarrow \rho(j)$; $\alpha \leftarrow \rho(i + \gamma_1)$. Note, that we do not have to include this piece of code into brackets $\rho(0) \leftarrow \gamma_1$ and $\gamma_1 \leftarrow \rho(0)$ as before because we took care of saving γ_1 elsewhere. We thus have (details are left to exercise 3).

Theorem 1: General address substitution can reduce the time complexity of RAM programs by at most a constant factor under both cost measures.

We discuss direct address calculation next. We extend the RAM model by a program store (PS) and call the extended model RASP (Random Access Stored Program Machine). PS consists of infinitely many locations, numbered 0,1,2,... . Each location has two parts. The first part contains the name of the instruction (opcode), the second part contains the operand, i.e. either an address or the number of an instruction.

Example continued: The RASP-version of our example program is shown below. We use the RAM-instruction as the opcode, data addresses are replaced by symbol a and instruction addresses are replaced by k.

	Opcode	Address
O	$\gamma_1 \leftarrow \rho(a)$	O
1	$\alpha \leftarrow a$	1
2	if $\gamma_1 = 0$ then goto k	6
3	$\alpha \leftarrow \alpha \cdot a$	2
4	$\gamma_1 \leftarrow \gamma_1 - a$	1
5	goto k	2
6	$\rho(a) \leftarrow \alpha$	1

□

The number of opcodes is finite because there are only four registers
and only a finite number of instructions. For the sequel, we assume a
fixed bijection between opcodes and some initial segment of the natural
numbers. We use Num to denote that bijection.

In addition to the RAM instruction set, the RASP instruction set contains so called π-instructions. π-instructions operate on the program
store. They are:

$$
\left.
\begin{array}{l}
\alpha \leftarrow \pi_k(i) \\
\quad \alpha \leftarrow \pi_k(i+\gamma_j) \\
\pi_k(i) \leftarrow \alpha \\
\pi_k(i+\gamma_j) \leftarrow \alpha
\end{array}
\right\}
\qquad
\begin{array}{l}
i \in \mathbb{N}_o, \\
1 \le k \le 2, \\
1 \le j \le 3,
\end{array}
$$

Instruction $\alpha \leftarrow \pi_k(i)$ loads the k-th component of location i of PS into
the accumulator α. If k = 1 then mapping Num is applied also. The semantic of all other instructions is defined similarly.

Execution times of RASP-instructions are defined as in the RAM case with
one change. RASP programs can grow during execution and therefore the
time required to modify the instruction counter cannot be neglected any
longer. We therefore add L(k) to the cost of an instruction stored in cell
k under the logarithmic cost measure. We have the following relations.

Theorem 2: Executing a RAM program of time complexity T(n) on a RASP
takes $\le$ c $\cdot$ T(n) time units, where c $\in$ |R is a constant, depending on
the RAM program but not on the input.

Theorem 3: There is a c > 0 such that every RASP program of time complexity T(n) can be simulated in $\le$ c $\cdot$ T(n) time units on a RAM. This
holds true under both cost measures.

Theorem 2 follows immediately from the observation, that a RAM program
uses only a fixed number of storage locations of the program store and
that therefore the additive factor L(k) (k being the content of the
program counter) can be bounded by a constant which is independent of
the particular input. Thus the "RASP-cost" of a RAM-instruction is at
most c times the "RAM-cost" where c = 1 + L(length of RAM program to
be executed on a RASP). Theorem 3 is somewhat harder to prove. One has
to write a RAM program which interprets RASP programs. Data store, pro-

gram store and registers of the RASP are stored in the data store of the RAM, more precisely, we use location 1 for the accumulator, locations 2, 3 and 4 for the index registers, locations 5, 8, 11, 14, ... for the data store, and locations 6, 7, 9, 10, 12, 13, ... for the program store. Two adjacent cells are used to hold the two components of a location of the program store of the RASP. Location 0 is used as an instruction counter; it always contains the number of the RASP instruction to be executed next. The interpreter has the following structure:

(1)   loop: load the opcode of the RASP-instruction to be executed into the accumulator.

(2)   decode the opcode and transfer control to a modul which simulates the instruction.

(3)   simulate the instruction and change the instruction counter.

(4)   goto loop

We leave the details for the reader (exercise 3). According to theorems 2 and 3, time complexity on RAMs and RASPs differ only by a constant factor. Since we will neglect constant factors anyway in most of what follows, the choice of machine model is not crucial. We prefer the RAM model because of its simplicity.

So far, RAMs (and RASPs) have no ability to interact with their environment, i.e. there are no I/O facilities. We will live with that defect except for chapter VI and always assume that the input (and output) is stored in the memory in some natural way. For chapter VI on NP-completeness we have to be more careful. We equip our machines with two semi-infinite tapes, a read only input tape and a write only output tape. The input tape contains a sequence of integers. There is one head on the input tape which is positioned initially on the first element of the input sequence. Execution of the instruction $\alpha \leftarrow$ Input transfers the integer under the input head into the accumulator and advances the input head by one position. The cost of instruction $\alpha \leftarrow$ Input is 1 in the unit cost measure and $1 + L(n)$ in the logarithmic cost measure where n is the integer to be read in. Similarly, the statement Output $\leftarrow \alpha$ transfers the content of α onto the output tape. Whenever a RAM attempts to read from the input tape and there is no element on the input tape left the computation blocks. We will then say that the output is undefined and that the time complexity of that particular compution is the number of time units consumed until blocking occurred.

I. 2. Randomized Computations

There are two important extensions of RAMs which we have to discuss: randomized RAMs and nondeterministic RAMs. We discuss randomized RAMs now and postpone discussion of nondeterministic RAMs to chapter VI. A randomized RAM (R-RAM) has the ability to toss a perfect coin and to make further computation dependent on the outcome of the coin toss, i.e. there is an additional instruction

$\alpha \leftarrow$ random

which assigns to α either 0 or 1 with probability 1/2 each. The cost of this instruction is 1 in both cost measures. We illustrate this new concept by a very simple example, an R-RAM which computes constant 0.

1: $\alpha \leftarrow$ random
2: if $\alpha \neq 0$ then goto 1

Apparently, the content of α is 0 when the program stops. However, the run time of the algorithm depends on the outcome of the coin tosses. More precisely, if the random choice comes out 0 at the k-th toss for the first time, $k \geq 1$, then the run time is 2k in the unit cost measure. Since the coin is assumed to be fair, the probability of this happening is 2^{-k} and therefore expected run time is $\sum_{k \geq 1} 2^{-k} 2k = 4$. Note that expected run time is small, although there is a chance that the program never halts.

The notion of R-RAM is most easily made precise by reducing it to ordinary RAMs, with two input facilities. The first input facility takes the actual input p for the randomized computation (as above, we leave the exact nature of that input facility unspecified), the second input facility is a read only input tape which contains a sequence of 0's and 1's. Execution of $\alpha \leftarrow$ random reads the next element (if there is one) from the input tape and transfers it into the accumulator α. Let

A be a RAM-program. For s a sequence of 0's and 1's it thus makes sense to talk about A(p,s), the output of A on input p and sequence s of coin tosses, and $T_A(p,s)$, the run time of A on input p and sequence s of coin tosses. Again, we leave it unspecified, whether the output is written into the memory or on an output tape. The expected run time of randomized algorithm A on input p is then defined by

$$T_A(p) = \lim_{k \to \infty} 2^{-k} \sum_{s \in \{0,1\}^k} T_A(p,s)$$

$T_A(p)$ is well defined because of

Lemma 1: for all k and p: $2^{-k} \sum_{s \in \{0,1\}^k} T_A(p,s) \le 2^{-k-1} \sum_{t \in \{0,1\}^{k+1}} T_A(p,t)$

Proof: Let $s \in \{0,1\}^k$, and let t = s0 or t = s1. If the computation of A on input p and sequence s of coin tosses stops regularly, i.e. is not blocked because sequence s is exhausted, then $T_A(p,s) = T_A(p,t)$. If it is not blocked but never halts then $T_A(p,s) = \infty = T_A(p,t)$. If it is blocked then $T_A(p,s) \le T_A(p,t)$. □

We can now define $T_A(n)$ and $T_A^{av}(n)$ as described above. Of course $T_A^{av}(n)$ is only defined with respect to a probability distribution on the inputs.

What does it mean to say, that a randomized algorithm A computes a function f : P → Y? Of course, the output of A can depend on the particular sequence s of coin tosses used in the computation.

Definition: Let f : P → Y and ε : IN → IR be functions. Randomized algorithm A computes f with error probability at most ε if for all p ∈ P

$$\lim_{k \to \infty} \frac{|\{s \in \{0,1\}^k;\ f(p) = A(p,s)\}|}{2^k} \ge 1 - \varepsilon(g(p)),$$

here g(p) is the size of input p. □

An argument similar to the one used in lemma 1 shows that the limit in the definition above always exists. Of course, only the case ε(n) < 1/2 is interesting. Then A gives the desired output with probability larger than 1/2. A randomized algorithm A is called a <u>Las Vegas</u> algorithm for function f if it computes f with probability 0 of error, i.e. $\varepsilon(n) = 0$ in the above definition. In particular, whenever A(p,s) stops and is defined then A(p,s) = f(p). Las Vegas algorithms are a particularly nice class of randomized algorithms because the output is completely reliable. We see examples of Las Vegas algorithms in II.1.3 and III.1.2.

Of course, we want the probability of error to be as small as possible. Suppose, that we have a randomized algorithm A which computes f : P → Y with probability of error at most $\varepsilon(n)$. If $\varepsilon(n)$ is too large we might just run A several times on the same input and then determine the output by a majority vote. This should increase our confidence in the output.

<u>Lemma 2:</u> Let $\delta > 0$. If randomized algorithm A computes f : P → Y with error probability at most $\varepsilon(n) = \varepsilon < 1/2$ in time $T_A(n)$ and if $T_A \circ g$ is computable in time $O(T_A)$ then there is a randomized algorithm B which computes f in time $c \cdot m \cdot (1/2 - \varepsilon)^{-1} T_A(n)$ with error at most δ. Here $m = (\log \delta)/\log(1-(1/2 - \varepsilon)^2)$ and c is a constant. Moreover, B always halts within $c \cdot m \cdot (1/2 - \varepsilon)^{-1} T_A(n)$ time units.

<u>Proof:</u> Consider any p ∈ P. Let n = g(p), $T = (4/(1 - 2\varepsilon))T_A(n)$ and $m = 2 \cdot (\log \delta)/\log(1-(1/2 - \varepsilon)^2)$. On input p, B computes T, chooses m random sequences $s_1, s_2, \ldots, s_m$ of length T each, and simulates A on inputs (p,s_1), ..., (p,s_m) for up to T time units each. It then outputs whatever the majority of the simulated runs of A output. Apparently B runs for at most $O((1 + m)T) = O(m(1/2 - \varepsilon)^{-1} T_A(n))$ time units. Moreover, $f(p) \neq B(p,s_1 \ldots s_m)$ iff $A(p,s_i) \neq f(p)$ for at least m/2 distinct i's. Next note that

$$\frac{|\{s \in \{0,1\}^T; \ f(p) \neq A(p,s)\}|}{2^T}$$

$$\leq \lim_{k \to \infty} \frac{|\{s \in \{0,1\}^k; \ f(p) \neq A(p,s)\}|}{2^k} + \frac{|\{s \in \{0,1\}^T; \ T_A(p,s) \geq T\}|}{2^T}$$

$$\leq \qquad \varepsilon \quad + \quad (1/2 - \varepsilon)/2 \qquad = 1/2 - 1/2(1/2 - \varepsilon)$$

since A computes f with error at most ε (and therefore the first term
is bounded by ε) and since for p ∈ P with g(p) = n we have

$$T_A(n) \geq T_A(p) \geq \Sigma\{T_A(p,s); \ s \in \{0,1\}^T\}/2^T$$

$$\geq \Sigma\{T_A(p,s); \quad s \in \{0,1\}^T \text{ and } T_A(p,s) \geq T\}/2^T$$

$$\geq \quad T \cdot |\{s \in \{0,1\}^T \text{ and } T_A(p,s) \geq T\}|/2^T$$

and therefore the second term is bounded by $T/T_A(n) = 4/(1-2\varepsilon)$. Let
$\gamma = 1/2 - 1/2(1/2-\varepsilon)$. Then

$$\frac{|\{s_1...s_m \in \{0,1\}^{Tm}; \ B(p,s_1,...s_m) \neq f(p)\}|}{2^{Tm}} \leq \sum_{i=m/2}^{m} \binom{m}{i} \gamma^i (1-\gamma)^{m-i}$$

$$\leq \sum_{i=m/2}^{m} \binom{m}{i} \gamma^{m/2}(1-\gamma)^{m/2} \qquad\qquad \text{since } \gamma < 1/2$$

$$\leq 2^m \gamma^{m/2}(1-\gamma)^{m/2} = (4\ \gamma(1-\gamma))^{m/2} \leq \delta \qquad \text{by definition of m.} \qquad \square$$

It is worth illustrating lemma 2 by an example. Assume that ε = 0.49 and
$\delta = 0.03$. Then m = 2 log δ/log$(1-(1/2-\varepsilon)^2)$ = 2 log 0.03/log 0.9999 ≈ 70127. Thus
we have to repeat a computation which gives the correct answer with prob-
ability 0.51 about 70 000 times in order to raise the level of confidence
to 0.97. If we start with a more reliable machine, say ε = 0.25, then m
reduces to 2 log 0.03/log 0.9375 ≈ 108. From this example we see that bring-
ing the error from 0.49 down to 0.25 is the hard part, increasing the
level of confidence further is easy. Randomized algorithms have a fair
coin available to them and deterministic algorithms do not. It is therefore important to know how good a randomized algorithm can be simulated
by a deterministic algorithm. We approach this problem from two sides.
First we show that for fixed problem size one can always replace the
fair coin by a fixed sequence of 0's and 1's of reasonable length   (Theorem 1), and then we show how to use good pseudo-random number generators
in randomized computations.

Theorem 1: Let n ∈ ℕ, N = |{p ∈ P; g(p) ≤ n}|, let δ = 1/(N+1) and let A,B,ε and
f as in lemma 2. Then there is a sequence s ∈ $\{0,1\}^{mT}$, m and T as in the
proof of lemma 2, such that f(p) = B(p,s) for all p ∈ P, g(p) ≤ n.

Proof: B computes f with error probability at most δ. Let
P_n = {p ∈ P; g(p) ≤ n}. Then for all p ∈ P_n

$$|\{s \in \{0,1\}^{Tm}; \ B(p,s) \neq f(p)\}| \leq \delta \cdot 2^{mT} = 2^{mT}/(N+1) \text{ and therefore}$$

$$\sum_{s \in \{0,1\}^{Tm}} \sum_{p \in P_n} \text{if } B(p,s) \neq f(p) \text{ then 1 else 0}$$

$$= \sum_{p \in P_n} \sum_{s \in \{0,1\}^{Tm}} \text{if } B(p,s) \neq f(p) \text{ then } 1 \text{ else } 0 = N2^{mT}/(N+1) < 2^{mT}$$

Thus there is at least one $s \in \{0,1\}^{Tm}$ such that

$$\sum_{p \in P_n} \text{if } B(p,S) \neq f(p) \text{ then } 1 \text{ else } 0 < 2^{mT}/2^{mT} = 1. \text{ Hence } B(p,s) = f(p)$$

for all $p \in P_n$. □

We illustrate Theorem 1 by an example. Assume that $P = \{0,1\}*$ and $g(p) = |p|$, the length of bit string p. Then $|P_n| \leq 2^{n+1}$. Assume also that we start with a randomized machine A with $\varepsilon = 1/4$ and running time $T_A(n) = n^k$ for some k. Taking $\delta = 1/(2^{n+1}+1)$. Lemma 2 yields a machine B with worst case running time $T_B(n) = O((-\log \delta)T_A(n)) = O(n^{k+1})$ and error probability at most δ. Moreover, by theorem 1, there is a fixed 0-1 sequence s of length $O(n^{k+1})$ which can be used by B instead of a true random number generator. Unfortunately, the proof of theorem 1 does not suggest on efficient method for finding a suitable s.

The question now arises whether we can use a pseudo-random number generator (say built-in procedure RANDOM on your favorite computer) to generate coin toss sequences for randomized algorithms. A typical pseudo-random number generator works as follows. It consists of a function T: $\{0,1\}^m \rightarrow \{0,1\}^m$ which is designed such that there is no "obvious" connection between argument x and value T(x). The most popular choice of function T is

$$T(x) = (ax + c) \mod 2^m$$

where the argument x is interpreted as a number between 0 and $2^m - 1$, multiplied by a multiplier a in the same range, incremented by an increment c in the same range, and finally truncated to the last m bits. A user of a pseudo-random number generator provides a "seed" $x_0 \in \{0,1\}^m$ and then uses the transformation T to generate a sequence $x_1, x_2, x_3, \ldots, x_k$ with $x_{i+1} = T(x_i)$. Thus a pseudo-random number generator takes a bit sequence x_0 of length m and produces a bit sequence (take the concatenation of $x_1, \ldots, x_k$) of length km for some k. We can therefore define a pseudo-random number generator as a mapping ρ: $\{0,1\}^m \rightarrow \{0,1\}^{E(m)}$ where $E(m) \geq m$. It takes a seed $x \in \{0,1\}^m$ and produces a sequence $\rho(x)$ of length $E(m)$.

The choice of the seed is left to the user and we will not further discuss it. We might use a physical device or actually toss a coin.

However, we will discuss the desirable properties of mapping ρ in more detail. The mapping ρ takes a bit string of length m and produces a bit string of length E(m). If E(m) > m then ρ(x) is certainly not a random (in the sense that all strings of lenth E(m) are equally likely) string even if x is a random string of length m. After all, only 2^m out of the $2^{E(m)}$ possible strings of length E(m) are in the range of ρ . Suppose now that we can generate random strings x of length m, is it then safe to use the pseudo-random strings ρ(x) of length E(m) in a randomized algorithm? At first glance the answer seems no because pseudo-random strings are <u>not</u> random strings.

However, they might be "random enough" to be used anyway instead of a true random sequence. In order to make this precise we need to introduce a measure of quality for pseudo-random number generators. We do so by introducing the concept of a <u>statistical test</u>. Consider for example the function h: $\{0,1\}^* \to \{0,1\}$ which yields one if the number of zeroes and ones in the argument differs by at most 10%. Then h applied to a random bit string yields one with very high probability and we might require the same for a random element in the range of ρ . If this were the case then the statistical test h cannot distinguish between true random sequences and the sequences obtained by applying ρ to shorter random sequences. If this were true for all statistical tests (a notion still to be defined) then the sequences generated by ρ are rightfully called pseudo-random.

In general, we define a statistical test to be any function h:$\{0,1\}^* \to \{0,1\}$ which yields a one for at least half of the arguments of any fixed length. A randomized algorithm A can easily be turned into a statistical test h_A. The test h_A calls a sequence s $\in \{0,1\}^*$ "good" (i.e. yields a one) if the run time of algorithm A when using sequence s of coin tosses does not exceed its expected run time by more than a factor of, say, two. Then most random sequences are good, i.e. h_A is a statistical test, and if pseudo-random number generator ρ "passes" test h_A, then this should also be true for many (a precise definition is given below) sequences in the range of ρ . Note that for this argument to work it suffices to know that ρ passes the statistical test h_A derived from algorithm A. Thus, if A's run time is polynomially bounded (we restrict attention to polynomially time bounded algorithms because we saw in the introduction of this chapter that algorithms with exponential run time are hopelessly inefficient) and ρ passes all statistical tests of polynomial time complexity then ρ will also pass the test h_A and hence we can hope to use the pseudo-random sequences generated by ρ instead of true random sequences in operating algorithm A.

We will now make these concepts precise. Part c) of the definition below defines in precise terms what we mean with the phrase that a mapping ρ passes a statistical test h. We give two variants of the definition which are geared towards the two applications of pseudo-random number generators to be described later: fast simulation of randomized algorithms by deterministic algorithms and reducing the number of coin tosses in randomized computations.

Definition: a)   A function h: $\{0,1\}^* \to \{0,1\}$ is polynomially time computable if there is a deterministic algorithm computing h whose running time is bounded by a polynomial.

   b)   A statistical test is a function
h: $\{0,1\}^* \to \{0,1\}$ with $|\{x \in \{0,1\}^k \; ; \; h(x) = 1\}| \geq 2^{k-1}$ for all k.

   c)   Let E: $\mathbb{N} \to \mathbb{N}$ be a function, let $\rho: \{0,1\}^* \to \{0,1\}^*$ be such that $|\rho(x)| = E(m)$ for $|x| = m$ and let $m_0: \mathbb{N} \to \mathbb{N}$ be a function. Let h be a statistical test and let h be computable in time tn^t for some t. Then ρ passes test h if for all $m \geq m_0(t)$
$$\{x \in \{0,1\}^{E(m)} \; ; \; x \in \text{range } \rho \text{ and } h(x) = 1\} \neq \emptyset$$
Furthermore, ρ passes test h well if for all $m \geq m_0(t)$
$$|\{x \in \{0,1\}^{E(m)} \; ; \; x \in \text{range } \rho \text{ and } h(x) = 1\}| \geq 2^m/8$$

Remark: If ρ passes test h well then a random element in the range of ρ makes h true (one) with probability exceeding 1/8 while a true random element of $\{0,1\}^{E(m)}$ makes h true with probability exceeding 1/2. The choice of cut-points $a_1 = 1/2$ and $a_2 = 1/8$ is arbitrary; however $0 < a_2 \leq a_1$ is essential.

   d)   A mapping ρ is a good (very good) pseudo-random number generator if it passes all polynomial time computable statistical tests (well).   □

The reader should pause at this point and should try to grasp the intuition behind this definition. We defined a statistical test to be any predicate on bit strings which at least half of the strings of any fixed length satisfy (part b). Furthermore, we restrict attention to simple (= polynomial time computable predicates) (parts a and c). A pseudo-random number generator ρ passes all statistical tests if the range of ρ has no simple structure, i.e. if there is no large and computationally simple subset of $\{0,1\}^{E(m)}$, namely a set $\{x \in (0,1)^{E(m)};\ h(x) = 1\}$ for some statistical test h, which either ρ misses completely or ρ does not hit with sufficiently high probability. In other words, the properties of a random element in range (ρ) are hard to predict, and hence the elements produced by ρ are rightfully called pseudo-random sequences. Note that "being random" is the same as "being hard to predict".

It is not known whether (very) good random number generators in the sense of this definition exist. However, it can be shown that very good random number generators with $E(m) = m^k$ for any k and ρ computable in polynomial time exist if any one of the following number theoretic problems is hard: the discrete logarithm problem or the problem of factoring integers. We have to refer the reader to the literature for a discussion of these results (cf. A.C. Yao: Theory and Applications of Trapdoor Functions, IEEE FOCS 1982, 80-91). We proceed under the assumption that a (very) good polynomially time computable pseudo-random number generator ρ exists with $E(m) = m^2$, say. We show that good pseudo-random number generators can be used to speed up the simulation of randomized algorithms by deterministic algorithms and that very good generators can be used to reduce the required number of true random choices. The latter consequence is important if generation of truely random bits would ever become possible, yet be expensive.

For concreteness and simplicity, let A be a Las Vegas algorithm with polynomial running time, i.e. $T_A(n) \le tn^t$ for some $t \in \mathbb{N}$ and let ρ be a good pseudo-random number generator with $E(m) = m^2$. Let $p \in P$, $n = g(p)$ be such that $\sqrt{2tn^t} \ge m_0$. Then $h_p:\ \{0,1\}* \to \{0,1\}$ with

$$h_p(s) = \begin{cases} 1 & \text{if } T_A(p,s) \le 2tn^t \\ 0 & \text{otherwise} \end{cases}$$

is computable in time tn^t and we have $h_p(s) = 1$ for at least fifty percent of the bit strings of length $2tn^t$. This follows from the fact that

the running time of T_A on p and s can exceed twice the expected value
for at most half of the sequences of coin tosses. Hence

$$\{s \in \{0,1\}^{E(m)}; \ s \in \text{range } \rho \text{ and } h_p(s) = 1\} \neq \emptyset$$

for all $m \geq \sqrt{2}tn^t$ or

$$\{s \in \{0,1\}^{E(m)}; \ s \in \text{range } \rho \text{ and } T_A(p,s) \leq 2n^t\} \neq \emptyset$$

This relationship directly leads to a deterministic simulation of probabilistic machines which is more efficient than the naive one. Let
$p \in P$, $g(p) = n$ and let $m = \sqrt{2}tn^t$. Consider the following piece of code:

```
for all x ∈ {0,1}^m
do      let s ← ρ(x);
        run A on p and s for up to  2tn^t steps;
        if A halts within that number of steps
        then output, whatever A outputs and halt fi
end
```

Since A is a Las Vegas algorithm and since there is an $s \in \rho(\{0,1\}^m)$
with $T_A(p,s) \leq 2n^t$, the simulation always produces the correct answer.
Also the running time of the simulation is $O(2^{\sqrt{2tn^t}}(tn^t + q(m)))$, where q is
the polynomial bound on the time needed to compute ρ. Thus the existence
of good pseudo-random number generators leads to more efficient simu-
lations of probabilistic machines by deterministic machines. Note that
the naive simulation has running time $O(2^{tn^t}tn^t)$.

Assume now that ρ is a very good pseudo-random number generator. Then

$$|\{s \in \{0,1\}^{E(m)}; \ s \in \text{range } \rho \text{ and } T_A(p,s) \leq 2tn^t\}| \geq 2^m/8$$

where m,n and p are as defined above. In other words, a random
$x \in \{0,1\}^m$ produces an $s = \rho(x)$ such that $T_A(p,s) \leq 2tn^t$ with probability
at least 1/8. This observation leads to the following implementation of
algorithm A which uses fewer coin tosses than A.

repeat generate a random sequence of m bits and call it x;

      $s \leftarrow \rho(x)$

until A on p and s halts within $2tn^t$ steps;

output, whatever A outputs on p and s.

Since a random $x \in \{0,1\}^m$ produces an $s = \rho(x) \in \{0,1\}^{E(m)}$ with
$T_A(p,s) \leq 2tn^t$ with probability at least 1/8 only 8 iterations of the
loop are required on the average. Hence the algorithm above simulates
A in time $O(T_A(n)) = O(n^t)$ and uses only $O(\sqrt{n^t})$ random choices. Thus
if true random choices are possible but costly, this is a significant
improvement. This finishes our discussion on the use of (very) good
pseudo-random number generators in randomized computations.

We close this section with a remark on the relation between the expected time complexity of deterministic algorithms and the running time
of probabilistic algorithms.

Let A be a Las Vegas algorithm which computes function f: P → Y. Let
us assume for simplicity that for every $n \in \mathbb{N}$ A makes at most $a(n)$ coin
tosses on any input $p \in P$ with $g(p) = n$. Then

$$T_A(p) = \sum_{s \in \{0,1\}^{a(n)}} T_A(p,s)/2^{a(n)}$$

Suppose also that we are given a probability distribution μ on the set
P of problem instances. Let B a deterministic algorithm for f, whose
expected running time on inputs of size n is minimal (B is certain to
exist if P_n, the set of problem instances size n, is finite), i.e. for
all deterministic algorithms C

$$E(\{T_B(p); p \in P \text{ and } g(p) = n\}) \leq E(\{T_C(p); p \in P \text{ and } g(p) = n\})$$

where expectations are taken with respect to probability distribution μ.
For every fixed $s \in \{0,1\}^{a(n)}$ algorithm A with sequence s of coin tosses
is a deterministic algorithm and hence

$$\sum_{p \in P_n} \mu(p) T_B(p) \leq \sum_{p \in P_n} \mu(p) T_A(p,s)$$

Since this inequality holds for every s we have

$$\sum_{p \in P_n} \mu(p) \, T_B(p) \leq \sum_{s \in \{0,1\}^{a(n)}} \sum_{p \in P_n} \mu(p) \, T_A(p,s)/2^{a(n)}$$

$$\leq \sum_{p \in P_n} \mu(p) \sum_{s \in \{0,1\}^{a(n)}} T_A(p,s)/2^{a(n)}$$

$$\leq \sum_{p \in P_n} \mu(p) \, T_A(p)$$

Thus the expected running time of Las Vegas algorithm A on inputs of size n can be no better than the expected running time of the best deterministic algorithm. We will use this fact to derive lower bounds on the randomized complexity of some sorting problems in chapter II. For sorting and some related problems we will derive $\Omega(n \log n)$ lower bounds on the expected running time of a large class of deterministic algorithms in chapter II. The inequality derived above immediately extends that lower bound to the corresponding class of randomized algorithms.

I. 3. A High Level Programming Language

Only a few algorithms in this book are formulated in RAM code, most algorithms are formulated in a high level Algol-like programming language. We feel free to introduce additional statements into the language, whenever the need arises and whenever translation to RAM code is obvious. Also we make frequent use of complex data structures such as lists, stacks, queues, trees and graphs. We choose this very high level description of many algorithms because it allows us to emphasize the principles more clearly.

Most statements of our programming language are known from Algol-like languages. In particular, we use the conditional statement
if <condition> then <statement> else <statement> fi,
the iterative statement
while <condition> do <statement> od,
the for-loop
for i from <expression> step <expression> to <expression>
do <statement> od.

If step size is unspecified then it is 1 by default. We also use a
second form of the for-loop

for i ∈ set do <statement> od

with the following semantics. The statement is executed |set|-times;
i runs through the members of set in some unspecified order. Assign-
ments are written in the form <variable> ← <expression>. Translation of
all statements above into RAM code is simple. We describe the translation in the case of a while-statement while B do S od. Let P_1 be a RAM
program for B_1, i.e. P_1 evaluates expression B and leaves a O (1) in
the accumulator, if B evaluates to false (true). Let P_2 be a RAM program
for A. Then the following piece of RAM code realizes the while-loop.

    P_1
    if α = O then goto exit;
    P_2
    goto first instruction of P_1;
exit:

This program also defines the complexity of the while-loop; it is the
sum of the time units spent on the repeated testing of the condition
and execution of the body.

Variables in our programs contain unstructured elementary values or
structured values. The elementary data types are integer, real, boolean,
pointer and an additional unspecified data type. We use this additional
data type in sorting algorithms; the data to be sorted will be of the
unspecified type. The operations defined on this additional data type
are given on a case by case basis. Structured data types are strings
over some alphabet, records, arrays, lists, stacks, queues, trees and
graphs. Strings are treated in II.2., graphs in IV.1., all other structured types are treated in I.4.. The type of a variable will be obvious
from the context in most cases; in this case we will not declare variables explicitly.

Procedures play a major role in our programs. Parameters are restricted
to elementary types. Then parameter passing takes constant time (cf.
I.5.). Non-recursive procedures are easily reduced to RAM code; one only has to substitute the procedure body at the place of call. The situation is more complicated for recursive procedures. We treat recursive
procedures in I.5..

I. 4. Structured Data Types

Records and arrays are the most simple ways of structuring data. An array A of n elements consists of n variables A[1],...,A[n] of the same type. An array is stored in n consecutive storage locations, e.g. in locations BA+1, BA+2, ... ,BA+n. Here BA stands for base address. If x is a variable stored in location i then accessing array element A[x] is realized by means of index registers. The following piece of code

$$\gamma_1 \leftarrow \rho(i)$$
$$\alpha \leftarrow \rho(BA+\gamma_1)$$

loads A[x] into the accumulator for a cost of 3 in the unit cost measure and $(2 + L(i) + L(BA) + 2L(x) + L(A[x]))$ in the logarithmic cost measure. Again the logarithmic cost is proportional to the length of the numbers involved.

Records are fixed size collections of variables of different type, e.g. record age : integer, income : real end. A variable x of this record type is easily simulated by two simple variables, a variable x.age of type integer and a variable x.income of type real.

Queues, stacks, lists and trees are treated in the sections below. They are all reduced to arrays.

I. 4.1 Queues and Stacks

Queues and stacks are used to represent sequences of elements which can be modified by insertions and deletions. In the case of queues insertions are restricted to the end of the sequence and deletions are restricted to the front of the sequence. A typical example is a waiting line in a student cafeteria. Queues are also known under the name FIFO (first in - first out) store. In the case of stacks, insertions and deletions are restricted to the end of the sequence: LIFO (last in - last out) store. Very often, the names Push and Pop are used instead of insertion into and deletion from a stack.

A stack K is most easily realized by an infinite array K[1], K[2], ... and an index TOP of type integer. The stack consists of elements K[1], ...,K[TOP]; K[TOP] is the top element of the stack. The following piece of code realizes operation push(K,a)

```
    TOP  ← TOP + 1;
  K[TOP] ← a
```

and the following piece of code deletes an element from the stack and
assigns it to variable x, i.e. it realizes x ← pop(K)

```
  if TOP = O then error fi;
  x ← K[TOP];
  TOP ← TOP - 1
```

Of course, infinite arrays are rarely available. Instead we have to
use a finite array of, say, n elements. In this case a push-operation
should also check whether overflow occurs. In either case, the stack
operations push and pop take constant time in the unit cost measure.

A queue S is also realized by an array. We immediately treat the case
of a finite array S[1.. n]. We conceptually think of array S as a closed
line, i.e. S[1] follows S[n], and use two indices FRONT and END to denote
the borders of the queue. More precisely, if FRONT < END then the queue
consists of S[FRONT],...,S[END-1], if FRONT > END then the queue con-
sits of S[FRONT],...,S[N],S[1],...,S[END-1] and if FRONT = END then the
queue is empty. Then deleting an element from S and assigning it to x
is realized by

```
  if FRONT = END then error fi;
  x ← S[FRONT];
  FRONT ← 1 + (FRONT mod n)
```

and inserting an element a into a queue is realized by

```
  S[END] ← a;
  END ← 1 + (END mod n);
  if FRONT = END then error fi
```

Insertions into and deletions from queues take constant time in the unit
cost measure.

I. 4.2 Lists

Linear lists are used to represent sequences which can be modified any-
where. In linear lists the elements of a sequence are not stored in
consecutive storage locations, rather each element explicitly points
to its successor.

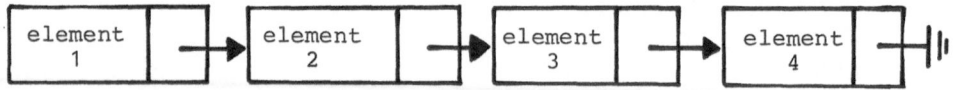

There are many versions of linear lists: singly linked, doubly linked,
circular, ... We discuss singly linked lists here and leave the
others for the exercises. In singly linked linear lists each element
points to its successor. There are two realizations of linear lists:
one by records and one by arrays. We discuss both, although internally
the record representation boils down to the array representation. We
use both representations throughout the book whichever is more convenient. In the record representation an element of a linear list is a
record of type element = record cont : real, next: ↑element end and
HEAD is a variable of type ↑element. HEAD always points to the first
element of the list. The pictorial representation is as given above.
Closer to RAM code is the realization by two arrays. Real array
CONTENT[1.. n] contains the contents of the elements and integer array
NEXT[1.. n] contains the pointers. HEAD is an integer variable. Our
example list can be stored as follows:

HEAD: 2

	CONTENT	NEXT
1	element 4	0
2	element 1	4
3	element 3	1
4	element 2	3

Here HEAD = 2 means that row 2 of the arrays contains the first element
of the list, the second element is stored in row 4, ... The last element of the list is stored in row 1; NEXT[1] = 0 indicates that this
element has no successor.

We will next describe insertion into, deletion from and creation of linear lists. We give two versions of each program, one using records and one using arrays. In either case we assume that there is a supply of unused elements and that a call of procedure newr (<u>var</u> p: ↑element) (newa(<u>var</u> p: <u>integer</u>)) takes a node from the supply and lets p point to it in the record (array) version and that a call of procedure disposer(<u>var</u> p: ↑element)(disposea (<u>var</u> p: integer)) takes the node pointed to by p and returns it to the supply. Suffixes r and a distinguish between the representations. We discuss later how the supply of elements is implemented. In our example a call newa(p) might assign 5 to p because the fifth row is unused and a call newr(p) results in

p: ⬛➡⬛⬛➡|··

Prodedure Create takes one parameter and makes it the head of an empty list. Again we use suffixes r and a to distinguish the record and the array version.

<u>proc</u> Creater(<u>var</u> HEAD: ↑element);   <u>proc</u> Creater(<u>var</u> HEAD: <u>integer</u>);
HEAD ← <u>nil</u>   HEAD ← 0
<u>end</u>   <u>end</u>

Procedure Insert takes two parameters, a pointer to the element after which we want to insert and the content of the new element.

    <u>proc</u> Insertr(p: ↑element,a:<u>real</u>); <u>proc</u> Inserta(p:<u>integer</u>, a:<u>real</u>);
    <u>var</u> q: ↑element;   <u>var</u> q: <u>integer</u>;
(1) newr(q);   newa(q);
(2) q↑.cont ← a;   CONTENT[q] ← a;
(3) q↑.next ← p↑.next;   NEXT[q] ← NEXT[p];
(4) p↑.next ← q   NEXT[p] ← q
    <u>end</u>   <u>end</u>

The following sequence of diagrams illustrates a call Insertr(p,a).

before the call

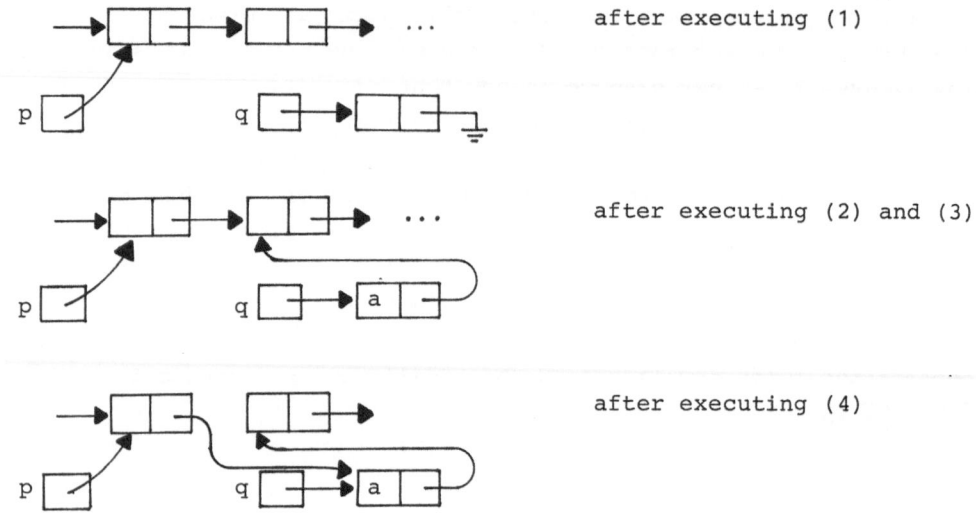

after executing (1)

after executing (2) and (3)

after executing (4)

Procedure Delete takes one parameter, a pointer to the element which precedes the element which we want to delete.

```
proc Deleter(p: ↑element);          proc Deletea(p: integer);
var q: ↑element;                    var q: integer;
q ← p↑. next;                       q ← NEXT[p];
p↑. next ← q↑. next;                NEXT[p] ← NEXT[q];
disposer(q)                         disposea(q)
end                                 end
```

Finally, we have a function to test whether a list is empty.

```
function Emtyr(HEAD: ↑element);     function Emtya(HEAD: ↑integer);
Emtyr ← (HEAD = nil)                Emtya ←(HEAD = 0)
end                                 end
```

It remains to discuss the supply of unused nodes in more detail. Supply is again a linear list with head FREE. We will only describe the array version of procedures new and dispose because these procedures are usually built-in functions in programming languages which contain records. Internally, records are always realized by arrays and therefore

newr(disposer) are identical to newa(disposea). A supply of n elements
is created by

```
proc Inita(n: integer);
var i: integer;
FREE ← 1;
for i from 1 to n-1
do NEXT[i] ← i+1 od;
NEXT[n] ← 0
end
```

and newa and disposea are realized by

```
proc newa(var q: integer);
q ← FREE;
if FREE = 0 then supply exhausted fi;
FREE ← NEXT[FREE];
NEXT[q] ← 0
end
```

and

```
proc disposea(var: q integer);
NEXT[q] ← FREE;
FREE ← q;
q ← 0
end
```

We summarize in

Theorem 1: Creating a supply of n nodes takes time $O(n)$ in the unit
cost measure, creation of an empty list, insertion into, deletion from
a linear list and testing for emptiness take time $O(1)$ in the unit
cost measure.   □

One often uses linear lists to realize stacks and queues. In particular, several stacks and queues may share the same supply of unused
nodes. This will guarantee high storage utilization if we have knowledge about the total length of all stacks and queues but no knowledge
about individual length. Typical examples can be found in chapter IV.

We store a graph by listing for each node its set of successors. In a graph of n nodes and m edges these lists have total length m, but nothing is known in advance about the length of individual lists.

I. 4.3 Trees

Trees consist of nodes (branching points) and leaves. Let $V = \{v_1, v_2, \ldots\}$ be an infinite set of nodes and let $B = \{b_1, b_2, b_3, \ldots\}$ be an infinite set of leaves. We define the set of trees over V and B inductively.

<u>Definition</u>: a) Each element $b_i \in B$ is a tree. Then b_i is also root of the tree.

b) If $T_1, \ldots, T_m (m \geq 1)$ are trees with pairwise disjoint sets of nodes and leaves and $v \in V$ is a new node then the m+1 tuple $T = <v, T_1, \ldots, T_m>$ is a tree. Node v is the root of the tree, $\rho(v) = m$ is its degree and T_i is the i-th subtree of T.   □

Trees can also be defined graph-theoretically. In graph-theoretic literature trees as defined above are usually called ordered rooted trees. We always draw trees with the root at the top and the leaves at the bottom. Nodes are drawn as circles and leaves are drawn as rectangles.

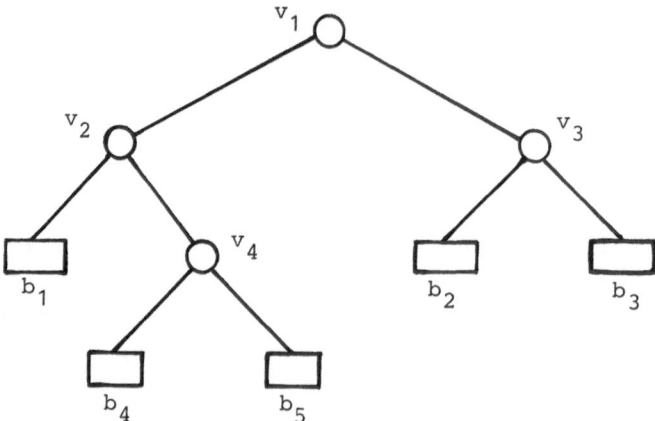

We use the following terms when we talk about trees. Let T be a tree with root v and subtrees T_i, $1 \leq i \leq m$. Let $w_i = \text{root}(T_i)$. Then w_i is the i-th <u>son</u> of v and v is the <u>father</u> of w_i. Descendant (ancestor)

denotes the reflexive, transitive closure of relation son (father). w_j is a brother of w_i, $j \neq i$. In the tree above, b_1 and v_4 are brothers, v_1 is father of v_3 and b_5 is descendant of v_2.

Definition (depth): Let v be a node or leaf of tree T. If v is the root of T then depth$(v,T) = 0$. If v is not the root of T then v belongs to T_i for some i. Then depth$(v,T) = 1 + $ depth(v,T_i). We mostly drop the second argument of depth when it is clear from the context.

Definition (height of a tree): Let T be a tree. Then height(T) = max {depth(b,T); b is leaf of T}.

In our example, we have depth$(v_3) = 1$, depth$(v_4) = 2$ and height$(T) = 3$.

Definition: Tree T is a binary tree if all nodes of T have degree exactly 2.

Our example tree is a binary tree. A binary tree with n nodes has n+1 leaves. The 1st (2nd) subtree is also called left (right) subtree.

Information can be stored in the leaves and nodes of a tree. In some applications we use only one possibility. A binary tree is realized by three arrays LSON, RSON and CONTENT or equivalently by records with three fields. Figure 1 gives the storage representation of our example tree. We have associated rows with nodes and leaves in some arbitrary way. If information is only stored in the nodes and not in the leaves then leaves do not have to be stored explicitly. All rows corresponding to leaves can be deleted and pointers pointing to leaves are set to 0. A 0-pointer then represents a subtree consisting of a single leaf. In the diagrams we will not draw leaves in this case. (cf. figures 2 and 3).

root

| 3 |

	CONTENT	LSOHN	RSOHN
1	Content of v_2	0	4
2	Content of v_4	0	0
3	Content of v_1	1	2
4	Content of v_3	0	0

figure 2

root

5

	CONTENT	LSOHN	RSOHN
1	Content of v_4	8	4
2	Content of v_2	3	1
3	Content of b_1	0	0
4	Content of b_5	0	0
5	Content of v_1	2	7
6	Content of b_2	0	0
7	Content of v_3	6	9
8	Content of b_4	0	0
9	Content of b_3	0	0

figure 1

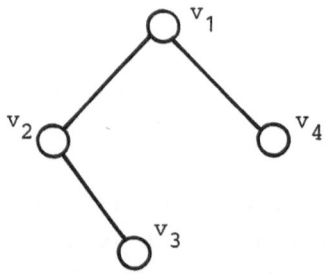

figure 3

Systematic exploration of a tree is needed frequently. A binary tree consists of three components: a root, a left subtree and a right sub-tree. Thus three methods of tree traversal come naturally:

Preorder traversal: visit the root, traverse the left subtree, traverse the right subtree: Root, L, R.

Postorder traversal: traverse the left subtree, traverse the right sub-tree, visit the root: L, R, Root.

Symmetric traversal: traverse the left subtree, visit the root, trav-erse the right subtree: L, Root, R.

Symmetrical variants are obtained by interchanging L and R. Procedure

Symord below traverses a tree in symmetrical order and prints the content of all nodes and leaves.

```
     proc SYMORD(v);
(1)  if v is leaf
(2)  then print(CONTENT[v])
(3)  else SYMORD(LSON[v]);
(4)       print(CONTENT[v]);
(5)       SYMORD(RSON[v])
     fi
     end
```

I. 5. Recursion

Recursive procedure SYMORD traverses a binary tree in symmetrical order. Before we can estimate time- and space - complexity of SYMORD we need to take a look at the implemention of recursive procedures in RAM-or RASP-code. Recursive procedures are realized by means of a stack. We associate with each call (incarnation, activation) of a procedure an element of the stack, called activation record. The activation record contains complete information about the call,

a) the values of the actual parameters,
b) the return address,
c) the local variables.

If a procedure has n parameters and m local variables then the activation record consists of $n + 1 + m$ storage locations. The i-th cell, $1 \leq i \leq n$, contains the value of the i-th actual parameter, the $(n+1)$-st cell contains the return address, i.e. the address of the instruction which follows the procedure call in the calling program, and the $(n+1+j)$-th cell contains the j-th local variable. Parameters and local variables are addressed indirectly via the activation record. More precisely, if TOP is the address of the storage location immediately preceeding the activation record then location $TOP + i$ contains the i-th actual parameter and cell $TOP + n + 1 + j$ contains the j-th local variable. TOP is best stored in an index register. After completion of the procedure call control is transfered to the address stored in location $TOP + n + 1$. Also TOP is reduced after completion, i.e. the

activation record is deleted from the stack. Parameters and return
address are computed by the calling program, i.e. the first n + 1
cells of an activation record are initialized by the calling program.
We are now ready to give the non-recursive version of SYMORD. Array
K[1.. ∞] is used as the stack

```
(1')              begin co the main program calls SYMORD(root);
(2')              TOP ← 0;
(3')              K[1] ← root;
(4')              K[2] ← "HP"
(5')              goto SYMORD ;
(6')      HP: Halt;
(7')  SYMORD: co here comes the code for SYMORD; node v  is stored in
                  K[TOP+1] and return address is stored in K[TOP+2];
(8')              if LSON[K[TOP+1]] = RSON[K[TOP+1]] = 0
                  then co K[TOP+1] is a leaf ;
                     print(CONTENT[K[TOP+1]]);
(1o')                goto FINISH
                  else co call SYMORD(LSON[v]);
(11')                TOP ← TOP + 2;
(12')                K[TOP+1] ← LSON[K[TOP-1]];
(13')                K[TOP+2] ← "M1"
(14')                goto SYMORD;
(15')     M1:        TOP ← TOP - 2;
(16')                print(CONTENT[K[TOP+1]]);
                     co call SYMORD(RSON[v]);
(17')                TOP ← TOP + 2;
(18')                K[TOP+1] ← RSON[K[TOP-1]];
(19')                K[TOP+2] ← "M2";
(2o')                goto SYMORD;
(21')     M2:        TOP ← TOP - 2;
(22')                goto FINISH
                  fi ;
(23') FINISH: goto K[TOP+2];
                  end
```

Call SYMORD(LSON[v]) (line (3) of the recursive program) is simulated
by lines (11') - (15') of the non-recursive program. In (11') storage
space for the activation record is reserved. The activation record is
initialized in lines (12') and (13'); in (12') the value of the actual

parameter and in (13') the return address is stored. In line (14') control is transfered to SYMORD and the recursive call is started. Upon
completion of the call control is transfered to label M1 (line (15')).
The space for the activation record is freed (line (16')) and execution
of SYMORD is resumed. Analogously, one can associate the other instructions of the non-recursive program with the instructions of the recursive program.

The program above is practically a RASP-program. Line (23') uses a
π-instruction. The program can be turned into a RAM program either by
the method described in the proof of I.3. theorem 3 or more simply by
replacing line (23') by

```
if K[TOP+2] = "M1"
then goto M1;
if K[TOP+2] = "M2"
then goto M2;
goto HP;
```

We have described a simplified method for translating recursive programs into non-recursive ones. The method suffices if global variables
can only come from the main program. This will be the case throughout
this book. In the general case a single register TOP does not suffice;
one has to replace it by a set of registers one for each activation
record which can contain global variables. We refer the reader to a
book on compiler construction for details.

We are now ready to analyse the time complexity of recursive procedures
in the unit cost measure. A constant number of instructions is required
to set up a recursive call, namely to increase TOP, to store the n actual parameters and the return address. Note that n is fixed and independent of the input; n can be infered from the program text. Also,
we allow only elementary types in parameter position and hence a single
parameter can be passed in constant time. Upon return from a recursive
procedure TOP has to be decreased. Altogether, the administrative overhead for a procedure call is bounded by a constant.

The following method for computing the time complexity of recursive
procedures is often useful. We associate with every procedure call the

cost of executing the procedure body, inclusive the administrative cost for initiating further recursive calls but <u>exclusive</u> the time spent inside recursive calls. Then we sum over all calls and obtain the total cost in this way. We illustrate this method on procedure SYMORD. Each line in the body of SYMORD takes constant time. Recall that we only count the time required to set up the recursive calls in lines (3) and (5) but do not count the time needed to execute the recursive calls. Thus one execution of the body of SYMORD takes constant time. SYMORD is called once for each leaf and node of a binary tree. Thus the total cost of SYNORD is O(n) where n is the number of leaves and nodes of the binary tree.

The summation over all calls of a procedure can be done more formally by means of recursion equations. Let T(v) be the run time of call SYMORD(v). Then

$$T(v) = \begin{cases} c_1 & \text{if v is a leaf} \\ c_2 + T(LSON[v]) + T(RSON[v]) & \text{otherwise} \end{cases}$$

for suitable constants c_1 and c_2. We can now show by induction on the height of (the tree with root) v that $T(v) = c_2$ # of nodes in the tree with root v + c_1 # of leaves in the tree with root v. Although the induction proof is very simple we include it for didactic purposes.

height(v) = 0 : Then v is a leaf and we have $T(v) = c_1$
height(v) > 0 : Then v is a node and we have
$$T(v) = c_2 + T(LSON[v]) + T(RSON[v])$$
$$= c_2 + c_2 \#_{nodes}(LSON[v]) + c_1 \#_{leaves}(LSON[v]) +$$
$$c_2 \#_{nodes}(RSON[v]) + c_1 \#_{leaves}(RSON[v])$$
$$= c_2 \#_{leaves}(v) + c_1 \#_{nodes}(v)$$

We used $\#_{leaves}(v)$ ($\#_{nodes}(v)$) to denote the number of leaves (nodes) in the tree with root v. A more detailed discussion of recursion equations can be found in II.1.3.

I. 6. Order of Growth

In most cases we will not be able to derive exact expressions for the
run time of algorithms; rather we have to be content with order of
growth analysis. We use the following notation.

Definition: Let f: $\mathbb{N}_o \to \mathbb{N}_o$ be a function. Then $O(f)$, $\Omega(f)$ and $\theta(f)$
denote the following sets of functions:

$O(f) = \{g: \mathbb{N}_o \to \mathbb{N}_o ; \exists c>0 \ \exists n_o: g(n) \le c \cdot f(n) \text{ for all } n \ge n_o\}$

$\Omega(f) = \{g: \mathbb{N}_o \to \mathbb{N}_o ; \exists c>0 \ \exists n_o: g(n) \ge c \cdot f(n) \text{ for all } n \ge n_o\}$

$\theta(f) = \{g: \mathbb{N}_o \to \mathbb{N}_o ; \exists c>0 \ \exists n_o: 1/c \cdot f(n) \le g(n) \le c \cdot f(n) \text{ for all } n \ge n_o\}$

□

We use O-notation in upper bounds, Ω-notation in lower bounds and θ-
notation whenever we can determine the order of growth exactly.

It is customary, to use the notations above together with the equality
sign instead of the symbols $\in$, $\subseteq$ for the relations element in and subset of, i.e. we write $n^2 + 5n = n^2 + O(n) = O(n^2)$ instead of
$n^2 + 5n \in n^2 + O(n) \subseteq O(n^2)$. More precisely, if $\circ$ is an n-ary operation
on functions and $A_1, \ldots, A_n$ are sets of functions, then $\circ(A_1, \ldots, A_n)$
denotes the natural extension to sets of functions, e.g.
$A_1 + A_2 = \{a_1 + a_2; a_1 \in A_1, a_2 \in A_2\}$. Singleton sets are identified
with their single member. Then expressions α and β which contain O-expressions denote sets of functions and α = β stands for α ⊆ β. Equalities, which contain O-expressions, can only be read from left to right.
The terms of a sequence $A_1 = A_2 = \ldots = A_k$ represent larger and larger
sets of functions; the bounds become coarser and coarser from left to
right.

I. 7. Secondary Storage

On a few occasions we consider algorithms which use secondary storage.
We make the following assumption. Data is transported in blocks (pages)
between main and secondary memory. A page consists of a fixed (say
$2^{10} = 1024$) number of storage locations. It takes 5000 time units to
transport a page from one memory to the other. This assumption approxi-
mates the behaviour of modern disk memory.

38

I. 8. Exercises

1) Develop a RAM-Program for computing 2^n which runs in $O(\log n)$ time units in the unit cost measure and $O(n)$ time units under the logarith-cost measure. Hint: Let $n = \sum_{i=o}^{k} a_i 2^i$, $a_i \in \{0,1\}$, be the binary representation of n. Note that $2^n = (...((2^{a_k})^2 \, 2^{a_{k-1}})^2 ... 2^{a_1})^2 \, 2^{a_o}$

2) Give a detailed proof of theorem I.1.1.. In particular, discuss the assumption that a RAM-Program does not use cell 0. Show, that one can add one to all addresses dynamically and hence free cell 0.

3) Give a detailed proof of theorem I.1.3..

4) Let $f: \{0,1\}^* \to \{0,1\}$ be computable in polynomial time on a deterministic RAM under the logarithmic cost measure, and let $f_n = f|_{\{0,1\}^n}$ be the restriction of f to inputs of length n. Show that there is a boolean circuit (in the sense of V.7.) for f_n of size polynomial in n. (Hint: read the proof of theorem VI.4.1.).

5) Let $f: \{0,1\}^* \to \{0,1\}$ be computable in polynomial time on a randomized RAM under the logarithmic cost measure with probability ϵ of error at most 1/4. Let $f_n = f|_{\{0,1\}^n}$. Show that there is a boolean circuit for f_n of size polynomial in n. (Hint: use exercise 4 and theorem I.2.1.).

6) Show how to translate conditional and iterative statements into RAM-code.

7) In doubly linked lists every list element points to its successor and its predecessor. Do section I.4.2. for doubly linked lists.

8) A tree is k-ary if every node has exactly k sons. Show that a k-ary tree with n nodes has exactly $k + (k-1)(n-1)$ leaves.

9) Prove

$f(n) = O(f(n))$
$O(f(n)) + O(f(n)) = O(f(n))$
$c \, O(f(n)) = O(f(n))$
$O(f(n)) \cdot O(g(n)) = O(f(n)g(n))$

I. 9. Bibliographic Notes

RAMs and RASPs were introduced by Shepherdson/Sturgis (63) and Elgot/
Robinson (64). Our notation follows Hotz (72). The theorems in section
I.1. are taken from Cook/Reckhow (72). The discussion of randomized
algorithms is based on Adleman (78), Reif (82), Yao (77) and Yao (82).
A more detailed account of linear lists can be found in Maurer (74)
and Knuth (68). For a detailed discussion of the implementation of
recursive procedure we recommend Gries (71).

II. Sorting

Sorting a set with respect to some ordering is a very frequently occuring problem. IBM estimates that about 25% of total computing time is
spent on sorting in commercial computing centers. The most important
applications of sorting are (according to Knuth (73)):

a) Collecting related things: In an airline reservation system one has
to manipulate a set of pairs consisting of passenger name and flight
number. Suppose that we keep that set in sorted order of passenger name.
Sorting according to flight number then gives us a list of passengers
for each flight.

b) Finding duplicates: Suppose that we are given a list of 1000 persons
and are asked to find out which of them are present in a group of 100
persons. An efficient solution is to create a list of the persons in
the group, sort both lists and then compare them in a sequential scan
through both lists.

c) Sorting makes searching simpler as we will see in chapter III.

We next give a formal definition of the sorting problem. Given is a set
of n objects $R_1, \ldots, R_n$. Each object R_i consists of a key (name) S_i and
some information associated with that name. For example, the objects
might be entries in a German-English dictionary, the keys are German
words, and the information part is gender, English translation, ...
An important fact is that the keys are drawn from some linearly ordered
universe U; we use ≤ to denote the linear order. In our example, the
ordering relation is the alphabetic order on words. We want to find a
rearrangement $R_{i_1}, R_{i_2}, \ldots, R_{i_n}$ of the objects such that

$$S_{i_1} \leq S_{i_2} \leq \ldots \leq S_{i_n}.$$

Apparently, the information associated with the keys does not play
any role in the sorting process. We will therefore never mention it in
our algorithms. There is one further remark in order. Frequently, the
information associated with the keys is much larger than the keys them-
selves. It is then very costly to move an object. Therefore it is better to replace the objects by records consisting of the key and a

pointer to the object and to sort the set of records obtained in this way. Sometimes it will also suffice, to only compute the permutation $i_1, i_2, \ldots, i_n$ and to not actually rearrange the set of objects. All algorithms described below are easily adopted to this modified sorting problem.

Let us reconsider example a) above. Suppose that we want for each flight the list of passengers in alphabetic order. Note that we start with a list of pairs sorted by passenger name. It would then be very nice if the sorting algorithm would not destroy that order when it re-arranges the pairs according to flight number because then the passenger lists would be in alphabetic order automatically. Move formally, we call a sorting algorithm <u>stable</u> if it produces a rearrangement $R_{i_1}, \ldots, R_{i_n}$ such that

$$S_{i_\ell} = S_{i_{\ell+1}} \quad \text{implies} \quad i_\ell < i_{\ell+1}$$

for all ℓ. Note that we can always produce a stable rearrangement by extending the keys to pairs (S_i, i) and by using the lexicographic ordering on these pairs as the linear order.

Sorting algorithms can be divided into two large groups: the algorithms in the first group are <u>comparison-based, i.e. they make only use of the fact that the universe is linearly ordered</u>. In these algorithms the only operation applied to elements of U is the comparison between elements. We will discuss four algorithms of the first kind: <u>Heapsort</u> which always runs in time $O(n \log n)$, <u>Quicksort</u> which runs in time $O(n \log n)$ on the average and is the algorithm with the smallest average running time, <u>Mergesort</u> which also runs in time $O(n \log n)$ and uses only sequential access and finally A-sort (section III. 5.3.2.) which works particularly well on almost sorted inputs. The algorithms in the first group are also called <u>general sorting algorithms</u> because they do not put any additional restriction on the universe. We will also see, that general sorting algorithms require $\Omega(n \log n)$ comparisons in the worst case as well as in the average case. Thus all algorithms mentioned above are optimal up to constant factors. The algorithms in the second group only work for keys in a restricted domain. We treat sorting reals and sorting words according to lexicographic order.

Remark: For this chapter we extend our machine model by two instructions, which are very helpful in sorting algorithms. One instruction exchanges the contents of accumulator and some storage cell.

$$\alpha \longleftrightarrow op \quad and \quad \alpha \longleftrightarrow mop$$

The second instruction addresses a second general purpose register, which we denote by $\bar{\alpha}$. We allow loads into and stores from $\bar{\alpha}$ and simple arithmetic operations, which leave their result in α, e.g.

$$\alpha \leftarrow \bar{\alpha} - op \text{ and } \alpha \leftarrow \bar{\alpha} - mop$$

Instructions of the second type allow us to compare with $\bar{\alpha}$ without destroying it. Both type of instructions are available on many machines.

II. 1. General Sorting Methods

II. 1.1 Sorting by Selection, a First Attempt

We begin with a very simple sorting method. Select the largest element from the input sequence, delete it and add it to the front of the output sequence. The output sequence is empty initially. Repeat this process until the input sequence is exhausted. We formulate the complete algorithm in our high level programming language first and then translate it into machine code. The input sequence is given by array S[1.. n].

```
(1)   j ← n;
(2)   while j > 1
      do co S[j+1.. n] contains the output sequence in increasing order,
         S[1.. j] contains the remainder of the input sequence;
(3)      k ← j; max ← j; s ← S[j];
(4)      while k > 1
         do co we search for the maximal elelment of S[1.. j]; s = S[max]
            is always a largest element of S[k.. j];
(5)         k ← k - 1;
(6)         if S[k] > s
(7)         then max ← k; s ← S[k] fi
         od;
(8)      S[max] ← S[j]; S[j] ← s;
(9)      j ← j - 1
      od;
```

Next we translate into machine code. We use the following storage assignment. Index register γ_1 holds j-1, γ_2 holds k-1 and index register γ_3 holds max-1. n is stored in location 0, S is stored in $\bar{\alpha}$ and array S[1.. n] is stored in locations m+1,...,m+n. We assume n > 1. In the right column the number of executions of each instruction is given.

0	:	$\gamma_1 \leftarrow \rho(0)$	$\left.\vphantom{\begin{array}{c}a\\b\end{array}}\right\}$ j $\leftarrow$ n	1
1	:	$\gamma_1 \leftarrow \gamma_1 - 1$		1
2	:	$\gamma_2 \leftarrow \gamma_1$	k $\leftarrow$ j	n - 1
3	:	$\gamma_3 \leftarrow \gamma_1$	max $\leftarrow$ j	n - 1
4	:	$\bar{\alpha} \leftarrow \rho(m+1+\gamma_3)$	S $\leftarrow$ S[max]	n - 1
5	:	$\gamma_2 \leftarrow \gamma_2-1$	k $\leftarrow$ k-1	A
6	:	$\alpha \leftarrow \bar{\alpha} - \rho(m+1+\gamma_2)$	$\left.\vphantom{\begin{array}{c}a\\b\end{array}}\right\}$ line (6)	A
7	:	if $\alpha \geq 0$ then goto 10		A
8	:	$\gamma_3 \leftarrow \gamma_2$	max $\leftarrow$ k	B
9	:	$\bar{\alpha} \leftarrow \rho(m+1+\gamma_3)$	S $\leftarrow$ S[max]	B
1o	:	if $\gamma_2 > 0$ then goto 5	line (4)	A
11	:	$\bar{\alpha} \longleftrightarrow \rho(m+1+\gamma_1)$	$\left.\vphantom{\begin{array}{c}a\\b\end{array}}\right\}$ line (8)	n - 1
12	:	$\rho(m+\gamma_3+1) \leftarrow \bar{\alpha}$		n - 1
13	:	$\gamma_1 \leftarrow \gamma_1 - 1$	j $\leftarrow$ j-1	n - 1
14	:	if $\gamma_1 > 0$ then goto 2	line (2)	n - 1

Lines 5,6,7,1o are executed for j = n, n-1,...,2 and k = j-1,...,1. Hence A = n(n-1)/2. Furthermore B $\leq$ A. Thus the run time is $\leq 3 \cdot 1 + 10 \cdot (n-1) + 5 \cdot A + 3 \cdot B = 2.5\, n^2 + 7.5\, n - 7 + 3B \leq 4\, n^2 + 6\, n - 7$ time units in the unit cost measure. Average case run time is slightly better. We compute it under the assumption that the keys are pairwise different and that all n! permutations of keys $S_1,...,S_n$ are equally likely. The first assumption is not crucial but it simplifies calculations.

In each execution of the body of the outer loop we exchange S_{max} with S_j. Since there are j different possibilities for max, this step transforms j possible arrangements of keys $S_1,..,S_j$ into one arrangement. Hence after the exchange all possible permutations of keys $S_1,.. S_{j-1}$ are equally likely. Therefore we always have a random permutation of keys $S_1,...,S_j$ during the sorting process. Sequence $S_1,...,S_j$ is scanned from right to left. Instruction 8 is executed whenever a new maximum is found. For example, if 4 5 3 1 2 is sequence $S_1,...,S_j$ (we assume w.l.o.g. that $\{S_1,...,S_j\} = \{1,...,j\}$; this convention facilitates the discussion), then the maximum changes twice: from 2 to 3 and then to 5. Key S_j is equal to i, $1 \le i \le j$, with probability $1/j$. If $S_j = j$ then the maximum is found. If $S_j = i < j$ then we may delete elements $1, \ldots, i-1$ from the sequence. They certainly do not change the maximum. Thus we are left with $(j-1)-(i-1) = j-i$ keys out of $S_1, \ldots, S_{j-1}$. The maximum changes once plus whatever times it will change in the remaining sequence. This gives the following recursion for a_j the expected number of changes of the maximum

$$a_1 = 0$$

$$a_j = 1/j \sum_{i=1}^{j-1} (1 + a_{j-i}) \quad \text{for } j > 1$$

Multiplying by j gives

$$j \cdot a_j = j-1 + \sum_{i=1}^{j-1} a_i$$

and similarly for j+1

$$(j+1)a_{j+1} = j + \sum_{i=1}^{j} a_i$$

Subtraction yields

$$(j+1)a_{j+1} - j a_j = 1 + a_j$$

or

$$a_{j+1} = a_j + 1/(j+1)$$

Thus

$$a_j = \sum_{i=2}^{j} 1/i = H_j - 1$$

where $H_j = \sum_{i=1}^{j} 1/i$ is the j-th harmonic number (cf. appendix). We have thus shown that lines (8) and (9) are executed a_{j_o} times on the average when the outer loop is executed with $j = j_o$. Hence

$$B = \sum_{j=2}^{n} a_j = \sum_{j=1}^{n} H_j - n = (n+1)H_n - 2n \qquad \text{(cf. appendix)}$$

$$\le (n+1)\ln n - (n-1)$$

since $H_n \le 1 + \ln n$ (cf. appendix).

Average case running time of our algorithm is $2.5\, n^2 + 3(n+1)\ln n + 4.5\, n - 4 = \Theta(n^2)$. Worst case and average running time are quadratic. It is also easy to see that the algorithm uses exactly $n(n-1)/2$ comparisons between keys.

II. 1.2 Sorting by Selection: Heapsort

Is the algorithm described in the preceeding section good? Can we improve upon the method for finding the maximum? The answer to the second question is no, at least, if we restrict ourselves to comparison-based algorithms. In comparison-based algorithms there is no operation other than the comparison of two elements which is applicable to elements of the universe from which the keys are drawn.

<u>Theorem 1:</u> Any comparison-based algorithm needs at least n-1 comparisons to find the maximum of n elements.

<u>Proof:</u> Interpret a comparison $S_i < S_j$? as a match between S_i and S_j. If $S_i < S_j$ then S_j is the winner and if $S_i > S_j$ then S_i is the winner. If an algorithm uses less than n-1 matches (comparisons) then there are at least two players (keys) which are unbeaten at the end of the tournament. Both players could still be best (the maximum), a contradiction. □

Theorem 1 implies that we have to look for a different sorting method if we want to improve upon the quadratic running time of the naive algorithm. Consider that algorithm on input 4 5 3 2 1. We compare 2 with 1, 2 with 3, 3 with 5 and finally 5 with 4. We can summarize our knowledge at the end of the first maximum selection in

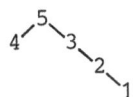

, here 5 means that 5 is larger than 3. Next we exchange 5 and 2 and
   ＼₃

obtain 4 2 3 1. In the second iteration we compare 1 with 3, 3 with 2,
3 with 4 and obtain.

 Two of these comparisons were unnecessary. We knew already from the first iteration that 3 is larger than
1 and 2. Let us take a more global look:
At the end of the first iteration we have a tree-like structure with
the following property: Whenever one considers a path through that tree
then the labels along that path are monotonically decreasing. This is
also called the heap property.

After removing the 5 we obtain:

4   3   It suffices now to compare 4 and 3. This gives us that 4
   ＼₂
     ＼₁   is larger than 3 and the second selection of a maximum
is completed. Let us consider another example, the sequence 1 2 3 4 5. We obtain at the end of the first iteration. After
removing 5 we have 4 uncorrelated elements, i.e. we have
not saved any information from the first iteration to
the second. We can see from these examples that the
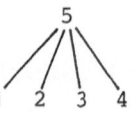 trees which we build should have small fan-out. In this
way only little information is lost when a maximum is
removed. Let us consider one more example, the sequence 2 10 3 5 1 7 9
6 4 8. The "ideal" tree has the form

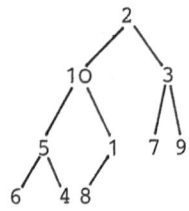 Unfortunately, the labelling does not satisfy the heap
property yet. We can install the heap property in a
bottom-up process. In the following tree the three bottom levels of the tree already satisfy the heap property but the root label does not satisfy it yet.

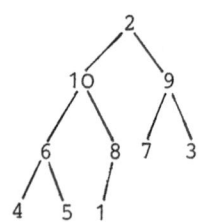 We sink the 2 to its proper position by interchanging
it with the larger of its sons and obtain:

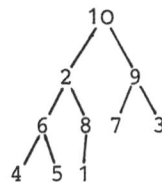

In this tree the 2 is still not larger than its two sons and so we have to interchange it again with the larger of its sons (the 8). We obtain:

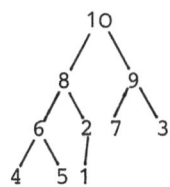

a tree having the heap property. So the maximum is the root label. We remove the maximum and obtain

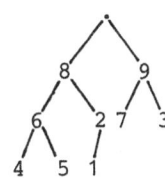

How should we restore the heap property? We might compare the 8 and the 9 and move up the 9. Next we compare the 7 and the 3 and obtain:

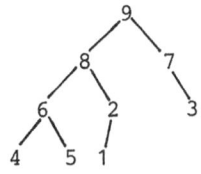

We can now remove the 9 and repeat the process. This gives us

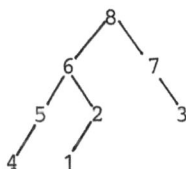

Although this approach leads to an O(n log n) sorting method there is one problem with it. After a few iterations the tree looses its perfect shape. There is another approach which avoids this problem. After removal of the 1o we take the 1, the label of the rightmost leaf on the bottom level, and move it to the root. Next we sink the 1 as described above. This method produces the following sequence of trees

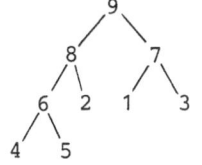

Removal
of 9
———>

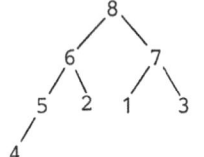

Removal
of 8
———>

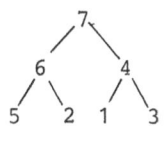

Removal
of 7

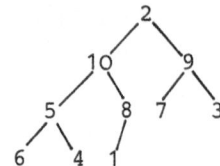

Removal of 6

In this way we always keep the tree an almost complete binary tree. All leaves are on two adjacent levels, all levels except the bottom level are complete, and the leaves on the bottom level are as far to the left as possible. Trees of this form can be stored in very compact form: Number the nodes starting at the root (with number 1) according to increasing depth and for fixed depth from left to right. Then the sons of node k are numbered 2k and 2k+1 and the father of node k is numbered $\lfloor k/2 \rfloor$ ($\lfloor x \rfloor$ is the largest integer $\leq x$). Thus we can store the tree in a single array and save the space for pointers.

Definition: An array S[1.. n] satisfies the heap property if

$$S[\lfloor k/2 \rfloor] \geq S[k]$$

for $2 \leq k \leq n$. The array is a heap starting at ℓ, $1 \leq \ell \leq n$, if

$$S[\lfloor k/2 \rfloor] \geq S[k]$$

for $\ell \leq \lfloor k/2 \rfloor < k \leq n$.   □

Notice that every array S[1.. n] is a heap starting at $\lfloor n/2 \rfloor + 1$. Tree

corresponds to array 2,10,9,5,8,7,3,6,4,1 and is a heap starting at position 2. We give next the complete program for Heapsort; we assume $n \geq 2$.

(1) $\ell \leftarrow \lfloor n/2 \rfloor + 1$; $r \leftarrow n$;
(2)   while $r \geq 2$ do
        begin co either r = n and then S[1.. n] is a heap starting at ℓ
            (build up phase) or $\ell=1$ and the n-r largest elements are stored
            in increasing order in S[r+1],...,S[n] (selection phase).

(3)   if ℓ > 1
         then co we are building the heap and add element S[ℓ-1]
(4)   ℓ ← ℓ - 1; j ← ℓ
         else co we are in the selection phase. S[1] is the maximum of
         S[1],...,S[r]. We exchange S[1] and S[r] and have to restore
         the heap property on S[1.. r-1].
(5)   exchange S[1] and S[r]; r ← r - 1; j ← 1 fi;
(6)   S ← S[j];
(7)   while 2j ≤ r do
         begin co we sink S[j] by interchanging it repeatedly with the
                   larger of its sons.
(8)   k ← 2j;
(9)   if k < r and S[k] < S[k+1] then k ← k + 1;
(10)   if S < S[k]
(11)   then S[j] ← S[k]; j ← k
(12)   else goto E
         end
(13) E: S[j] ← S;
     end

Line 10 is executed in each iteration of the inner loop and the inner
loop is entered at least once in each iteration of the outer loop.
Hence total running time is proportional to the number of comparisons
in line (10). We count the number of comparisons. For simplicity, let
$n = 2^k - 1$.

Build-up Phase: The tree has 2^i nodes of depth i, $0 \le i < k$. In the
build-up phase we add to the heap the nodes of depth k-2, then the nodes
of depth k-3, ... When we add a node at level i then it can sink down
to level k-1 for a cost of 2 comparisons per level. Thus the total cost
of the build-up phase is bounded by

$$\sum_{i=0}^{k-2} 2(k-1-i)2^i = 2^{k+1} - 2(k+1)$$

(cf. appendix, formula S1).

Selection phase: In the selection phase we repeatedly   remove the root
and bring up element S[r]. This element can then sink down all the way
to the bottom level of the tree. More precisely, if an element of
depth i is moved up then restoring the heap property can cost us up to

2i comparisons. Thus the total number of comparisons in the selection phase is at most

$$2 \cdot \sum_{i=0}^{k-1} i \, 2^i = 2(k-2)2^k + 4$$

Altogether, Heapsort uses at most $2k(2^k-1)-2(2^k-1) = 2n \log(n+1)-2n$ comparisons. For $n \neq 2^k-1$ counting is slightly more complicated.

Theorem 2: Heapsort sorts n elements in at most $2n \log(n+1)-2n$ comparisons and time $O(n \log n)$.

Compiling into RAM-Code gives a run time of $\leq 20n \log(n+1)-n-7$ time units in the worst case. Average run time of Heapsort is only slightly better because of the following two reasons. We put new elements into the root and sink them to their proper position. Since most nodes of a binary tree are close to the leaves most elements will sink almost down to the leaves. Furthermore, in the selection phase we sink elements which we get from a leaf and hence tend to be small. A complete average case analysis of Heapsort still needs to be written.

II. 1.3 Sorting by Partitioning: Quicksort

Quicksort is an example for a very powerful problem solving method: divide and conquer. A problem is split into several smaller parts (divide) which are then solved using the same algorithm recursively (conquer). Finally the answer is put together from the answers to the subproblems. In the case of Quicksort this means: Choose an element from sequence $S_1,\ldots,S_n$, say S_1, and partition the sequence into two parts. The first subsequence consists of all S_i with $S_i < S_1$ and no S_j with $S_j > S_1$ and the second subsequence consists of all S_j with $S_j > S_1$ and no S_i with $S_i < S_1$. The partitioning algorithm stores the first sequence in positions 1 through k-1 of an array, S_1 in position k, and the second sequence in positions $k+1,\ldots,n$. Then the same algorithm is applied recursively to the two subsequences. Putting the sorted subsequences and the partitioning element S_1 together to a single sorted sequence is trivial. Nothing has to be done. One could think of splitting the sequence into three parts; the third part consisting of all $S_i = S_1$. In general, this is not worth the additional effort (cf. exercise 8).

We take next a closer look at the partitioning phase. A good solution encloses array S[1.. n] with two additional elements S[0] and S[n+1] such that S[0] ≤ S[i] ≤ S[n+1] for all i and uses two pointers with starting values 1 and n+1. Pointers i and k have the following meaning: the first subproblem consists of S[2],...,S[i], the second subproblem consists of S[k],...,S[n], and elements S[i+1],...,S[k-1] still have to be distributed. We increase i until we find S[i] ≥ S[1] and we decrease S[k] until S[k] ≤ S[1]. Note that no test for "index out of bounds" is required because of the addition of elements S[0] and S[n+1]. Two cases can arise. If k > i then we exchange S[k] and S[i] and repeat the process. If k ≤ i we are done. (it is easy to see that either k = 1 (if S[i] = S[1]) or k = i-1 (if S[i] ≠ S [1] in this case). Interchanging S[k] and S[1] finishes partioning.

```
    procedure Quicksort(ℓ,r);
    co Quicksort(ℓ,r)  sorts the subarray S[ℓ],...,S[r] into increas-
    ing order;
(1) begin i ← ℓ; k ← r + 1; S ← S[ℓ];
(2) while i < k do
(3) begin repeat i ← i + 1 until S[i] ≥ S;
(4)       repeat k ← k - 1 until S[k] ≤ S;
(5)       if k > i then exchange S[k] and S[i]
    end;
(6) exchange S[ℓ] and S[k];
(7) if ℓ < k-1 then Quicksort(ℓ,k-1);
(8) if k+1 < r then Quicksort(k+1,r)
    end
```

A remark on correctness of the algorithm is in order. We assume in lines (3) and (4) the existence of keys S[ℓ-1] and S[k+1] with S[ℓ-1] ≤ S[i] ≤ S[k+1] for all i with ℓ ≤ i ≤ r. Existence of these keys is ensured for call Quicksort(1,n) by adding S[0] and S[n+1] with the required properties, for recursive calls it is immediate from the description of the algorithm. Since we only have S[ℓ-1] ≤ S[i] ≤ S[r+1] we have to test for ≥ and ≤ in lines (3) and (4) in order to save the test for index out of bounds.

Worst case behaviour of Quicksort is easily determined. Consider lines (1) through (6) for fixed values of ℓ and r, say ℓ = 1 and r = n. In line (3) we compare and increase i, in line (4) we compare and decrease k. Before entering the loop in line (2) we have k - i = r - ℓ + 1 = n, after termination of the loop we have k - i = 0 or k - i = - 1. Hence k and i are changed for a total of n or n + 1 times and n or n + 1 comparisons are made. Actual run time of lines (2) to (5) is O(number of comparisons) = O(n). The cost of lines (1) and (6) - (8) is O(1) per call of Quicksort. Since there are ≤ n - 1 calls altogether including the call in the main program (exercise 6) the total cost of lines (1) and (6) - (8) summed over all calls is O(n).

Let us return to the maximal number QS(n) of key comparisons which are needed on an array of n elements. We have

QS(0) = QS(1) = 0
QS(n) ≤ n + 1 + max {QS(k-1) + QS(n-k); 1 ≤ k ≤ n}

It is easy to show by induction that QS(n) ≤ (n+1)(n+2)/2 - 3. This bound is sharp as can be seen from the example 1,2,...,n. Here the partitioning phase splits off exactly one element and therefore subproblems of size n,n-1,n-2,...,2 have to be solved. This requires (n+1) + n + (n-1) + ... + 3 comparisons which sums exactly to the bound given above. Quicksort's worst case behaviour is quadratic.

Average case behaviour is much better. We analyse it under the assumption that keys are pairwise distinct and that all permutations of the keys are equally likely. We may then assume w.l.o.g. that the keys are the integers 1,...,n. Key S_1 is equal to k with probability 1/n, 1 ≤ k ≤ n. Then subproblems of size k - 1 and n - k have to be solved recursively and these subproblems are again random sequences, i.e. they satisfy the probability assumption set forth above. This can be seen as follows. If S_1 = k then array S looks as follows just prior to execution of line (6):

$$k \ i_1 \ i_2 \ \cdots \ i_{k-1} \ j_{k+1} \ j_{k+2} \ \cdots \ j_n$$

Here $i_1,...,i_{k-1}$ is a permutation of integers 1,..,k-1 and $j_{k+1},...,j_n$ is a permutation of integers k+1,...,n. How did the array look like before the partitioning step? If ℓ interchanges occured in line (5) then there are ℓ positions in the left subproblem, i.e. among array indices 2,...,k, and ℓ positions in the right subproblem, i.e. among k+1,...,n, such that the entries in these positions were interchanged pairwise, namely the leftmost selected entry in the left subproblem with the rightmost selected entry in the right subproblem, ... Thus there are exactly

$$\sum_{\ell \geq 0} \binom{k-1}{\ell} \binom{n-k}{\ell}$$

arrays before partitioning which produce the array above by the partitioning process. The important fact to observe is that this expression only depends on k but not on the particular permutations $i_1, \ldots, i_{k-1}$ and $j_{k+1}, \ldots, j_n$. Thus all permutations are equally likely, and hence the subproblems of size $k - 1$ and $n - k$ are again random. Let $QS_{av}(n)$ be the expected number of comparisons on an input of size n. Then

$$QS_{av}(0) = QS_{av}(1) = 0$$

and

$$QS_{av}(n) = 1/n \sum_{k=1}^{n} (n+1 + QS_{av}(k-1) + QS_{av}(n-k))$$

$$= n+1 + 2/n \sum_{k=0}^{n-1} QS_{av}(k) \qquad \text{for } n \geq 2$$

We solve this recurrence by the method already used in II.1.1.. Multiplication by n gives us

$$n \ QS_{av}(n) = n(n+1) + 2 \cdot \sum_{k=0}^{n-1} QS_{av}(k) \qquad \text{for } n \geq 2$$

Subtracting from the equality for $n + 1$ instead of n, yields

$$QS_{av}(n+1) = 2 + \frac{n+2}{n+1} QS_{av}(n)$$

This recurrence is of the form

$$a_1 = b_1$$

$$a_{n+1} = b_n + c_{n+1} a_n$$

with $b_1 = 0$, $b_i = 2$ and $c_i = (i+1)/i$ for $i > 1$ and has solution

$$a_{n+1} = \sum_{i=1}^{n+1} (\prod_{j=i+1}^{n+1} c_j) b_i$$

as is easily verified by induction. Thus

$$QS_{av}(n) = \sum_{i=2}^{n} \frac{n+1}{i+1} 2$$

$$= 2(n+1)(H_{n+1} - 3/2) \leq 2(n+1) \ln(n+1)$$

where H_{n+1} is the (n+1)-th harmonic number (cf. appendix). Let us return to run time. We argued above, that run time of the partitioning phase is proportional to the number of comparisons and that the total cost of all other operations is O(n). Thus

Theorem 3: Quicksort sorts n elements with at most $(n^2 + 3n - 4)/2$ key comparisons and run time $O(n^2)$ in the worst case. It uses $\leq 2(n+1) \ln(n+1)$ comparisons and time O(n log n) on the average.

Translating into RAM-Code as described in I.4 produces a program which sorts n numbers in expected time $\leq 13(n+1) \ln(n+1) + 29n - 33 \approx 9(n+1) \log(n+1) + 29n - 33$. (exercise 7). Quicksort has quadratic worst case behaviour; the worst case behaviour occurs on the completely sorted sequence. Also almost sorted sequences, which occur frequently in practice, are unfavourable to Quicksort. There is an interesting way out of this dilemma : randomized Quicksort. We change the algorithm by replacing line (1) by

(1a)   begin i ← ℓ; k ← r + 1;
(1b)   j ← a random element of {0,...,r-ℓ};
(1c)   interchange S[ℓ] and S[ℓ+j];
(1d)   S ← S[ℓ];

What does that do for us? Let Π be any permutation of numbers 1,...,n and let $QS_{ran}(\Pi)$ be the expected number of comparisons in randomized Quicksort applied to sequence $\Pi(1),\Pi(2),...,\Pi(n)$. In lines (1a) - (1d) we choose a random element of Π as the partitioning element, i.e. S = S[h] with probability 1/n for $1 \leq h \leq n$. Then subproblems Π_1 and Π_2

of size S[h] - 1 and n - S[h] respectively have to be solved recursive-
ly. Of course, Π_1 and Π_2 depend on Π and h (= ℓ+j). We write $\Pi_1(\Pi,h)$
and $\Pi_2(\Pi,h)$ in order to make the dependency explicit. Then

$$QS_{ran}(\Pi) = 1/n \sum_{h=1}^{n} (n+1 + QS_{ran}(\Pi_1(\Pi,h)) + QS_{ran}(\Pi_2(\Pi,h)))$$

It is now trivial to prove that $QS_{ran}(\Pi) = QS_{av}(n)$ where n is the
number of elements in permutation Π (use induction on n). Hence
$QS_{ran}(\Pi) \leq 2(n+1) \ln(n+1)$ for any permutation Π of n elements, i.e. randomized Quicksort sorts any <u>fixed</u> sequence in expected time O(n log n).
The reader should think for a moment about the meaning of this sentence.
Standard Quicksort has average running time O(n log n). When deriving
this result we postulated a distribution on the set of inputs, and the
user of Quicksort has to behave according to that postulate if he wants
to observe small run times. If the user has a preference for nearly
sorted sequences he should better keep away from standard Quicksort.
Not so far randomized Quicksort. Expected run time is O(n log n) on
every single problem instance (and worst case running time is $O(n^2)$ on
every single problem instance). There are no bad inputs for randomized
Quicksort, randomized Quicksort behaves the same on all input sequences.

It is worthwhile, to consider divide and conquer strategies in more detail at this point. Let us assume, that a problem of size n is split
into a(n) problems of size b(n) and that the cost of dividing into subproblems and pasting together the answers is f(n). Then we obtain the
following recurrence for T(n), the run time on a problem of size n.

$$T(n) = f(n) \qquad \text{for } 1 \leq n < b^{-1}(1)$$
$$T(n) = a(n) \ T(b(n)) + f(n) \text{ for } \quad n \geq b^{-1}(1)$$

Here we assumed that the recursion stops as soon as we arrive at a problem of size $< b^{-1}(1)$. We solve the recurrence for T(n) in a two step
process. In the first step we solve the "simpler" homogeneous recurrence

$$h(n) = 1 \qquad \text{for } 1 \leq n < b^{-1}(1)$$
$$h(n) = a(n) \ h(b(n)) \qquad \text{for } \quad n \geq b^{-1}(1)$$

In all our applications the solution of the homogeneous recurrence will
be very easy to obtain explicitely. Setting $R(n) = T(n)/h(n)$ the recurrence for $T(n)$ transforms into

$\qquad R(n) = f(n) \qquad\qquad\qquad$ for $1 \le n < b^{-1}(1)$

and

$\qquad R(n) \; h(n) = a(n) \; h(b(n)) \; R(b(n)) + f(n)$ for $n \ge b^{-1}(1)$

or

$\qquad\qquad R(n) = R(b(n)) + f(n)/h(n)$

Thus $R(n)$ can be computed by a simple summation. With $g(n) = f(n)/h(n)$
we have $R(n) = g(n) + q(b(n))) + \ldots$.

Theorem 4: Let $a, b, f : [1, \infty) \to \mathbb{R}_+$, b strictly increasing and $b(n) < n$
for all n. Then the recurrence

$\qquad T(n) = f(n) \qquad\qquad\qquad$ for $1 \le n < b^{-1}(1)$

$\qquad T(n) = a(n) \; T(b(n)) + f(n)$ for $n \ge b^{-1}(1)$

has solution

$$T(n) = h(n) \sum_{i=o}^{rd(n)} g(b^{(i)}(n))$$

where

$\qquad rd(n) = \min\{d; \; b^{(d)}(n) < b^{-1}(1)\}$

$\qquad h(n) = 1 \qquad\qquad\qquad$ for $1 \le n < b^{-1}(1)$

$\qquad h(n) = a(n) \; h(b(n)) \qquad\quad$ for $n \ge b^{-1}(1)$

and

$\qquad g(n) = f(n)/h(n)$

Proof: By the discussion above. $\qquad\qquad\qquad\qquad\qquad\qquad\qquad$ □

Theorem 4 can be visualized as follows. Define the notion of a recurrence tree by induction on n. If $n < b^{-1}(1)$ then the recurrence tree
consists of a single leaf labelled $f(1)$. If $n \ge b^{-1}(1)$ then the tree for
n consists of a root labelled $f(n)$ and $a(n)$ subtrees, each being a recurrence tree for $b(n)$. Then $rd(n)$ is the depth of this tree and $h(n)$
is the number of leaves of this tree. More generally, the number of
leaves below a node of depth d is $h(b^{(d)}(n))$. $T(n)$ is the sum of the

labels of all nodes and leaves of the tree. We can determine $T(n)$ by summing the labels by depth. A node of depth d has label $f(b^{(d)}(n))$. If we distribute that label over all leaves below the node then each leaf receives a portion $f(b^{(d)}(n))/h(b^{(d)}(n)) = g(b^{(d)}(n))$. Thus

$$T(n) = h(n) \sum_{d=o}^{rd(n)} g(b^{(d)}(n)).$$

We can now classify the solutions of the recurrence according to the growth of function g.

Corollary 5: Under the assumptions of theorem 4 we have

a) $T(n) = O(h(n))$ if $g(n) = O(q^{-rd(n)})$ for some $q > 1$

b) $T(n) = O(h(n))$ if $g(n) = O(rd(n)^p)$ for some $p < -1$

c) $T(n) = O(h(n) \log rd(n))$ if $g(n) = O(1/rd(n))$

d) $T(n) = O(h(n)(rd(n))^{p+1})$ if $g(n) = O(rd(n)^p)$ for some $p > -1$

e) $T(n) = \Omega(h(n) q^{rd(n)})$ if $g(n) = \Omega(q^{rd(n)})$ for some $q > 1$

f) $T(n) = \Theta(f(n))$ if $g(n) = \Theta(q^{rd(n)})$ for some $q > 1$.

Proof: Let $n_o = b^{(rd(n))}(n)$. Then we can rewrite the conclusion of theorem 4 as

$$T(n) = h(n) \sum_{i=o}^{rd(n)} g(b^{(i)}(n))$$

$$= h(n) \sum_{i=o}^{rd(n)} g(b^{(-rd(n)+i)}(n_o))$$

$$= h(n) \sum_{i=o}^{rd(n)} g(b^{(-i)}(n_o))$$

a) From $g(n) = O(q^{-rd(n)})$ and hence $g(b^{(-i)}(n_o)) = O(q^{-i})$ we conclude

$$T(n) = O(h(n) \sum_{i=o}^{rd(n)} q^{-i}) = O(h(n))$$

b,c and d) From $g(n) = O(rd(n)^p)$ and hence $g(b^{(-i)}(n_o)) = O(i^p)$ we conclude

$$T(n) = O(h(n) \sum_{i=0}^{rd(n)} i^p)$$

$$= \begin{cases} O(h(n)) & \text{if } p < -1 \\ O(h(n) \log rd(n)) & \text{if } p = -1 \\ O(h(n) rd(n)^{p+1}) & \text{if } p > -1 \end{cases}$$

e) From $g(n) = \Omega(q^{rd(n)})$ and hence $g(b^{(-i)}(n_o)) = \Omega(q^i)$ we conclude

$$T(n) = \Omega(h(n) \sum_{i=0}^{rd(n)} q^i)$$

$$= \Omega(h(n) \ q^{rd(n)})$$

f) As in part e) we conclude

$$T(n) = \Theta(h(n) \sum_{i=0}^{rd(n)} q^i)$$

$$= \Theta(h(n)) q^{rd(n)} = \Theta(h(n) \ g(n))$$

$$= \Theta(f(n)) \qquad\qquad \square$$

Again it is very helpful to visualize corollary 5 in terms of recurrence trees. In cases a) and b) of corollary 5 the cost of the leaves dominates, in case f) the cost in the root dominates and in case d), p = 0 the cost is the same on all levels of the tree. We close with a brief discussion of a frequently occuring special case: a(n) = a and b(n) = n/b for all n.

Corollary 6: Let $a,b \in \mathbb{R}_+$, b > 1, and let f: $[1,\infty] \to \mathbb{R}_+$. Then recurrence

$$T(n) = f(n) \qquad\qquad \text{if } 1 \le n < b$$
$$T(n) = a \ T(n/b) + f(n) \qquad \text{if } n \ge b$$

has solution

$$T(n) = \sum_{i=0}^{\lfloor \log_b n \rfloor} a^i \ f(n/b^i)$$

In particular,

$$
T(n) = \begin{cases}
O(n^{\log_b a}) & \text{if } f(n) = O(n^p) \text{ with } p < \log_b a \\[1mm]
O(n^{\log_b a}(\log_b n)^{p+1}) & p > -1 \\[1mm]
O(n^{\log_b a} \log \log n) & \text{if } f(n) = \Theta(n^{\log_b a}(\log_b n)^p) \text{ and } \begin{cases} p = -1 \end{cases} \\[1mm]
O(n^{\log_b a}) & p < -1 \\[1mm]
O(n^p) & \text{if } f(n) = \Theta(n^p) \text{ with } p > \log_b a
\end{cases}
$$

<u>Proof:</u> Using the notation of theorem 4 and corollary 5 we have $a(n) = a$, $b(n) = n/b$, $rd(n) = \llcorner \log_b n \lrcorner$ and $h(n) = a^{\llcorner \log_b n \lrcorner} = O(a^{\log_b n}) = O(2^{(\log n)(\log a)/\log b}) = O(n^{\log_b a})$. Thus

$$
T(n) = a^{\llcorner \log_b n \lrcorner} \sum_{i=o}^{\llcorner \log_b n \lrcorner} f(n/b^i)/a^{\llcorner \log_b n - i \lrcorner}
$$

$$
= \sum_{i=o}^{\llcorner \log n \lrcorner} a^i \, f(n/b^i)
$$

Next note that $f(n) = O(n^p)$ for some $p < \log_b a$ implies $g(n) = O(q^{-rd(n)})$ for some $q > 1$ and hence $T(n) = O(h(n))$. Also, if $f(n) = \Theta(n^{\log_b a}(\log_b n)^p)$ then $g(n) = O((\log_b n)^p) = O(rd(n)^p)$. Thus $T(n)$ is as given by corollary 5, cases b) - d). Finally case f) handles $f(n) = \Theta(n^p)$ with $p > \log_b a$. $\quad\square$

II. 1.4 Sorting by Merging

Quicksort's bad worst case behaviour stems from the fact that the size of the subproblems created by partitioning is badly controlled. Corollary 6 tells us that a = b = 2 would produce an efficient method. How can we achieve the splitting into two subproblems of size n/2 each? There is a simple answer: Take the first half of the input sequence and sort it, take the second half of the input sequence and sort it. Then merge the two sorted subsequences to a single sorted sequence. These considerations lead to the follow algorithm.

```
procedure Mergesort(S);
begin      let n = |S|; split S into two subsequences S₁ and S₂ of
```

procedure Mergesort(S);

begin   let $n = |S|$; split S into two subsequences S_1 and S_2 of
           length $\lceil n/2 \rceil$ and $\lfloor n/2 \rfloor$ respectively;
           Mergesort(S_1);
           Mergesort(S_2);
           suppose that the first recursive call produces sequence
           $x_1 \leq x_2 \leq \ldots \leq x_{\lceil n/2 \rceil}$, and the second call produces
           $y_1 \leq y_2 \leq \ldots \leq y_{\lfloor n/2 \rfloor}$;
           merge the two sequences into a single sorted sequence
           $z_1 \leq z_2 \leq \ldots \leq z_n$

end

Let us take a closer look at the merge algorithm. An obvious approach
is to repeatedly compare the front elements of the sequences, to remove
the smaller one and to add it to the end of the z-sequence. Thus

$i \leftarrow 1$; $j \leftarrow 1$; $k \leftarrow 1$;

while $i \leq \lceil n/2 \rceil$ and $j \leq \lfloor n/2 \rfloor$ do
begin if $x_i < y_i$
       then $z_k \leftarrow x_i$; $i \leftarrow i + 1$; $k \leftarrow k + 1$
       else $z_k \leftarrow y_j$; $j \leftarrow j + 1$; $k \leftarrow k + 1$
end;
if $i \leq \lceil n/2 \rceil$
then while $i \leq \lceil n/2 \rceil$ do begin $z_k \leftarrow x_i$; $i \leftarrow i + 1$; $k \leftarrow k + 1$ end
else while $j \leq \lfloor n/2 \rfloor$ do begin $z_k \leftarrow y_j$; $j \leftarrow j + 1$; $k \leftarrow k + 1$ end

This algorithm merges two sequences with at most $\lceil n/2 \rceil + \lfloor n/2 \rfloor - 1 =$
$n - 1$ comparisons and total run time $\Theta(n)$. Note that at least one
element is added to the z-sequence without a comparison. This is optimal.

Theorem 7: Every comparison-based algorithm for combining two sorted
sequences $x_1 \leq x_2 \leq \ldots \leq x_{\lceil n/2 \rceil}$ and $y_1 \leq y_2 \leq \ldots \leq y_{\lfloor n/2 \rfloor}$ into a single
sorted sequence $z_1 \leq z_2 \leq \ldots \leq z_n$ needs $n - 1$ comparisons in the worst
case.

Proof: We choose the x- and y-sequence such that the elements are pairwise different and such that the following relations between the ele-

ments hold: $x_1 < y_1 < x_2 < y_2 < \ldots < x_{\lfloor n/2 \rfloor} < y_{\lfloor n/2 \rfloor} (< x_{\lceil n/2 \rceil})$. Element $x_{\lceil n/2 \rceil}$ only exists if n is odd. Let us assume that some algorithm produces the correct z-sequence and uses less than n - 1 comparisons in doing so. Then it has not compared a pair x_i, y_i or y_i, x_{i+1}. Let us assume the former case, i.e. it has not compared x_i with y_i for some i, $1 \le i \le n/2$. Then let us consider the algorithm on an input where the following relations hold: $x_1 < y_1 < x_2 < \ldots < y_{i-1} < y_i < x_i < x_{i+1} < \ldots$. All comparisons which are made by the algorithm have the same outcome on the original and the modified input and hence the algorithm produces the same z-sequence on both inputs, a contradiction. □

We will next compute the exact number of comparisons which Mergesort uses on an input of length n in the worst case. We use M(n) to denote that number. Apparently

$$M(1) = 0 \text{ and}$$
$$M(n) = n - 1 + M(\lceil n/2 \rceil) + M(\lfloor n/2 \rfloor) \text{ if } n > 1$$

We use induction on n to show

$$M(n) = n\lceil \log n \rceil - 2^{\lceil \log n \rceil} + 1$$

This is correct for n = 1. So let n > 1.

Case 1: $n \ne 2^k + 1$. Then $\lceil \log\lceil n/2 \rceil \rceil = \lceil \log\lfloor n/2 \rfloor \rceil = \lceil \log n \rceil - 1$ and therefore

$$M(n) = n - 1 + \lceil n/2 \rceil \cdot \lceil \log\lceil n/2 \rceil \rceil - 2^{\lceil \log\lceil n/2 \rceil \rceil} + 1$$
$$+ \lfloor n/2 \rfloor \cdot \lceil \log\lfloor n/2 \rfloor \rceil - 2^{\lceil \log\lfloor n/2 \rfloor \rceil} + 1$$
$$= n + n(\lceil \log n \rceil - 1) - 2^{\lceil \log n \rceil} + 1$$
$$= n \cdot \lceil \log n \rceil - 2^{\lceil \log n \rceil} + 1.$$

Case 2: $n = 2^{k+1}$. Then $\lceil \log\lfloor n/2 \rfloor \rceil = \lceil \log\lceil n/2 \rceil \rceil - 1 = \lceil \log n \rceil - 2$ and therefore

$$M(n) = n - 1 + \lceil n/2 \rceil (\lceil \log n \rceil - 1) - 2^{\lceil \log n \rceil - 1} + 1$$

$$+ \lfloor n/2 \rfloor (\lceil \log n \rceil - 2) - 2^{\lceil \log n \rceil - 2} + 1$$

$$= n \cdot \lceil \log n \rceil - \lfloor n/2 \rfloor - 2^{\lceil \log n \rceil} + 2^{\lceil \log n \rceil - 2} + 1$$

$$= n \cdot \lceil \log n \rceil - 2^{\lceil \log n \rceil} + 1$$

We introduced Mergesort by way of a recursive program. It is easy to replace recursion by iteration in the case of Mergesort. Split the input sequence into n sequences of length 1. A sequence of length 1 is sorted. Then we pair the sequences of length 1 and merge them. This gives us $\lfloor n/2 \rfloor$ sorted sequences of length 2 and maybe one sequence of length 1. Then we merge the sequences of length 2 into sequences of length 4, and so on. It is clear that the run time of this algorithm is proportional to the number of comparisons.

<u>Theorem 8:</u> Mergesort sorts n elements with at most $n\lceil \log n \rceil - 2^{\lceil \log n \rceil} + 1$ comparisons and run time $\Theta(n \log n)$.

Translating into RAM-Code results in a run time of 12n log n + 4on + 97 log n + 29 in the worst case. (Exercise 1o).

Sorting by merging accesses data in a purely sequential manner. Hence it is very appropriate for sorting with secondary memory, such as disks and tapes. In this context the following problem is of interest. Very often we do not start with sorted sequences of length one but are given n sorted sequences $S_1, \ldots, S_n$ of length $w_1, \ldots, w_n$ respectively. The problem is to find the optimal order of merging these sequences into a single sequence. Here we assume that it costs x + y time units to merge a sequence of length x with a sequence of length y. Any merging pattern can be represented as a binary tree with n leaves. The n leaves represent the n initial sequences and the n - 1 internal nodes represent the sequences obtained by merging.

Tree 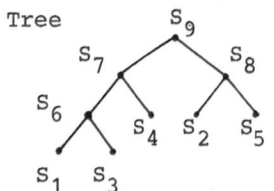 represents the following merging pattern:

$S_6 \leftarrow$ Merge(S_1, S_3)
$S_7 \leftarrow$ Merge(S_6, S_4)
$S_8 \leftarrow$ Merge(S_2, S_5)
$S_9 \leftarrow$ Merge(S_7, S_8)

Definition: Let T be a binary tree with n leaves $v_1, \ldots, v_n$, let CONT: leaves of T $\rightarrow$ $\{w_1, \ldots, w_n\}$ be a bijection and let d_i be the depth of leave v_i. Then

$$COST(T) = \sum_i d_i \ CONT[v_i]$$

is called the cost of tree T with respect to labelling CONT. $\square$

This definition requires a little bit of explanation. Tree T is a merging pattern, the leaves of T are labelled by the n initial sequences, respectively their lengths (weights). What is the cost of merging the n sequences according to pattern T? Note that in our example above sequence S_1 is merged three times into larger sequences, namely first with S_3, then as a part of S_6 with S_4 and then as a part of S_7 with S_8. Also three is the depth of the leaf labelled S_1. In general, a leaf v of depth d is merged d times into larger sequences for a total cost of d CONT[v]. Thus the cost of a merging pattern T is as given in the definition above. We want to find the merging pattern of minimal cost.

Definition: Tree T with labelling CONT is optimal if Cost(T) $\leq$ Cost(T') for any other tree T' and labelling CONT'.

Theorem 9: If $0 \leq w_1 \leq w_2 \leq \ldots \leq w_n$ then an optimal tree T and labelling CONT can be found in linear time.

Proof: We construct tree T in a bottom-up fashion. We start with a set $V = \{v_1, \ldots, v_n\}$ of n leaves and labelling $CONT(v_i) = w_i$ for $1 \leq i \leq n$ and an empty set I of internal nodes and set k to zero; k counts the number of internal nodes constructed so far.

<u>while</u> k < n-1
<u>do</u> select $x_1, x_2 \in I \cup V$ with the two smallest values of CONT; ties are
    broken arbitrarily; construct a new node x with CONT(x) =
    $CONT(x_1) + CONT(x_2)$ and add x to I; k $\leftarrow$ k+1;
    delete x_1 and x_2 from I $\cup$ V
<u>od</u>

Before we prove correctness and analyse run time we illustrate the algorithm on an example. Let n = 5 and $\{w_1, \ldots, w_5\} = \{1, 2, 4, 4, 4\}$. We start with 5 leaves of weight 1, 2, 4, 4, 4. In the first step we combine the leaves of weight 1 and 2 and obtain a node with weight (content) 3, ...

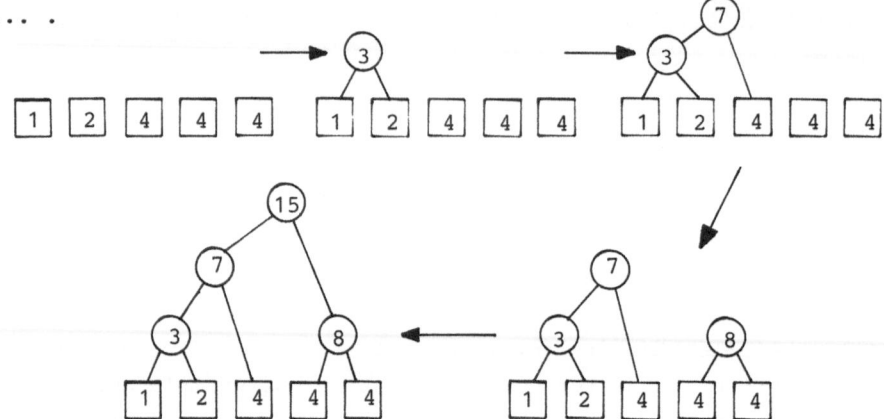

Let T_{opt} with labelling $CONT_{opt}$ be an optimal tree. Let $\{y_1,\ldots,y_n\}$ be the set of leaves of T_{opt}. Assume w.l.o.g. that $CONT_{opt}(y_i) = w_i$ for $1 \leq i \leq n$. Let d_i^{opt} be the depth of leaf y_i in tree T_{opt}.

<u>Lemma 1:</u> If $w_i < w_j$ then $d_i^{opt} \geq d_j^{opt}$ for all i,j.

<u>Proof:</u> Assume otherwise, say $w_i < w_j$ and $d_i^{opt} < d_j^{opt}$ for some i and j. If we interchange the labels of leaves y_i and y_j then we obtain a tree with cost

$$\text{Cost}(T_{opt}) - d_i^{opt} w_i + d_j^{opt} w_i - d_j^{opt} w_j + d_i^{opt} w_j$$

$$= \text{Cost}(T_{opt}) - (w_j - w_i)(d_j^{opt} - d_i^{opt}) < \text{Cost}(T_{opt}),$$

a contradiction.   □

<u>Lemma 2:</u> There is an optimal tree in which the leaves with content w_1 and w_2 are brothers.

<u>Proof:</u> Let y be a node of maximal depth in T_{opt} and let y_i and y_j be its sons. Then y_i and y_j are leaves. Assume w.l.o.g. that $CONT_{opt}(y_i) \leq CONT_{opt}(y_j)$. From lemma 1 we infer that either $CONT(y_i) = w_1$ or $d_i \leq d_1$ and hence $d_i = d_1$ by the choice of y. In either case we may exchange leaves y_1 and y_i without affecting cost. This shows that there is an optimal tree such that y_1 is a son of y. Similarly, we infer from lemma 1 that either $CONT(y_j) = w_2$ or $d_j \leq d_2$ and hence $d_j = d_2$. In

either case we may exchange leaves y_2 and y_j without affecting cost. In this way we obtain an optimal tree in which y_1 and y_2 are brothers.

□

Lemma 3: The algorithm above constructs an optimal tree.

Proof: (by induction on n). The claim is obvious for $n \leq 2$. So let us assume that $n \geq 3$ and let T_{alg} be the tree constructed by our algorithm for weights $w_1 \leq w_2 \leq \dots \leq w_n$. The algorithm combines weights w_1 and w_2 first and constructs a node of weight (content) $w_1 + w_2$. Let T'_{alg} be the tree constructed by our algorithm for set $\{w_1 + w_2, w_3, w_4, \dots, w_n\}$ of weights. Then

$$\text{Cost}(T_{alg}) = \text{Cost}(T'_{alg}) + w_1 + w_2$$

because T_{alg} can be obtained from T'_{alg} by replacing a leaf of weight $w_1 + w_2$ by a node with two leaf sons of weight w_1 and w_2 respectively. Also T'_{alg} is optimal for the set of $n - 1$ weights $w_1 + w_2, w_3, \dots, w_n$ by induction hypothesis.

Let T_{opt} be an optimal tree satisfying lemma 2, i.e. the leaves with content w_1 and w_2 are brothers in T_{opt}. Let T' be the tree obtained from T_{opt} by replacing leaves w_1 and w_2 and their father by a single leaf of weight $w_1 + w_2$. Then

$$\begin{aligned}
\text{Cost}(T_{opt}) &= \text{Cost}(T') + w_1 + w_2 \\
&\geq \text{Cost}(T'_{alg}) + w_1 + w_2 \\
&= \text{Cost}(T_{alg})
\end{aligned}$$

since $\text{Cost}(T') \geq \text{Cost}(T'_{alg})$ by induction hypothesis.   □

It remains to analyse the run time of the algorithm. The crucial observation is:

Lemma 4: Let $z_1, z_2, \dots, z_{n-1}$ be the nodes created by the algorithm in order. Then $\text{CONT}[z_1] \leq \text{CONT}[z_2] \leq \dots \leq \text{CONT}[z_{n-1}]$. Furhtermore, we always have $V = \{v_i, \dots, v_n\}$, $I = \{z_j, \dots, z_k\}$ for some $i \leq n+1$, $j \leq k+1 \leq n$ when entering the body of the loop.

Proof: (by induction on k). The claim is certainly true when $k = 0$. In

each iteration of the loop we increase k by one and $i + j$ by two. Also
$CONT[z_{k+1}] \geq CONT[z_k]$ is immediately obvious from the construction.

□

Lemma 4 suggests a linear time implementation. We keep the elements of
V and I in two separate sets both ordered according to CONT. Since
$w_1 \leq \ldots \leq w_n$ a queue will do for V and since $CONT[z_1] \leq \ldots \leq$
$CONT[z_{n-1}]$ a queue will do for I. It is then easy to select
$x_1, x_2 \in I \cup V$ with the two smallest values of CONT by comparing the
front elements of the queues. Also x_1, x_2 can be deleted in time $O(1)$
and the newly created node can be added to the I-queue in constant time.

□

Theorem 9 can be generalized to non-binary trees.

II. 1.5 Comparing Different Algorithms

We saw four sorting methods so far: maximum selection, Heapsort, Quicksort, and Mergesort. We see one more in section III.5.3.2.: A-sort. The
following table summarizes our knowledge.

	Single Maximum selection	Heapsort	Quicksort	Mergesort	A-Sort
# of comparisons worst case average case	$n^2/2$ $n^2/2$	$2 n \log n$ $\approx 2 n \log n$	$n^2/2$ $1.44 n \log n$	$n \log n$ $n \log n$	$O(n \log F/n)$ $O(n \log F/n)$
run time worst case average case	$2.5 n^2$ $2.5 n^2$	$2o n \log n$ $\leq 2o n \log n$	$\Theta(n^2)$ $9 n \log n$	$12 \log n$ $12 n \log n$	$O(n \log F/n)$ $O(n \log F/n)$
storage requirement	$n + const$	$n + const$	$n + \log n + const$	$2 n + const$	$5 n$
access	random			sequential	random
stable	no	no	no	yes	yes

F denotes the number of inversions in the input sequence; $0 \leq F \leq$
$n(n-1)/2$ (cf. III.5.3.2. for details).

Access: Heapsort, Quicksort and A-sort require random access, Mergesort

accesses the keys in a purely sequential manner. Therefore Mergesort
is well suited for usage with secondary storage which allows only sequential access (e.g. tapes).

Storage Requirement: Heapsort needs on top of the storage required for
the input sequence space for a few pointers. Quicksort also needs space
for a pushdown store which holds the arguments of pending recursive
calls. Maximal stack height is n/2, namely if k = r - 2 always and
therefore the size of the subproblem which has to be solved in line (7)
is only two smaller than the size of the original problem. Maximal
stack height can be kept to log n by a slight modification of the program: always solve the smaller subproblem first, i.e. replace lines (7)
and (8) by:

```
if k ≤ (ℓ + r)/2
then if ℓ < k-1   then Quicksort(ℓ,k-1) fi;
     if k + 1 < r then Quicksort(k + 1,r) fi
else if k + 1 < r then Quicksort(k + 1,r) fi;
     if ℓ < k-1   then Quicksort(ℓ,k-1) fi
fi
```

This modification has the following effect. The size of the subproblem
which is solved first has at most 1/2 the size of the original problem.
Therefore there are never more than log n recursive calls pending.
Mergesort requires two arrays of length n and space for some additional
pointers. A-sort is based on (a,b)-trees (cf. III.5.2. and III.5.3.).
For a = 2 and b = 3 a node of an (a,b)-tree requires 5 storage locations and may contain only one key. Hence A-sort requires up to 5n
storage locations.

Average asymptotic run time: The table contains the dominating terms of
the bounds on run time derived above. The relation of the run times of
Quicksort: Mergesort: Heapsort is 1: 1.33: 2.22 which is typical for
many computers. Note however, that the worst case run time of Mergesort
and Heapsort is not much larger than their expected run time. The re-
lative efficiency of Quicksort is based on the following facts: All
comparisons in the partitioning phase are made with the same element
and therefore this element can be kept in a special register. Also an
exchange of keys is required only after every fourth comparison on the
average, after every second in Heapsort and after every comparison in

Mergesort. However, Heapsort compares twice as often as Mergesort does. For small n, the relations somewhat change. Simple maximum selection is better than Quicksort for n ≤ 22. Therefore Quicksort may be improved by terminating recursion for some n > 2 and switching to maximum selection for small n (exercise 11). A-sort is inferior to all other methods with respect to average and worst case run time. However, A-sort has one major advantage. It runs fast on nearly sorted inputs, i.e. if F is small, say F = O(n log n), then A-sort runs in time O(n log log n). This is in marked contrast to the other methods. Heapsort's and Mergesort's behaviour hardly depends on the statistical properties of the input and Quicksort even runs slower on nearly sorted inputs.

II. 1.6 Lower Bounds

In this section we prove a lower bound on the number of comparisons required for sorting and related problems. We will first show an $\Omega(n \log n)$ lower bound on the average and worst case complexity of general sorting algorithms. We will then extend this lower bound to randomized general sorting algorithms and to decision tree algorithms allowing comparisons of rational functions of the inputs.

General sorting algorithms are comparison based, i.e. the only operation applicable to elements of the universe from which the keys are drawn is the comparison between two elements with outcome ≥ or >. In particular, the pair of keys compared at any moment of time depends only on the outcome of previous comparisons and nothing else. For purposes of illustration let us consider sorting by simple maximum selection on sequence S_1, S_2, S_3. The first comparison is $S_2 : S_3$. If $S_3 > S_2$ then S_3 is compared with S_1 next, if $S_3 \leq S_2$ then S_2 is compared with S_1, next, ... We can illustrate the complete sorting algorithm by a tree, a decision tree.

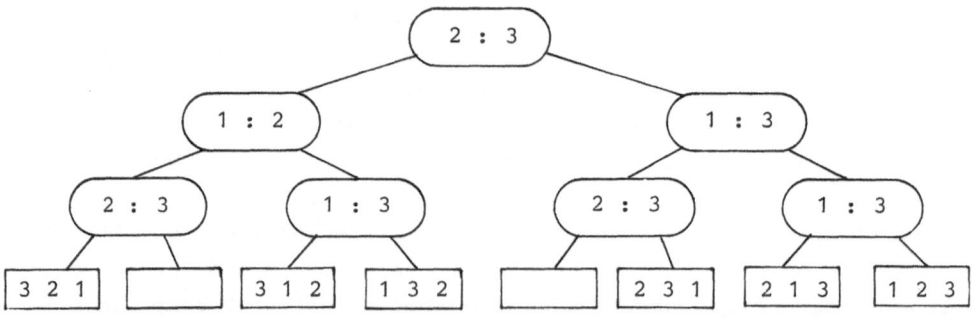

Node i : j denotes a comparison between S_i and S_j. The edge to the right son corresponds to $S_i > S_j$, the edge to the left corresponds to $S_i \leq S_j$.

Definition: A decision tree is a binary tree whose nodes have labels of the form $S_i : S_j$. The two outgoing edges are labelled $\leq$ and $>$.   □

Let $S_1, \ldots, S_n$ be elements of universe U. The computation of decision tree T on input $S_1, \ldots, S_n$ is defined in a natural way. We start in the root of the tree. Suppose now that we reached node v which is labelled $S_i : S_j$. We then compare S_i with S_j and proceed to one of the sons of v depending on whether $S_i \leq S_j$ or $S_i > S_j$. The leaves of a decision tree represent the different outcomes of the algorithm.

Definition: Let T be a decision tree. T solves the sorting problem of size n if there is a labelling of the leaves of T by permutations of $\{1, \ldots, n\}$ such that for every input $S_1, \ldots, S_n \in U$: if the leaf reached on $S_1, \ldots, S_n$ is labelled by π then $S_{\pi(1)} \leq S_{\pi(2)} \leq \cdots \leq S_{\pi(n)}$.   □

We can now define the worst case and average case complexity of the sorting problem. For a decision tree T and permutation π let ℓ_π^T be the depth of the leaf which is reached on input $S_1, \ldots, S_n$ with $S_{\pi(1)} < S_{\pi(2)} < \cdots < S_{\pi(n)}$. Define

$$S(n) = \min_T \max_\pi \ell_\pi^T$$

$$A(n) = \min_T 1/n! \sum_\pi \ell_\pi^T$$

where T ranges over all decision trees for sorting n elements and π ranges over all permutations of n elements. ℓ_π^T is the number of comparisons used on input π by decision tree T. Thus $S(n)$ is the minimal worst case complexity of any algorithm and $A(n)$ is the minimal average case complexity of any algorithm. We prove lower bounds on $S(n)$ and $A(n)$.

Suppose $S(n) \leq k$. A tree of depth $\leq k$ has at most 2^k leaves. A decision tree for sorting n elements has at least n! leaves. Thus

$$2^{S(n)} \geq n!$$

or

$$S(n) \geq \lceil \log n! \rceil$$

since S(n) is an integer. Stirling's approximation for n! gives us

$$\log n! = (n+1/2) \log n - n/\ln 2 + O(1)$$
$$= n \log n - 1.43 n + O(\log n)$$

An upper bound for S(n) comes from the analysis of sorting algorithms. In particular, we infer from the analysis of Mergesort

$$S(n) \leq n \lceil \log n \rceil - 2^{\lceil \log n \rceil} + 1$$

and hence

$$\lim_{n \to \infty} S(n)/n \log n = 1$$

We have thus determined the exact asymptotic worst case complexity of sorting. The result derived above is often called the information-theoretic bound. Any sorting algorithm has to distinguish n! possibilities, and thus has to gain log n! bits of information. One comparison gives at most 1 bit of information. The bound follows.

We turn to A(n) next. We give a different interpretation of $1/n! \sum_{\pi} \ell^T_{\pi}$ first. Let $b_1, b_2, \ldots$ be the leaves of T. Define

$$\alpha_i = \begin{cases} 1/n! & \text{if leaf } b_i \text{ is reached on some input sequence} \\ 0 & \text{otherwise} \end{cases}$$

Then $1/n! \sum_{\pi} \ell^T_{\pi} = \sum_i \alpha_i \text{ depth}(b_i)$ and hence $1/n! \sum_{\pi} \ell^T_{\pi}$ is equal to the weighted path length of tree T with respect to distribution $\alpha_1, \alpha_2, \alpha_3 \ldots$ (cf. III.4. for a detailed discussion of weighted path length). We show in III.4. in a more general context that

$$\sum_{\pi} \ell^T_{\pi} 1/n! \geq H(1/n!, \ldots, 1/n!)$$

$$= \sum_{\pi} 1/n! \log n! = \log n!$$

for any tree T. Here H is the entropy of the distribution (cf. III.4.).

Theorem 1o: Every decision tree algorithm for sorting n elements needs $\geq \lceil \log n! \rceil$ comparisons in the worst case and $\geq \log n!$ comparisons on the average.

Theorem 10 can be used to prove lower bounds on other problems then sorting. The element uniqueness problem is defined as follows. Given n elements $S_1, \ldots, S_n$ in U one has to decide whether $S_i \neq S_j$ for $i \neq j$.

Theorem 11: Every decision tree algorithm for the element uniqueness problem of size n needs at least log n! comparisons in the worst case.

Proof: Let T be a decision tree for the element uniqueness problem of size n, i.e. the nodes of T are labelled by comparisons $S_i : S_j$ and the leaves are labelled yes or no. On input $(S_1, \ldots, S_n) \in U^n$ a leaf labelled yes is reached iff $S_i \neq S_j$ for $i \neq j$. We will show that one can use T to sort.

For permutation π of n elements let $v(\pi)$ be the leaf reached on an input $(S_1, \ldots, S_n) \in U^n$ with $S_{\pi(1)} < S_{\pi(2)} < \cdots < S_{\pi(n)}$. Note that this leaf is well-defined because the computation on any input $(S_1, \ldots, S_n) \in U^n$ with $S_{\pi(1)} < S_{\pi(2)} < \cdots < S_{\pi(n)}$ will end in the same leaf.

Claim: $v(\pi) \neq v(\rho)$ if $\pi \neq \rho$ (π, ρ permutations).

Proof: Assume otherwise, i.e. there are permutations π and ρ such that $v(\pi) = v(\rho)$. Note that leaf $v(\pi)$ is labelled yes. We will now construct an input $(S_1, \ldots, S_n)$ such that the computation on input $(S_1, \ldots, S_n)$ ends in leaf $v(\pi)$, yet $S_i = S_j$ for some $i \neq j$. This is a contradiction. $(S_1, \ldots, S_n)$ is constructed as follows. Let $w_1, \ldots, w_t$ be the nodes on the path to leaf $v(\pi)$. Consider partial order $P(v(\pi))$ on $(S_1, \ldots, S_n)$ defined as follows. For k, $1 \le k \le t$: if w_k is labelled $S_i : S_j$ and the $\le$ - edge ($>$ - edge) is taken from w_k to w_{k+1} then $S_i < S_j$ ($S_i > S_j$) in partial order $P(v(\pi))$. Then $P(v(\pi))$ is the smallest partial order (with respect to set inclusion) satisfying these constraints. In particular, if $(R_1, \ldots, R_n) \in U^n$ is such that $R_{\sigma(1)} < R_{\sigma(2)} < \cdots < R_{\sigma(n)}$ for $\sigma \in \{\pi, \rho\}$ then $(R_1, \ldots, R_n)$ satisfies partial order $P(v(\pi))$. Hence $P(v(\pi))$ is not a linear order and therefore there are a and b, $a \neq b$, such that S_a, S_b are not related in partial order $P(v(\pi))$. Let $(S_1, \ldots, S_n) \in U^n$ be such that $(S_1, \ldots, S_n)$ satisfies partial order $P(v(\pi))$ and $S_a = S_b$. Then the computation on input $(S_1, \ldots, S_n)$ ends in leaf $v(\pi)$ and hence has result yes, a contradiction. □

Can a randomized sorting algorithm, i.e. an algorithm which uses random choices in order to determine which comparison to make next, be any faster? After all, we saw that Quicksort's quadratic worst case behaviour vanishes when we switch to randomized Quicksort. The answer is no. A randomized comparison-based algorithm can be represented by a random decision tree. In a random decision tree there are two types of nodes. The first type of node is the ordinary comparison node; the second type is a coin tossing node. It has two outgoing edges labelled 0 and 1 which are taken with probability 1/2 each. For the sake of simplicity we restrict attention to finite random decision trees, i.e. we assume that the number of coin tosses on inputs of size n is bounded by $k(n)$. The notion "a random decision tree solves the sorting problem of size n" is defined exactly as above. Note however, that the leaf reached not only depends on the input but also on the sequence $s \in \{0,1\}^{k(n)}$ of outcomes of coin tosses. For any permutation π and sequence $s \in \{0,1\}^{k(n)}$ let $\ell_{\pi,s}^T$ be the depth of the leaf reached on sequence s of coin tosses and input sequence $S_1,\ldots,S_n$ where $S_{\pi(1)} < S_{\pi(2)} < \ldots < S_{\pi(n)}$. Define

$$S_{ran}(n) = \min_{T} \max_{\pi} \ 1/2^{k(n)} \sum_{s \in \{0,1\}^{k(n)}} \ell_{\pi,s}^T$$

and

$$A_{ran}(n) = \min_{T} 1/n! \sum_{\pi} [1/2^{k(n)} \sum_{s \in \{0,1\}^{k(n)}} \ell_{\pi,s}^T]$$

where T ranges over all random decision trees which solve the sorting problem of size n and π ranges over all permutations of n elements. A_{ran} (S_{ran}) is the minimal average (worst) case complexity of any randomized comparison-based sorting algorithm. We can now use the argument outlined at the end of section I.2. to show that randomization cannot improve the complexity of sorting below log n!. We have

$$S_{ran}(n) \geq A_{ran}(n)$$

$$\geq \min_{T} 1/n! \sum_{\pi} 1/2^{k(n)} \sum_{s \in \{0,1\}^{k(n)}} \ell_{\pi,s}^T$$

$$\geq \min_{T} 1/2 \underset{s \in \{0,1\}^{k(n)}}{\Sigma} 1/n! \underset{\pi}{\Sigma} \ell^{T}_{\pi,s}$$

$$\geq \min_{T} 1/2^{k(n)} \underset{s \in \{0,1\}^{k(n)}}{\Sigma} A(n)$$

since for every <u>fixed</u> sequence s of coin tosses random decision tree T defines an ordinary decision tree

$$\geq A(n)$$

Thus randomization cannot improve expected running time below log n!

We will next strengthen our basic lower bound in a different direction. Suppose that the inputs are not taken from an arbitrary ordered universe but from the set of real numbers. Reals cannot only be compared but can also be added, multiplied, ... This leads to the concept of rational decision trees.

<u>Definition:</u> A rational decision tree for inputs $S_1, \ldots, S_n$ is a binary tree whose nodes are labelled by expressions $p(S_1, \ldots, S_n) : q(S_1, \ldots, S_n)$ where p and q are rational functions, whose edges are labelled by $\leq$ and >, and whose leaves are labelled by rational functions $r(S_1, \ldots, S_n)$ of $S_1, \ldots, S_n$.

Rational decision trees compute functions $f : \mathbb{R}^n \to \mathbb{R}$ in an obvious way. Let $S_1, \ldots, S_n \in \mathbb{R}^n$. Computation starts in the root. Suppose that computation has reached node v which is labelled $p(S_1, \ldots, S_n) : q(S_1, \ldots, S_n)$. We evaluate rational functions p and q and proceed to the appropriate son of v depending on the outcome of the comparison. If the computation reaches a leaf labelled by rational function $r(S_1, \ldots, S_n)$ then r is evaluated and the value of r is the result of the computation.

<u>Theorem 12:</u> Let $f : \mathbb{R}^n \to \mathbb{R}$ be a function and let T be a rational decision tree which computes f. Let $W_1, \ldots, W_q$ be pairwise disjoint subsets of $\mathbb{R}$ of non-zero measure and let $r_1, \ldots, r_q$ be pairwise different rational functions. If $f|_{W_i} = r_i$ for $1 \leq i \leq q$ then rational decision tree T has depth at least log q.

<u>Proof:</u> Let T be a rational decision tree which computes f. For v a leaf

of T let $D_v = \{(S_1,\ldots,S_n) \in \mathbb{R}^n;$ the computation on input $(S_1,\ldots,S_n)$ ends in leaf v}. Then $\{D_v;$ v leaf of T} is a partition of $\mathbb{R}^n$ and hence

$$W_i = \bigcup_{\text{v leaf of T}} (D_v \cap W_i)$$

for every i, $1 \le i \le q$. Since W_i has non-zero measure there must be a leaf v(i) such that $D_{v(i)} \cap W_i$ has non-zero measure. Note that T has a finite number of leaves. Let r(v(i)) be the rational function which labels leaf v(i). Then functions r(v(i)) and r_i agree on set $D_{v(i)} \cap W_i$. Since $D_{v(i)} \cap W_i$ has non-zero measure we must have that functions r(v(i)) and r_i are identical. Hence v(i) $\neq$ v(j) for i $\neq$ j and T must have at least q leaves. Thus the depth of T is at least log q.   □

We give two applications of theorem 12. The first application is to sorting. For $(x_1,\ldots,x_n) \in \mathbb{R}^n$ define $f(x_1,\ldots,x_n) = x_1^{r_1} + x_2^{r_2} + \ldots + x_n^{r_n}$ where $r_i = |\{j;\ x_j < x_i\}|$ is the rank of x_i. We call f the <u>rank function</u>. For π a permutation of n elements let $W_\pi = \{(x_1,\ldots,x_n) \in \mathbb{R}^n; x_{\pi(1)} < x_{\pi(2)} < \ldots < x_{\pi(n)}\}$. Then W_π has non-zero measure, $f|_{W_\pi}$ is a polynomial and $f|_{W_\rho} \neq f|_{W_\rho}$ for $\pi \neq \rho$. Hence the depth of any rational decision tree for the rank function is at least log n!

<u>Theorem 13:</u> Any rational decision tree for the rank function of n arguments has depth at least log n!

The second application is to searching. For $(y,x_1,\ldots,x_n) \in \mathbb{R}^{n+1}$ define $f(y,x_1,\ldots,x_n) = |\{j;\ x_j < y\}|$. We call f the <u>searching function</u>. For k, $0 \le k \le n$, let $W_k = \{(y,x_1,\ldots,x_n) \in \mathbb{R}^{n+1};$ exactly k x_j's are smaller than y}. Then W_k has non-zero measure and $f|_{W_k} = k$. Thus $f|_{W_k}$ is a rational function and $f|_{W_k} \neq f|_{W_\ell}$ for k $\neq$ ℓ. We have

<u>Theorem 14:</u> Any rational decision tree for the searching function of size n has depth at least log(n+1).

We will see in chapter III that log(n+1) is also an upper bound to the complexity of the searching function. Further applications of theorem 12 can be found in the exercises. Unfortunately, theorem 12 is not strong enough for the element uniqueness problem. Note that there is a rational decision tree of depth one which decides the element uniqueness problem,

namely $\prod_{1\le i<j\le n} (x_i - x_j) = 0$? This shows that there are problems which
are difficult in the restricted model of decision trees but become
simple if tests between rational functions are allowed and no charge
is made for computing those functions. Note however that the best
algorithm known for computing the product $\prod_{1\le i<j\le n} (x_i - x_j)$ requires
$\Omega(n\log n)$ multiplications and divisions. Hence, if we charge for tests
and algebraic operations then an $\Omega(n\log n)$ lower bound for the element
uniqueness problem is conceivable. We will use the remainder of the
section to prove such a lower bound. We start by fixing the model of
computation.

Definition: An algebraic computation tree for inputs $S_1,\ldots,S_n$ is a
binary tree T with a function that assigns
    a) to each leaf an output yes or no
    b) to each vertex v with exactly one son (= simple node) an assign-
ment (statement) of the form
$$Y(v) \leftarrow Y(v_1) \text{ op } Y(v_2) \ , \ Y(v) \leftarrow c \text{ op } Y(v_2) \ , \ \text{or } Y(v) \leftarrow \sqrt{Y(v_1)}$$
where op $\in \{+,-,x,/\}$, v_i is a simple node and a proper ancestor of v in
tree T or $Y(v_i) \in \{S_1,\ldots,S_n\}$, and $c \in \mathbb{R}$
    c) to each vertex of v with exactly two sons (= branching node) a
comparison of the form
$$Y(v_1) \ge 0, \ Y(v_1) > 0, \ \text{or } Y(v_1) = 0$$
where v_1 is a simple node and a proper ancestor of v or
$$Y(v_1) \in \{S_1,\ldots,S_n\}.$$
    □

Algebraic computation trees compute functions $f: \mathbb{R}^n \to \{yes,no\}$ in an
obvious way. Given an input $S = (S_1,\ldots,S_n) \in \mathbb{R}^n$ the program traverses
a path $P(S)$ in the tree. In simple nodes an arithmetical operation is
performed and the value of the operation is assigned to the variable
associated with the simple node. In branching nodes the value of a
variable is tested and the computation proceeds to the appropriate
son. We require that no computation leads to a division by zero or to
taking the square root of a negative number. The cost of an algebraic
computation tree is its depth, the complexity of (the membership problem
of) a set $V \subseteq \mathbb{R}^n$ is the minimum cost of any algebraic computation
tree which computes the characteristic function of V. The lower bounds
on the cost of algebraic computation trees are based on the following
fact from algebraic topology.

<u>Fact:</u> Let $q_1, \ldots, q_M$ be polynomials in N variables of degree at most d.
Let $V \subseteq \mathbb{R}^N$ be defined by

$$q_1(x_1, \ldots, x_N) = 0, \qquad \ldots \qquad , q_M(x_1, \ldots, x_N) = 0$$

Then the number of components of V is at most $d(2d - 1)^{N-1}$.

<u>Remark:</u> A proof of this can be found in J. Milnor: On the betti numbers
of real algebraic varieties, Proc. AMS 15 (1964), 275-280, and is far
beyond the scope of this book. We restrict ourselves to a short informal
discussion. Two points x and x' of V belong to the same component if
there is a line running inside V and connecting them, i.e. if there is
a continous function h: $[0,1] \to V$ with $h(0) = x$ and $h(1) = x'$. The
components of V are the equivalence classes under this relation.

The fact above becomes particularly simple if N = 1. In this case it
is equivalent to the fact that a polynomial of degree d in one variable
has at most d real roots. Consider the case N = 2 and d = 2 next. Then
$q_1(x_1, x_2) = 0$ defines an ellipse (parabola, or hyperbola) and so do
$q_2, q_3, \ldots$. The crucial observation is now that $q_1(x_1, x_2) = 0$,
$q_2(x_1, x_2) = 0$ defines a set of at most 6 <u>points</u>, i.e. six zero-
dimensional sets. All further equations $q_3(x_1, x_2) = 0, \ldots, q_M(x_1, x_2) = 0$
can only weed out some of these points and cannot increase the number
of components.

By analogy the truth of the fact is now conceivable for larger degree
and larger number of variables as well. The set defined by
$q_1(x_1, \ldots, x_N) = 0$ has at most d components, each of which has dimension
N - 1. Intersecting this set with the set $q_2(x_1, \ldots, x_N) = 0$ yields at
most $d(2d - 1)$ components each of which has dimension N - 2. Iterating
in this way we arrive at $d(2d - 1)^{N-1}$ components of dimension 0 each
defined by polynomials $q_1, \ldots, q_N$. Considering more polynomials weeds
out some of these points but does not increase the number of components.

We close with the warning that the argument above is at most a hint
towards a proof.   □

We are now ready for the lower bound. We use #V to denote the number of
components of set V.

<u>Theorem 15:</u> Let T be an algebraic computation for inputs $S_1, \ldots, S_n$
which decides the membership problem for $V \subseteq \mathbb{R}^n$, and let h be the
depth of T. Then

a) $\max(\#V, \#(\mathbb{R}^n - V)) \le 2^h 3^{h+n}$

b) $h \ge (\log \max(\#V, \#(R^n - V)) - n\log 3)/\log 6$

<u>Proof:</u> Part b) follows from part a) by taking logarithms. It remains to prove part a). Since tree T has depth h it has at most 2^h leaves. If w is a leaf of T let $D(w) \subseteq \mathbb{R}^n$ be the set of inputs S for which the computation ends in leaf w. We claim that $\#D(w) \le 3^{h+n}$. Note first that this claim implies part a) since there are at most 2^h leaves w and each leaf satisfies $\#D(w) \le 3^{h+n}$. Thus $\#V \le 2^h 3^{h+n}$ and similarly $\#(R^n - V) \le 2^h 3^{h+n}$.

It remains to prove $\#D(w) \le 3^{h+n}$ for every leaf w. In order to do so we characterize $D(w)$ by a set of polynomial equations and inequalities of degree at most 2. Let P be the path from the root to leaf w. We traverse down the path P and set up a system Γ of equalities and inequalities as follows. Let v be a node on path P.
If v is a simple node then

operation	equation
$Y(v) \leftarrow Y(v_1) \pm Y(v_2)$	$Y(v) = Y(v_1) \pm Y(v_2)$
$Y(v) \leftarrow Y(v_1) \cdot Y(v_2)$	$Y(v) = Y(v_1) \cdot Y(v_2)$
$Y(v) \leftarrow Y(v_1) / Y(v_2)$	$Y(v_1) = Y(v) \cdot Y(v_2)$
$Y(v) \leftarrow \sqrt{Y(v_1)}$	$Y(v_1) = Y(v)^2$

and if v is a branching node with a test

$\quad\quad Y(v_1) > 0 \quad\quad\quad\quad Y(v_1) \ge 0 \quad\quad\quad\quad Y(v_1) = 0$

then we add this (in-)equality to Γ if the positive outcome is taken on path P and we add

$\quad\quad -Y(v_1) \ge 0 \quad\quad\quad\quad -Y(v_1) > 0 \quad\quad\quad\quad Y(v) Y(v_1) - 1 = 0$

otherwise. Note that in the last case $Y(v)$ is a <u>new</u> variable which is not used in any assignment. Also note that the equation $Y(v) Y(v_1) - 1 = 0$ has a solution iff $Y(v_1) \ne 0$.

The system Γ involves variables $S_1, \ldots, S_n, Y(v_1), \ldots, Y(v_r)$ for some integer r. Also Γ contains exactly r equalities and some number s of inequalities. Clearly $r + s \le h$ since each node on P adds one equality or inequality. Let $W \subseteq \mathbb{R}^{n+r}$ be the set of solutions to the system Γ. Then the projection of W onto the first n coordinates is $D(w)$. Since the projection function is continous we conclude that $\#D(v) \le \#W$ and it therefore suffices to show $\#W \le 3^{h+n}$.

What have we obtained at this point? The set W is defined by a set of r equalities and s inequalities. Each equality or inequality is given by a polynomial of degree at most 2 in $n + r$ variables which we call $x_1,\ldots,x_{n+r}$ for simplicity from now on, i.e. we have a system

$$
\begin{array}{lll}
p_1(x_1,\ldots,x_{n+r}) = 0, & \ldots & , \; p_r(x_1,\ldots,x_{n+r}) = 0 \\
q_1(x_1,\ldots,x_{n+r}) > 0, & \ldots & , \; q_m(x_1,\ldots,x_{n+r}) > 0, \\
q_{m+1}(x_1,\ldots,x_{n+r}) \geq 0, & \ldots & , \; q_s(x_1,\ldots,x_{n+r}) \geq 0
\end{array}
$$

where each p_i, q_j has degree at most 2.

In order to apply the fact above we transform this system into a set of equalities in a higher dimensional space. Let $t = \#W$ and let $p_1,\ldots,p_t$ be points in the different components of W. Let

$$\varepsilon = \min \{q_j(p_i) \; ; \; 1 \leq j \leq m, \; 1 \leq i \leq t\}$$

Then $\varepsilon > 0$. Let W_ε be defined by the system

$$
\begin{array}{lll}
p_1(x_1,\ldots,x_{n+r}) = 0, & \ldots & , \; p_r(x_1,\ldots,x_{n+r}) = 0 \\
q_1(x_1,\ldots,x_{n+r}) \geq \varepsilon, & \ldots & , \; q_m(x_1,\ldots,x_{n+r}) \geq \varepsilon \\
q_{m+1}(x_1,\ldots,x_{n+r}) \geq 0,\ldots & & , \; q_s(x_1,\ldots,x_{n+r}) \geq 0
\end{array}
$$

Then $W_\varepsilon \subseteq W$ and $p_i \in W_\varepsilon$ for all i. Hence $\#W \leq \#W_\varepsilon$. It therefore suffices to show $\#W_\varepsilon \leq 3^{n+h}$.

Let $Z \subseteq \mathbb{R}^{n+r+s}$ be defined by the system

$$
\begin{array}{lll}
p_1(x_1,\ldots,x_{n+r}) = 0, & \ldots & , \; p_r(x_1,\ldots,x_{n+r}) = 0 \\
q_1(x_1,\ldots,x_{n+r}) = x_{n+r+1}^2 + \varepsilon, & \ldots & , \; q_m(x_1,\ldots,x_{n+r}) = x_{n+r+m}^2 + \varepsilon \\
q_{m+1}(x_1,\ldots,x_{n+r}) = x_{n+r+m+1}^2, & \ldots & , \; q_s(x_1,\ldots,x_{n+r}) = x_{n+r+s}^2
\end{array}
$$

where $x_{n+r+1},\ldots,x_{n+r+s}$ are new variables. Then W_ε is the projection of Z onto the first $n+r$ coordinates and hence $\#W_\varepsilon \leq \#Z$. Furthermore, Z is defined by a system of polynomial equations of degree at most two in $n + r + s \leq n + h$ variables. Hence

$$\#Z \leq 2(4 - 1)^{n+h-1} \leq 3^{n+h}$$

by the fact above. □

We close this section with three applications of Theorem 15.

Theorem 16: The complexity of the element uniqueness problem in the model of algebraic computation is $\Omega(n\log n)$.

Proof: Let $V \subseteq \mathbb{R}^n$ be defined by $\prod\limits_{1 \leq i < j \leq n} (x_i - x_j) \neq 0$. Then $\#V \geq n!$ as we will now argue. For $x = (x_1,\ldots,x_n) \in \mathbb{R}^n$, $x_i \neq x_j$ for $i \neq j$, let σ

be the order type of x, i.e. σ is a permutation with $x_{\sigma(1)} < x_{\sigma(2)} <$ $\cdots < x_{\sigma(n)}$. Then it is easy to see that if $x, x \in \mathbb{R}^n$ have different order types then any line connecting them must go through a point with two equal coordinates, i.e. a point outside V, and hence x and x' belong to different components of V. This proves $\#V \geq n!$ Since $\log n! = \Omega(n\log n)$ the proof is completed by an application of theorem 15. □

Our second application is the convex hull problem (cf. section VIII.2): Given n points in the plane, does their convex hull have n vertices?

<u>Theorem 17:</u> The complexity of the convex hull problem in the model of algebraic decision trees is $\Omega(n\log n)$.

<u>Proof:</u> Let $V = \{(x_1,y_1,\ldots,x_n,y_n);$ the convex hull of point set $\{(x_i,y_i); 1 \leq i \leq n\}$ has n vertices$\} \subseteq \mathbb{R}^{2n}$. As in the proof of theorem 16 we assign an order type to every element of V. Let $(x_1,y_1,\ldots,x_n,y_n) \in V$, and let p be any point in the interior of the convex hull of point set $\{(x_i,y_i); 1 \leq i \leq n\}$. Then the order type of this tuple is the circular ordering of the points around p. Note that there are $(n - 1)!$ different order types and that any line in $\mathbb{R}^{2n}$ connecting tuples of different order types must go through a point outside V. Hence $\#V \geq (n - 1)!$ and the theorem follows from theorem 15. □

Our last application is the computation of the elementary symmetric functions: Given $x_1,\ldots,x_n \in \mathbb{R}$, compute the elementary symmetric functions $p_0(x_1,\ldots,x_n), p_1(x_1,\ldots,x_n),\ldots,p_n(x_1,\ldots,x_n)$.

Here $p_j(x_1,\ldots,x_n) = (-1)^j \sum_{i_1 < i_2 < \ldots < i_j} x_{i_1} x_{i_2} \cdots x_{i_j}$. It is a well known fact from algebra that the elementary symmetric functions are the coefficients of the interpolation polynomial through points $(x_1,0),\ldots,(x_n,0),(0,(-1)^n x_1 \cdots x_n)$.

<u>Theorem 18:</u> The complexity of computing the elementary symmetric functions is $\Omega(n\log n)$ in the model of algebraic computation trees.

<u>Proof:</u> Let $a_i = p_i(1,2,\ldots,n)$, $1 \leq i \leq n$. An algorithm that computes $p_1(x_1,\ldots,x_n),\ldots,p_n(x_1,\ldots,x_n)$ can be used to test $a_i = p_i(x_1,\ldots,x_n)$, $1 \leq i \leq n$, in n more steps. Since this is true iff $\{x_1,\ldots,x_n\} = \{1,\ldots,n\}$

(This is a direct consequence of the uniqueness of the interpolation polynomial) it suffices to show that $\#V = n!$ where $V = \{(x_1,\ldots,x_n);\ \{x_1,\ldots,x_n\} = \{1,\ldots,n\}\}$. A proof that $\#V = n!$ can be given along the lines of the proof of theorem 15. □

Theorems 16, 17, and 18 show the strength of theorem 15. It can be used to prove lower bounds for a great variety of algorithmic problems. We should also note that theorem 15 is not strong enough to imply lower bounds on the complexity of RAM computations because indirect addressing is a "non-algebraic" operation (a lower bound on the complexity of RAM computaion will be shown in section II.3) and that is not strong enough to imply lower bounds for computations over the integers when integer division belongs to the instruction repertoire.

II. 2. Sorting by Distribution

II. 2.1 Sorting Words

Let Σ be a finite alphabet of size m and let $\leq$ be a linear order on Σ. We may assume w.l.o.g. that $\Sigma = \{1,2,\ldots,m\}$ with the usual ordering relation. The ordering on Σ is extended to an ordering on the words over Σ as usual.

<u>Definition:</u> Let $x = x_1 \ldots x_k$ and $y = y_1 \ldots y_\ell$ be words over Σ, i.e. $x_i, y_j \in \Sigma$. Then x is smaller than y in the alphabetic ordering (denoted $x < y$) if there is an i, $0 \leq i \leq k$ such that $x_j = y_j$ for $1 \leq j \leq i$ and either $i = k < \ell$ or $i < k$, $i < \ell$ and $x_{i+1} < y_{i+1}$. □

The definition of alphabetic ordering conforms with every day usage, e.g. we have $x = ABC < AD = y$ because $x_1 = y_1$ and $x_2 < y_2$.

We treat the following problem in this section: Given n words $x^1, x^2, \ldots, x^n$ over alphabet $\Sigma = \{1,\ldots,m\}$ sort them according to alphabetic order.

There are many different ways of storing words. A popular method stores all words in a common storage area called string space. The characters of any word are stored in consecutive storage locations. Each string variable then consists of a pointer into the string space and a location containing the current length of the word. The figure below shows an example for $x^1 = ABD$, $x^2 = DBA$ and $x^3 = Q$.

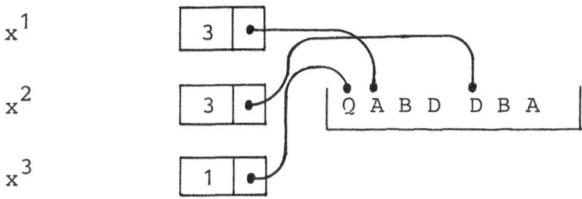

The basic idea of bucketsort is most easily explained when we consider
a special case first: all words $x^1, \ldots, x^n$ have length 1, i.e. the input
consists of n numbers between 1 and m. Bucketsort starts with m empty
buckets. Then we process word by word, throwing x^i into the x^i-th
bucket. Finally, we step through the buckets in order and collect the
words in sorted order. This description of Bucketsort is fairly poetic
in style; let us fill in some implementation details next. Buckets are
linear lists, the heads of the lists are stored in array K[1.. m].
Initially, we have to create m empty lists. This is easily done in time
O(m) by initializing array K. In order to process x^i we have to access
$K[x^i]$ and to insert x^i into the list with head $K[x^i]$. This can be done
in time O(1) if we insert x^i at the front end of the list or at the
back end of the list. In the latter case $K[x^i]$ must also contain a
pointer to the end of the list. Thus we can distribute n words in time
O(n). Finally we have to collect the buckets. We step through array
K[1.. m] and concatenate the front of the (j+1)-st list with the end of
the j-th list. This takes time O(m), if array K also contains pointers
to the back ends of the lists, and time O(n+m) otherwise. Note that the
total length of all m lists is n. In either case total running time is
O(n+m). We have to discuss one more detail before we proceed. Should we
add x^i to the front or to the rear end of the x^i-th list? If we always
add to the rear, then the order of elements x^i, x^j with $x^i = x^j$ is unchanged, i.e. bucketsort is stable. This will be important for what
follows.

We proceed to a slightly more difficult case next. The x^i's, $1 \leq i \leq n$,
are proper words and all of them have equal length, say k. Then $x^i =$
$x_1^i \, x_2^i \, \ldots \, x_k^i$ with $x_j^i \in \Sigma$. There are two ways of extending our basic
algorithm to the more general case. In the first approach we sort
according to the first letter first. This divides our set of words into
m groups, some of which may be empty. Then we sort each group seperately
according to the second character, ... until each group consists of a

single word only. This approach has a serious disadvantage. Groups
become smaller and smaller, but the complexity of bucketsort is at
least the size of the alphabet, i.e. the overhead may be large for
small group size. It is shown in exercise 18 that total running time of
this approach may be as large as $\Omega(n \cdot k \cdot m)$. In the second approach one
sorts according to the last letter first. After having done so we sort
the entire list of n words, which is sorted according to the last
letter, according to the next to last letter. Here comes the crucial
observation. The words are sorted according to the last two letters
now, because bucketsort is stable. Next we sort according to the
(k-2)-th letter, and so on. The second approach requires k passes over
the set of n words, each pass having a cost of $O(n+m)$ time units. Thus
total running time is $O(k(n+m))$.

Can we improve upon this? Let us consider an example with m = 4, n = 5
and k = 3. The 5 words are: 123, 124, 223, 324, 321. The first pass
yields:

bucket one : 321		and hence the input sequence for the
bucket two :		second pass is 321, 123, 223, 124, 324.
bucket three: 123, 223		The second pass yields:
bucket four : 124, 324		

bucket one :		and hence the input sequence for the third
bucket two : 321, 123,		pass is 321, 123, 223, 124, 324. The third
	223, 124, 324	pass yields:
bucket three:		
bucket four :		

bucket one : 123, 124	and hence the final result sequence is
bucket two : 223	123, 124, 223, 321, 324.
bucket three: 321, 324	
bucket four :	

Note that we collected a total of 3·4 = 12 buckets, but only 7 buckets
where non-empty altogether. It would improve running time if we knew
ahead of time which buckets to collect in each pass. Let us assume that
s_j buckets are non-empty in the j-th pass, $1 \le j \le k$. If we could avoid
looking at empty buckets then the cost of the j-th pass were only
$O(s_j + n)$. Since $s_j \le n$, the cost of a pass would be only $O(n)$ instead
of $O(n + m)$.

There is a very simple method for determining which buckets are non-empty in the j-th pass, i.e. which letters occur in the j-th position. Create set $\{(j,x_j^i),\ 1 \le j \le k,\ 1 \le i \le n\}$ of size $n \cdot k$ and sort it by bucketsort according to the second component and then according to the first. Then the j-th bucket contains all characters which appear in the j-th position in sorted order. The cost of the first pass is $O(n \cdot k + m)$, the cost of the second pass is $O(n \cdot k + k)$. Total cost is thus $O(nk + m)$.

Before we give a complete algorithm for bucketsort we discuss the extension to words of arbitrary length. Let $x^i = x_1^i\ x_2^i\ \ldots\ x_{\ell_i}^i$, $1 \le i \le n$; ℓ_i is the length of x_i. We basically proceed as above, however we have to make sure that x^i has to be considered for the first time when we sort according to the ℓ_i-th letter. This leads to the following algorithm. Let $L = \Sigma\ \ell_i \ge n$

1) Determine the length of x^i, $1 \le i \le n$, and create pairs (ℓ_i, pointer to x^i). This takes time $O(L)$.

2) Sort the pairs (ℓ_i, pointer to x^i) by bucketsort according to the first component. Then the k-th bucket contains all x^i with $\ell_i = k$, i.e. all these strings are contained in a linear list. Call this list length[k]. The cost of step 2) is $O(n + L)$ because L buckets certainly suffice.

3) Create L pairs (j, x_j^i), $1 \le i \le n$, $1 \le j \le \ell_i$ and sort them according to the second and then according to the first component. Let Nonempty[j], $1 \le j \le \ell_{max} = \max(\ell_1, \ldots, \ell_n)$ be the j-th bucket after the second pass. Nonempty[j] contains all letters which appear in the j-th position in sorted order. Delete all duplicates from Nonempty[j]. The cost of step 3 is $O(L + m) + O(L + \ell_{max}) = O(L + m)$.

4) We finally sort words x^i by distribution. All lists in the following program are used as queues; the head of each list contains a pointer to the last element. Also x is a string variable and x_j is the j-th letter of string x.

```
(1)    W ← empty queue;
(2)    for k from 1 to m do S[k] ← empty queue od;
(3)    for j from ℓ_max to 1
(4)    do add length[j] to the front of W and call the new queue W;
(5)        while W ≠ ∅
(6)        do let x be the first element of W; delete x from W;
(7)            add x to the end of S[x_j];
           od
(8)        while Nonempty[j] ≠ ∅
(9)        do let k be the first element of Nonempty[j];
(1o)           delete k from Nonempty[j];
(11)           add S[k] to the end of W;
(12)           set S[k] to the empty queue;
           od
       od
```

Correctness of this algorithm is immediate from the preceding discussion. Line (2) costs $O(m)$ time units, a single execution of any other line has a cost of $O(1)$. Note that only a pointer to string x is moved in line (7). Lines (3) and (4) are executed ℓ_{max} times. In lines (5), (6) and (7) we operate exactly ℓ_i times on string x^i. Hence the total cost of these lines is $O(L)$. We associate the cost of a single execution of lines (9) to (12) with the first element of S[k]; k as in line (9). In this way we associate at most $O(\ell_i)$ time units with x^i, $1 \le i \le n$, and hence the total cost of lines (8) - (12) is $O(L)$. Altogether we have shown that total cost of steps (4) - (12) is $O(m + L)$.

Theorem 1: Bucketsort sorts n words of total length L over an alphabet of size m in time $O(m + L)$.

II. 2.2 Sorting Reals by Distribution

We briefly describe distribution sort applied to real numbers. For simplicity, we assume that we are given a sequence x_i, $1 \le i \le n$, of reals from the interval [0,1]. We use the following very simple algorithm, called Hybridsort. α is some fixed real and k is equal to αn.

1) Create k empty buckets. Put x_i into bucket $\lceil kx_i \rceil$ for $1 \le i \le n$.

2) Apply Heapsort to every bucket and concatenate the buckets.

The correctness of this algorithm is obvious.

Theorem 2: a) Worst case running time of Hybridsort is $O(n \log n)$.

b) If the x_i's are drawn independently from a uniform distribution over the interval $[0,1]$, then Hybridsort has expected running time $O(n)$.

Proof: a) Running time of the first phase is clearly $O(n)$. Let us assume that t_i elements end up in the i-th bucket, $1 \le i \le k$. Then the cost of the second phase is $O(\Sigma_i t_i \log t_i)$ where $0 \cdot \log 0 = 0$ and $\Sigma_i t_i = n$. But $\Sigma_i t_i \log t_i \le \Sigma_i t_i \log n = n \log n$.

b) Let B_i be the random variable representing the number of elements in the i-th bucket after pass 1. Then $\text{prob}(B_i = h) = \binom{n}{h}(1/k)^h(1-1/k)^{n-h}$ since any single x_j is in the i-th bucket with probability $1/k$. Expected running time of phase 2 is

$$E(\sum_{i=1}^{k} B_i \log B_i) = k \cdot \sum_{h=2}^{n} (h \cdot \log h) \binom{n}{h}(1/k)^h(1-1/k)^{n-h}$$

$$\le k \cdot \sum_{h=2}^{n} h^2 \binom{n}{h}(1/k)^h(1-1/k)^{n-h}$$

$$= k(n(n-1)/k^2 + n/k)$$

since $h^2\binom{n}{h} = (h(h-1) + h)\binom{n}{h} = n(n-1)\binom{n-2}{h-2} + n\binom{n-1}{h-1}$

$$= O(n)$$

since $k = \alpha n$ □

II. 3. Lower Bounds on Sorting, Revisited

In section II.1.6. we proved an $\Omega(n \log n)$ lower bound on the average and worst case complexity of sorting. However, in II.2.2. we showed an $O(n)$ upper bound on the average case complexity of sorting reals. What

went wrong? An upper bound which is smaller than the corresponding
lower bound? The answer is that we have to keep the models of computation in mind for which we proved the bounds. The lower bound of II.1.6
was shown for rational decision trees. In rational decision trees we
can compare rational functions of the inputs at every step. Hybridsort
uses a larger set of primitives; in particular it uses division and
rounding and it uses indirect addressing. Note that indices into arrays
are computed as functions of the inputs. Also the upper bound on
running time is expected case and not worst case. It is open whether
any variant of Hybridsort can sort numbers in linear worst case time.
However, it can be shown that any RAM (in the sense of I.1.) which
operates on natural numbers and has basic operations $+$, $\doteq$ (subtraction
in $\mathbb{N}_o$), $\cdot$ in addition to the comparison operator $\leq$ requires time
$\Omega(n \log n)$ in the unit cost measure for sorting in the worst case. This
is even true for coin tossing RAMs (in the sense of I.2.). It is open
whether the result stays true if division is also a basic operation.

Before we state the precise result we briefly recall the RAM model. It
is convenient to use indirect addressing instead of index registers as
the means for address calculations. We saw in I.1. that this does not
affect running time by more than a constant; however it makes the proof
more readable. The basic operations are (i, $k \in \mathbb{N}$):

$$\alpha \leftarrow i, \qquad \alpha \leftarrow \rho(i) \qquad , \alpha \leftarrow \rho(\rho(i))$$

$$\rho(i) \leftarrow \alpha \qquad , \rho(\rho(i)) \leftarrow \alpha$$

$$\alpha \leftarrow \alpha \text{ op } \rho(i) \qquad , \text{where op} \in \{+, \cdot, \doteq\}$$

goto k

if $\rho(i) > \alpha$ then goto k_1 else goto k_2 fi

$\alpha \leftarrow$ random

$$\text{Here } x \doteq y = \begin{cases} x - y & \text{if } x \geq y \\ 0 & \text{if } x < y \end{cases} \quad \text{and}$$

$\alpha \leftarrow$ random assigns 0 or 1 to α with probability 1/2 each. A RRAM program is a sequence of instructions numbered starting at 1. The labels
in the goto instructions refer to this numbering.

Definition: Let A be an RRAM. A solves the sorting problem of size n
if for all x = $(x_1, \ldots, x_n) \in \mathbb{R}^n$: if A is started with x_i in location
i, $1 \leq i \leq n$, and 0 in the accumulator and all locations j, j > n, and
if π is a permutation such that $x_{\pi(1)} \leq x_{\pi(2)} \leq \ldots \leq x_{\pi(n)}$ then A
stops and $x_{\pi(i)}$ is in location i, $1 \leq i \leq n$, when A stops.

Theorem 1: Let A be any RRAM which solves the sorting problem of size
n. Then there is an $x \in \mathbb{R}^n$ such that the expected running time of A on
x is at least log n!, i.e. the worst case running time of A is at least
log n!.

Proof: Let A be any RRAM which solves the sorting problem of size n and
stops on all inputs $x \in \mathbb{R}^n$ and all sequences of coin tosses in at most
t steps. Here t is some integer. The proof is by reduction to the decision tree model studied in section II.1.6.. The first step is to re-
place all instructions of the form $\alpha \leftarrow \alpha \doteq \rho(i)$ by the equivalent
sequence if $\rho(i) \geq \alpha$ then $\alpha \leftarrow 0$ else $\alpha \leftarrow \alpha - \rho(i)$ fi. After the modification A uses only true subtractions. In the second step we associate
with program A a (maybe infinite) decision tree T(A) by unfolding. T(A)
is a binary tree whose nodes are labelled by instructions and tests and
some of whose edges are labelled by 0 or 1. More precisely, let A consist of m instructions. Then $T_i(A)$, $1 \leq i \leq m+1$ is defined by

(1) $T_{m+1}(A)$ a single leaf

(2) if line i of A is instruction $\alpha \leftarrow i$, $\alpha \leftarrow \rho(i)$, $\alpha \leftarrow \rho(\rho(i))$,
$\rho(i) \leftarrow \alpha$, $\rho(\rho(i)) \leftarrow \alpha$ or $\alpha \leftarrow \alpha$ op $\rho(i)$ then $T_i(A)$ consists of a root
labelled by that instruction with a single son. The single subtree is
$T_{i 1}(A)$.

(3) if line i is goto k then $T_i(A)$ is equal to $T_k(A)$.

(4) if line i is if $\rho(i) > \alpha$ then goto k_1 else goto k_2 fi then

$T_i(A) =$

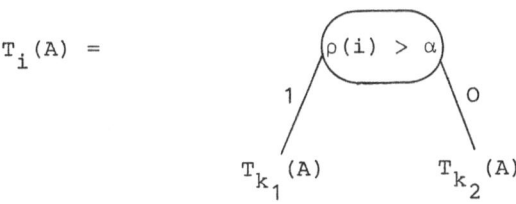

(5) if line i is $\alpha \leftarrow$ random then

$$T_i(A) =$$

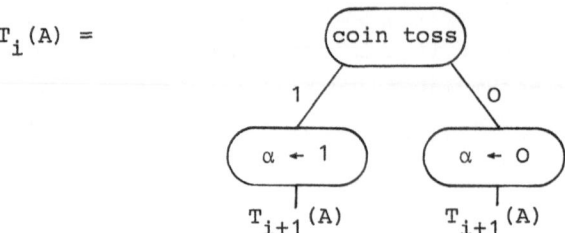

Finally $T(A) = T_1(A)$. Tree $T(A)$ simulates RRAM A in an obvious way; in coin tossing nodes the two outgoing edges are taken with equal probability. Tree $T(A)$ might be infinite but because A stops on every input $x \in \mathbb{R}^n$ within t steps no node of depth $> 2t$ is ever reached in any computation. Therefore we may prune $T(A)$ at depth $2t$.

In the third step we associate with every edge e of the decision tree a set $\{p_{e,i}, i \in \mathbb{N}_0\}$ of polynomials in indeterminates $X_1, \ldots, X_n$. The intended meaning of $p_{e,i}(x)$ is the content of location i (the accumulator for $i = 0$) if the input is $x \in \mathbb{R}^n$ and control has reached edge e. Polynomials $p_{e,i}$ are defined inductively by induction on the depth of e. Polynomials $p_{e,i}$ will not have the intended meaning for all inputs x but only for a sufficiently large set of nice inputs as made precise below. If p and q are polynomials we write $p \equiv q$ to denote the fact that p and q define the same rational function. The inductive definition is started by:

If e is the (conceptual) edge entering the root then

$$p_{e,i}(X) = \begin{cases} X_i & \text{if } 1 \le i \le n \\ 0 & \text{otherwise} \end{cases}$$

For the induction step let e be an edge leaving node v, let d be the edge into v and let ins(v) be the label of node v.

(1) if ins(v) is $\rho(i) > \alpha$ or coin toss then $p_{e,i} = p_{d,i}$ for all $i \ge 0$

(2) if ins(v) is $\alpha \leftarrow \alpha$ op $\rho(i)$, op $\in \{+,-,\cdot\}$ then

$$p_{e,j} = \begin{cases} p_{d,0} \text{ op } p_{d,i} & \text{if } j = 0 \\ p_{d,j} & \text{otherwise} \end{cases}$$

(3)   if ins(v) is $\alpha \leftarrow i$ then

$$p_{e,j} = \begin{cases} i & \text{if } j = 0 \\ p_{d,j} & \text{otherwise} \end{cases}$$

(4)   if ins(v) is $\alpha \leftarrow \rho(i)$ or $\alpha \leftarrow \rho(\rho(k))$ and

$p_{d,k} \equiv i$ for some $i \in \mathbb{N}_0$ then

$$p_{e,j} = \begin{cases} p_{d,i} & \text{if } j = 0 \\ p_{e,j} & \text{otherwise} \end{cases}$$

(5)   if ins(v) is $\alpha \leftarrow \rho(\rho(k))$ and $p_{d,k} \neq i$ for all $i \in \mathbb{N}_0$ then let w be the closest ancestor (i.e. an ancestor of maximal depth) of v such that the label of w is $\rho(\rho(\ell)) \leftarrow \alpha$ for some $\ell \in \mathbb{N}$ and $p_{f,\ell} \equiv p_{d,k}$ where f is the edge entering w. If w does exist then

$$p_{e,j} = \begin{cases} p_{f,0} & \text{if } j = 0 \\ p_{d,j} & \text{otherwise} \end{cases}$$

and if w does not exist then

$$p_{e,j} = \begin{cases} 0 & \text{if } j = 0 \\ p_{d,j} & \text{otherwise} \end{cases}$$

(6)   if ins(v) is $\rho(i) \leftarrow \alpha$ or $\rho(\rho(k)) \leftarrow \alpha$ and $p_{d,k} \equiv i$ for some $i \in \mathbb{N}_0$ then

$$p_{e,j} = \begin{cases} p_{d,0} & \text{if } j = i \\ p_{d,j} & \text{otherwise} \end{cases}$$

(7)   if ins(v) is $\rho(\rho(k)) \leftarrow \alpha$ and $p_{d,k} \neq i$ for all $i \in \mathbb{N}_0$ then $p_{e,j} = p_{d,j}$ for all j.

We will next derive a sufficient condition for the "correctness" of the intended meaning of polynomials $p_{e,j}$. Let $I = \{1,\ldots,n\} \cup \{j;$ there is some instruction with address j in $T(A)$ or $p_{e,i} \equiv j$ for some edge e and $i \in \mathbb{N}_0\}$. Note that I is finite since for every edge e there are only finitely many (at most n + depth of e) i's with $p_{e,i} \neq 0$. This is easily seen by induction on the depth of e. Let Q_A, a set of polynomials, be defined by $Q_A = I \cup \{p_{e,i};$ e is edge of T(A) and $i \geq 0\}$. Q_A is a finite set of polynomials by the remark above. A point $x \in \mathbb{R}^n$ is admissible if $p(x) \neq q(x)$ for any $p, q \in Q_A$ with $p \neq q$.

Lemma 1: If $x \in \mathbb{R}^n$ is admissible for Q_A then all $p_{e,j}$'s have their intended meaning for all edges e and all $j \in I$, i.e. $p_{e,j}(x)$ is the content of location j if the input is x and control reaches e for all $j \in I$.

Proof: The proof is by induction on the depth of e. The claim is clearly true for the edge entering the root. So let us consider the case that edge e emanates from node v. Let d be the edge entering v. The induction step is by case analysis paralleling the definition of $p_{e,j}$. The induction step is easy in cases (1), (2), (4) and (6) and therefore left to the reader. The two remaining cases are cases (5) and (7).

Case (5): Let w, f and ℓ be defined as above. Let us consider the case that w exists first. Let $h = p_{f,\ell}(x) = p_{d,k}(x)$. Then $p_{f,o}(x)$ was stored in location h by instruction ins(w). It remains to be shown that location h was not written into on the path from w to v. Let z be any node on that path excluding v and w. If ins(z) is not a store instruction then there is nothing to show. So let us assume that ins(z) is either $\rho(i) \leftarrow \alpha$ or $\rho(\rho(i)) \leftarrow \alpha$. In the former case we have $i \neq h = p_{d,k}(x)$ since $i \in I \subseteq Q_A$, x is admissible for Q_A, and $p_{d,k}$ is not constant, in the latter case we have $p_{g,i}(x) \neq h = p_{f,\ell}(x)$, where g is the edge entering z, since $p_{g,i} \in Q_A$ and x is admissible for Q_A. In either case ins(z) does not write into location z.

If w does not exist then one proves in the same way that nothing was ever written in location $h = p_{d,k}(x)$ before control reaches edge e.

Case (7): Then ins(v) is $\rho(\rho(k)) \leftarrow \alpha$ and $p_{d,k} \neq i$ for all $i \in \mathbb{N}_o$. Hence $p_{d,k}(x) \notin I$ since x is admissible for Q_A and $I \subseteq Q_A$. Thus the content of locations with addresses in I is not changed by ins(v).   □

Let π be a permutation of $\{1, 2, \ldots, n\}$. $x \in \mathbb{R}^n$ is of order type π if $x_{\pi(1)} < x_{\pi(2)} < \cdots < x_{\pi(n)}$. Let $P = |\{\pi;$ there is $x \in \mathbb{R}^n$ of order type π which is admissible for $Q_A\}|$. We show below that $P = n!$ Let $x(\pi)$ be admissible for Q_A of order type π. Execution of $T(A)$ on input $x(\pi)$ ends in some leaf with ingoing edge e; of course, the leaf depends on sequence $s \in \{0,1\}^{2t}$ of coin tosses used in the computation. We have $p_{e,i}(x(\pi)) = x_{\pi(i)}(\pi)$ for all $i \in \{1,\ldots,n\}$. Since $X_1,\ldots,X_n \in Q_A$ and $x(\pi)$ is admissible for Q_A this is only possible if $p_{v,i} \equiv X_{\pi(i)}$ for all $i \in \{1,\ldots,n\}$. Thus for every sequence $s \in \{0,1\}^{2t}$ of coin tosses at least $n!$ different leaves are reachable   one for each order type. Let $d(\pi,s)$ be the number of nodes of outdegree 2 on the path from the root to the leaf which is reached on input $x(\pi)$ when sequense s of coin tosses is used. Then

$$1/n! \; \Sigma_\pi \; d(\pi,s) \geq \log n!$$

(compare the proof of II.1.6., Theorem 10) for every $s \in \{0,1\}^{2t}$ and hence

$$1/2^{2t} \quad \Sigma_{s\in \{0,1\}^{2t}} \quad (1/n! \; \Sigma_\pi \; d(\pi,s)) \geq \log n!$$

or

$$1/n! \; \Sigma_\pi \; (1/2^{2t} \quad \Sigma_{s\in \{0,1\}^{2t}} \quad d(\pi,s)) \geq \log n!$$

Thus there must be some π such that

$$1/2^{2t} \quad \Sigma_{s\in \{0,1\}^{2t}} \quad d(\pi,s) \geq \log n!$$

, i.e. the expected running time of A on input $x(\pi)$ is at least $\log n! \geq n \log n - 2n$.

It remains to prove that $P = n!$. Q_A is a finite set of polynomials. x is admissible for Q_A if $p(x) \neq q(x)$ for any pair $p,q \in Q_A$ with $p \neq q$, i.e. if $R(x) \neq 0$ where $R_A = \Pi\{p-q;\ p,q \in Q_A,\ p \neq q\}$. R_A is a single polynomial. It therefore suffices to prove lemma 2.

Lemma 2: Let $R \neq 0$ be a polynomial of degree m in variables $\{X_1,\ldots,X_n\}$ and let π be any permutation of $\{1,\ldots,n\}$. Then there is an $x \in \{1,\ldots,n+m\}^n$ of order type π with $R(x) \neq 0$.

Proof: Since $R(X_{\pi(1)}, \ldots, X_{\pi(n)})$ is again a polynomial of degree m it suffices to prove the claim for π being the identity. This is done by induction on n. For n = 1 the claim follows from the fact that a univariate polynomial of degree m has at most m zeroes. For the induction step let

$$R(X) = \sum_{i=0}^{s} R_i(X_1, \ldots, X_{n-1}) \; X_n^i$$

where $R_s \neq 0$. Let r be the degree of R_s. Then $r + s \leq m$. By induction hypothesis there is some $x \in \{1, \ldots, r+n-1\}^{n-1}$, $x_1 < x_2 < \ldots < x_{n-1}$ with $R_s(x) \neq 0$. Choose $x_n \in \{r+n, \ldots, n+r+s\}$ such that the s-th degree polynomial

$$\sum_{i=0}^{s} R_i(x_1, \ldots, x_{n-1}) \; X_n^i$$

in X_n is non-zero.   □□

Similar lower bounds can be shown for related problems, e.g. the nearest neighbour problem (exercise 2o) and the problem of searching an ordered table (exercise 21). It is open whether theorem 1 stays true if integer division is added as an additional primitive operation. It should be noted however that one can sort in linear time (in the unit cost model) if bitwise boolean operations (componentwise negation and componentwise AND of register contents, which are imagined to be binary representations of numbers) and integer division are additional primitives.

Theorem 2: RAMs with integer division and bitwise boolean operations can sort n numbers in time O(n) in the unit cost model.

Proof: The idea of the proof is to exploit the parallelism provided by bitwise boolean operations and to use integer division for cutting large numbers into pieces. The details are as follows.

Let $x_1, x_2, \ldots, x_n$ be integers. We first find the maximum, say x_m, compute $x_m \vee \overline{x_m}$ (bitwise) and add 1. This produces 10^k where k is the length of the binary representation of x_m. Note that 10^k is the binary representation of 2^{k+1}.

We shall compute the rank of every x_i, i.e. compare each x_i with all x_j and count how many are smaller than it. Note that if we have

```
A          ... 1 x_i 1 ...
B          ... 0 x_j 0 ...
                 ↑
           indicator
```

in registers A and B, with x_i and x_j in matching positions, then regardless to the rest of registers A and B, C = A - B will contain a 1 at the indicated position iff $x_i \geq x_j$.

So, to sort, we obtain in a single register n copies of $1 \ x_n \ 11 \ x_{n-1} \ 11 \ x_{n-2} \ \cdots \ 1 \ x_1 \ 1$ concatenated to each other, and $(0 \ x_n \ 0)^n \ (0 \ x_{n-1} \ 0)^n \ \cdots \ (0 \ x_1 \ 0)^n$ in another with the length of all x_i's padded out to k with leading zeroes. This can be done in time O(n) as follows. We show the construction for $(0 \ x_n \ 0)^n \ (0 \ x_{n-1} \ 0)^n \ \cdots \ (0 \ x_1 \ 0)^n$. Note first that we have 2^{k+1} available and therefore can compute $a := 2^{(k+2)n}$ in time O(n). Next note that

$$b := \sum_{i=1}^{n} x_i \ 2^{(k+2)n(i-1)+1}$$ has binary representation.

$$\underbrace{0 \ \cdots \ 0 \ x_n \ 0}_{(k+2)n \text{ bits}} \quad \underbrace{0 \ \cdots \ 0 \ x_{n-1} \ 0}_{(k+2)n \text{ bits}} \quad \cdots \quad \underbrace{0 \ \cdots \ 0 \ x_1 \ 0}_{(k+2)n \text{ bits}}$$

and can be computed in time O(n) given a, $x_1, \ldots, x_n$. Finally observe, that $\sum_{i=0}^{n-1} b \ 2^{(k+2)i}$ is the desired result.

At this point, a single subtraction yields all comparisons. An AND with bit string $(10^{k+1})^{n^2}$, which can be constructed in time O(n), retrieves all the indicator bits. More precisely, we have a bitstring of length $(k+2)n^2$ such that bit $(k+2)n \ (j-1) + (k+2)i$ is one iff $x_i \geq x_j$ and all other bits are zero. We cut this bit string into pieces of length $(k+2)n$ by repeatedly dividing it by $2^{(k+2)n}$ and sum all the pieces. This yields

$$\text{rank}(x_n) \ \cdots \ 0 \ \cdots \ 0 \ \underbrace{\text{rank}(x_2)}_{(k+2) \text{ bits}} \quad \underbrace{0 \ \cdots \ 0 \ \text{rank}(x_1)}_{(k+2) \text{ bits}} \quad \underbrace{0 \ \cdots \ 0}_{(k+1) \text{ bits}}$$

The ranks are now easily retrieved and the sort is completed in time
$O(n)$.   □

II. 4. The Linear Median Algorithm

Selection is a problem which is related to but simpler than sorting. We
are given a sequence $S_1, \ldots, S_n$ of pairwise distinct elements and an integer i, $1 \leq i \leq n$, and want to find the i-th smallest element of the
sequence, i.e. an S_j such that there are i-1 keys S_ℓ with $S_\ell < S_j$ and
n-i keys S_ℓ with $S_\ell > S_j$. For i = n/2 such a key is called median. Of
course, selection can be reduced to sorting. We might first sort
sequence $S_1, \ldots, S_n$ and then find the i-th smallest element by a single
scan of the sorted sequence. This results in an $O(n \log n)$ algorithm.
However, there is a linear time solution. We describe a simple, linear
expected time solution (procedure Find) first and then extend it to a
linear worst case time solution (procedure Select).

Procedure Find is based on the partitioning algorithm used in Quicksort.
We choose some element of the sequence, say S_1, as partitioning element
and then divide the sequence into the elements smaller than S_1 and the
elements larger than S_1. We then call Find recursively on the appropriate subsequence.

```
(1)    procedure Find(M,i);
       co finds the i-th smallest element of set M;
(2)    S ← some element of M;
(3)    M₁ ← {m ∈ M; m < S};
(4)    M₂ ← {m ∈ M; m > S};
(5)    case |M₁| of
(6)       < i - 1 : Find(M₂, i - |M₁| - 1);
(7)       = i - 1 : return S;
(8)       > i - 1 : Find(M₁, i)
(9)    esac
(1o)   end
```

When set M is stored in an array then lines (2) - (4) of Find are best
implemented by lines (2) - (6) of Quicksort. Then a call of Find has
cost $O(|M|$ + the time spent in the recursive call). The worst case
running time of Find is clearly $O(n^2)$. Consider the case i = 1 and

$|M_1| = |M| - 1$ always. Expected running time of algorithm Find is
linear as we show next. We use the same randomness assumption as for
the analysis of Quicksort, namely the elements of M are pairwise distinct and each permutation of the elements of M is equally likely. In
particular, this implies that element S chosen in line (2) is the k-th
largest element of M with probability $1/|M|$. It also implies that both
subproblems M_1 and M_2 again satisfy the randomness assumption (cf. the
analysis of Quicksort). Let $T(n,i)$ be the expected running time of
Find(M,i) where $|M| = n$ and let $T(n) = \max_i T(n,i)$.

We have $T(1) = c$ for some constant c and

$$T(n,i) \le cn + 1/n[\sum_{k=1}^{i-1} T(n-k,\ i-k) + \sum_{k=i+1}^{n} T(k-1,i)]$$

since the partitioning process takes time cn and the recursive call
takes expected time $T(n-k,i-k)$ if $k = |M_1| + 1 < i$ and time $T(k-1,i)$
if $k = |M_1| + 1 > i$. Thus

$$T(n) \le cn + 1/n \max_i[\sum_{k=1}^{i-1} T(n-k) + \sum_{k=i}^{n-1} T(k)]$$

We show $T(n) \le 4cn$ by induction on n. This is clearly true for $n = 1$.
For $n > 1$ we have

$$T(n) \le cn + 1/n \max_i[\sum_{k=n-i+1}^{n-1} 4ck + \sum_{k=i}^{n-1} 4ck]$$

$$\le cn + 4c/n \max_i[n(n-1) - (n-i)(n-i+1)/2 - i(i-1)/2]$$

$$\le 4cn$$

since the expression in square brackets is maximal for $i = (n+1)/2$
(note that the expression is symmetric in i and n-i+1) and then has
value $n(n-1) - n(n-1)/4 \le 3n^2/4$. We have thus shown.

Theorem 1: Algorithm Find has linear expected running time.

The expected linearity of Find stems from the fact that the expected size of the subproblem to be solved is only a fraction of the size of the original problem. However, the worst case running time of Find is quadratic because the size of the subproblem might be only one smaller than the size of the original problem. If one wants a linear worst case algorithm one has to choose the partitioning element more carefully. A first approach is to take a reasonable size sample of M, say of size $|M|/5$, and to take the median of the sample as partitioning element. However, this idea is not good enough yet because the sample might consist of small elements only. A better way of choosing the sample is to divide M into small groups of say 5 elements each and to make the sample the set of medians of the groups. Then it is guaranteed that a fair fraction of elements are smaller (larger) than the partitioning element. This leads to the following algorithm.

(1) <u>proc</u> Select(M,i);
     <u>co</u> finds the i-th smallest element of set M;
(2) n ← |M|;
(3) <u>if</u> n ≤ 1oo <u>then</u> sort M and find the i-th smallest element directly
     <u>else</u>
(4) divide M in $\lceil n/5 \rceil$ subsets $M_1, \ldots, M_{\lceil n/5 \rceil}$ of 5 elements each (the last subset may contain less than 5 elements);
(5) sort M_j; $1 \leq j \leq \lceil n/5 \rceil$;
(6) let m_j be the median of M_j;
(7) call Select($\{m_1, \ldots, m_{\lceil n/5 \rceil}\}$, $\lceil n/1o \rceil$) and determine $\bar{m}$, the median of the medians;
(8) let $M_1 = \{m \in M; m < \bar{m}\}$ and $M_2 = \{m \in M; \bar{m} \leq m\}$;
(9) <u>if</u> i ≤ |M_1|
(1o) <u>then</u> Select(M_1,i)
(11) <u>else</u> Select(M_2,i - |M_1|)
     <u>fi</u>
     <u>fi</u>
     <u>end</u>

It is very helpful to illustrate algorithm Select pictorially. In line (4) M is divided into groups of 5 elements each and the median of each group is determined in lines (5) and (6). At this point we have n/5 linear orders of 5 elements each. Next we find $\bar{m}$, the median of the medians. Assume w.l.o.g. that $m_1, \ldots, m_{n/1o} < \bar{m}$ and $\bar{m} \leq m_{n/1o+1}, \ldots, m_{n/5}$. This may be represented by the following diagram.

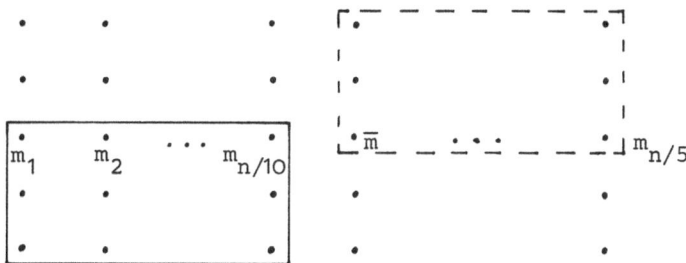

where each of the groups is represented by a vertical line of 5 elements, largest element at the top. (Note that all elements in the solid rectangle are smaller than $\overline{m}$ and hence belong to M_1 and that all points in the dashed rectangle are at least as large as $\overline{m}$ and hence belong to M_2. Each rectangle contains $3n/10$ points, provided that 10 divides n.

Lemma 1: $|M_1|, |M_2| \leq 8n/11$.

Proof: Almost immediate from the discussion above. Note that $|M_1| + |M_2| = n$ and that $|M_1|, |M_2| \geq 3n/10$ if 10 divides n. If 10 does not divide n then $|M_1|, |M_2| \geq 3n/11$ for $n \geq 100$. Details are left to the reader.   □

Let T(n) be the maximal running time of algorithm Select on any set M of n elements and any i.

Lemma 2: There are constants a,b such that

$$T(n) \leq a \cdot n \qquad\qquad \text{for } n \leq 100$$
$$T(n) \leq T(21n/100) + T(8n/11) + b \cdot n \qquad \text{for } n \geq 100.$$

Proof: The claim is obvious for $n \leq 100$. So let us assume $n \geq 100$. Select is called twice within the body of Select, once for a set of $\lceil n/5 \rceil \leq 21n/100$ elements and once for a set of size at most $8n/11$. Furthermore, the total cost of Select outside recursive calls is clearly O(n).   □

Theorem 2: Algorithm Select works in linear time.

Proof: We show $T(n) \leq c \cdot n$ where $c = \max(a, 1100b/69)$ by induction on n.

For n ≤ 1oo there is nothing to show. For n > 1oo we have

$$T(n) \le T(21n/1oo) + T(8n/11) + bn$$
$$\le c \ 21n/1oo + c \ 8n/11 + bn \le cn$$

by definition of c.   □

II. 5. Exercises

1) Let S[n] and P[1.. n] be two arrays. Let P[1],...,P[n] be a permutation of the integers 1,...,n. Describe an algorithm which rearranges S as given by P, i.e. $S_{after}[i] = S_{before}[P[i]]$.

2) Write a RAM-program for Heapsort and analyse it.

3) Is there a sequence of n numbers which forces Heapsort to use $2n(\log(n+1)-1)$ comparisons?

4) When discussing Heapsort we first derived a method which does not keep the heap balanced. Analyse this variant of Heapsort. In particular, treat the following questions. Is it possible to store the tree without explicite father-son pointers? Storage requirement of the method? Number of comparisons? Running time on a RAM?

5) Discuss Heapsort based on ternary trees.

6) Procedure Quicksort is called at most n-1 times on a problem of size n (use induction). Conclude, that the expected number of calls in lines (7) and (8) are n/2-1 each. Also show that line (5) is executed at most n/4 times on the average.

7) Translate Quicksort into RAM-code and analyse it. (Use exercise 6).

8) Do you recommend to modify Quicksort such that a separate list is built for the elements S_i with $S_i = S_1$? Assume that every element S_i occurs exactly k times in the initial sequence. At what value of k does it pay off to partition into three sequences?

9) Solve the following recurrences:

a)
$$T(n) = \begin{cases} n^{3/2} \log n & \text{for } 1 \leq n < 10 \\ \sqrt{n}\, T(\sqrt{n}) + n^{3/2} \log n & \text{for } \quad n \geq 10 \end{cases}$$

b)
$$T(n) = \begin{cases} f(n) & \text{for } 1 \leq n < 100 \\ 2T(n/2) + f(n) & \text{for } \quad n \geq 100 \end{cases}$$

Use $f(n) = n$, $f(n) = n \log n$, $f(n) = n^{3/2}$

c)
$$T(n) = \begin{cases} \sqrt{n} & \text{for } 1 \leq n < 10 \\ \log n\, T(\log \log n) + \sqrt{n} & \text{for } \quad n \geq 10 \end{cases}$$

10) Write a RASP-program for Mergesort and analyse it.

11) Modify Quicksort such that sequences of length at most M are sorted by repeatedly searching for the maximum. What is the best value for M. (Compare the proof of theorem V.4.2.). Running time?

12) Would you recommend to use the linear median algorithm of section II.4. in the partitioning phase of Quicksort?

13) Prove theorem 9 (of section II.1.4.) for ternary trees.

14) Let T be any binary tree with n leaves. Interpret the tree as a merging pattern and assume that all initial sequences have length 1. In section III.5.3.3., theorem 14 we give an algorithm which merges two sequences of length x and y in time $O(\log(\genfrac{}{}{0pt}{}{x+y}{y}))$. Show that the total cost of merge pattern T is $O(n \log n)$.

15) Does theorem II.1.6. 12 stay true if we allow exponentiation as an additional operation?

16) For $(x_1, \ldots, x_n) \in \mathbb{R}^n$ let $f(x_1, \ldots, x_n) = \min\{i;\ x_i \geq x_j \text{ for all } j\}$ be the maximum function. Use theorem 12 of section II.1.6. to prove a $\log n$ lower bound on the depth of rational decision trees for the maximum function. Can you achieve depth $O(\log n)$?

17) For $n \in \mathbb{N}$, $x \in \mathbb{R}$ let $f(x) = \begin{cases} 0 & \text{if } x < 0 \\ \lfloor x \rfloor & \text{if } 0 \leq x \leq n \\ n & \text{if } x > n \end{cases}$

be the floor-function restricted to interval [0...n]. Use theorem 12 to prove a lower bound on the complexity of the floor function. Does theorem 12 stay true if the floor-function is added as an additional operation?

18) Let x^i, $1 \le i \le n$, be words of length k over alphabet $\Sigma = \{1,...,m\}$. Discuss the following variant of bucketsort. In phase 1 the input set is divided into m groups according to the first letter. Then the algorithm is applied recursively to each group. Show that the worst case running time of this method is $\Omega(n\,m\,k)$. Why does the German postal service use this method to distribute letters?

19) Use Bucketsort to sort n integers in the range $[0...n^k]$, k fixed, in worst case time $O(n)$.

20) A program solves the nearest neighbour problem of size n if for all inputs $(x_1,...,x_n,y_1,...,y_n)$ the first n outputs produced by the program are $(x_{i_1},...,x_{i_n})$ where for all ℓ: $i_\ell \in \{i;\ |x_i-y_\ell| \le |x_j-y_\ell|$ for all $j\}$. Show an n log n lower bound for the nearest neighbour problem in the PRAM-model of section II.1.6. (Hint: for π a permutation of $\{1,...,n\}$ say that $(x_1,...,x_n,y_1,...,y_n)$ is of order type π if for all i,j: $|x_{\pi(i)}-y_i| < |x_j-y_i|$. Modify lemma 1 in the proof of theorem 1).

21) A program solves the searching problem of size n if for all inputs $(x_1,...,x_n,y)$ with $x_1 < x_2 < ... < x_n$ it computes the rank of y, i.e. it outputs $|\{i,\ x_i < y\}|$. Prove an $\Omega(\log n)$ lower bound in the PRAM-model of section II.1.6..

II. 6. Bibliographic Notes

Heapsort is by Williams (64) and Floyd (64). Hoare (62) developed Quicksort and procedure Find. Sorting by merging and distribution was already known to von Neumann and dates back to methods used on mechanical sorters. Bucketsort as described here is due to Aho/Hopcroft/Ullmann (74). Hybridsort is by Meijer/Akl (80). The treatment of recurrences is based on Bentley/Haken/Saxe (80). Theorem 9 (of section II.1.) is by Huffmann (52), the linear time implementation was described by van Leeuwen (76). The sections on lower bounds are based on A. Schmidt(82) (theorems 12-14 of II. 1.6) and Hong (79)(theorems 12-14 of II. 1.6

and theorem 1 of II. 3.), Paul/Simon (80) (theorems 1 and 2 of II. 3.), and Ben-Or (83) (theorems 15 - 18 of II. 1.6). Weaker versions of theorems 17 - 18 were obtained previously by Yao (81) and Strassen (73) respectively. Finally, the linear time median algorithm is taken from Blum/Floyd/Pratt/Rivest/Tarjan (72).

III. Sets

Many algorithms manipulate sets. We consider some typical examples.
A compiler uses a symboltable to keep track of the identifiers which
are used in the program. An identifier together with relevant information (e.g. type, scope, address, ...) is entered into the symboltable when its declaration is processed by the compiler. Applied
occurences of the same identifier refer to the defining occurence;
the compiler has to access the symboltable and to look up the relevant information. More abstractly, a compiler deals with a set ST of
objects consisting of a name (key) and associated information. Two
kinds of operations are performed on the set ST. New objects (x, I)
are added to set ST, i.e. ST is replaced by ST ∪ $\{(x, I)\}$, and the
objects are accessed via their key, i.e. given an identifier x we
want to find I such that (x, I) ∈ ST. In most programming languages
identifiers are strings of letters and digits of some bounded length,
say at most length 6. Then the number of possible identifiers is
$(26 + 10)^6 \approx 10^9$; in every program only a small subset of the set of
all possible identifiers is used. Set ST is small compared to the
very large universe of all possible identifiers.

A second example is the author catalogue of a library. The name of
the author is the key, the associated information are titles of books,
their locations on the shelf, ... This example exhibits all charac-
teristica of the problem above; however, at least one additional operation is performed on the set: print a library catalogue in ascending
lexicographic order.

Let us consider a third example: the set of accounts in a bank. The
account number is the key, the associated information is the holder
of the account, the balance, etc. Typical operations are Access,
Insert, Delete, List in ascending order; i.e. the same operations as
in our previous example. However, there is one major difference to
the previous examples: the size of the universe. A bank might have
$5 \cdot 10^5$ different accounts and use account numbers with 6 decimal
digits, i.e. there are 10^6 possible account numbers and half of them
are actually used. The universe of possible keys and the set of keys
used are of about the same size. Graph algorithms (chapter IV) also
provide us with plenty of examples for this phenomenon.

We treat the case of drastic size difference between the universe and the set stored first (sections 1 to 7) and discuss the case of equal size later (section 8). The major difference between the solutions is based on the fact that accessing an information via a key is a diffi- cult problem in the first case, but can be made trivial in the second case by the use of an array.

Sets consist of objects. An object is typically a pair consisting of key (name) and information associated with the key. As in chapter II we will concentrate on the key part and identify object and key.

Let $S \subseteq U$ be the subset of a universe U. We consider the following operations:

Name of operation	effect
Access(x,S) or	if $x \in S$
Member(x,S)	then the information associated with x
	else a message, that x is not element
	of S
Insert(x,S)	$S \leftarrow S \cup \{x\}$
Delete(x,S)	$S \leftarrow S - \{x\}$

Operations Insert und Delete change set S, i.e. the old version of set S is destroyed by the operations. Operation names Access and Member are used interchangeable; we will always use Member when the particular application only requires yes/no answers.

For the following operations we assume in addition, that $(U, \leq)$ is linearly ordered.

Ord(k,S)	the k-th element of the linear arrange- ment of set S
List(S)	a list of the elements of set S in ascen- ding order.

Additional operations will be considered in later sections.

We know already one data structure which supports all operations men- tioned above, the linear list of section I.3.2. . A set $S = \{x_1, \ldots, x_n\}$

is represented as a list, whose i-th element is x_i. All operations above can be realized by a single traversal of the list and hence take time $O(n)$ in the worst case.

In this chapter we study data structures which are considerably more efficient than linear lists. These data structures can be divided in two large groups: comparison based methods (sections 3 to 7) and methods based on representation (sections 1 and 2). The former methods only use comparisons ($\leq$, $<$, $=,>$,$\geq$) between elements to gain information, the latter methods use the representation of keys as strings over some alphabet to gain information. Search trees and hashing are typical representatives of the two classes.

III. 1. Digital Search Trees

III. 1.1 TRIES

One of the most simple ways to structure a file is to use the digital representation of its elements; e.g. we may represent S = {121, 102, 211, 120, 210, 212} by the following TRIE

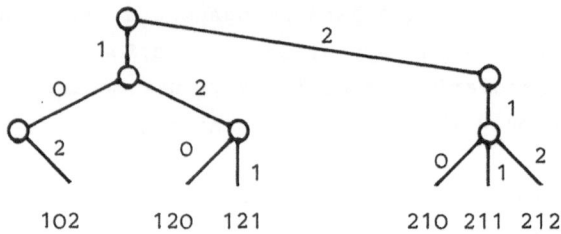

The general situation is as follows: the universe U consists of all strings of length ℓ over some alphabet of say k elements, i.e. $U = \{0, \ldots, k-1\}^{\ell}$. A set $S \subseteq U$ is represented as the k-ary tree consisting of all prefixes of elements of S. An implementation which immediately comes to mind is to use an array of length k for every internal node of the tree. (We will see a different implementation in section 6.3). Then operations Access, Insert and Delete are very fast and are very simple to program; in particular, if the reverse of all elements of S are stored (in our example this would be set {121, 201, 112, 021, 012, 212}), then the following program will realize operation Access(x)

```
v ← root;
y ← x;
do ℓ times (i,y) ← (y mod k, y div k);
              v ← i-th son of v
od;
if x = CONTENT[v] then "yes" else "no".
```

This program takes time $O(ℓ) = O(\log_k N)$ where $N = |U|$. Unfortunately, the space requirement of a TRIE as described above can be horrendous: $O(n \cdot ℓ \cdot k)$. For each element of set S, $|S| = n$, we might have to store an entire path of ℓ nodes, all of which have degree one and use up space $O(k)$.

There is a very simple method to reduce storage requirement to $O(n \cdot k)$. We only store internal nodes which are at least binary. Since a TRIE for a set S of size n has n leaves there will be at most n-1 internal nodes of degree 2 or more. Chains of internal nodes of degree 1 are replaced by a single number, the number of nodes in the chain. In our example we obtain:

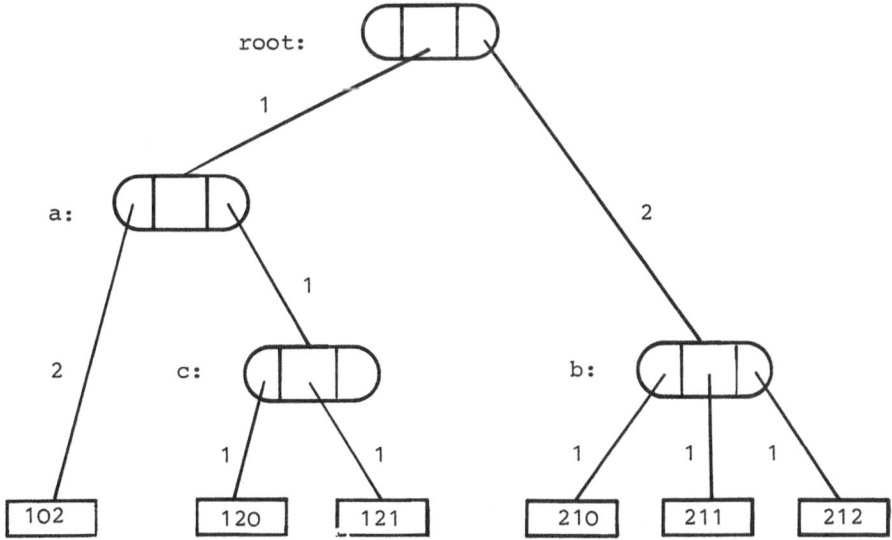

Here internal nodes are drawn as arrays of length 3. On the pointers
from fathers to sons the numbers indicate the increase in depth, i.e.
1 + the length of the eliminated chain of nodes of degree one. In our
example the 2 on the pointer from the root to the son with name b indicates that after branching on the first digit in the root we have to
branch on the third (1 + 2) digit in the son. The algorithms for
Access, Insert und Delete become slightly more complicated for compressed TRIES but still run in time $O(\ell)$.

Theorem 1: A compressed TRIE supports operations Access, Insert and
Delete with time bound $O(\log_k N)$, where N is the size of the universe
and k is the branching factor of the TRIE. A set S of n elements requires space $O(k \cdot n)$.

Proof: by the discussion above. □

Note that TRIES exhibit an interesting time space trade-off. Choosing
k large will make TRIES faster but more space consuming, choosing k
small will make TRIES slower but less space consuming. For static sets,
i.e. only operation Access is supported, we describe a further compression technique below.

A disturbing fact about TRIES is that the worst case running time depends on the size of the universe rather than the size of the set
stored. We will next show that the average case behaviour of TRIES is
$O(\log_k n)$; i.e. average access time is logarithmic in the size of the
set stored. We use the following probability assumption:

Every subset $S \subseteq U$, $|S| = n$, is equally likely.

Theorem 2: Let $E(d_n)$ be the expected depth of a k-ary compressed
TRIE for a set of n elements. Then

$$E(d_n) \leq 2 \cdot \log_k n + O(1)$$

Proof: Let q_d be the probability that the TRIE has depth d or more.
Then $E(d_n) = \sum_{d \geq 1} q_d$. Let $S = \{x_1, .., x_n\} \subseteq U = \{0, ..., k-1\}^\ell$ be a subset
of U of size n. The compressed TRIE for S has depth less than d if the
function $trunc_{d-1}$ which maps an element of U into its first d-1 digits
is injective on S. Furthermore, $trunc_{d-1}$ is an injective mapping on

set S iff $\{trunc_{d-1}(x), x \in S\}$ is a subset of size n of $\{0,..,k-1\}^{d-1}$.

Thus there are exactly $\binom{k^{d-1}}{n} \cdot k^{(\ell-(d-1)) \cdot n}$ subsets S of size n of U

such that $trunc_{d-1}$ is injective on S. Hence

$$q_d \leq 1 - \frac{\binom{k^{d-1}}{n} \cdot k^{[\ell-(d-1)] \cdot n}}{\binom{k^{\ell}}{n}}$$

$$\leq 1 - \frac{k^{d-1} \cdot (k^{d-1}-1) \cdot \ \cdots \ \cdot (k^{d-1}-(n-1)) \cdot k^{n \cdot [\ell-(d-1)]}}{(k^{\ell})^n}$$

$$= 1 - \prod_{i=0}^{n-1} (1-i/k^{d-1})$$

Next note that

$$\prod_{i=0}^{n-1} (1-i/k^{d-1}) = e^{\sum_{i=0}^{n-1} \ell n(1-i/k^{d-1})}$$

$$\geq e^{\int_0^n \ell n(1-x/k^{d-1})\,dx}$$

$$= e^{-n^2/k^{d-1}}$$

The inequality follows from the fact that $f(x) = \ell n(1-x/k^{d-1})$ is a decreasing function in x and hence $f(i) \geq \int_i^{i+1} f(x)\,dx$. The last equality
can be seen by evaluating the integral using the substitution
$x = k^{d-1}(1-t)$. Hence

$$q_d \leq 1 - e^{-n^2/k^{d-1}}$$

$$\leq n^2/k^{d-1}$$

since $e^x - 1 \geq x$ and hence $1 - e^x \leq - x$. Let $c = 2 \lceil \log_k n \rceil$. Then

$$E(d_n) = \sum_{q=1}^{c} q_d + \sum_{d \geq c+1} q_d$$

$$\leq c + \sum_{d \geq c} n^2/k^d$$

$$\leq 2\lceil \log_k n \rceil + (n^2/k^c) \cdot \sum_{d \geq 0} k^{-d}$$

$$\leq 2\lceil \log_k n \rceil + 1/(1-1/k) \qquad\qquad \square$$

Theorem 2 shows that the expected depth of a random TRIE is at most $2 \log_k n + O(1)$ and so the expected ACCESS-, INSERT- and DELETE-time is $O((\log n)/(\log k))$. Space requirement is $O(n \cdot k)$. Parameter k, the basis of the digital representation, allows us to trade between space and time.

III. 1.2 STATIC TRIES or Compressing Sparse Tables

In this section we show that the space requirement can be drastically reduced for static TRIES without an increase in access time. Static TRIES only support operation ACCESS. The reduction is done in two steps. In the first step we describe a general overlay technique for compressing large sparse tables. This technique is not only applicable to TRIES but also to other areas where large sparse tables arise, e.g. parsing tables. The first step reduces space requirement to $O(n \log \log n)$. In a second step we reduce the space requirement further to $O(n)$ by packing several numbers into one storage location.

A TRIE for a set of n elements requires space $O(k \cdot n)$. There are at most n-1 internal nodes each of which requires storage for an array of k elements. Of the $(n-1) \cdot k$ possible outgoing pointers at most 2n-2 will be non-nil, because the TRIE has n leaves and at most n-2 internal nodes unequal the root. This suggests to use an overlay technique to reduce storage requirement (An alternative approach is discussed in section 2.3).

In our example, we might use an array of length 10

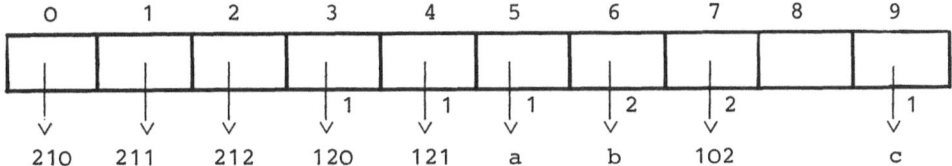

to store all four arrays of length 3. The root node starts at location 4, node a starts at 7, node b starts at 0 and c starts at location 3. This information is stored in an additional table

a	b	c	root
7	0	3	4

Suppose now that we search for 121. We follow the 1-st pointer out of
the root node, i.e. the pointer in location 4 + 1 of the large array.
This brings us to node a. We follow the 2-nd pointer out of a, i.e.
the pointer in location 7 + 2 of the big array which brings us to node
c, ... It is also instructive to perform an unsuccessful search, say
to search for 012. We follow the 0-th pointer out of the root, i.e.
the pointer in location 4 + 0. This brings us to a leaf with content
121 ≠ 012. So 012 is not member of the set.

We will now describe one particular compression technique in more detail. Let A be a r by s 0 - 1 matrix with exactly m entries equal to
one. We want to find small row displacements $rd(i)$, $0 \leq i \leq q - 1$,
such that $A[i,j] = 1 = A[i',j']$ and $(i,j) \neq (i',j')$ implies $rd(i) + j$
$\neq rd(i') + j'$ for all pairs (i,j) and (i',j'), i.e. if we store the
i-th row of matrix A beginning at position $rd(i)$ of a one-dimensional
array $C[0..]$ then no two ones will collide. In our example the 0's
correspond to the nil pointers and the 1's correspond to the non-nil
pointers. One method for computing the row displacements is the first-
fit decreasing method.

1) Sort the rows in nonincreasing order according to the number of
    ones in the row, i.e. the row with the maximal number of ones
    comes first.

2) Set $rd(0) = 0$. For $i \geq 1$ choose $rd(i) \geq 0$ minimal such that no
    collision with the previously placed rows 0 to i - 1 occurs.

110

In our example step 1 could produce the following matrix.

b:	1	1	1
c:	1	1	0
root:	0	1	1
a:	1	0	1

0	1	2	3	4	5	6	7	8	9
1	1	1							
			1	1	0				
				0	1	1			
							1	0	1

In step 2 we choose rd(b) = 0, rd(c) = 3, rd(root) = 4 and rd(a) = 7. These choices are illustrated by the second matrix.

The first fit decreasing method produces small row displacements if the ones of matrix A are evenly distributed across the matrix.

Theorem 3: Let $m(\ell)$ be the total number of ones in rows of A which contain $\ell + 1$ or more ones. If $m(\ell) \leq m/(\ell+1)$ for all ℓ then the first-fit decreasing method produces row displacements rd(i) $\leq m$ for $0 \leq i \leq r - 1$ in time $O(r \cdot m \cdot s)$.

Proof: Consider a row with exactly ℓ ones. When that row is placed in step 2 only rows with $\geq \ell$ ones have been placed and hence the array C can contain at most $m(\ell-1)$ ones. Each such one can block at most ℓ possible choices for the row displacement. Since $\ell \cdot m(\ell-1) \leq m$ by assumption we can always find rd(i) $\leq m$ for all i, $0 \leq i \leq r-1$.

It remains to prove the time bound. In time $O(r \cdot s)$ we compute the number of ones in each row. Bucket sort will then sort the rows according to the number of ones in time $O(r+m)$. Finally, in order to compute rd(i) one has to try up to m candidates. Testing one candidate takes time $O(s)$. We obtain a total of $O(r \cdot s + r+m + r \cdot m \cdot s) = O(r \cdot m \cdot s)$ time units.   □

The hypothesis of theorem 3, the harmonic decay property, puts a severe restriction on the distribution of ones in matrix A. We have $m(1) \leq m/2$ and thus at least half of the ones have to lie in rows with exactly one entry equal to one. Also $m(\sqrt{m}) < m/\sqrt{m} = \sqrt{m}$ and hence no row of A can contain $\sqrt{m}$ or more ones. What can we do if A does not have the harmonic decay property? We try to find column displacements cd(j), $0 \leq j \leq s-1$, such that matrix B obtained from matrix A by displacing columns has the harmonic decay property. Then we apply the previously described compression technique to matrix B.

In our example we might choose cd(0) = 0, cd(1) = cd(2) = 1 and obtain the following 5 by 3 matrix B. We can now choose

	0	1	2
0	1		
1	1	1	1
2	0	1	0
3	1	1	1
4		0	1

	0	1	2
cd	0	1	1

row displacements according to the first fit decreasing method. Note that step 1 of that algorithm reorders the rows of B into order 1, 3, 0, 2, 4. Step 2 of that algorithm chooses rd(1) = 0, rd(3) = 3, rd(0) = 6, rd(2) = 6 and rd(4) = 6

	0	1	2	3	4	5	6	7	8
0							1	0	0
1	1	1	1						
2							0	1	0
3				1	1	1			
4							0	0	1

and hence matrix C is the following array of length 9

	0	1	2	3	4	5	6	7	8	9
C	1	1	1	1	1	1	1	1	1	1

The important fact to remember is that all ones of matrix A are mapped on distinct ones of matrix C, namely A[i,j] = 1 implies A[i,j] = = B[i + cd[j],j] = C[rd[i + cd[j]] + j]. The question remains how to choose the column displacements? We will use the first fit method.

Let m_j be the number of ones in columns $0,\ldots,j$ of matrix A. We choose $cd(0)$, $cd(1)$, $\ldots$ in that order. Suppose we have chosen $cd(0)$, $\ldots$, $cd(j-1)$ and applied these displacements to the first j columns of matrix A. Let B_{j-1} be the matrix obtained in that way and let $m_{j-1}(\ell)$ be the number of ones in rows of B_{j-1} with $\ell + 1$ or more ones. We want that $B = B_{s-1}$ has the harmonic decay property, i.e.

$$m_{s-1}(\ell) \leq m/(\ell+1) \qquad \text{for all } \ell \geq 0$$

In order to ensure the harmonic decay property after all colunm displacements have been chosen we enforce a more stringent restriction during the selection process, i.e. we enforce

$$m_j(\ell) \leq m/f(\ell,m_j)$$

where f will be chosen later. The boundary conditions for f are $f(\ell,m_{s-1}) \geq \ell + 1$ and $f(0,m_j) \leq m/m_j$. The former condition ensures the harmonic decay property at the end of the construction, the latter condition makes sure that we can choose $cd(0) = 0$ and that the requirement can be satisfied for $\ell = 0$. Note that $m_j(0) = m_j$ for all j and $m_0(\ell) = 0$ for $\ell > 0$.

We use the first fit method to choose the column displacements: Choose $cd(0) = 0$. For $j > 0$ choose $cd(j) \geq 0$ minimal such that $m_j(\ell) \leq m/f(\ell,m_j)$ for all $\ell \geq 0$.

We need an upper bound on the values $cd(j)$ obtained in that way. We ask the following question: Consider a fixed $\ell \geq 1$. How many choices of $cd(j)$ may be blocked because of violation of requirement $\ell : m_j(\ell) \leq m/f(\ell,m_j)$? If a particular choice, say k, of $cd(j)$ is blocked then

$$m_j(\ell) > m/f(\ell,m_j)$$

where $m_j(\ell)$ is computed using displacement k for the j-th column. Since requirement ℓ was satisfied after choosing $cd(j-1)$ we also have

$$m_{j-1}(\ell) \leq m/f(\ell,m_{j-1})$$

and hence

$$m_j(\ell) - m_{j-1}(\ell) > m/f(\ell,m_j) - m/f(\ell,m_{j-1}).$$

Let $q = m/f(\ell,m_j) - m/f(\ell,m_{j-1})$. We can interpret q as follows: In matrix B_j the number of ones in rows with $\geq \ell + 1$ ones is at least q more than in matrix B_{j-1}. We can count these q ones in a different way. There are at least $q/(\ell+1)$ pairs (a row of B_{j-1} with $\geq \ell$ ones, a one in column j) which are aligned when column displacement $cd(j) = k$ is chosen. Note that any such pair contributes either 1 (if the row of B_{j-1} has $\geq \ell + 1$ ones) or $\ell + 1$ (if the row of B_{j-1} has exactly ℓ ones) to q. Since the number of rows of B_{j-1} with $\geq \ell$ ones is bounded by $m_{j-1}(\ell-1)/\ell \leq m/\ell \cdot f(\ell-1,m_{j-1})$ and since the j-th column of A contains exactly $m_j - m_{j-1}$ ones the number of such pairs is bounded by

$$p := (m_j - m_{j-1}) \cdot m/(\ell \cdot f(\ell-1,m_{j-1})).$$

Hence there are at most $p/[q/(\ell+1)]$ possible choices k for $cd(j)$ which are blocked because of violation of requirement ℓ, $\ell \geq 1$. Hence the total number of blocked values is bounded by

$$BV := \sum_{\ell=1}^{\ell_0} \frac{(\ell+1) \cdot (m_j - m_{j-1}) \cdot m}{\ell \cdot f(\ell-1,m_{j-1}) \cdot [m/f(\ell,m_j) - m/f(\ell,m_{j-1})]}$$

where $\ell_0 = \min\{\ell; m/f(\ell,m_{j-1}) < \ell\}$. Note that there are no rows of B_{j-1} with $\geq \ell_0$ ones and hence p (as defined above) will be 0 for $\ell > \ell_0$. Hence we can we can always choose $cd(j)$ such that $0 \leq cd(j) \leq BV$.

It remains to derive a bound on BV. We rewrite the expression for BV as follows:

$$BV = \sum_{\ell=1}^{\ell_0} \frac{\ell+1}{\ell} \cdot \frac{(m_j - m_{j-1})}{(f(\ell,m_{j-1})/f(\ell,m_j)-1)} \cdot \frac{f(\ell,m_{j-1})}{f(\ell-1,m_{j-1})}$$

This expression involves only quotients of f and therefore we set $f(\ell,m_j) = 2^{g(\ell,m_j)}$ for some function g to be chosen later. We obtain

$$BV = \sum_{\ell=1}^{\ell_0} \frac{\ell+1}{\ell} \cdot \frac{(m_j - m_{j-1})}{(2^{g(\ell,m_{j-1})-g(\ell,m_j)}-1)} \cdot 2^{g(\ell,m_{j-1})-g(\ell-1,m_{j-1})}$$

$$\leq \sum_{\ell=1}^{\ell_0} \frac{\ell+1}{\ell} \cdot \frac{(m_j - m_{j-1})}{(g(\ell,m_{j-1}) - g(\ell,m_j)) \cdot \ell n \, 2} \cdot 2^{g(\ell,m_{j-1})-g(\ell-1,m_{j-1})}$$

since $2^x-1 \geq x \cdot \ln 2$. Next we note that the two differences involve on-ly one argument of g. This suggests to set $g(\ell,m_j) = h(\ell) \cdot k(m_j)$ for functions h and k to be chosen later. The upper bound for BV simpli-fies to

$$BV \leq \sum_{\ell-1}^{\ell_0} \frac{\ell+1}{\ell} \cdot \frac{(m_j - m_{j-1})}{h(\ell)(k(m_{j-1}) - k(m_j))\ell n\ 2} \cdot 2^{(h(\ell)-h(\ell-1)) \cdot k(m_{j-1})}$$

This sum will further simplify if we choose h and k to be linear func-tions, say $h(\ell) = \ell$ and $k(m_j) = (2-m_j/m) \leq 2$. Then

$$BV \leq \sum_{\ell=1}^{\ell_0} \frac{\ell+1}{\ell} \cdot \frac{(m_j - m_{j-1})}{\ell \cdot (m_j/m - m_{j-1}/m) \cdot \ell n\ 2} \cdot 2^2$$

$$\leq \sum_{\ell=1}^{\ell_0} (4/\ln 2)m \cdot (\ell+1)/\ell^2 = (4 \cdot m/\ell n\ 2)(\sum_{\ell=1}^{\ell_0} 1/\ell + \sum_{\ell=1}^{\ell_0} 1/\ell^2)$$

$$\leq (4 \cdot m/\ell n\ 2)(\ell n\ \ell_0 + 1 + \pi^2/6)$$

since $\sum_{\ell=1}^{\ell_0} 1/\ell \leq 1 + \ell n\ \ell_0$ (cf. appendix) and $\sum_{\ell \geq 1} 1/\ell^2 = \pi^2/6$

$$\leq 4 \cdot m \cdot \log\ \ell_0 + 15.3\ m$$

Finally notice that $f(\ell,m_j) = 2^{\ell \cdot (2-m_j/m)} \geq 2^\ell$ and therefore $\ell_0 \leq \log m$. Also $f(\ell,m_{s-1}) = 2^\ell \geq \ell + 1$ for all ℓ and $f(0,m_j) = 2^0 = 1 \leq m/m_j$ for all j and so f satisfies the boundary conditions. Thus we can always find cd(j) such that $0 \leq cd(j) \leq 4 \cdot m \cdot \log\log m + 15.3 \cdot m$.

Theorem 4: Given a matrix A[0..r-1, 0..s-1] with m nonzero entries one can find column displacements cd(j), $0 \leq j \leq s-1$, such that $0 \leq cd(j) \leq 4 \cdot m \cdot \log\log m + 15.3m$ and such that matrix B obtained from A using those displacements has the harmonic decay property. The column displacements can be found in time $O(s(r + m \cdot \log\log m)^2)$.

Proof: The bound on the column displacements follows from the discus-sion above. The time bound can be seen as follows. For every row of B_j we keep a count on the number of ones in the row and we keep the num-

bers $m_j(i)$ and m_j. In order to find $cd(j+1)$ we have to test up to
$4 \cdot m \cdot \log\log m + O(m)$ possible values. For each candidate we have to update the $m_j(i)$'s in time $O(r + m \cdot \log\log m)$ and to test for violation
of requirement ℓ, $1 \leq \ell \leq \ell_0$, in time $O(\ell_0) = O(\log m)$. Hence the total time spent on computing the column displacements is
$O(s \cdot (r+m \cdot \log\log m)^2)$.   □

Let us put theorems 3 and 4 together. Given a matrix $A[0..r-1, 0..s-1]$
with m nonzero entries, theorem 4 gives us column displacements $cd(j)$,
$0 \leq j < s$, and a matrix B such that

    $A[i,j] \neq 0$ implies $B[i+cd(j),j] = A[i,j]$

B has s columns and $r' \leq r + 4 \cdot m \cdot \log\log m + 15.3 \cdot m$ rows. Of course, B
has at most m rows with at least one nonzero entry. Next we apply theo-
rem 3 and obtain row displacements $rd(i)$, $0 \leq i < r'$ and a one-dimensional matrix C such that

    $B[h,j] \neq 0$ implies $C[rd(h)+j] = B[h,j]$

or in other words

    $A[i,j] \neq 0$ implies $C[rd(i+cd(j))+j] = A[i,j]$.

Since B has only m nonzero entries there are at most m different h's
such that $rd(h) \neq 0$. Furthermore, array C has length at most $m + s$
since $rd(h) \leq m$ for all h.

So far, we obtained the following reduction in space: C uses $m + s$
storage locations, cd uses s storage locations and rd uses
$r' \leq r + 4 \cdot m \cdot \log\log m + 15.3 \cdot m$ storage locations.

Let us apply our compression technique to a TRIE for a set of n elements with branching factor $k \leq n$; $k = n$ will give the best result with
respect to access time. We can view the array representation of the
internal nodes as an r, $r \leq n - 1$, by s, $s = k$, array with $\leq 2n - 2$
non-nil entries. Compression gives us a matrix C with $O(k + n) = O(n)$
locations, a set of $k = O(n)$ column displacements and a set of
$O(n \cdot \log\log n)$ row displacements. So total space requirement is
$O(n \cdot \log\log n)$.

The entries of arrays rd, cd and C are numbers in the range 0 to $O(n)$, i.e. bitstrings of length $\leq \log n + O(1)$. As we observed above, array rd has $\leq c\, n\, \log\log n$ entries for some constant c all but $2n$ of which are zero. We will next describe a compression of vector rd based on the following assumption: A storage location can hold several numbers if their total length is less than $\log n$.

Let $i_0, i_1, \ldots, i_{t-1}$, $t \leq 2\,n - 2$, be the indices of the nonzero elements of vector rd. We compress vector rd into a vector crd of length t by storing only the nonzero entries, i.e. $crd[\ell] = rd[i_\ell]$ for $0 \leq \ell \leq t - 1$. It remains to describe a way of finding ℓ given i_ℓ.

Let $d = \lfloor \log\log n \rfloor$. We divide vector rd into $c \cdot n \cdot \log\log n / d \leq 2 \cdot c \cdot n$ blocks of length d each. For each block we write down the minimum ℓ such that i_ℓ lies in that block, if any such ℓ exists. This defines a vector base of length $2 \cdot c \cdot n$. For any other element of a block we store the offset with respect to ℓ in a two-dimensional array offset, i.e.

$$
base[v] = \begin{cases} \min \{\ell;\ i_\ell \text{ div } d = v\} & \text{if } \exists \ell\ i_\ell \text{ div } d = v \\[2ex] -1 & \text{otherwise} \end{cases}
$$

for $0 \leq v < 2 \cdot c \cdot n$ and

$$
offset[v,j] = \begin{cases} \ell - base[v] & \text{if } v \cdot d + j = i_\ell \text{ for some } \ell \\[2ex] -1 & \text{otherwise} \end{cases}
$$

for $0 \leq j < d$.

Then $rd[h] = 0$ iff offset $[h \text{ div } d,\ h \bmod d] = -1$ and $rd[h] \neq 0$ implies $rd[h] = crd[base[h \text{ div } d] + offset[h \text{ div } d,\ h \bmod d]]$.

For any fixed v, $offset[v, \ ]$ is a list of d numbers in the range $-1, \ldots, d - 1$. We combine these numbers into a single number $off[v]$

$$
\text{by } off[v] = \sum_{j=0}^{d-1} (offset[v,j] + 1)(d + 1)^j
$$

Then $0 \leq off[v] \leq (d + 1)^d \leq n$ and thus $off[v]$ fits into a single storage location. Also

$$offset[v,j] = ((off[v] \; div \, (d+1)^j) \; mod \, (d+1)) - 1$$

and so $offset[v,j]$ can be computed in time $O(1)$ from $off[v]$ and a table of the powers of $d + 1$. Altogether we decreased the space requirement to $O(n)$, namely $O(n)$ each for arrays crd, base and off, and increased access time only by a constant factor.

We illustrate these definitions by an example, $d = 3$, $i_0 = 1$, $i_1 = 3$, $i_2 = 5$ and $i_3 = 11$.

rd:

| 0 1 0 | 1 0 1 | 0 0 0 | 0 0 1 |

Then

crd:

| rd(1) | rd(3) | rd(5) | rd(11) |

base:

| 0 | 1 | -1 | 3 |

offset:

-1	0	-1
0	-1	1
-1	-1	-1
-1	-1	0

and off:

4
33
0
16

Note that $off[1] = (1 + offset[1,0]) \cdot 4^0 + (1 + offset[1,1]) \cdot 4^1 +$
$+ (1 + offset[1,2]) \cdot 4^2 = 1 \cdot 4^0 + 0 \cdot 4^1 + 2 \cdot 4^2 = 33$.

Theorem 5: Let $S \subseteq U$, $|S| = n$ and $|U| = N$. Then a n-ary TRIE supports operation Access in time $O(\log_n N)$ worst case and $O(1)$ expected case. The TRIE can be stored in $O(n)$ storage locations (of $O(\log n)$ bits each).

Proof: The time bound follows from theorems 1 and 2. The space bound follows from the preceding discussion.   □

118

We will improve upon theorem 5 in section III.2.3. on perfect hashing and show how to obtain O(1) access time in the worst case. We included theorem 5 because the compression technique used to prove theorem 5 is of general interest. In particular, it compresses large sparse tables without seriously degrading access time. Note that an access to array A is replaced by an access to three arrays rd, cd and c and only a few additions, at least as long as we are willing to tolerate the use of O(n log log n) storage locations.

III. 2. Hashing

The ingredients of hashing are very simple: an array T[0..m-1], the hash table, and a function h : U → [0..m-1], the hash function. U is the universe; we will assume U = [0..N-1] throughout this section. The basic idea is to store a set S as follows: x ∈ S is stored in T[h(x)]. Then an access is an extremely simple operation: compute h(x) and look up T[h(x)].

Suppose m = 5, S = {03, 15, 22, 24} ⊆ [0..99] and h(x) = x mod 5. Then the hash table looks as follows:

0	15
1	
2	22
3	3
4	24

There is one immediate problem with this basic idea: what to do if h(x) = h(y) for some x, y ∈ S, x ≠ y. Such an event is called a collision. There are two main methods for dealing with collisions: chaining and open adressing.

III. 2.1 Hashing with Chaining

The hash table T is an array of linear lists. A set S ⊆ U is represented as m linear lists. The i-th list contains all elements x ∈ S with h(x) = i.

The following figure shows the representation of set S = {1,3,4,7,1o,
17,21} in a table of length m = 3. We use hash function h(x) = x mod 3.

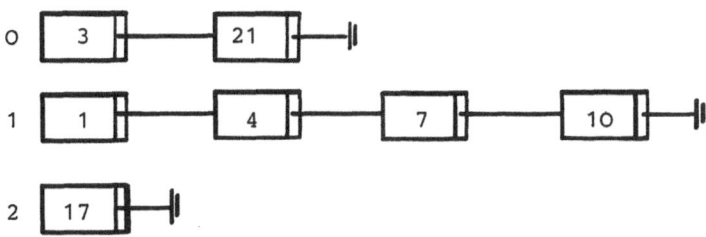

Operation Access(x,S) is realized by the following program:

    1)   compute h(x)

    2)   search for element x in list T[h(x)]

Operations Insert(x,S) and Delete(x,S) are implemented similarly. We
only have to add x to or delete x from list T[h(x)]. The time complexity of hashing with chaining is easy to determine: the time to evaluate
hash function h plus the time to search through list T[h(x)]. We assume in this section that h can be evaluated in constant time and
therefore define the cost of an operation referring to key x as
$O(1 + \delta_h(x,S))$ where S is the set of stored elements and

$$\delta_h(x,S) = \sum_{y \in S} \delta_h(x,y) \qquad , \text{ and}$$

$$\delta_h(x,y) = \begin{cases} 1 & \text{if } h(x) = h(y) \text{ and } x \neq y \\ 0 & \text{otherwise.} \end{cases}$$

The worst case complexity of hashing is easily determined. The worst
case occurs when the hash function h restricted to set S is a constant,
i.e. $h(x) = i_0$ for all x ∈ S. Then hashing deteriorates to searching
through a linear list; any one of the three operations costs O(|S|)
time units.

Theorem 1: The time complexity (in the worst case) of operations
Access(x,S), Insert(x,S) and Delete(x,S) is O(|S|).

Average case behaviour is much better. We analyse the complexity of a
sequence of n insertions, deletions and accesses starting with an empty

table, i.e. of a sequence $Op_1(x_1),\ldots, Op_n(x_n)$, where $Op_k \in \{Insert, Delete, Access\}$ and $x_k \in U$, under the following probability assumptions (we will discuss these assumptions later).

1) Hash function $h : U \to [0\ldots m-1]$ distributes the universe uniformly over the interval $[0\ldots m-1]$, i.e. for all i, $i' \in [0\ldots m-1]$: $|h^{-1}(i)| = |h^{-1}(i')|$.

2) All elements of U are equally likely as argument of any one of the operations in the sequence, i.e. the argument of the k-th operation of the sequence is equal to a fixed $x \in U$ with probability $1/|U|$.

Our two assumptions imply that value $h(x_k)$ of the hash function on the argument of the k-th operation is uniformely distributed in $[0\ldots m-1]$, i.e. $prob(h(x_k) = i) = 1/m$ for all $k \in [1\ldots n]$ and $i \in [0\ldots m-1]$.

Theorem 2: Under the assumptions above, a sequence of n insertions, deletions and access-operations takes time $O((1 + \beta/2)n)$ where $\beta = n/m$ is the (maximal) load factor of the table.

Proof: We will first compute the expected cost of the (k+1)-st operation. Assume that $h(x_{k+1}) = i$, i.e. the (k+1)-st operation accesses the i-th list. Let $prob(\ell_k(i) = j)$ be the probability that the i-th list has length j after the k-th operation. Then

$$EC_{k+1} = \sum_{j \geq 0} prob(\ell_k(i) = j)(1+j)$$

is the expected cost of the (k+1)-st operation. Next note that $prob(\ell_k(i) = j) \leq \binom{k}{j}(1/m)^j(1-1/m)^{k-j}$ (with equality if the first k operations are insertions) and hence

$$EC_{k+1} \leq 1 + \sum_{j \geq 0} \binom{k}{j}(1/m)^j(1-1/m)^{k-j} \cdot j$$

$$= 1 + (k/m) \sum_{j \geq 1} \binom{k-1}{j-1}(1/m)^{j-1}(1-1/m)^{k-j}$$

$$= 1 + k/m$$

Thus the total expected cost of n operations is

$$\sum_{k=1}^{n} EC_k = O(\sum_{k=1}^{n} (1+(k-1)/m)) = O(n + \frac{(n-1)n}{2m})$$

$$= O(1 + \beta n/2) \qquad\qquad \square$$

We will next discuss the probability assumptions used in the analysis of hashing. The first assumption is easily satisfied. Hash function h distributes the universe U uniformly over the hash table. Suppose U = [0...N-1], and m/N. Then h(x) = x mod m will satisfy the first re-quirement (division method). If m does not divide N but N is much larger than m then the division method almost satisfies assumption 1); theorem 2 stays true.

The second assumption is more critical because it postulates a certain behaviour of the user of the hash function. In general, the exact con-ditions of latter use are not known when the hash function is designed and therefore one has to be very careful about applying theorem 2. We discuss one particular application now and come back to the general problem in the sections on perfect and universal hashing.

Symboltabels in compilers are often realized by hash tabels. Identifiers are strings over the alphabet {A,B,C,...}, i.e. U = {A,B,C,...}*. The usage of identifiers is definitely not uniformly distributed over U. Identifiers I1, I2, I3, J1,... are very popular and XYZ is not. We can use this nonuniformity to obtain even better behaviour than predicted by theorem 2. Inside a computer identifiers are represented as bit-strings; usually 8 bits (a byte) is used to represent one character. In other words, we assign a number num(C) $\in$ [0...255] to each character of the alphabet and interpret a string $C_r C_{r-1}...C_0$ as a number in base 256, namely $\sum_{i=0}^{r} num(C_i) \cdot 256^i$.; moreover, consecutive numbers are usually assigned to characters 1,2,3,... . Then strings I0, I1, I2, and X0, X1, X2 lead to arithmetic progressions of the form a + i and b + i respec-tively where i = 0,1,2,... and 256|(a-b). Because identifiers of the form I0, I1, I2, and X0, X1, X2 are used so frequently, we want

$$h(a + i) \neq h(b + j) \qquad \text{for } 0 \le i,j \le 9 \text{ and } 256|(a-b)$$

i.e. if h(x) = x mod m then we want

   (b - a)+(j - i) ≠ 0 mod m

Since 256|(b - a) we should choose m such that m does not divide numbers
of the form 256·c + d where |d| ≤ 9. In this way one can obtain even
better practical performance than predicted by theorem 2.

load factor	0.5	0.6	0.7	0.8	0.9
access time					
experiment	1.19	1.25	1.28	1.34	1.38
theory	1.25	1.30	1.35	1.40	1.45

(the expected behaviour of hashing (Lum (1971)).

Assumption 2) is not the only problem with hashing as we described it.
The expected behaviour of hashing depends on the load factor $\beta = n/m$.
An operation can be executed in time O(1) if β is bounded by a constant.
This implies that either one has to choose m large enough to begin
with or one has to increase (decrease) the size of the hash table from
time to time. The first solution increases storage requirement, which
in many environments also implies an increased running time. If the hash
table is too large to be stored in main storage, then a small load factor will increase the number of page faults.

In the second case we can use a sequence $T_0, T_1, T_2, \ldots$ of hash tables
of size m, 2m, 4m, ... respectively. Also, for each i we have a hash
function h_i. We start with hash table T_0. Suppose now, that we use
hash table T_i and the load factor reaches 1 or 1/4. In the first case,
we move to hash table T_{i+1} by storing all $2^i m$ elements which are present in T_i in table T_{i+1}. On the average, this will cost $O(2^i m)$ time
units. Also, the load factor of table T_{i+1} is 1/2 and therefore we can
execute at least $(1/4) \cdot 2^{i+1} \cdot m = (1/2) \cdot 2^i \cdot m$ operations until the next
restructuring is required. In the second case, we move to hash table
T_{i-1} by storing all $(1/4) \cdot 2^i \cdot m$ elements which are present in T_i in
table T_{i-1}. On the average, this will cost $O((1/4) \cdot 2^i \cdot m)$ time units.
Also, the load factor of table T_{i-1} is 1/2 and therefore we can execute

at least $(1/4) \cdot 2^{i-1} \cdot m$ operations without any further restructuring. In either case, the cost of restructuring is twice the number of subsequent operations which can be performed without further restructuring. Hence we can distribute (conceptually) the cost of restructuring to the operations following it but preceding the next restructuring process. In this way we will assign cost $O(1)$ to each operation and so the average cost of an operation is still $O(1)$. Also the load factor is always at least $1/4$ (except when table T_O is in use).

We continue this section with a remark on operations $Ord(k,S)$ and $List(S)$. Since the elements of set S are completely scattered over the hash table T both operations cannot be realized at reasonable cost. One of the main applications of operation $List(S)$ is batching of requests. Suppose that we want to perform n_1 operations Access, Insert, Delete on set S. Instead of performing n_1 single operations it is often better to sort the requests by the key referred to and to perform all requests by a single sweep of set S. If set S is stored in a hash table we may still use this method. We apply the hash function to the requests and sort the requests by the hashed key. Then we process all requests during a single scan through the hash table.

We close this section with a second look at the worst case behaviour of hashing and discuss the expected worst case behaviour of hashing with chaining. Suppose that a set of n elements is stored in the hash table. Then $\max_{x \in U} \delta_h(x,S)$ is the worst case cost of an operation when set S is stored. We want to compute the expected value of the worst case cost under the assumption that S is a random subset of the universe. More precisely, we assume that $S = \{x_1, \ldots, x_n\}$ and that $prob(h(x_k) = i) = 1/m$ for all $k \in [1 \ldots n]$ and $i \in [0 \ldots m-1]$. The very same assumption underlies theorem 2.

Theorem 3: Under the assumption above, the expected worst case cost of hashing with chaining is $O((\log n)/\log \log n)$ provided that $\beta = n/m \leq 1$.

Proof: Let $\ell(i)$ be the number of elements of S which are stored in the i-th list. Then $prob(\ell(i) \geq j) \leq \binom{n}{j}(1/m)^j$. Also

$$prob((\max_i \ell(i)) \geq j) \leq \sum_{i=0}^{m-1} prob(\ell(i) \geq j)$$

$$\leq m \binom{n}{j} (1/m)^j$$

$$\leq n(n/m)^{j-1}(1/j!)$$

Thus the expected worst case cost EWC, i.e. the expected lenth of the longest chain, is

$$EWC = \sum_{j\geq 1} \text{prob}((\max_{i} \ell(i)) \geq j)$$

$$\leq \sum_{j\geq 1} \min(1, n(n/m)^{j-1}(1/j!))$$

Let $j_o = \min \{j; n(n/m)^{j-1}(1/j)! \leq 1\} \leq \min \{j; n \leq j!\}$ since $n/m \leq 1$. From $j! \geq (j/2)^{j/2}$ we conclude $j_o = O((\log n)/\log \log n)$. Thus

$$EWC \leq \sum_{j=1}^{j_o} 1 + \sum_{j>j_o} 1/j_o^{j-j_o}$$

$$= O((\log n)/\log \log n). \qquad \Box$$

III. 2.2 Hashing with Open Addressing

Each element $x \in U$ defines a sequence $h(x,i)$, $i = 0, 1, 2, \ldots$ of table positions. This sequence of positions is searched through whenever an operation referring to key x is performed.

A very popular method for defining function $h(x,i)$ is to use the linear combination of two hash functions h_1 and h_2:

$$h(x,i) = [h_1(x) + i\, h_2(x)] \bmod m$$

We illustrate this method by an example; let $m = 7$, $h_1(x) = x \bmod 7$ and $h_2(x) = 1+(x \bmod 4)$. If we insert 3, 17, 6, 9, 15, 13, 1o in that order, we obtain

0	13
1	15
2	9
3	3
4	10
5	17
6	6

$h(3,i)\ \ = (3 + 4i) \bmod 7$, $i = 0$ works
$h(17,i) = (3 + 2i) \bmod 7$, $i = 1$ works
$h(6,1)\ \ = (6 + 3i) \bmod 7$, $i = 0$ works
$h(9,i)\ \ = (2 + 2i) \bmod 7$, $i = 0$ works

```
h(15,i) = (1 + 4i) mod 7, i = 0 works
h(13,i) = (6 + 2i) mod 7, i = 4 works
h(1o,i) = (3 + 3i) mod 7, i = 5 works
```

Hashing with open addressing does not require any additional space. However, its performance becomes poorly when the load factor is nearly one and it does not support deletion.

We analyse the expected cost of an operation Insert(x) into a table with load factor $\beta = n/m$ under the following assumption: Sequence $h(x,i)$, $i = 0, 1, \ldots, m-1$ is a random permutation of the set $\{0, \ldots, m-1\}$. The cost of operation Insert(x) is $1 + \min \{i; T[h(x,i)]$ is not occupied$\}$.

Theorem 4: The expected cost of an Insert into a table with load factor $\beta = n/m$ is $(m+1)/(m-n+1) \approx 1/(1-\beta)$ provided that $n/m < 1$.

Proof: Let $C(n,m)$ be the expected cost of an Insert into a table with m positions, n of which are occupied. Let $q_j(n,m)$ be the probability that table positions $h(x,0), \ldots, h(x,j-1)$ are occupied. Then $q_0(n,m) = 1$, $q_j(n,m) = [n/m] \cdot [(n-1)/(m-1)] \ldots [(n-(j-1))/(m-(j-1))]$ and

$$C(n,m) = \sum_{j=0}^{n} (q_j(n,m) - q_{j+1}(n,m))(j+1)$$

$$= \sum_{j=0}^{n} q_j(n,m) - (n+1)q_{n+1}(n,m)$$

$$= \sum_{j=0}^{n} q_j(n,m).$$

The expression for $q_j(n,m)$ can be justified as follows. Position $h(x,0)$ is occupied in n out of m cases. If $h(x,0)$ is occupied then position $h(x,1)$ is occupied in n-1 out of m-1 cases (note that $h(x,1) \neq h(x,0)$),...

We prove $C(n,m) = (m+1)/(m-n+1)$ by induction on m and for fixed m by induction on n. Note first that $C(0,m) = q_0(0,m) = 1$. Next note that $q_j(n,m) = (n/m) \cdot q_{j-1}(n-1,m-1)$ for $j \geq 1$. Hence

$$C(n,m) = \sum_{j=0}^{n} q_j(n,m)$$

$$= 1 + (n/m) \cdot \sum_{j=0}^{n-1} q_j(n-1,m-1)$$

$$= 1 + (n/m) \cdot C(n-1,m-1)$$

$$= 1 + (n/m) \cdot m/(m-n+1)$$

$$= (m+1)/(m-n+1) \qquad \square$$

The expected cost of a successful Access operation is now easy to determine. Suppose that set S is stored. When Access(x), x ∈ S, is executed we step through sequence h(x,0), h(x,1), ... until we find an i with T[h(x,i)] = x. Of course, the very same i determined the cost of inserting element x ∈ S in the first place. Hence the expected cost of a successful search in a table with n elements is

$$\frac{1}{n} \sum_{i=0}^{n-1} C(i,m) = \frac{1}{n} \sum_{i=0}^{n-1} \frac{m+1}{(m-i+1)}$$

$$= \frac{m+1}{n} \cdot [\sum_{j=1}^{m+1} 1/j - \sum_{j=1}^{m-n+1} 1/j]$$

$$\approx (1/\beta) \cdot \ln[(m+1)/(m-n+1)]$$

$$\approx (1/\beta) \cdot \ln 1/(1-\beta)$$

<u>Theorem 5</u>: The expected cost of a successful search in a table with load factor $\beta = n/m$ is $O((1/\beta)\ln(1/(1-\beta)))$.

<u>Proof</u>: By the discussion above. $\square$

Theorems 4 and 5 state that Insert and Access time will go up steeply as β approaches 1, and

β	0.5	0.7	0.9	0.95	0.99	0.999
$1/(1-\beta)$	2	3.3	10	20	1oo	1ooo
$(1/\beta)\,\ell n(1-\beta)$	1.38	1.70	2.55	3.15	4.65	6.9

that open addressing works fine as long as β is bounded away from one,
say β ≤ 0.9.

III. 2.3 Perfect Hashing

We based our analysis of the expected performance of hashing with
chaining on two assumptions, the second of which is very critical. It
postulates uniformity on the key space, an assumption which is almost
always violated. However, we saw in section 2.1. that it is possible to
tune the hash function according to the bias which is present in the
key space. In this section we will consider the ultimate form of tun-
ing. Set S is known when hash function h is chosen, h is chosen such
that it operates injectively on S.

Definition: a) A function $h : [0...N-1] \to [0...m-1]$ is a perfect hash
function for $S \subseteq [0...N-1]$ if $h(x) \neq h(y)$ for all $x,y \in S$, $x \neq y$.

b) A set H of functions $h : [0...N-1] \to [0...m-1]$ is called
(N,m,n) - perfect (or perfect for short) if for every $S \subseteq [0...N-1]$,
$|S| = n$, there is $h \in H$ such that h is perfect for S.   □

Of course, every set S has a perfect hash function. In our example of
the beginning of section 2 we can take h(x) = (last digit of x) mod 4.
The most interesting questions concerning perfect hash functions are:

a) How large are the programs for perfect hash functions, i.e. is there
always a short program computing a perfect hash function?

b) How hard is it to find a perfect hash function given S, m and N?

c) How hard is it to evaluate perfect hash functions?

In this section we will essentially answer all three questions
completely. We first have to give a more precise definition of
program size. The size of a program is just

the length of the program written as a string over some finite alphabet. We prove upper bounds on program size by explicitly exhibiting programs of a certain length. We prove lower bounds on program length by deriving a lower bound on the number of different programs required and then using the fact that the number of words (and hence programs) of length $\leq L$ over an alphabet of size c is $\leq c^{L+1}/(c-1)$.

<u>Theorem 6</u>: Let $N, m, n \in \mathbb{N}$ and let H be a (N, m, n) - perfect class of hash functions. Then

a) $|H| \geq \binom{N}{n} / ((N/m)^n \cdot \binom{m}{n})$

b) $|H| \geq \log N / \log m$

c) There is at least one $S \subseteq [0...N-1]$, $|S| = n$, such that the length of the shortest program computing a perfect hash function for S is

$$\max(\frac{n(n-1)}{2m \, \ln 2} - \frac{n(n-1)}{2N \, \ln 2} (1 - \frac{n-1}{N}), \; \log \log N - \log \log m)/\log c - 1,$$

here c is the size of the alphabet used for coding programs.

<u>Proof</u>: a) There are $\binom{N}{n}$ different subsets of $[0...N-1]$ of size n. It therefore suffices to show that any fixed function $h : [0...N-1] \to [0...m-1]$ is perfect for at most $(N/m)^n \cdot \binom{m}{n}$ different subsets $S \subseteq [0...N-1]$, $|S| = n$. If h is perfect for S then $|h^{-1}(i) \cap S| \leq 1$ for all $i \in [0...m-1]$. Hence the number of sets S such that h is perfect for S is bounded by

$$\sum_{0 \leq i_1 < i_2 < \, ... \, < i_n < m} |h^{-1}(i_1)| \cdot |h^{-1}(i_2)| \; ... \; |h^{-1}(i_n)|$$

This expression is maximal if $|h^{-1}(i)| = N/m$ for all $i \in [0...m-1]$ and its value is equal to $(N/m)^n \cdot \binom{m}{n}$ in this case.

b) Let $H = \{h_1, ..., h_t\}$. We construct $U_i \subseteq U$, $0 \leq i \leq t$, such that for every $S \subseteq U$, $|S \cap U_i| \geq 2$, functions $h_1, ..., h_i$ are not perfect for S. Then we must have $|U_t| \leq 1$. Let $U_0 = U$ and

$$U_{i+1} = U_i \cap h_{i+1}^{-1}(j) \qquad \text{for } i < t$$

where j is such that $|U_i \cap h_{i+1}^{-1}(j)| \geq |U_i \cap h_{i+1}^{-1}(\ell)|$ for every $\ell \in [0...m-1]$. Then $|U_{i+1}| \geq |U_i|/m$ and hence $|U_{i+1}| \geq N/m^{i+1}$. Also functions $h_1, ..., h_{i+1}$ are constant on U_{i+1} and hence $|U_t| \leq 1$. Thus $1 \geq N/m^t$ or $t \geq \log N/\log m$.

c) Let LBa and LBb be the lower bounds for $|H|$ proven in parts a) and b). Since there are at most c^{L+1} different programs of length $\leq L$ and different functions require different programs we conclude that there is at least one $S \subseteq [0...N-1]$, $|S| = n$, such that the shortest program computing a perfect hash function for S has length $\max(\log LBa, \log LBb)/\log c - 1$. But

$$\log LBb = \log \log N - \log \log m$$

and

$$\log LBa = \log \frac{N \ ... \ (N-n+1) \cdot m^n}{N^n \ m \cdot \ ... \ (m-n+1)}$$

$$= \log \left[\prod_{i=0}^{n-1} \frac{N-i}{N} / \prod_{i=0}^{n-1} \frac{m-i}{m} \right]$$

$$= \left[\sum_{i=0}^{n-1} \ln(1-i/N) - \sum_{i=0}^{n-1} \ln(1-i/m) \right]/\ln 2$$

$$\geq \left[(1 - \frac{n-1}{N}) \cdot \sum_{i=0}^{n-1} (i/N) + \sum_{i=0}^{n-1} (i/m) \right]/\ln 2$$

since $\ln(1-i/m) \leq -i/m$ and hence $-\ln(1-i/m) \geq i/m$ and $\ln(1-i/N) \geq -(i/N)(1-(n-1)/N)$ for $0 \leq i \leq n-1$ (cf. appendix)

$$\geq n \cdot (n-1)/2m \cdot \ln 2 - n \cdot (n-1) \cdot (1-(n-1)/N)/(2 \cdot N \cdot \ln 2) \qquad \square$$

Informally, we can state part c) of theorem 6 as follows. The length of the shortest program for a perfect hash function is at least $[(\beta/(2 \ln 2)) \cdot n + \log \log N]/\log c$, i.e. there is an initial cost $\log \log N$ due to the size of the universe and there is an incremental cost of $\beta/(2 \ln 2)$ bits per element stored. The incremental cost depends on the load factor $\beta = n/m$.

How good is that lower bound? We give our answer in two steps. We will
first show by a non-constructive argument that the lower bound is almost achievable (theorems 7 and 8). Unfortunately, the programs constructed in theorem 8 are extremely inefficient, i.e. theorem 8 settles
question a) concerning the program size of perfect hash functions but
does not give convincing answers to questions b) and c). In a second
step we will then derive answers for questions b) and c).

Theorem 7: Let $N,m,n \in \mathbb{N}$. If

$$t \geq n \cdot \ln N \cdot e^{n^2/m}$$

then there is a (N,m,n) - perfect class H with $|H| = t$.

Proof: We may represent any class $H = \{h_1, \ldots, h_t\}$ by a N by t matrix
$M(H) = (h_i(x))_{0 \leq x \leq N-1, 1 \leq i \leq t}$ with entries in $[0 \ldots m-1]$, i.e. the i-th
column of matrix $M(H)$ is the table of function values for h_i. Converse-
ly, every N by t matrix M is the representation of a class H of hash
functions. There are $m^{N \cdot t}$ matrices of dimension N by t with entries in
$[0 \ldots m-1]$.

We want to derive an upper bound on the number of non-perfect matrices,
i.e. matrices which correspond to non-perfect classes of hash functions.
If H does not contain a perfect hash function for $S = \{x_1 < x_2 < \ldots < x_n\}$,
then the submatrix of $M(H)$ given by rows $x_1, x_2, \ldots, x_n$ cannot have a
column with n different values. Hence the columns of that submatrix can
be chosen out of $m^n - m(m-1) \ldots (m-n+1)$ possibilities (namely, the number of functions from n points into a set of m elements minus the number of injective functions), and hence the number of such submatrices
is bounded by $[m^n - m(m-1) \ldots (m-n+1)]^t$. Recall that the submatrix has
t columns. Since S can be chosen in $\binom{N}{n}$ different ways, the number of
non-perfect matrices is bounded by

$$\binom{N}{n} [m^n - m(m-1) \ldots (m-n+1)]^t \, m^{(N-n) \cdot t}$$

Note that the rows corresponding to elements not in S may be filled ar-
bitrarily. Thus there is a perfect class H, $|H| = t$, if

$$\binom{N}{n} [m^n - m(m-1)\ldots(m-n+1)]^t \, m^{(N-n)\cdot t} < m^{N\cdot t}$$

or

$$\binom{N}{n} [1 - \frac{m\cdot(m-1)\ldots(m-n+1)}{m^n}]^t < 1$$

or

$$t \ge (\ell n\binom{N}{n})/(- \ell n(1 - m(m-1)\ldots(m-n+1)/m^n))$$

Since $\ell n\binom{N}{n} \le n\cdot \ell n\, N$, $- \ell n(1 - m(m-1)\ldots(m-n+1)/m^n) \ge \prod_{i=0}^{n-1} (1-i/m)$

$$= e^{\sum_{i=0}^{n-1} \ell n(1-i/m)} \quad \text{and} \quad \sum_{i=0}^{n-1} \ell n(1-i/m) \ge \int_0^n \ell n(1-x/m)\,dx =$$

$m[(1-n/m)(1-\ell n(1-n/m))-1] \ge m[(1-n/m)(1+n/m)-1] = n^2/m$ there will be a perfect class H with $|H| = t$ provided that

$$t \ge n\cdot (\ell n\, N)\cdot e^{n^2/m} \qquad\qquad\qquad\qquad \square$$

Theorem 7 gives us an upper bound on the cardinality of perfect classes of hash functions; it does not yet give us an upper bound on program size. The upper bound on program size is given by the next theorem.

Theorem 8: Let $N,m,n \in \mathbb{N}$. For every $S \subseteq [0\ldots N-1]$, $|S| = n$, there is a program of length

$$O(n^2/m + \log\log N + 1)$$

which computes a perfect hash function $h : [0\ldots N-1] \to [0\ldots m-1]$ for S.

Proof: We will explicitly describe a program. The program implements the proof of theorem 7 ; it has essentially 4 lines:

(1) $k \leftarrow \lceil \ell n\, N \rceil$ written in binary;

(2) $t \leftarrow \lceil n\cdot k\cdot e^{n^2/m} \rceil$ written in binary;

(3) $i \leftarrow$ some number between 1 and t depending on S written in binary;

(4) search through all 2^k by t matrices with entries in $[0\ldots m-1]$ until a (N,m,n) - perfect matrix is found; use the i-th column of that matrix as the table of the hash function for S;

The correctness of this program is immediate from theorem 7 ; by theorem 7 there is a 2^k by t perfect matrix and hence we will find it in step (4). One column of that matrix describes a perfect hash function for S, say the i-th. We set i to the appropriate value in line (3).

The length of this program is log log N + O(1) for line (1), log n + log log N + n^2/m + O(1) for lines (2) and (3) and O(1) for line (4). Note that the length of the text for line (4) is independent of N, t and m. This proves the claim.   □

Theorems 6 and 8 characterize the program size of perfect hash functions; upper and lower bounds are of the same order of magnitude. Unfortunately the program constructed in theorem 8 is completely useless. It runs extremely slow and it uses an immense amount of work space. Therefore, we have to look for constructive upper bounds if we also want to get some insight on questions b) and c).

Our constructive upper bounds are based on a detailed investigation of the division method for hashing. More precisely, we consider hash functions of the form

$$x \rightarrow ((kx) \bmod N) \bmod m$$

where k, $1 \le k < N$, is a multiplier, N is the size of the universe and m is the size of the hash table. The following lemma is crucial.

<u>Lemma 9</u> : Let N be a prime, let $S \subseteq [0...N-1]$, $|S| = n$. For every k, $1 \le k < N$, and $m \in \mathbb{N}$ let

$$b_i^k = |\{x \in S; ((kx) \bmod N) \bmod m = i\}|$$

for $0 \le i < m$.

a) For every m there is a k such that $\sum_{i=0}^{m-1} (b_i^k)^2 \le n + 2n(n-1)/m$. Moreover, such a k can be found in time O(nN).

b) For every m, a k satisfying $\sum_{i=0}^{m-1} (b_i^k)^2 \le n + 4n(n-1)/m$ can be found in random time O(n).

Proof: a) For k, $1 \le k < N$, let $h_k(x) = ((kx) \bmod N) \bmod m$ be the hash function defined by multiplier k. Then

$$\sum_{k=1}^{N-1} (\sum_{i=o}^{m-1} (b_i^k)^2 - n) = \sum_{k=1}^{N-1} (\sum_{i=o}^{m-1} |\{x \in S;\ h_k(x) = i\}|^2 - n)$$

$$= \sum_{k=1}^{N-1} \sum_{i=o}^{m-1} |\{(x,y);\ x,y \in S,\ x \ne y,\ h_k(x) = h_k(y) = i\}|$$

$$= \sum_{\substack{x,y \in S \\ x \ne y}} |\{k;\ h_k(x) = h_k(y)\}|$$

Next note that $h_k(x) = h_k(y)$ iff $[(kx) \bmod N - (ky) \bmod N] \bmod m = 0$. We are asking for the number of solutions k with $1 \le k < N$. Since $k \to (kx) \bmod N$ is a permutation of $\{1,\dots,N-1\}$ we may assume w.l.o.g. that $x = 1$ and hence $y \ne 1$. Thus

$$\sum_{k=1}^{N-1} (\sum_{i=0}^{m-1} (b_i^k)^2 - n) = |S| \sum_{y \in S, y \ne 1} |\{k;\ h_k(1) = h_k(y)\}|.$$

Consider a fixed y and let $g_y(k) = k - (ky) \bmod N$. We need to count the number of k with $1 \le k < N$ and $g_y(k) \bmod m = 0$. Note first that $-N + 2 \le g_y(k) \le N - 2$. We can therefore rewrite the sum above as

$$|S| \sum_{i=1}^{\lfloor (N-2)/m \rfloor} \sum_{y \in S, y \ne 1} |\{k;\ g_y(k) = \pm im\}|$$

We show $|\{k;\ g_y(k) = \pm im\}| \le 2$. Let $k_1, k_2 \in \{1,\dots,N-1\}$ be such that $g_y(k_1) = a g_y(k_2)$ where $a \in \{-1, +1\}$. Then

$$k_1 - (k_1 y) \bmod N = a(k_2 - (k_2 y) \bmod N)$$

or

$$k_1 - ak_2 = (k_1 y) \bmod N - (ak_2 y) \bmod N$$

and hence

$$(k_1 - ak_2) \bmod N = ((k_1 - ak_2)y) \bmod N$$

Since y ≠ 1 and N prime this implies $(k_1 - ak_2) \bmod N = 0$.
and hence $k_1 = k_2$ or $k_1 = N - k_2$. Hence

$$\sum_{k=1}^{N-1} \left(\sum_{i=0}^{m-1} (b_i^k)^2 - n \right) \leq |S| \cdot \sum_{i=0}^{\lfloor (N-2/m \rfloor} \sum_{y \in S, y \neq 1} 2$$

$$\leq 2n(n-1)(N-2)/m$$

Thus there is at least one k such that

$$\sum_{i=0}^{m-1} (b_i^k)^2 \leq n + 2n(n-1)/m.$$

Finally note that k can be found by exhaustive search in time $O(Nn)$.

b) In part a) we have shown that $\sum_{k=1}^{N-1} \left(\sum_{i=0}^{m-1} (b_i^k)^2 - n \right) \leq 2n(n-1)(N-2)/m$.
Since $\sum_{i=0}^{m-1} (b_i^k)^2 - n \geq 0$ for all k we conclude that we must have
$\sum_{i=0}^{m-1} (b_i^k)^2 - n \leq 4(n-1)n/m$ for at least fifty percent of the k's between
1 and N-1. Thus the expected number of tries needed to find a k with
$\sum_{i=0}^{m-1} (b_i^k)^2 - n \leq 4n(n-1)/m$ is at most two. Testing a particular k for
that property takes time $O(n)$. □

We will make use of lemma 9 in two particular cases:
$m = n$ and $m \approx n^2$.

<u>Corollary 1o:</u> Let N be a prime and let $S \subseteq [0...N-1]$, $|S| = n$. Let b_i^k
be defined as in lemma 9 .

a) If $n = m$ then a k satisfying $\sum_{i=o}^{m-1} (b_i^k)^2 < 3n$ can be found in time

$O(nN)$ deterministically, and a k satisfying $\sum_{i=o}^{m-1} (b_i^k)^2 < 4n$ can be found

in random time $O(n)$.

b) If $m = 1 + n(n-1)$ $(m = 2n(n-1) + 1)$ then a k such that
$x \to ((kx) \bmod N) \bmod m$ operates injectively on S can be determined deterministically in time $O(nN)$ (in random time $O(n)$).

Proof: a) follows immediately from lemma 9 by substituting $m = n$. For
part b) we observe first that substituting $m = 1 + n(n-1)$
$(m = 2n(n-1) + 1$ respectively) into lemma 9a (9b resp.) shows the
existence of a k, $1 \le k < N$, such that $\sum_i (b_i^k)^2 < n + 2$. Next note that
$b_i^k \in \mathbb{N}_o$ for all i and that $\sum_i b_i^k = n$. Thus $b_i^k \ge 2$ for some i implies
$\sum_i (b_i^k)^2 \ge n + 2$, a contradiction. We conclude that $b_i^k \le 1$ for all i,
i.e. the hash function induced by k operates injectively on S.   □

Corollary 1o can be interpreted as follows. If $m > n(n-1)$ then the
general division method directly provides us with a perfect hash function. Of course, nobody wants to work with a load factor as small as $1/n$.
However, part a) of corollary 1o suggests a method to improve upon the
load factor by using a two step hashing function. In the first step we
partition set S into n subsets S_i, $0 \le i < n$, such that $\sum |S_i|^2 < 3n$ as
described in part a) of corollary 10. In the second step we apply part
b) to every subset. The details are spelled out in

Theorem 11: Let N be a prime and let $S \subseteq [0...N-1]$, $|S| = n$.

a) A perfect hash function $h : S \to [0...m-1]$, $m = 3n$, with $O(1)$ evaluation time and $O(n \log N)$ program size can be constructed in time $O(nN)$.

b) A perfect hash function $h : S \to [0...m-1]$, $m = 4n$, with $O(1)$ evaluation time and $O(n \log N)$ program size can be constructed in random
time $O(n)$.

Proof: a) By corollary 1o a) there is a k, $1 \le k < N$, such that
$\sum_{i=o}^{n-1} |S_i|^2 < 3n$ where $S_i = \{x \in S; ((kx) \bmod N) \bmod n = i\}$. Moreover, k

can be found in time $O(nN)$. Let $b_i = |S_i|$ and let $c_i = 1 + b_i(b_i-1)$
For every i, $0 \le i < n$, there is k_i, $1 \le k_i < N$, such that
$x \to ((k_i x) \bmod N) \bmod c_i$ operates injectively on S_i by corollary 10 b).
Moreover, k_i can be determined in time $O(b_i N)$.

The following program computes an injective function from S into
$[0...m-1]$ where $m = \sum\limits_{i=o}^{n-1} c_i = n + (\sum\limits_i b_i^2 - \sum\limits_i b_i) < n + 3n-n = 3n$

(1) $i \gets ((kx) \bmod N) \bmod n$

(2) $j \gets ((k_i x) \bmod N) \bmod c_i$

(3) output $\sum\limits_{\ell=o}^{i-1} c_\ell + j$

The size of this program is $O(n \log N)$; namely, $O(\log N)$ bits each for
integers k, k_i and $\sum\limits_{\ell=o}^{i-1} c_\ell$, $0 \le i < n - 1$. The running time is clearly
$O(1)$ in the unit cost measure. Finally, the time to find the program is
bounded by $O(nN + \sum\limits_i b_i N) = O(nN)$.

b) The proof of part b) is very similar to the proof of part a). Note
first that a k with $\sum\limits_{i=o}^{n-1} |S_i|^2 < 4n$ can be found in random time $O(n)$.

Also, k_i's such that $x \to ((k_i x) \bmod N) \bmod (2b_i(b_i-1) + 1)$ operates injectively on S_i can be found in random time $\sum\limits_i O(b_i) = O(n)$. Putting
these functions together as described above yields an injective func-
tion from S into $[0...m-1]$ where $m = \sum\limits_{i=o}^{n-1} (2b_i(b_i-1) + 1) = \sum\limits_i b_i^2 < 4n$ □

Theorem 11 provides us with very efficient perfect hash functions. After
all, evaluating the hash functions constructed in the proof of theorem 9
requires only two multiplications and four divisions. However, the programs are hard to find, at least deterministically, and they are very
large. Let us take a closer look. The method devised in part a) of theorem 11 requires a hash table of size 3n and storage space for 2n integers in the range 1...N. Thus a total of 5n storage locations are
needed. The situation is even worse for the hash functions constructed
by probabilistic methods. They require a total of 6n storage locations,
4n for the hash table and 2n for the program. We will improve upon both
methods in the sequel and cut down the storage requirement for the
hash function to $O(n \log n + \log \log N)$ bits.

The key to the improvement is another variant of the division method
which we will use to reduce the size of the universe. More precisely,
we will show that for every $S \subseteq [0...N-1]$ there is $p = O(n^2 \ln N)$ such
that $x \to x \bmod p$ operates injectively on S. We can then apply theorems
1o and 11 to set $S' = \{x \bmod p; x \in S\}$. Since the members of S' have
size $O(n^2 \ln N)$ this will reduce the space requirement considerably.

Theorem 12: Let $S = \{x_1 < x_2 < ... < x_n\} \subseteq [0..N-1]$.

a)   There is a prime $p = O(n^2 \ln N)$ such that $x_i \bmod p \neq x_j \bmod p$ for
     $i \neq j$.

b)   A number p satisfying $p = O(n^2 \ln N)$ and $x_i \bmod p \neq x_j \bmod p$ for
     $i \neq j$ can be found in time $O(n \cdot \log n \cdot (\log n + \log\log N))$ by a prob-
     abilistic algorithm, and in time $O(n^3 \log N \log n)$ deterministically.

Proof: a) let $d_{ij} = x_j - x_i$ for $1 \le i < j \le n$. Then $x_1 \bmod p \neq x_j \bmod p$
iff $d_{ij} \neq 0 \bmod p$. Let $D = \prod_{i<j} d_{ij} \le N^{(n^2)}$. We need to find a bound on
the size of the smallest prime which does not divide D.

Claim 1:   Let $m \in \mathbb{N}$. Then m has at most $O(\ln m / \ln \ln m)$ different
prime divisors.

Proof: Let m have q different prime divisors and let $p_1, p_2, p_3, ...$
be the list of primes in increasing order. Then

$$m \ge p_1 \cdot p_2 \cdots \cdots p_q \ge q! = e^{\sum_{i=1}^{q} \ln i}$$

$$\ge e^{\int_1^q \ln x \, dx} = e^{q \ln(q/e) + 1} \ge (q/e)^q.$$

Hence there is a constant c such that $q \le c(\ln m)/\ln \ln m$.   □

We infer from claim 1 that D has at most $c(\ln D)/(\ln \ln D)$ different
prime divisors. Hence at least half of the $2 \cdot c(\ln D)/(\ln \ln D)$ smallest
primes will not divide D and hence not divide any d_{ij}. The prime number theorem gives us a bound on the size of this prime.

Fact: There is $d \in \mathbb{R}$ such that $p_q \leq d \, q \, \ell n \, q$ for all $q \geq 1$; p_q is the q-th smallest prime.

Proof: Cf. I. Niven/H.S. Zuckermann: Introduction to the Theory of Numbers, Vol. 2, theorem 8.2.   □

We infer from this fact that at least half of the primes
$p \leq d(2 \cdot c \, \ell n \, D/\ell n \, \ell n \, D) \, \ell n(2 \cdot c \, \ell n \, D/\ell n \, \ell n \, D) = O(\ell n \, D) = O(n^2 \, \ell n \, N)$
satisfy part a).

b) We proved in part a) that there is a constant a such that at least
half of the primes $p \leq a \, n^2 \, \ell n \, N$ will not divide D and hence satisfy a).
Furthermore, the prime number theorem tells us that there are at least
$b \cdot (a \, n^2 \, \ell n \, N)/\ell n(a \, n^2 \, \ell n \, N)$ primes less than $a \, n^2 \, \ell n \, N$ for some constant
$b > 0$. These observations suggest a probabilistic algorithm for finding
a number p (not necessarily prime) satisfying $p \leq a n^2 \, \ell n \, N$ and x_i mod $p \neq$
x_j mod p for $i \neq j$. We select a number $p \leq a \, n^2 \, \ell n \, N$ at random
and check whether x_i mod $p \neq x_j$ mod p for $i \neq j$ in time O(n log n) by
sorting the numbers x_i mod p, $1 \leq i \leq n$. If p does not work then we try
again, ... It remains to derive a bound on the expected number of
unsuccessful attempts. Note first that a random number $p \leq a \, n^2 \, \ell n \, N$ is
a prime with probability $\Omega(1/\ell n(a \, n^2 \, \ell n \, N))$ and that a random prime
satisfies a) with probability $\geq 1/2$. Hence a random number $p \leq a \, n^2 \, \ell n \, N$
leads to a mapping $x \rightarrow x$ mod p which is injective on S with probability
$\Omega(1/\ell n(a \, n^2 \, \ell n \, N))$; therefore the expected number of unsuccessful attempts is $O(\ell n(a \, n^2 \, \ell n \, N))$. Since each attempt costs O(n log n) time
units the total expected cost is O(n log n(log n + loglog N)).

Deterministically, we search through numbers $p = O(n^2 \, \ell n \, N)$ exhaustive-
ly. This will cost at most $O(n^3 \log n \log N)$ time units. □□

We close this section by combining theorems 1o, 11 and 12.

Theorem 13: Let $S \subseteq [0...N-1]$, $|S| = n$. There is a program P of size
O(n log n + log log N) bits and evaluation time O(1) which computes a
perfect hash function from S into $[0...m-1]$, $m = 3n$. P can be found
in random time $O(n^3 + n \log n \log \log N)$.

<u>Proof:</u> Let $S \subseteq [0...N-1]$, $|S| = n$. By theorem 12a) there is a prime
$p = O(n^2 \log N)$ such that h_1: $x \to x \bmod p$ operates injectively on S.
Moreover, p can be found in random time $O(n \log n(\log n + \log \log N))$.
Let $S_1 = h_1(S) \subseteq [0...p-1]$. By theorem 1ob) there is k, $1 \leq k \leq p$,
such that h_2: $x \to ((kx) \bmod p) \bmod n^2$ operates injectively on $h_1(S)$.
Moreover, k can be found in random time $O(n)$. Let $S_2 = h_2(S_1) \subseteq [0...n^2-1]$.
By theorem 11a) there is an injective function h_3: $S_2 \to [0...m-1]$,
$m = 3n$/with evaluation time $O(1)$ snd program size $O(n \log n)$. More-
over, h_3 can be found in time $O(n^3)$ deterministically.

$h = h_3 \circ h_2 \circ h_1$ is the desired hash function. A program for h can be
found in time $O(n^3 + n \log n \log \log N)$ by a probabilistic algorithm.
The program has size $O(\log p + \log p + n \log n) = O(n \log n + \log \log N)$
bits. Moreover, it can be evaluated in time $O(1)$. □

Theorem 13 essentially settles all questions about perfect hashing.
The program constructed in the proof of theorem 13 has almost minimal
size, namely $O(n \log n + \log \log N)$ bits instead of $O(n + \log \log N)$
bits, they achieve a load factor $\beta = n/m$ exceeding $1/3$, they are not
too hard to find, and they are quite efficient. More precisely, evaluation requires one division of numbers of length $O(\log N)$, a multiplication and two divisions on numbers of length $O(\log n + \log \log N)$, and
two multiplications and four divisions on numbers of length $O(\log n)$.

III. 2.4 Universal Hashing

Universal hashing is a method to deal with the basic problem of hashing:
its linear worst case behaviour. We saw in section 2.1. that hashing
provides us with $O(1)$ expected access time and $O(n)$ worst case access
time. The average was taken over all sets $S \subseteq [0...N-1]$, $|S| = n$. In
other words, a fixed hash function $h : [0...N-1] \to [0...m-1]$ works well
for a random subset $S \subseteq U$, but there are also some very "bad" inputs
for h. Thus it is always very risky to use hashing when the actual distribution of the inputs is not known to the designer of the hash function. It is always conceivable, that the actual distribution favours
worst case inputs and hence will lead to large average access times.

Universal hashing is a way out of this dilemma. We work with an entire
class H of hash functions instead of a single hash function; the specific

hash function in use is selected randomly from the collection H. If H
is chosen properly, i.e. for every subset S ⊆ U almost all h ∈ H distribute S fairly evenly over the hash table, then this will lead to
small expected access time for every set S. Note that the average is
now taken over the functions in class H, i.e. the randomization is
done by the algorithm itself not by the user: the algorithm controls
the dices.

Let us reconsider the symbol table example. At the beginning of each
compiler run the compiler chooses a random element h ∈ H. It will use
hash function h for the next compilation. In this way the time needed
to compile any fixed program will vary over different runs of the compiler, but the time spent on manipulating the symbol table will have
small mean.

What properties should the collection H of hash functions have? For
any pair $x,y \in U$, $x \neq y$, a random element h ∈ H should lead to collision,
i.e. $h(x) = h(y)$, with fairly small probability.

Definition: Let $c \in \mathbb{R}$, $N,m \in \mathbb{N}$. A collection
$H \subseteq \{h; \; h : [0...N-1] \to [0...m-1]\}$ is c-universal, if for all
$x,y \in [0...N-1]$, $x \neq y$

$$|\{h; \; h \in H \text{ and } h(x) = h(y)\}| \leq c \cdot |H|/m \qquad \qquad \square$$

A collection H is c-universal if only a fraction c/m of the functions
in H lead to collision on any pair $x,y \in [0...N-1]$. It is not obvious
that universal classes of hash functions exist. We exhibit an almost
1-universal class in theorem 14; in exercise 6 it is shown that there
are no c-universal classes for $c < 1 - m/N$. Thus theorem 14 is almost
optimal in that respect.

Theorem 14: Let $m,N \in \mathbb{N}$ and let N be a prime. Then

$$H_1 = \{h_{a,b}; \; h_{a,b}(x) = [(ax + b) \bmod N] \bmod m, \; a,b \in [0...N-1]\}$$

is a c-universal class, where $c = [\lceil N/m \rceil/(N/m)]^2$.

Proof: Note first that $|H_1| = N^2$. Let $x,y \in [0...N-1]$, $x \neq y$. We have to show that

$$|\{(a,b); h_{a,b}(x) = h_{a,b}(y)\}| \leq cN^2/m$$

If $h_{a,b}(x) = h_{a,b}(y)$ then there are $q \in [0...m-1]$ and $r,s \in [0...\ulcorner N/m \urcorner -1]$ such that

$$ax + b = q + rm \quad \text{mod } N$$
$$ay + b = q + sm \quad \text{mod } N$$

Since $\mathbb{Z}_N$ is a field (N is a prime) there is exactly one solution in a,b of these equations for each choice of q,r and m. Hence

$$|\{(a,b); h_{a,b}(x) = h_{a,b}(y)\}| = m\ulcorner N/m \urcorner^2$$

and therefore class H_1 is c-universal. □

Universal class H_1 has size N^2, i.e. $O(\log N)$ bits are required to specify a function of the class. A random element of H_1 may be selected by choosing two random numbers a,b in the range $0...N-1$. In theorem 17 we exhibit a smaller universal class; $O(\log m + \log \log N)$ bits suffice to specify a member of that class. We will also show that this is best possible.

We analyse the expected behavior of universal hashing under the following assumptions:

1) The hash function h is chosen at random from some c-universal class H, i.e. each $h \in H$ is chosen with probability $1/|H|$.

2) Hashing with chaining is used.

Theorem 15: Let $c \in \mathbb{R}$ and let H be a c-universal class of hash functions.

a) Let $S \subseteq [0...N-1]$, $|S| = n$ and let $x \in [0...N-1]$. Then

$$\sum_{h \in H} (1 + \delta_h(x,S))/|H| \leq \begin{cases} 1 + cn/m & \text{if } x \notin S \\ 1 + c(n-1)/m & \text{if } x \in S \end{cases}$$

b)   The expected cost of an Access, Insert or Delete operation is
      $O(1 + c\beta)$, where $\beta = n/m$ is the load factor.

c)   The expected cost of a sequence of n Access, Insert and Delete
      operations starting with an empty table is $O((1 + c\beta/2)n)$ where
      $\beta = n/m$ is the (maximal) load factor.

Proof: a)

$$\sum_{h \in H} (1 + \delta_h(x,S)) = |H| + \sum_{h \in H} \sum_{y \in S} \delta_h(x,y), \text{ by definition of } \delta_h$$

$$= |H| + \sum_{y \in S} \sum_{h \in H} \delta_h(x,y), \text{ reordering}$$

$$\leq |H| + \sum_{y \in S - \{x\}} c \, |H|/m \, , \text{ since } \delta_h(x,x) = 0$$
$$\text{and H is c-universal}$$

$$\leq \begin{cases} |H| \, (1 + c \cdot n/m) & \text{if } x \notin S \\ |H| \, (1 + c \cdot (n-1)/m) & \text{if } x \in S \end{cases}$$

b) immediate from part a)

c) immediate from part b) and the observation that the expected cost of
the i-th operation in the sequence is $O(1 + c \cdot i/m)$.   □

Theorem 15, c reads the same as theorem 2 (except for the factor c).
However, there is a major difference between the two theorems. They are
derived under completely different assumptions. In theorem 2 each sub-
set $S \subseteq U$, $|S| = n$, was assumed to be equally likely, in theorem 15, c
each element $h \in H$ is assumed to be equally likely. So universal hashing gives exactly the same performance as standard hashing, but the
dices are now controlled by the algorithm not by the user.

For every fixed set $S \subseteq U$, a random element $h \in H$ will distribute S
fairly evenly over the hash table, i.e. almost all functions $h \in H$
work well for S and only very few will give us bad performance on any
fixed set S. Theorem 16 gives us a bound on the probability of bad performance.

Theorem 16:   Let c ∈ IR and let H be a c-universal class. Let
S ⊆ [0...N-1], |S| = n and x ∈ [0...N-1]. Let μ be the expected value
of $\delta_h(x,S)$, i.e. μ = ($\sum_{h \in H} \delta_h(x,S)$)/|H|. Then the probability that
$\delta_h(x,S)$ ≥ t·μ is less than 1/t.

Proof: Let H' = {h∈H; $\delta_h(x,S)$ ≥ t·μ}. Then

$$\mu = (\sum_{h \in H} \delta_h(x,S))/|H|$$

$$\geq (\sum_{h \in H'} \delta_h(x,S))/|H| \qquad \text{since } \delta_h(x,S) \geq 0$$

$$\geq t \cdot \mu \cdot |H'|/|H| \qquad \text{since } \delta_h(x,S) \geq t \cdot \mu \text{ for } h \in H'$$

and hence |H'| ≤ |H|/t   □

We infer from theorem 16 that the probability that the performance is
more than t times the expected performance is at most 1/t. Much better
bounds can often be obtained for specific universal classes; cf exercise 7 where a 1-universal class with an $O(1/t^2)$ bound is described.
We close this section with an estimate of the size of universal classes
of hash functions.

Theorem 17:   a) Let H ⊆ {h; h : [0...N-1] → [0...m-1]} be a c-universal
class. Then

$$|H| \geq m \cdot (\lceil \log_m N \rceil - 1)/c$$

and hence log |H| = Ω(log m + log log N - log c).

b) Let N,m ∈ IN , N ≥ m. Then there is a 8-universal class
H_2 ⊆ {h; h : [0...N-1] → [0...m-1]} of hash functions with

$$\log |H_2| = O(\log m + \log \log N)$$

Proof: a) Let H = {$h_1,...,h_t$}. As in the proof of theorem 6, a) we
construct a sequence U_0 = [0...N-1], U_1, U_2, ... such that $h_1,...,h_i$
are constant functions on U_i and |U_i| ≥ |U_{i-1}|/m ≥ N/m^i. Let
t_0 = $\lceil \log_m N \rceil$ - 1. Then |U_{t_0}| > 1. Let x,y ∈ U_{t_0}, x ≠ y. Then

$$t_0 \leq |\{h \in H; \ h(x) = h(y)\}| \leq c \cdot |H|/m$$

since H is c-universal. Thus $|H| \geq m \cdot (\lceil \log_m N \rceil - 1)/c$.

b) Let $N, m \in \mathbb{N}$ and let t be minimal such that $t \cdot \ln p_t \geq m \cdot \ln N$. Here p_t denotes the t-th prime. Then $t = O(m \ln N)$. Let

$$H_2 = \{g_{c,d}(h_\ell(x)); \ t < \ell \leq 2t, \ 0 \leq c,d < p_{2t}\}$$

where

$$h_\ell(x) = x \bmod p_\ell$$

and

$$g_{c,d}(z) = [(cz + d) \bmod p_{2t}] \bmod m.$$

Then $|H_2| = t \cdot p_{2t}^2$ and hence $\log |H_2| = O(\log t) = O(\log m + \log \log N)$ since $\log p_{2t} = O(\log t)$ by the prime number theorem. It remains to show that H_2 is 8-universal.

Let $x,y \in [0 \dots N-1]$, $x \neq y$, be arbitrary. We have to show that

$$|\{(c,d,\ell); \ g_{c,d}(h_\ell(x)) = g_{c,d}(h_\ell(y))\}| \leq 8 \cdot |H_2|/m$$

If $g_{c,d}(h_\ell(x)) = g_{c,d}(h_\ell(y))$ then by definition of h_ℓ and $g_{c,d}$

$$[c(x \bmod p_\ell) + d] \bmod p_{2t} = [c(y \bmod p_\ell) + d] \bmod p_{2t} \bmod m$$

Thus there have to exist $q \in [0 \dots m-1]$ and $r,s \in [0 \dots \lceil p_{2t}/m \rceil -1]$ such that

$$[c(x \bmod p_\ell) + d] \bmod p_{2t} = q + r \cdot m$$

$$[c(y \bmod p_\ell) + d] \bmod p_{2t} = q + s \cdot m$$

We have to count the number of triples (c,d,ℓ) which solve this pair of equations. We count the solutions in two groups. The first group contains all solutions (c,d,ℓ) with $x \bmod p_\ell \neq y \bmod p_\ell$ and the second group contains all solutions (c,d,ℓ) with $x \bmod p_\ell = y \bmod p_\ell$.

Group 1: Of course, there are at most t different ℓ's such that
$x \bmod p_\ell \neq y \bmod p_\ell$. For each such ℓ and any choice of q,r and s there
is exactly one pair c,d which solves our equations. This follows from
the fact that $\mathbb{Z}_{p_{2t}}$ is a field. Hence the number of solutions in group
one is bounded by

$$t \, m(\ulcorner p_{2t}/m \urcorner)^2 \leq t \, m(1 + p_{2t}/m)^2 \leq (t \cdot p_{2t}^2/m) \cdot (1 + m/p_{2t})^2$$

$$\leq (|H_2|/m) \cdot (1 + m/p_{2t})^2$$

Group 2: Let $L = \{\ell;\ t < \ell \leq 2t$ and $x \bmod p_\ell = y \bmod p_\ell\}$ and let
$P = \Pi \{p_\ell;\ \ell \in L\}$. Then $P \geq p_t^{|L|}$. Also P divides $x - y$ and hence $P \leq N$.
Thus $|L| \leq (\ln N)/\ln p_t \leq t/m$ by definition of t.

Consider any fixed $\ell \in L$ and any choice of q,r and s. If $r \neq s$ then
there is no pair (c,d) solving our pair of equations. If $r = s$ then
there are exactly p_{2t} pairs (c,d) solving our pair of equations. Hence
the number of solutions in group two is at most

$$|L| \, m^{\ulcorner} (p_{2t}/m)^{\urcorner} p_{2t} \leq (t \cdot p_{2t}^2/m)(1 + m/p_{2t}) = (|H_2|/m)(1 + m/p_{2t})$$

Altogether, we have shown that the number of solutions (c,d,ℓ) is
bounded by $2(1 + \varepsilon)^2 |H_2|/m$ where $\varepsilon = m/p_{2t} \leq 1$. (Note that $p_{2t} \leq m$
would imply $t \ln p_t < p_{2t} \ln p_{2t} \leq m \ln m \leq m \ln N$, a contradiction to
the definition of t). Hence H_2 is 8-universal.   □

III. 2.5 Extendible Hashing

Our treatment of hashing in sections 2.1. to 2.4. was based on the
assumption that main memory is large enough to completely contain the
hash table. In this section we discuss application of hashing to secondary storage. We assume that secondary storage is divided into
buckets (pages) of size b; i.e. each bucket can hold up to b elements
of universe U.

Again, we start with a hash function $h : U \to \{0,1\}^k$ where k is some integer. h is assumed to be injective. For d, $0 \leq d \leq k$, we use h_d to denote the function which maps $x \in U$ onto the first d digits of $h(x)$, i.e. $h_d : U \rightarrow \{0,1\}^d$ and $h_d(x)$ is a prefix of $h(x)$ for all $x \in U$. Let $S \subseteq U$, $|S| = n$, be a subset of U. The depth $d(S)$ of S with respect to bucket size b and hash function h is defined as

$$d(S) = \min\{d; \, |\{x \in S; \, h_d(x) = a\}| \leq b \text{ for all } a \in \{0,1\}^d\}$$

In other words, if we use a TRIE to partition $h(S)$ into subsets of size at most b then this TRIE has depth $d(S)$.

Extendible hashing uses a table $T[0...2^{d(S)} - 1]$, called the directory, and some number of buckets to store set S. More precisely, the entries of table T are pointers to buckets. If x is an element of S then the bucket containing x can be found as follows.

(1) Compute $h_{d(s)}(x)$ and interpret it as the binary representation of an integer, say i, in the range $0...2^{d(S)} - 1$.

(2) Use this integer to index directory T; pointer $T[i]$ points to the bucket containing x.

Example: Let $h(S) = \{0000, 0000, 0100, 1100\}$ and let $b = 2$. Then $d(S) = 2$.

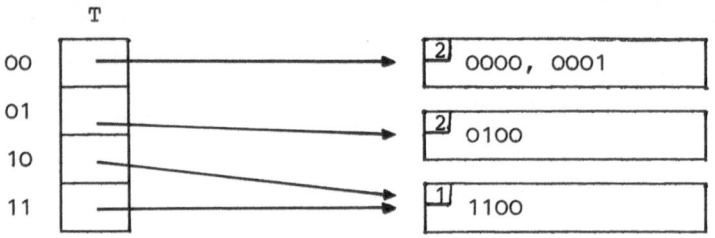

As one can see from the example, we allow entries of T to point to the same bucket. However, we require that sharing of buckets must conform to the buddy principle. More precisely, if $r < d(S)$, $a \in \{0,1\}^r$, $a_1, a_2 \in \{0,1\}^{d(S)-r}$, $a_1 \neq a_2$ and $T[aa_1] = T[aa_2]$ then $T[aa_1] = T[aa_3]$ for all $a_3 \in \{0,1\}^{d(S)-r}$. In other words, if we represent $\{0,1\}^{d(S)}$ as a TRIE then the table entries sharing a bucket form a subtree of the TRIE. Finally, if B is a bucket and $2^{d(S)-r}$ table entries point to B then r is the local depth of B. In our example the local depth of buckets is shown in their left upper corner.

The insertion algorithm for extendible hashing is quite simple. Suppose that we want to insert x $\in$ U. We first compute bucket B which should contain x. If B is not full, i.e. B contains less than b keys, then we insert x into B and are done. If B is full, say B contains $x_1, \ldots, x_b$, then additional work is required. Let r be the local depth of page B and let B' be a new page. If r = d(S) then we double the size of directory T, i.e. we increase d(S) by 1, create a directory T' of size $2^{d(S)+1}$ and initialize T'. Note that initializing T' essentially means to make two copies of T and to merge them. At this point we have r < d(S) in either case, i.e. if r < d(S) initially or if r = d(S) and directory size was doubled. We finish the insertion by setting the local depth of B and B' to r + 1 and by inserting $x_1, \ldots, x_b$, x into B or B' whatever is appropriate. Note that this might cause B or B' to overflow (in some rare case). In this case we go through the routine once more.

Example (continued): Suppose that we want to insert x with h(x) = 0010. It will cause the first bucket to overflow. We obtain

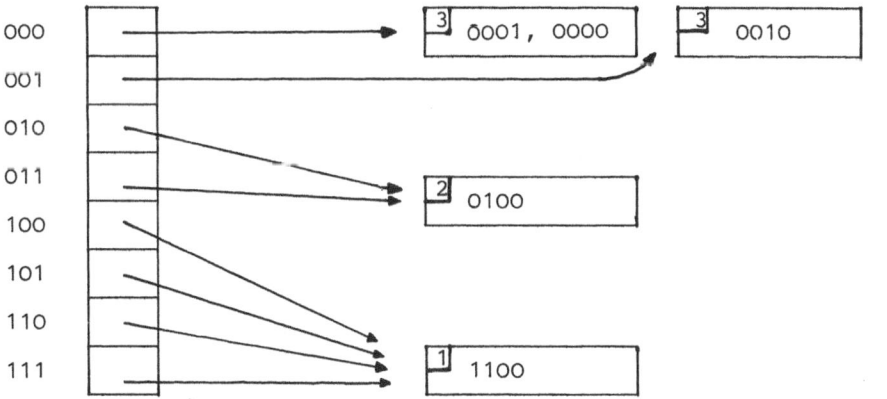

The deletion algorithm is also quite simple. Suppose that we want to delete x from S. We first determine bucket B containing x and delete x from B. Let B' be the buddy of B, i.e. if r is the local depth of B and a $\in \{0,1\}^{r-1}$ and z $\in \{0,1\}$ are such that all directory entries $T[aza_1]$, $a_1 \in \{0,1\}^{d(S)-r}$, point to B then B' is the buddy of B if all entries

$T[a\bar{z}a_1]$, $a_1 \in \{0,1\}^{d(S)-r}$ and $\bar{z} = 1 - z$, point to B'. Note that B' does not necessarily exist. If B' does exist and B and B' contain together at most b keys then we merge B and B' to a single bucket of local depth $r - 1$. In addition, if $r = d(S)$ and B and B' were the only buckets of depth $d(S)$ then we half the size of the directory. This completes the description of the deletion algorithm.

What can we say about the behaviour of extendible hashing? What are the relevant quantities? We have seen already that an Access operation requires only two accesses to secondary memory. This is also true for an Insert, except in the case that a bucket overflows. In this case we have to obtain a new bucket, a third access, and to distribute the elements of the bucket to be split over the new buckets. In rare cases we will also have to double the directory. These remarks show that the time complexity of extendible hashing is very good. The space complexity requires further investigation. The two main questions are: What is the size of directory T? How many buckets are used? First of all, as for all hashing schemes worst case behaviour can be very, very bad. So let us discuss expected behaviour. The analysis is based on the following assumption. We have $k = \infty$, i.e. hash function h maps U into bit strings of infinite length. Furthermore, h(x) is uniformly distributed in interval [0,1]. Note that h(x) can be interpreted as the binary representation of a real number. A discussion of expected behaviour is particularly relevant in view of our treatment of universal hashing. Note that the behaviour of extendible hashing heavily depends on the hash function in use and that universal hashing teaches us how to choose good hash functions. Unfortunately, a complete analysis of the expected behaviour of extendible hashing is quite involved and far beyond the scope of the book.

Theorem 18: a) The expected number of buckets required to store a set of n elements is approximately $n/b \ln 2$.

b) The expected size of the directory for a set of n elements is approximately $(e/b \ln 2)n^{1+1/b}$.

Proof: A complete analysis of extendible hashing can be found in Flajolet/Steyaert (82). The exact formula for the expected size of the directory is

$$Q((1 + 1/b) \log n) \; n^{1+1/b}(1 + o(1))$$

where Q is a periodic function given by $Q(z) = \sum_{k \geq 0} q_k e^{-2ik\pi z}$ with

$$q_o = (-1/b \; \ln 2)[(b+1)!]^{1/b} \; \Gamma(-1/b)$$

and

$$q_k = (-1/b \; \ln 2) \; [(b+1)!]^{1/b-\lambda_k} \; \Gamma(\lambda_k - 1/b) \quad \text{where}$$

$$\lambda_k = 2ik\pi/b \; \ln 2$$

$\Gamma(z)$ is the gamma function. Q is periodic with mean value q_o; q_o is numerically close to $e/b \; \ln 2$. In part b) of theorem 18 we only quoted the leading term of the exact formula for expected directory size. More-over, we replaced Q by its mean value. An approximate and simpler anal-ysis of extendible hashing is contained in A. Yao (1980). □

We finish this section with a discussion of theorem 18. Part a) states that the expected number of buckets is $n/(b \; \ln 2)$; in other words the expected number of elements per bucket is $b \; \ln 2 \approx 0.69 \; b$. Expected storage utilization is 69 %. This result is not too surprising. After all, buckets can contain between 0 and b keys. Once a bucket overflows it is split into two buckets. The size of the two parts is a random variable; however, it is very likely that each of the two buckets receives about 50 % of the elements. We should thus expect that the expected number of elements per bucket is somewhere between 0 and b with a small inclination towards b.

Part b) is more surprising. Expected directory size is non-linear in the number of elements stored. The following table lists expected di-rectory size for various choices of b and n.

b \ n	10^5	10^6	10^8	10^{10}
2	$6.2 \cdot 10^7$	$1.96 \cdot 10^8$	$1.96 \cdot 10^{11}$	$1.96 \cdot 10^{14}$
10	$1.2 \cdot 10^5$	$1.5 \cdot 10^6$	$2.4 \cdot 10^8$	$3.9 \cdot 10^{10}$
50	$9.8 \cdot 10^3$	$1.0 \cdot 10^6$	$1.1 \cdot 10^8$	$1.2 \cdot 10^{10}$
100	$4.4 \cdot 10^3$	$4.5 \cdot 10^4$	$4.7 \cdot 10^6$	$4.9 \cdot 10^8$

We can see from this table that the non-linear growth is clearly perceptible for small b, say b ≈ 1o, and that directory size exceeds the size of the file even for moderate n, say n = 10^6. If b is larger, say b ≈ 1oo, then the non-linearity is hardly noticible for practical values of n, say n ≤ 10^{10}. Moreover, the size of the directory will be only about 5 % of the size of the file.

Why does directory size grow non-linearly in the size of the file? In the case b = 1 this is not too hard to see and follows from the birthday paradox. If b is 1 then directory size doubles whenever two elements of S hash to the same entry of the directory (have the same birthday). If directory size is m (the year has m days) and the size of S is n then the probability $p_{n,m}$ that no two elements of S hash to the same entry of the directory is

$$p_{n,m} = m(m-1) \ldots (m-n+1)/m^n$$

$$= \prod_{i=0}^{n-1} (1 - i/m)$$

$$= e^{\sum_{i=0}^{n-1} \ln(1-i/m)}$$

$$\approx e^{-\sum_{i=0}^{n-1} i/m} \approx e^{-n^2/m}$$

Thus $p_{n,m} \le 1/e$ if n exceeds $\sqrt{m}$. In other words, a directory of size m suffices for a set of n = $\sqrt{m}$ elements with probability less than 1 - 1/e. So directory size must grow non-linearly in file size and should in fact be quadratic in file size.

III. 3. Searching Ordered Sets

We will now turn to comparison based methods for searching. We assume
that U is linearly ordered and denote the linear ordering by $\leq$. The
assumption of U being linearly ordered is no real restriction; there
is always an ordering on the internal representations of the elements
of U. The basis for all comparison-based methods is the following algorithm for searching ordered arrays. Let $S = \{x_1 < x_2 <...< x_n\}$ be
stored in array S[1.. n], i.e. $S[i] = x_i$, and let a $\in$ U. In order to
decide a $\in$ S, we compare a with some table element and then proceed
with either the lower or the upper part of the table.

```
(1)    low ← 1; high ← n;
(2)    next ← an integer in [low.. high];
(3)    while a ≠ S[next] and high > low
(4)    do     if a < S[next]
(5)           then high ← next - 1
(6)           else low ← next + 1 fi;
(7)           next ← an integer in [low.. high]
(8)    od;
(9)    if a = S[next] then "successful"  else "unsuccessful";
```

Various algorithms can be obtained from this scheme by replacing lines
(2) and (7) by specific strategies for choosing next. Linear search is
obtained by next ← low, binary search by next ← $\lceil$(low + high)/2$\rceil$ and
interpolation search by next ← (low-1) + $\lceil \frac{a-S[low-1]}{S[high+1]-S[low-1]}(high-low+1) \rceil$.
We discuss these strategies in greater detail below.

The correctness of the program is independent of the particular choice
made in line (2) and (7). This can be seen from the fact that the following predicate P is an invariant of the body of the while-loop:
(a $\in$ S $\Rightarrow$ a $\in$ {S[low],..., S[high]}) and ((low $\leq$ high) $\Rightarrow$ low $\leq$ next $\leq$ high)
P is certainly true before execution of the while-loop. If the loop
body is entered then a ≠ S[next] and hence either a < S[next] or
a > S[next]. If a < S[next] then certainly a $\notin$ {S[next],..., S[high]}
and hence a $\in$ S implies a $\in$ {S[low],..., S[next - 1]}. The case
a > S[next] is treated similarly. Also a number in [low ..high] is assigned to next in line (7) provided that low $\leq$ high.

Thus when the while-loop terminates we have P and ((a = S[next]) or high ≤ low). If a = S[next] then the search is successful. Suppose now that a ≠ S[next]. Since P holds we know that a ∈ S implies a ∈ {S[low],..., S[high]}. If high < low then certainly a ∉ S. If high = low then next = high by P and hence a ∉ S. In either case the search is unsuccessful.

Finally, the program terminates because high - low is decreased by at least one in each execution of the loop body.

III. 3.1. Binary Search and Search Trees

Binary search is obtained by replacing lines (2) and (7) by next ← ⌈(low + high)/2⌉. It is very helpful to illustrate the behaviour of the algorithm by a binary tree. We do so for n = 6. In this tree node S[4] represents a comparison with S[4].

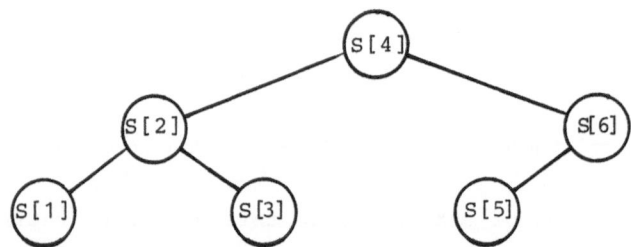

If a < S[4] then we go left, if a > S[4] then we go right, if a = S[4] then we are done. We start the search by comparing a and S[4]. If a > S[4] then a can only be equal to S[5] or S[6]. Next we compare a and S[6],... . We can also see from this picture that an unsuccessful search gives us information about the rank of a in S.

Since the value of high - low + 1 is halved in each iteration of the loop, the loop body is executed at most log n times. Thus an operation Access(a,S) takes time O(log |S|). Operations Ord(k,S) and Sequ(S) are trivial in this structure, however Insert and Delete cannot be done efficiently. An Insert would require to move part of the array, a costly process. An elegant way out is to represent the tree above explicitly by pointers and not implicitly by an array. Then operations Insert and Delete can also be executed fast as we will see shortly. This leads to the following definition.

<u>Definition:</u> A binary search tree for set $S = \{x_1 < x_2 < \ldots < x_n\}$ is a binary tree with n nodes $\{v_1, \ldots, v_n\}$. The nodes are labelled with the elements of S, i.e. there is an injective mapping CONTENT: $\{v_1, \ldots, v_n\} \rightarrow S$. The labelling preserves the order, i.e. if $v_i (v_j)$ is a node in the left (right) subtree of the tree with root v_k then $\text{CONTENT}[v_i] < \text{CONTENT}[v_k] < \text{CONTENT}[v_j]$.

An equivalent definition is as follows: a traversal of a search tree for S in symmetric order reproduces the order on S. We will mostly identify nodes with their labellings, i.e. instead of speaking of node v with label x with speak of node x and write ⊗ or simply x. Node x corresponds to the test: if a < x <u>then</u> go to the left son <u>else if</u> a = x <u>then</u> terminate search <u>else</u> go to the right son <u>fi fi</u>. The n + 1 leaves represent unsuccessful access operations. It is not necessary to store leaves explicitly. Each leaf represents one of the n + 1 open intervals of U generated by the elements of S. We draw the leaf corresponding to interval $x_i < a < x_{i+1}$ as $\boxed{(x_i, x_{i+1})}$.

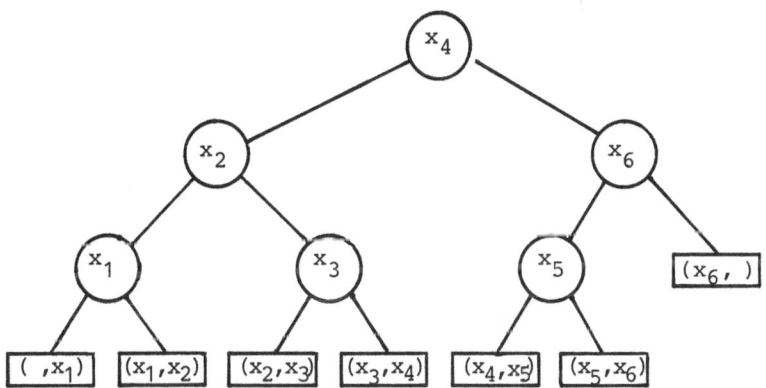

In the text we simply speak about leaf (x_i, x_{i+1}). Leaf $(, x_1)$ represents all $a \in U$ with $a < x_1$. Sometimes we will write (x_0, x_1) instead of $(, x_1)$. A similar remark applies to leaf $(x_n,)$. So let T be a binary search tree for set S. Then the following piece of code realizes operation Access(a,S).

```
v ← root of T;
while v is a node and a ≠ CONTENT[v]
do if a < CONTENT[v]
```

```
    then v ← LSON[v]
    else v ← RSON[v]
    fi
od
```

If this algorithm terminates in node v then a = CONTENT[v]. Otherwise
it terminates in a leaf, say (x_i, x_{i+1}). Then $x_i < a < x_{i+1}$. Operation Insert(a,S) is now very easy to implement. We only have to replace
leaf (x_i, x_{i+1}) by the tree

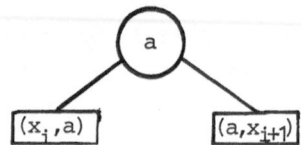

Deletion is slightly more difficult. A search for a yields node v with
content a. We have to distinguish two cases.

Case 1: At least one son of v is a leaf, say the left. Then we replace
v by its right son and delete v and its left son from the tree.

Case 2: No son of v is a leaf. Let w be the rightmost node in the left
subtree of v. Node w can be found by following the left pointer out of
v and then always the right pointer until a leaf is hit. We replace
CONTENT[v] by CONTENT[w] and delete w as described in case 1. Note that
w's right son is a leaf.

The following figure illustrates both cases. The node with content 4 is
deleted, leaves are not drawn.

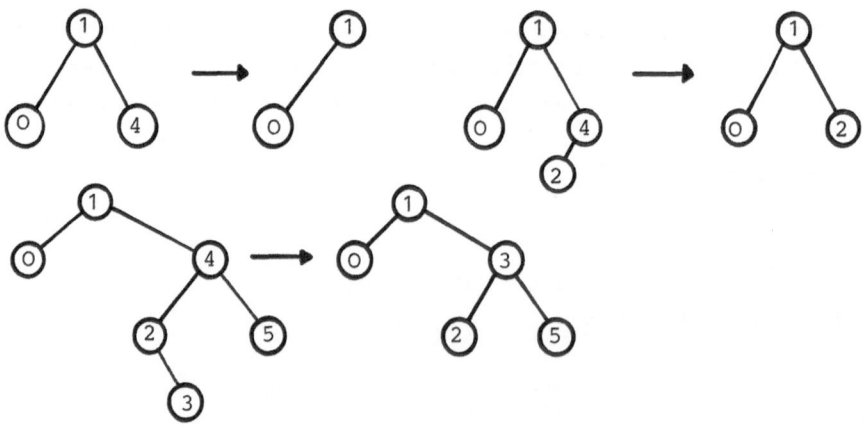

Operations Access, Insert and Delete essentially consist of a single
pass down the tree followed by some local updating. Updating takes
time O(1) and hence the total cost is O(h(T)), where h(T) is the height
of tree T. Operation Sequ(S) is equivalent to the traversal of tree T
in symmetric order. We have already seen (see I.4.) that tree trav-
ersal takes time O(|S|). Finally, we show how to realize operation
Ord(k,S) in time O(h(T)) by extending the data structure slightly. We
store in each node the number of elements stored in the left subtree.
These numbers are easily updated during insertions and deletions. With
the use of these numbers Ord(k,S) takes time O(h(T)).

The considerations above show that the height of the search tree
plays a crucial role for the efficiency of the basic set operations.
We will see in III.5. that h(T) = O(log |S|) can be achieved by the use
of various balanced tree schemes. In the exercises it is shown that the
average height of a randomly grown tree is O(log n).

III. 3.2 Interpolation Search

Interpolation search is obtained by replacing lines (2) and (7) by

$$\text{next} \leftarrow (\text{low}-1) + \left\lceil \frac{a - S[\text{low}-1]}{S[\text{high}+1] - S[\text{low}-1]} \cdot (\text{high}-\text{low}+1) \right\rceil$$

It is assumed that positions S[0] and S[n+1] are added and filled with
artificial elements. The worst case complexity of interpolation search
is clearly O(n); consider the case that S[0] = 0, S[n+1] = 1,
a = 1/(n+1) and S ⊆ (0,a). Then next = low always and interpolation
search deteriorates to linear search. Average case behaviour is
much better. Average access time is O(log log n) under the assumption
that keys $x_1, \ldots, x_n$ are drawn independently from a uniform distribution
over the open interval (x_0, x_{n+1}). An exact analysis of interpolation
search is beyond the scope of this book. However, we discuss a variant
of interpolation search, which also has O(log log n) expected behaviour:
quadratic binary search.

Binary search has access time O(log n) because it consists of a single
scanning of a path in a complete binary tree of depth log n. If we
could do binary search on the paths of the tree then we would obtain
log log n access time. So let us consider the question, whether there

is a fast (at least on the average) way to find the node on the path of
search which is halfway down the tree, i.e. the node on the path of
search which has depth 1/2 log n. There are $2^{1/2 \log n} = \sqrt{n}$ of these
nodes and they are $\sqrt{n}$ apart in the array representation of the tree.
Let us make an initial guess by interpolating and then search through
these nodes by linear search. Note that each step of the linear search
jumps over $\sqrt{n}$ elements of S and hence as we will see shortly only O(1)
steps are required on the average. Thus an expected cost of O(1) has
reduced the size of the set from n to $\sqrt{n}$ (or in other words determined
the first half of the path of search) and hence total expected search
time is O(log log n).

The precise algorithm for Access(a,S) is as follows. Let low = 1,
high = n and let next = $\lceil p \cdot n \rceil$ be defined as above; here
$p = (a-x_0)/(x_{n+1}-x_0)$. If $a > S[next]$ then compare a with $S[next + \sqrt{n}]$,
$S[next + 2\sqrt{n}]$, ... until an i is found with $a \leq S[next + (i-1) \cdot \sqrt{n}]$.
This will use up i comparisons. If $a < S[next]$ then we proceed analogously. In any case, the subtable of size $\sqrt{n}$ thus found is then
searched by applying the same method recursively.

We must determine the expected number C of comparisons required to determine the subtable of size $\sqrt{n}$. Let p_i be the probability that i or
more comparisons are required to find the subtable. Then

$$C = \sum_{i \geq 1} i(p_i - p_{i+1}) = \sum_{i \geq 1} p_i$$

It remains to estimate p_i. Note first that $p_1 = p_2 = 1$ since two comparisons are always required. So let $i > 2$. If i or more comparisons are
needed then

   |actual rank of a - next| $\geq$ (i-2)$\cdot \sqrt{n}$

where actual rank of a denotes the number of x_j's smaller than a. Hence

   $p_i \leq$ Prob (|actual rank of a - next| $\geq$ (i-2)$\sqrt{n}$)

We use Chebyshev's inequality (cf. W. Feller, An Introduction to Prob-
abtility Theory, and its Applications, John Wiley, New York 1968) to
derive a bound on p_i:

$$\text{Prob}(|X - \mu| \geq t) \leq \sigma^2/t^2$$

for a random variable X with mean μ and variance σ^2

Let random variable X be the number of x_j's smaller than a. Recall, that we assume that $x_1,\ldots,x_n$ are drawn independently from a uniform distribution over (x_0,x_{n+1}). Then, since the x_i are independent and since $p = (a-x_0)/(x_{n+1}-x_0)$ is the probability that any one of them is less than a, the probability that exactly j out of n are less then a is $\binom{n}{j}p^j(1-p)^{n-j}$. Thus the expected number of keys less than a, i.e. the expected rank of a is

$$\mu = \sum_{j=0}^{n} j\binom{n}{j}p^j(1-p)^{n-j} = pn$$

with variance

$$\sigma^2 = \sum_{j=0}^{n} (j-\mu)^2 \binom{n}{j}p^j(1-p)^{n-j} = p\cdot(1-p)\cdot n$$

Thus

$$P_i \leq \text{Prob}(|\text{actual rank of } a - p\cdot n| \geq (i-2)\cdot\sqrt{n})$$

$$\leq p\cdot(1-p)n/((i-2)\sqrt{n})^2$$

$$\leq p\cdot(1-p)/(i-2)^2$$

$$\leq 1/(4\cdot(i-2)^2)$$

since $p(1-p) \leq 1/4$ for $0 \leq p \leq 1$. Substituting into our expression for C yields

$$C \leq 2 + \sum_{i\geq 3} 1/(4(i-2)^2) = 2 + \pi^2/24 \approx 2.4$$

Finally, let $\overline{T}(n)$ be the average number of comparisons used in searching a random table of n keys for a. Since the subtables of size $\sqrt{n}$ are again random, we have

$$\overline{T}(n) \le C + \overline{T}(\sqrt{n}) \qquad \text{for } n \ge 3$$

and $\overline{T}(1) \le 1$, $\overline{T}(2) \le 2$ and thus

$$\overline{T}(n) \le 2 + C \cdot \log \log n \qquad \text{for } n \ge 2$$

as is easily verified by induction on n.

<u>Theorem 1:</u> The expected cost of quadratic binary search is $O(\log \log n)$.

The worst case access time of quadratic binary search is $O(\sqrt{n})$. Note that the maximal number of comparisons used is $n^{1/2} + n^{1/4} + n^{1/8} + \ldots$ $= O(\sqrt{n})$. This worst case behaviour can be reduced to $O(\log n)$ without sacrificing the $O(\log \log n)$ expected behaviour as follows. Instead of using linear search to determine the i with $S[\text{next} + (i-2) \cdot \sqrt{n}] < a$ $\le S[\text{next} + (i-1) \cdot \sqrt{n}]$ with i comparisons we use exponential + binary search (cf. III. 4.2., theorem 10) for a cost of only $O(\log i)$ comparisons. Since $\log i \le i$ the expected behaviour stays the same. However, the maximal number of comparisons is now $\log n^{1/2} + \log n^{1/4} + \log n^{1/8}$ $+ \ldots = (1/2 + 1/4 + 1/8 + \ldots) \log n = \log n$. Thus worst case behaviour is $O(\log n)$ if exponential + binary search is used.

III. 4. Weighted Trees

In this section we consider operation Access applied to weighted sets S. We associate a weight (access probability) with each element of S. Large weight indicates that the element is important and accessed frequently; it is desirable that these elements are high in the tree and can therefore be accessed fast.

<u>Definition:</u> Let $S = \{x_1 < x_2 < \ldots < x_n\}$ and let $\beta_i (\alpha_j)$ be the probability of operation Access (a, S) where $a = x_i (x_j < a < x_{j+1})$ for $1 \le i \le n (0 \le j \le n)$. Then $\beta_i \ge 0$, $\alpha_j \ge 0$ and $\Sigma\beta_i + \Sigma\alpha_j = 1$. The $(2n + 1)$-tuple $(\alpha_0, \beta_1, \alpha_1, \ldots, \beta_n, \alpha_n)$ is called access (probability) distribution.

Let T be a search tree for set S, let b_i^T be the depth of node x_i and let a_j^T be the depth of leaf (x_j, x_{j+1}). Consider a search for element a of the universe. If $a = x_i$ then we compare a with $b_i^T + 1$ elements in the tree, if $x_j < a < x_{j+1}$ then we compare a with a_j^T elements in the tree. Hence

$$P^T = \sum_{i=1}^{n} \beta_i (1 + b_i^T) + \sum_{j=0}^{n} \alpha_j a_j^T$$

is the average number of comparisons in a search. P^T is called (normalized) weighted path length of tree T. We take P^T as our basic measure for the efficiency of operation Access; the actual search time is proportional to P^T. We will mostly suppress index T if tree T can be inferred from the context. The following figure shows a search tree for set $S = \{x_1, x_2, x_3, x_4\}$ with $(\alpha_0, \beta_1, \ldots, \beta_4, \alpha_4) = (1/6, 1/24, 0, 1/8, 0, 1/8, 1/8, 0, 5/12)$

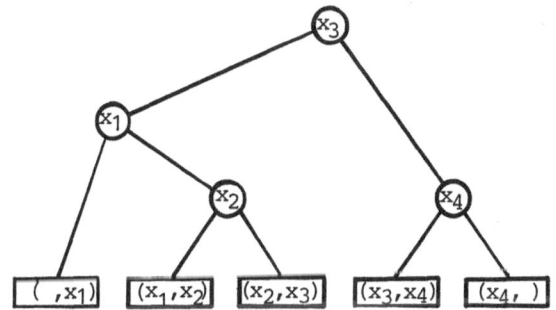

In this tree, $b_1 = 1$, $b_2 = 2$, $b_3 = 0$, $b_4 = 1$, $a_0 = a_3 = a_4 = 2$ and $a_1 = a_2 = 3$. Weighted path length P is equal to 2. There is no search tree for set S with smaller weighted path length; the tree shown above is optimal with respect to the given access distribution.

III. 4.1 Optimum Weighted Trees, Dymamic Programming and Pattern Matching

We associated with every search tree for set S a single real number, its weighted path length. We can therefore ask for the tree with the minimal weighted path length. This tree will then also optimize average access time.

Definition: Let $S = \{x_1 < x_2 < \ldots < x_n\}$ be a set and let $(\alpha_0, \beta_1, \alpha_1,$

$\ldots, \beta_n, \alpha_n)$ be an access distribution. Tree T is an optimum binary search tree for set S if its weighted path length is minimal among all search trees for set S. We use T_{opt} to denote an optimum binary search tree and P_{opt} to denote its weighted path length.

Theorem 1: An optimum binary search tree for set S and distribution $(\alpha_0, \beta_1, \ldots, \beta_n, \alpha_n)$ can be constructed in time $O(n^2)$ and space $O(n^2)$.

Proof: We use dynamic programming, i.e. we will construct in a systematic way optimal solutions for increasingly larger subproblems. In our case this means the construction of optimum search trees for all pairs, triples, ... of adjacent nodes. A search tree for set S has nodes $x_1, \ldots, x_n$ and leaves $(x_0, x_1), \ldots, (x_n, x_{n+1})$. A subtree might have nodes $x_i, \ldots, x_j$ and leaves $(x_{i-1}, x_i), \ldots, (x_j, x_{j+1})$ with $1 \le i, j \le n$, $i \le j + 1$. Such a subtree is a search tree for set $\{x_i, \ldots, x_j\}$ with respect to the universe (x_{i-1}, x_{j+1}). The access probabilities are given by the conditional probabilities

$$\bar{\beta}_k = \beta_k/w_{ij} \quad \text{and} \quad \bar{\alpha}_h = \alpha_h/w_{ij}$$

where $w_{ij} = \alpha_{i-1} + \beta_i + \ldots + \beta_j + \alpha_j$, $i \le k \le j$ and $i - 1 \le h \le j$.

We use T_{ij} to denote an optimum binary search tree for set $\{x_i, \ldots, x_j\}$ with access distribution $(\bar{\alpha}_{i-1}, \bar{\beta}_i, \ldots, \bar{\beta}_j, \bar{\alpha}_j)$. Let P_{ij} be the weighted path length of T_{ij} and let r_{ij} be the index of the root of T_{ij}, i.e. x_m with $m = r_{ij}$ is the root of T_{ij}.

Lemma 1:   a) $P_{i,i-1} = 0$

b) $w_{ij} P_{ij} = w_{ij} + \min_{i \le m \le j} (w_{i,m-1} P_{i,m-1} + w_{m+1,j} P_{m+1,j})$ for $i \le j$

Proof: a) $T_{i,i-1}$ consists of a single leaf which has depth zero. Thus $P_{i,i-1} = 0$.

b) Let T_{ij} be an optimum tree for set $\{x_i, \ldots, x_j\}$. Then T_{ij} has weighted path length P_{ij} and root x_m with $m = r_{ij}$. Let $T_\ell (T_r)$ be the left (right) subtree of T_{ij} with weighted path length $P_\ell (P_r)$. Since

$$b_k^{T_{ij}} = 1 + b_k^{T_\ell} \qquad \text{for } i \le k \le m - 1$$

$$b_m^{T_{ij}} = 0$$

$$b_k^{T_{ij}} = 1 + b_k^{T_r} \qquad \text{for } m + 1 \le k \le j$$

and analogously for the leaf weights we have $w_{ij} P_{ij} = w_{ij} + w_{i,m-1} P_\ell$ $+ w_{m+1,j} P_r$. T_ℓ is a search tree for set $x_i, \ldots, x_{m-1}$ and therefore $P_\ell \ge P_{i,m-1}$. We must have $P_\ell = P_{i,m-1}$ because otherwise we could replace T_ℓ by $T_{i,m-1}$ and obtain a tree with smaller weighted path length. This proves b).   □

Lemma 1 suggests a way for computing all values $w_{ij} P_{ij}$. Initialization is given in part a) and the iterative step is given in part b). In the complete program below we use $\bar{P}_{ij}$ to denote $w_{ij} P_{ij}$.

(1)   <u>for</u> i <u>from</u> 0 <u>to</u> n

(2)   <u>do</u> $w_{i+1,i} \leftarrow \alpha_i$; $\bar{P}_{i+1,i} \leftarrow 0$ <u>od</u>;

(3)   <u>for</u> k <u>from</u> 0 <u>to</u> n - 1

(4)   <u>do</u> <u>for</u> i <u>from</u> 1 <u>to</u> n - k

(5)   <u>do</u> j ← i + k;

(6) $w_{ij} \leftarrow w_{i,j-1} + \beta_j + \alpha_j$;

(7)   let m, $i \le m \le j$, be such that $\bar{P}_{i,m-1} + \bar{P}_{m+1,j}$ is minimal; in case of ties choose the largest such m

(8) $r_{ij} \leftarrow m$;

(9) $\bar{P}_{ij} \leftarrow w_{ij} + \bar{P}_{i,m-1} + \bar{P}_{m+1,j}$

(1o)   <u>od</u>

(11) <u>od</u>

The program above is a direct implementation of the recursion formula in lemma 1. After termination the optimum search tree is given implicitly by the array r_{ij}. Node x_m with m = $r_{1,n}$ is the root of the search tree. The root of the left subtree is x_k with k = $r_{1,m-1}$, ... It is easy to see that the search tree can be explicitly constructed in time $O(n)$ from array r_{ij}.

So let us consider the complexity of the algorithm above. The program uses three arrays $\bar{P}_{ij}$, w_{ij} and r_{ij} and hence has space complexity $O(n^2)$. We turn next to the time complexity. Note first that one execution of lines (5), (6), (8), (9) takes time $O(1)$ and one execution of line (7) takes time $O(j-i+1) = O(k+1)$ for fixed i and k. Thus the total running time is

$$\sum_{k=0}^{n-1} \sum_{i=1}^{n-k} O(k+1) = O(n^3)$$

This falls short of the $O(n^2)$ bound promised in the theorem. Before we sketch an improvement we illustrate the algorithm on the example from the beginning of III.4.. Arrays P_{ij}, w_{ij}, $1 \le i \le 5$, $0 \le j \le 4$ and r_{ij}, $1 \le i \le 4$, $1 \le j \le 4$ are given below:

$$24P = \begin{pmatrix} 0 & 5 & 11 & 24 & 48 \\ & 0 & 3 & 12 & 31 \\ & & 0 & 6 & 22 \\ & & & 0 & 13 \\ & & & & 0 \end{pmatrix} \qquad 24w = \begin{pmatrix} 4 & 5 & 8 & 14 & 24 \\ & 0 & 3 & 9 & 19 \\ & & 0 & 6 & 16 \\ & & & 3 & 13 \\ & & & & 10 \end{pmatrix}$$

$$r = \begin{pmatrix} 1 & 1 & 2 & 3 \\ & 2 & 3 & 4 \\ & & 3 & 4 \\ & & & 4 \end{pmatrix}$$

We learn one important fact from this example: Matrix r is monotone in each row and column, i.e. $r_{i,j-1} \le r_{i,j} \le r_{i+1,j}$ for all i,j. We postpone the proof of this fact for a while (cf. lemma 3 below). The monotonicity of r has an important consequence; we may change line (7), the search for r_{ij}, into

let m, $r_{i,j-1} \le m \le r_{i+1,j}$ be such ...

without affecting the correctness of the algorithm. However, the change does have a dramatic effect on the running time. It is now

$$O(\sum_{k=0}^{n-1} \sum_{i=1}^{n-k} (1+r_{i+1,i+k} - r_{i,i+k-1}))$$

$$= O(\sum_{k=0}^{n-1} (n-k + r_{n-k,n} - r_{1,k}))$$

$$= O(\sum_{k=0}^{n-1} n) = O(n^2)$$

This proves theorem 1. $\qquad\qquad\qquad\qquad\qquad\qquad\qquad\qquad\qquad\qquad\qquad$ $\square$

We still have to justify the monotonicity of r. We will do so in a more general context: Dynamic programming with quadrangle inequalities.

Let $w(i,j) \in \mathbb{R}$ for $1 \le i < j \le n$ and let $c(i,j)$ be defined by

$$c(i,i) = 0$$

$$c(i,j) = w(i,j) + \min_{i<k\le j} (c(i,k-1) + c(k,j)) \text{ for } i < j$$

Optimum binary search trees are a special case of these recursion equations: take $w(i,j) = w_{i+1,j} = \alpha_i + \beta_{i+1} + \ldots + \beta_j + \alpha_j$; then $c(i,j) = \overline{P}_{i+1,j}$.

The algorithm given in the proof of theorem 1 also allows us to compute $c(i,j)$, $1 \le i < j \le n$, in time $O(n^3)$. There is however a faster way to compute $c(i,j)$ if function $w(i,j)$ satisfies the quadrangle inequality (QI)

$$w(i,j) + w(i',j') \le w(i',j) + w(i,j') \text{ for } i \le i' < j \le j'$$

Theorem 2: If w satisfies QI and is monotone with respect to set inclusion of intervals, i.e. $w(i,j') \le w(i',j)$ if $i \le i' < j \le j'$, then function c as defined above can be computed in time $O(n^2)$

Remark: Before we give a proof of theorem 2 we apply it to optimum binary search trees. Function $w(i,j) = w_{i+1,j}$ is obviously monotone and satisfies QI, in fact with equality.

Proof of theorem 2: Theorem 2 is proven by establishing the following two lemmas.

Lemma 2: If w satisfies QI and is monotone then function c defined
above also satisfies QI, i.e. $c(i,j) + c(i',j') \leq c(i,j') + c(i',j)$
for $i \leq i' \leq j \leq j'$.
We use $c_k(i,j)$ to denote $w(i,j) + c(i,k-1) + c(k,j)$ and we define
$K(i,j) = \max \{k; c_k(i,j) = c(i,j)\}$ for $i < j$. Also $K(i,i) = i$. Then
$K(i,j)$ is the largest index where the minimum is achieved in the definition of $c(i,j)$. Then

Lemma 3: If c satisfies QI then K is monotone, i.c.

$$K(i,j) \leq K(i,j+1) \leq K(i+1,j+1) \quad \text{for } i \leq j$$

Lemma 3 is the key for improving the running time of dynamic programming to $O(n^2)$ as we have seen above. It remains to prove lemmas 2 and 3.

Proof of lemma 2: We use induction on the "length" $\ell = j'-i$ of the
quadrangle inequality for c(QIc)

$$c(i,j) + c(i',j') \leq c(i,j') + c(i',j) \text{ for } i \leq i' \leq j \leq j'$$

This inequality is trivially true if $i = i'$ or $j = j'$. This proves QIc
for $\ell \leq 1$. For the induction step we have to distinguish two cases:
$i' = j$ or $i' < j$

Case 1: $i < i' = j < j'$. In this case QIc reduces to

$$c(i,j) + c(j,j') \leq c(i,j')$$

, an (inverse) triangle inequality. Let $k = K(i,j')$. We distinguish two
symmetric subcases: $k \leq j$ or $k \geq j$.

Case 1.1: $k \leq j$. We have $c(i,j') = w(i,j') + c(i,k-1) + c(k,j')$ and
therefore

$$
\begin{aligned}
c(i,j) + c(j,j') &\leq w(i,j) \quad + c(i,k-1) + c(k,j) + c(j,j') \\
&\qquad\qquad \text{(def. of } c(i,j)) \\
&\leq w(i,j') + c(i,k-1) + c(k,j) + c(j,j') \\
&\qquad\qquad \text{(monotonicity of w)} \\
&\leq w(i,j') + c(i,k-1) + c(k,j') \\
&\qquad\qquad \text{(triangle inequality for } k \leq j \leq j')
\end{aligned}
$$

$$\leq c(i,j')$$

Case 1.2: $k \geq j$. This is symmetric to case 1.1 and left to the reader.

Case 2: $i < i' < j' < j$. Let $y = K(i',j)$ and $z = K(i,j')$. Again we have to distinguish two symmetric cases : $z \leq y$ or $z \geq y$. We only treat the case $z \leq y$. Note first that $z \leq y \leq j$ by definition of y and $i < z$ by definition of z. We have

$$c(i',j') + c(i,j) = c_y(i',j') + c_z(i,j)$$
$$= w(i',j') + c(i',y-1) + c(y,j') + w(i,j) + c(i,z-1) + c(z,j)$$
$$\leq w(i,j') + w(i',j) + c(i',y-1) + c(i,z-1) + c(z,j) + c(y,j')$$

,by QI for w

$$\leq w(i,j') + w(i',j) + c(i',y-1) + c(i,z-1) + c(y,j) + c(z,j')$$

,by the induction hypothesis, i.e. QI for c, applied to $z \leq y \leq j \leq j'$

$$= c(i,j') + c(i',j)$$

,by definition of y and z. This completes the induction step and thus proves lemma 2. □

Proof of lemma 3: Lemma 3 is trivially true when $i = j$, and so we only have to consider $i < j$. We will only prove $K(i,j) \leq K(i,j+1)$. Recall that $K(i,j)$ is the largest index where the minimum is assumed in the definition of $c(i,j)$. It therefore suffices to show

$$[c_{k'}(i,j) \leq c_k(i,j)] \Rightarrow [c_{k'}(i,j+1) \leq c_k(i,j+1)]$$

for all $i < k \leq k' \leq j$, i.e. if $K(i,j)$ prefers k' over k then so does $K(i,j+1)$. In fact, we will show the stronger inequality

$$c_k(i,j) - c_{k'}(i,j) \leq c_k(i,j+1) - c_{k'}(i,j+1)$$

or equivalently

$$c_k(i,j) + c_{k'}(i,j+1) \leq c_{k'}(i,j) + c_k(i,j+1)$$

or equivalently by expanding all four terms using their definition

$$c(k,j) + c(k',j+1) \leq c(k',j) + c(k,j+1)$$

However, this is simply the QI for c at $k \leq k' \leq j \leq j+1$. ◻◻

Dynamic programming is a very versatile problem solving method. The reader finds many applications in exercises 10 - 12 and in sections V.2. and VI.6.1.. Dynamic programming is closely related to problem solving by backtracking. We illustrate the connection with two examples: optimum binary search trees and simulating 2-way deterministic pushdown automata on random access machines.

A call OST(1,n) of the following recursive procedure computes the cost of an optimum search tree.

```
(1) real function OST(i,j : integer);
    --    OST computes the weighted path length of an optimum
    --    tree for x_i,...,x_j.
(2) if i = j + 1
(3) then OST ← 0
(4) else OST ← ∞;
(5)      for k from i to j
(6)      do OST ← min(OST, w_ij + OST(i,k-1) + OST(k+1,j))
(7)      od
(8) fi
(9) end
```

The running time of procedure OST is exponential. If $T(n)$ is the time required by OST to find the optimum cost of a tree for a set of n elements then $T(n) = O(n) + \sum_{i=0}^{n-1} (T(i) + T(n-i-1)) = O(n) + 2 \sum_{i=0}^{n-1} T(i)$. Subtracting the equations for $T(n+1)$ and $T(n)$ yields $T(n+1) - T(n) = O(1) + 2 T(n)$ and hence $T(n+1) = O(1) + 3 T(n)$. This shows that $T(n)$ grows exponentially.

Of course, the exponential running time of OST stems from the fact that subproblems OST(i,j) are solved repeatedly. It is therefore a good idea to introduce a global table P[i,j] and to record the values computed by OST in this table. This leads to

```
(1')   real function OST(i,j : integer);
(2')   if P[i,j] is defined
(3')   then OST ← P[i,j]
(4')   else if i = j + 1
(5')          then   OST ← 0
(6')          else   OST ← ∞;
(7')                 for k from i to j
(8')                 do  OST ← min(OST,w_ij + OST(i,k-1) + OST(k+1,j))
(9')                 od
(1o')         fi;
(11')         P[i,j] ← OST
(12') fi
(13') end
```

Note that lines (4') - (11') are executed at most once for every pair
(i,j), i + 1 ≤ j. Hence the total time spent in lines (4') - (11') of
OST is $O(n^3)$. Also note that the total number of calls of OST is $O(n^3)$
since lines (4') - (11') are executed at most once for every pair (i,j).
Thus the total time spent in lines (1') - (3') and (12') - (13') of OST
is also $O(n^3)$.

We can see from this example that tabulating function values in exhaustive search algorithms can have a dramatic effect on running time.
In fact, the revised program above is essentially our dynamic programming algorithm. The only additional idea required for the dynamic
programming algorithm is the observation that recursion can be replaced
by iteration.

We describe one more application of this approach. A two-way deterministic pushdown automaton consists of a finite set of states, an input
tape with a two-way reading head and a pushdown store

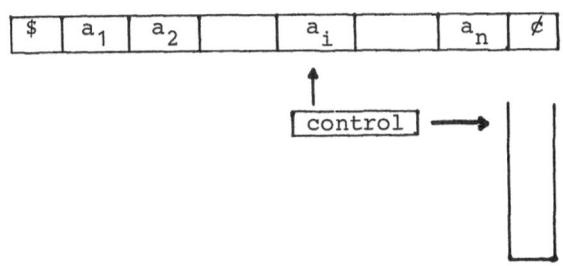

Formally, a 2DPDA is a 7-tuple (S,A,B,F,q_0,C,δ) consisting of a finite set S of states, an input alphabet A, a pushdown alphabet B, a set $F \subseteq S$ of accepting states, a start state $q_0 \in S$, initial pushdown symbol $C \in B$ and a transition function $\delta : S \times (A \cup \{\$, \rlap{/}c\}) \times B \to S \times (\{\varepsilon\} \cup B^2) \times \{-1,1\}$.

On input $a_1 a_2 \ldots a_n \in A*$ the machine is started in state q_0 with $\$ a_1 \ldots a_n \rlap{/}c$ on its input tape, its reading head on a_1 and with C in the pushdown store. The machine then operates as given by δ. More presicely, if the machine is in state $q \in S$, reads $a \in A \cup \{\$,\rlap{/}c\}$, has βD, $\beta \in B*$, $D \in B$, in its pushdown store and $\delta(q,a,D) = (q',\alpha,\Delta)$ then the new state is q', the new content of the pushdown store is $\beta\alpha$ and the input head is moved by Δ. Note that $\alpha \in \{\varepsilon\} \cup B^2$. If $\alpha = \varepsilon$ then the move is called a pop move, if $\alpha \in B^2$ then the move is called a push move. A 2DPDA is not allowed to leave the portion of the input tape delimited by $ and $\rlap{/}c$, i.e. $\delta(,\$,) = (, , + 1)$ and $\delta(,\rlap{/}c,) = (, , - 1)$. A 2DPDA halts if it empties its pushdown store. It accepts if it halts in an accepting state.

Example: We describe a 2DPDA M which does pattern matching, i.e. it accepts all strings $a_1 \ldots a_m \# b_1 \ldots b_n$, $a_i,b_j \in \{0,1\}$ such that there is a j with $a_i = b_{j+i-1}$ for $1 \le i \le m$. In other words, M decides whether pattern $a_1 \ldots a_m$ occurs in text $b_1 \ldots b_n$. Machine M operates as follows.

(1) move the head to the right endmarker $\rlap{/}c$ and then move left and store $b_n,b_{n-1},\ldots,b_1$ in the pushdown store; b_1 is at the top of the pushdown store. Position the input head on a_1.

(2) while the symbol under the input head and the top pushdown symbol agree
    do   move the input head to the right and delete one symbol from the pushdown store
    od

(3) if the symbol under the input head is #
    then empty the pushdown store and accept fi

(4) if the top symbol on the pushdown store is C (the special symbol)
    then empty the pushdown store and reject fi

(5) Move the input head to a_1. While moving left push all symbols
scanned onto the pushdown store

(6) Remove one symbol from the pushdown store and go to (2).

The correctness of this machine follows from the following observation.
Before step (2) the input head is on a_1 and the pushdown store contains
$b_j \, b_{j+1} \, \cdots \, b_n$ with b_j being at the top. If in step (2) we move the input head to a_{i+1} then $a_h = b_{j+h-1}$ for $1 \le h \le i$ and $a_{i+1} \ne b_{j+i}$. Next
observe, that $i = m$ implies that we found an occurrence of the pattern
and that $j + i = n + 1$ implies that the text is too short to contain an
occurrence of the pattern. In step (5) we push $b_{j+i-1}, \, b_{j+i-2}, \ldots, b_j$
in that order onto the pushdown store. Thus restoring the initial configuration. In (6) we remove b_j from the stack and then search for an
occurrence of the pattern starting at b_{j+1}.   □

Of course, a 2DPDA can be directly implemented on a RAM. The disadvantage of this approach is that the running time might be quite large. In
our example, the worst case running time of the 2DPDA and hence the RAM
is $O(m \cdot n)$. We can do a lot better.

Theorem 3: If a language L is accepted by a 2DPDA then there is RAM
which accepts L in linear time.

Proof: We will first define a recursive procedure which accepts L and
then improve its running time by tabulating function values.

Let $M = (S, A, B, F, q_0, C, \delta)$ be a 2DPDA and let $a_1 \, a_2 \, \cdots \, a_n \in A^*$ be an input. A triple (q, D, i) with $q \in S$, $D \in B$ and $0 \le i \le n + 1$ is called a
surface configuration of M; here i denotes the position of the input
head on the input tape. Note that the number of surface configurations
on input $a_1 \, \cdots \, a_n$ is $|S| \cdot |B| \, (n+2) = O(n)$. Define partial function
term: $S \times B \times [0 \ldots n+1] \to S \times [0 \ldots n+1]$ by $\text{term}(q, D, i) = (p, j)$ if M
started in configuration (q, D, i) will eventually empty its pushdown
store and is in state p and input position j in this case.

Next note that $\text{term}(q_0, C, 1) = (p, j)$ for some $p \in F$ iff M accepts
$a_1 \, a_2 \, \cdots \, a_n$. It thus suffices to compute term. The following (inefficient) recursive procedure TERM computes term

170

```
(1)    function TERM(q,D,i)
(2)    if δ(q,D,a_i) = (p,ε,Δ)
(3)    then TERM ← (p,i+Δ)
(4)    else let δ(q,D,a_i) = (p,GH,Δ) where G, H ∈ B;
(5)         (r,j) ← TERM(p,H,i+Δ);
(6)         TERM ← TERM(r,G,j)
(7)    fi
(8)    end
```

The correctness of this program is almost immediate. Procedure TERM certainly computes term if line (3) applies. If lines (4) - (6) apply then the computation out of configuration (q,D,i) starts with a push move. When the pushdown store has length 1 for the next time, the machine is in state r and scans position j (line 5). The content of the pushdown store is G at this point. Therefore term is correctly computed in line 6. The running time of this program is equal to the running time of the underlying 2DPDA. As in our previous example we observe that TERM may be called repeatedly for the same argument. This suggests to tabulate function values in a table which we call TE. In table TE we store terminators which were already computed and we store * in order to indicate that a call of TERM was initiated but not yet completed. Initially, all entries of TE are undefined. We obtain

```
(1')    function TERM(q,D,i)
(2')    if TE[q,D,i] = *
(3')    then halt and reject because the 2DPDA is in an infinite loop;
(4')    fi;
(5')    if TE[q,D,i] is defined
(6')    then TERM ← TE[q,D,i]
(7')    else TE[q,D,i] ← *;
(8')         if δ(q,D,a_i) = (p,ε,Δ)
(9')         then TERM ← TE[q,D,i] ← (p,i+Δ)
(10')        else let δ(q,D,a_i) = (p,GH,Δ) where G,H ∈ B;
(11')             (r,j) ← TERM(p,H,i+Δ);
(12')             TERM ← TE[q,D,i] ← TERM(r,G,j)
(13')        fi
(14')   fi
(15')   end
```

Claim: a) The total running time of call TERM(q_o,C,1) is O(n).

b) A call TERM(q_o,C,1) correctly computes term(q_o,C,1).

Proof: a) Recall that the number of surface configurations is O(n). Observe next, that lines (7') - (13') are executed at most once for each surface configuration. Hence the total time spent in lines (7') - (13') is O(n) and the total number of calls of TERM is O(n). Thus the total time spent in lines (1') - (6'), (14') - (15') of TERM is also O(n). This shows that the total running time is O(n).

b) Observe first that if term(q,D,i) returns pair (r,j) then term(q,D,i) =(r,j). It remains to consider the case that the simulation stops in line (3'). This can only be the case if there is a call TERM(q',D',i') which (indirectly) initiates call TERM(q',D',i') before its own completion. In this case we detected an infinite loop in the computation of M.   □□

Theorem 3 has a very pleasant consequence. Pattern matching can be done in linear time on a RAM. Of course, the algorithm obtained by applying theorem 3 to the 2DPDA described in the exercise above is quite involved and will be hard to understand intuitively. We therefore give an alternate simple linear time algorithm for pattern matching next.

Let a_1 ... a_n be a pattern and let b_1 b_2 ... b_m be a text, $a_i, b_j \in \{0,1\}$. We want to find all occurrences of the pattern in the text. Define f : [1...n] → [0...n], the failure function for the pattern, by

$$f(i) = \max\{h < i; a_{i-k} = a_{h-k} \text{ for } 0 \le k < h\}$$

The significance of function f is as follows. Suppose that we started to match the pattern at position j of the text and succeeded up to position i of the pattern, i. e. $a_\ell = b_{j+\ell-1}$ for $1 \le \ell \le i$ and $a_{i+1} \ne b_{j+i}$. At this point we can slide the pattern to the right and start

```
..... b_j b_{j+1}      .....        b_{j+i-1} b_{j+i}   .....

        ‖   ‖                           ‖        #
       a_1  a_2                        a_i      a_{i+1}

            a_1 ......              a_h      a_{h+1}
```

matching at some later position in text b. If we move the pattern to the right such that a_h is below b_{j+i-1} then a match can only succeed if we have $a_{i-k} = a_{h-k}$ for $0 \leq k < h$. Thus the only sensible values for h to try are $f(i)$, $f(f(i))$, ... We obtain the following algorithm. In this algorithm we assume that we added a special symbol a_{n+1} to the pattern which does not match any symbol in the text.

```
(1)    i ← 0; j ← 0;
(2)    while j ≤ m
(3)    do -- a₁...aᵢ = b_{j-i+1}...b_j and (ℓ > i implies a₁...a_ℓ ≠
                                                    b_{j-ℓ+1}...b_j)
(4)         if a_{i+1} = b_{j+1}
(5)         then i ← i + 1; j ← j + 1
(6)         else if i = n then report match starting at b_{j-n+1} fi;
(7)              if i = 0
(8)              then j + j + 1
(9)              else i ← f(i)
(1o)             fi
(11)        fi
(12) od
```

Lemma 4: The program above determines all occurences of pattern $p = a_1 \ldots a_n$ in text $b_1 \ldots b_m$ in time $O(m)$.

Proof: In order to prove correctness it suffices to verify the loop invariant. It is certainly true initially, i.e. if i = j = 0. So assume the invariant is true before executing the loop body. If $a_{i+1} = b_{j+1}$ then the invariant trivially holds after execution of the body, if $a_{i+1} \neq b_{j+1}$ and i = 0 then it also holds trivially and if i > 0 then it holds by definition of f.

The bound on the running time is shown as follows. In each iteration either line (5), line (8) or line (9) is executed. Lines (5) and (8) increase j and are therefore together executed exactly m + 1 times. In line (9) the value of i is decreased since $f(i) < i$. Since i is only increased in line (5) and $i \geq 0$ always we conclude that line (9) is executed at most m + 1 times.   □

Lemma 4 shows that pattern matching requires linear time if failure function f is available. Fortunately, f can be computed in time $O(n)$.

In fact, the same algorithm can be used because f is the result of matching the pattern against itself.

```
i ← 0; j ← 1; f(1) ← 0;
while j ≤ n
do -- a₁...aᵢ = a_{j-i+1}...aⱼ and (i < ℓ < j implies a₁...a_ℓ ≠
                                              a_{j-ℓ+1}...aⱼ)
    if a_{i+1} = a_{j+1}
    then f(j+1) ← i + 1; i ← i + 1; j ← j + 1
    else if i = 0
         then f(j+1) ← 0; j ← j + 1
         else i ← f(i)
         fi
    fi
od
```

Lemma 5: The program above computes failure function f in time O(n).

Proof: Similar to the proof of lemma 4.   □

We summarize in

Theorem 4: All occurrences of pattern $a_1...a_n$ in string $b_1...b_m$ can be found in linear time O(n + m).

Proof: Immediate from lemmas 4 and 5.   □

The dynamic programming algorithm for optimum binary search trees has quadratic space and time requirement. It can therefore only be used for small or medium size n. In the next section we will discuss algorithms which construct nearly optimal binary search trees in linear time. Note that giving up optimality is really not that bad because the access probabilities are usually only known approximatively anyhow. There is one further advantage of nearly optimal trees. We will be able to bound the cost of every single access operation and not only expected cost. Recall that average and worst case behaviour can differ by large amounts, e.g. in Quicksort; a similar situation could arise here.

We will not be able to relate weighted path length of optimum trees and nearly optimal trees directly. Rather we compare both of them to an independent yardstick, the entropy of the access distribution.

Definition: Let $(\gamma_1, \ldots, \gamma_n)$ be a discrete probability distribution, i.e. $\gamma_i \geq 0$ and $\Sigma \gamma_i = 1$. Then

$$H(\gamma_1, \ldots, \gamma_n) = - \sum_{i=1}^{n} \gamma_i \log \gamma_i$$

is called the **entropy** of the distribution. We use the convention $0 \cdot \log 0 = 0$. □

Some basic properties of the entropy function can be found in the appendix. In the sequel we consider a fixed search tree T for set $S = \{x_1, \ldots, x_n\}$ and access distribution $(\alpha_0, \beta_1, \ldots, \beta_n, \alpha_n)$. We use H to denote the entropy of the distribution, i.e. $H = H(\alpha_0, \beta_1, \ldots, \beta_n, \alpha_n)$ and we use b_i (a_j) for the depth of node x_i (leaf (x_j, x_{j+1})) for $1 \leq i \leq n (0 \leq j \leq n)$. P is the weighted path length of T. We will prove lower bounds on the search times in tree T. These lower bounds are independent of the structure of T; in particular, they are valid for the optimum tree. The proofs follow classical proofs of the noiseless coding theorem.

Lemma 6: Let $c \in \mathbb{R}$ with $0 \leq c < 1$. Let

$$\bar{\beta}_i = ((1-c)/2)^{b_i} c \qquad , 1 \leq i \leq n$$

$$\bar{\alpha}_j = ((1-c)/2)^{a_j} \qquad , 0 \leq j \leq n$$

Then $\bar{\beta}_i, \bar{\alpha}_j \geq 0$ and $\Sigma \bar{\beta}_i + \Sigma \bar{\alpha}_j = 1$, i.e. $(\bar{\alpha}_0, \bar{\beta}_1, \ldots, \bar{\beta}_n, \bar{\alpha}_n)$ is a probability distribution.

Proof: (By induction on n). If $n = 0$ then $a_0 = 0$ and hence $\bar{\alpha}_0 = 1$. So assume $n > 0$. Let x_k be the root of T, $T_\ell (T_r)$ the left (right) subtree of T. Let $b_i' (b_i'')$, $1 \leq i \leq k-1$ $(k+1 \leq i \leq n)$ be the depth of x_i in tree $T_\ell (T_r)$. Define a_j' and a_j'' analogously. Then

$$b_i = \begin{cases} b_i' + 1 & \text{for } 1 \leq i \leq k-1 \\ 0 & \text{for } i = k \\ b_i'' + 1 & \text{for } k+1 \leq i \leq n \end{cases}$$

and

$$a_j = \begin{cases} a'_j + 1 & \text{for } 0 \le j \le k-1 \\ a''_j + 1 & \text{for } k \le j \le n \end{cases}$$

Also by induction hypothesis

$$S_\ell = \sum_{i=1}^{k-1} ((1-c)/2)^{b'_i} c + \sum_{j=0}^{k-1} ((1-c)/2)^{a'_j} = 1$$

An analogous statement holds for T_r. Furthermore, $\bar{\beta}_k = c$. Thus

$$\sum_i \bar{\beta}_i + \sum_j \bar{\alpha}_j = ((1-c)/2)S_\ell + c + ((1-c)/2)S_r = 1 \qquad \square$$

__Theorem 5:__ (Lower Bound on weighted path length). Let $B = \Sigma\beta_i$. Then

a) max $\{(H-dB)/\log(2+2^{-d}); \ d \in \mathbb{R}\} \le P$

b) $H \le P + B[\log e - 1 + \log (P/B)]$

where we used the notation as defined above.

__Proof:__ a) Define $\bar{\beta}_i$ and $\bar{\alpha}_j$ as in lemma 6. Then

$$b_i + 1 = 1 + (\log \bar{\beta}_i - \log c)/\log \bar{c}$$

$$a_j = (\log \bar{\alpha}_j)/\log \bar{c}$$

where $\bar{c} = (1-c)/2$. An application of property 3) of the entropy function (cf. appendix) yields (note that $\log \bar{c} < 0$)

$$P = \Sigma\beta_i(b_i+1) + \Sigma\alpha_j a_j$$

$$= B(1 - \log c/\log \bar{c}) + (1/\log \bar{c})[\Sigma\beta_i \log \bar{\beta}_i + \Sigma\alpha_j \log \bar{\alpha}_j]$$

$$\ge B(1 - \log c/\log \bar{c}) - (1/\log \bar{c}) \cdot H$$

$$= (H - B \log(\bar{c}/c))/\log(1/\bar{c})$$

Setting $d = \log(\bar{c}/c)$ and observing that $c/\bar{c} = 2c/(1-c)$ is a surjective mapping from $0 \le c < 1$ onto the reals finishes the proof of part a).

b) Unfortunately, there is no closed form expression for the value of d which maximizes the left side of a). Numerical methods have to be used to compute d_{max} in every single application. A good approximation for d_{max} is $d = \log(P/2B)$. It yields

$$H \le P \cdot \log(2+2^{-d}) + dB$$

$$= P \log(2+2B/P) + B \log(P/2B)$$

$$\le P(1+(B/P)\log e) + B(\log P/B-1)$$

since log x ≤ (x-1) log e

$$= P + B(\log e - 1 + \log P/B) \qquad \square$$

Special case d = O is also useful in some occasions. It yields P ≥ H/log 3. We will next turn to the behavior of single access operations. Theorem 5a reads in expanded form

$$\Sigma \beta_i [(-\log \beta_i - d)/\log(2+2^{-d})] + \Sigma \alpha_j [-\log \alpha_j/\log(2+2^{-d})]$$

$$\leq \Sigma \beta_i [(b_i+1)] + \Sigma \alpha_j [a_j]$$

We show that the inequality above is almost true componentwise for the expressions in square brackets; more precisely, for h ∈ ℝ , h > O define

$$N_h = \{i; \ (-\log \beta_i - d - h)/\log(2+2^{-d}) \geq b_i + 1\}$$

and

$$L_h = \{j; \ (-\log \alpha_j - h) \ /\log(2+2^{-d}) \geq a_j\}$$

Then

$$\sum_{i \in N_h} \beta_i + \sum_{j \in L_h} \alpha_j \leq 2^{-h},$$

i.e. for a set of leaves and nodes, whose total weight exceeds $1 - 2^{-h}$, theorem 5a "almost" holds componentwise. "Almost" has to be interpreted as: up to the additive factor $-h/\log(2 + 2^{-d})$. The proof of this claim goes as follows. Let $d = \log(\bar{c}/c)$ with $\bar{c} = (1 - c)/2$ and $0 \leq c < 1$. Then $d = \log \bar{c} - \log c$ and $\log(2 + 2^{-d}) = \log(1/\bar{c})$. A simple computation shows that the definitions of N_h and L_h are equivalent to

$$N_h = \{i; \ \beta_i \leq 2^{-h} \bar{\beta}_i\} \ \text{and}$$

$$L_h = \{j; \ \alpha_j \leq 2^{-h} \bar{\alpha}_j\}$$

where $\bar{\beta}_i$ and $\bar{\alpha}_j$ are defined as in lemma 6. Thus

$$1 = \Sigma \bar{\beta}_i + \Sigma \bar{\alpha}_j$$

$$\geq \sum_{i \in N_h} \bar{\beta}_i + \sum_{j \in L_h} \bar{\alpha}_j \geq 2^h [\sum_{i \in N_h} \beta_i + \sum_{j \in L_h} \alpha_j]$$

We summarize in

Theorem 6: (Lower Bounds for single access operations). Let c,h ∈ ℝ with o ≤ c < 1 and h > O. Define $\bar{\beta}_i, \bar{\alpha}_j$ as in lemma 6 and let

$$N_h = \{i; \ \beta_i \leq 2^{-h} \bar{\beta}_i\}$$

and

$$L_h = \{j; \; \alpha_j \leq 2^{-h} \; \bar{\alpha}_j\}$$

Then

$$\sum_{i \in N_h} \beta_i + \sum_{j \in L_h} \alpha_j \leq 2^{-h} \qquad\qquad \square$$

We give an explicit example for theorems 5 and 6 at the end of section III.4.2.

III. 4.2 Nearly Optimal Binary Search Trees

In binary search (cf. III.3.1.) we always compare the argument of the access operation with the middle element of the remaining array and hence exclude at least half of the set in every step of the search. We deal now with the more general situation that elements have different weights (probabilities). We should therefore try to exclude in every step one half of the elements in probability. Let us consider the example from the beginning of III.4. and let us draw the distribution on the unit line.

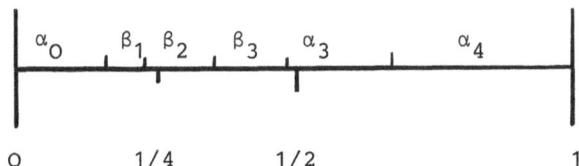

Point 1/2 lies within a β_i or an α_j. In the first case we should choose x_i as the root of the search tree, in the second case we should either choose x_j if 1/2 lies in the left half of α_j or x_{j+1} if 1/2 lies in the right half of α_j. In our example we choose x_3 as the root. This also fixes the right subtree. For the left subtree we still have the choice of choosing either x_1 or x_2 as the root.

Method 1: The restriction of our access distribution to set $\{x_1, x_2\}$ is given by (1/6 W, 1/24 W, 0, 1/8 W, 0) where $W = (1/6 + 1/24 + 1/8)^{-1}$. We proceed as described above and look for the middle of this distribution. In this way we will choose x_1 as the root of the left subtree. Method 1 is analysed in exercise 20.

<u>Method 2:</u> We proceed by strict bisection, i.e. we choose the root of
the left subtree by considering reference point 1/4. Point 1/4 is contained in β_2 and therefore x_2 is chosen as the root of the left subtree.
In this way the following tree with weighted path length P_{BB} = 5o/24 is
constructed.

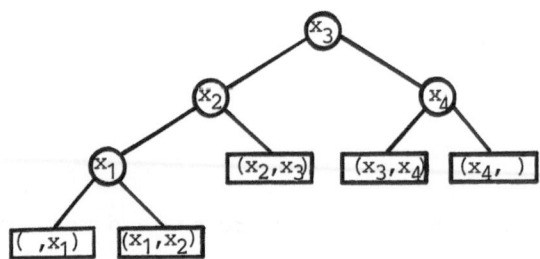

We now describe method 2 in more detail. Let

$$s_o = \alpha_o/2$$

$$s_i = s_{i-1} + \alpha_{i-1}/2 + \beta_i + \alpha_i/2 \qquad \text{for } 1 \leq i \leq n$$

Then a call construct-tree(0,n,0,1) constructs a search tree according
to method 2.

<u>procedure</u> construct-tree(i,j,cut,ℓ);

<u>comment</u> we assume that the actual parameters of any call of construct-
tree satisfy the following conditions.

(1) i and j are integers with $0 \leq i < j \leq n$,

(2) ℓ is an integer with $\ell \geq 1$,

(3) cut = $\Sigma_{p=1}^{\ell-1} x_p 2^{-p}$ with $x_p \in \{0,1\}$ for all p,

(4) cut $\leq s_i \leq s_j \leq$ cut + $2^{-\ell+1}$.

A call construct-tree (i,j, ,) will construct a binary search tree for
nodes i + 1, ... ,j and leaves i, ... ,j;

<u>begin</u>

<u>if</u> i + 1 = j (Case A)

<u>then</u> return tree

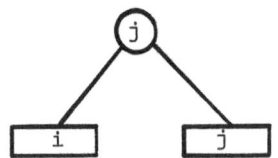

else

determine k such that

(5) $i < k \le j$

(6) $k = i + 1$ or $s_{k-1} \le cut + 2^{-\ell}$

(7) $k = j$ or $s_k \ge cut + 2^{-\ell}$

comment k exists because the actual parameters are supposed to satisfy condition (4);

if k = i + 1 (Case B)
then return   fi;

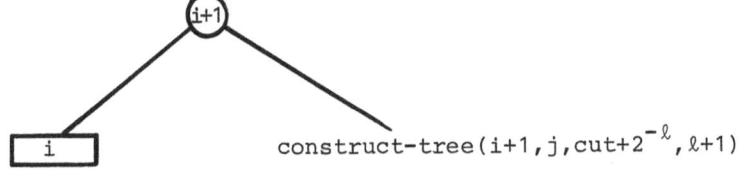

construct-tree $(i+1, j, cut+2^{-\ell}, \ell+1)$

if k = j (Case C)
then return   fi;

construct-tree $(i, j-1, cut, \ell+1)$

if i + 1 < k < j (Case D)
then return   k   fi

construct-tree $(i, k-1, cut, \ell+1)$ construct-tree $(k, j, cut+2^{-\ell}, \ell+1)$

fi

end

Theorem 7: Let b_i be the depth of node x_i and let a_j be the depth of leaf (x_j, x_{j+1}) in tree T_{BB} constructed by construct-tree$(0, n, 0, 1)$. Then

$$b_i \leq \lfloor \log 1/\beta_i \rfloor \quad , \quad a_j \leq \lfloor \log 1/\alpha_j \rfloor + 2$$

Proof: We state several simple facts.

Fact 1: If the actual parameters of a call construct-tree(i, j, cut, ℓ) satisfy conditions (1) to (4) and $i + 1 \neq j$, then a k satisfying conditions (5) to (7) exists and the actual parameters of the recursive calls of construct-tree initiated by this call again satisfy conditions (1) to (4).

Proof: Assume that the parameters satisfy conditions (1) to (4) and that $i + 1 \neq j$. In particular, $cut \leq s_j \leq cut + 2^{-\ell+1}$. Suppose, that there is no $k, i < k \leq j$, with $s_{k-1} \leq cut + 2^{-\ell}$ and $s_k \geq cut + 2^{-\ell}$. Then either for all $k, i < k \leq j, s_k < cut + 2^{-\ell}$ or for all $k, i < k \leq j$, $s_{k-1} > cut + 2^{-\ell}$. In the first case $k = j$ satisfies (6) and (7), in the second case $k = i + 1$ satisfies (6) and (7). This shows that k always exists. It remains to show that the parameters of the recursive calls satisfy again (1) and (4). This follows immediately from the fact that k satisfies (5) to (7) and that $i + 1 \neq j$ and hence $s_k \geq cut + 2^{-\ell}$ in Case B and $s_{k-1} \leq cut + 2^{-\ell}$ in Case C. □

Fact 2: The actual parameters of every call of construct-tree satisfy conditions (1) to (4) (if the arguments of the top-level call do).

Proof: The proof is by induction, Fact 1 and the observation that the actual parameters of the top-level call construct-tree $(0, n, 0, 1)$ satisfy (1) to (4). □

We say that node h (leaf h resp.) is constructed by the call construct-tree(i, j, cut, ℓ) if $h = j (h = i$ or $h = j)$ and Case A is taken or if $h = i + 1 (h = i)$ and Case B is taken or if $h = j (h = j)$ and Case C is taken or if $h = k$ and Case D is taken. Let b_i be the depth of node i and let a_j be the depth of leaf j in the tree returned by the call construct-tree $(0, n, 0, 1)$.

Fact 3: If node h (leaf h) is constructed by the call construct-tree (i,j,cut,ℓ), then $b_h + 1 = \ell (a_h = \ell)$.

Proof: The proof is by induction on ℓ. ☐

Fact 4: If node h (leaf h) is constructed by the call construct-tree (i,j,cut,ℓ), then $\beta_h \leq 2^{-\ell+1}$ $(\alpha_h \leq 2^{-\ell+2})$.

Proof: The actual parameters of the call satisfy condition (4) by fact 2. Thus

$$2^{-\ell+1} \geq s_j - s_i = (\alpha_i + \alpha_j)/2 + \beta_{i+1} + \alpha_{i+1} + \dots + \beta_j$$

$$\geq \beta_h (\text{resp. } \alpha_h/2).$$ ☐

We infer from facts 3 and 4, $\beta_h \leq 2^{-b_h}$ and $\alpha_h \leq 2^{-a_h+2}$. Taking logarithms and observing that b_h and a_h are integers proves the theorem. ☐

Theorems 6 and 7 together give fairly detailed information about the tree constructed by procedure construct-tree. In particular, we have

$$b_i \approx \log 1/\beta_i \qquad a_j \approx \log 1/\alpha_j$$

for most nodes and leaves of tree T_{BB}. Substituting the bounds on b_i and a_j given in theorem 7 into the definition of weighted path length we obtain

Theorem 8: Let P_{BB} be the weighted path length of the tree constructed by construct-tree. Then

$$P_{BB} \leq \Sigma \beta_i \lfloor \log 1/\beta_i \rfloor + \Sigma \alpha_j \lfloor \log 1/\alpha_j \rfloor + 1 + \Sigma \alpha_j$$

$$\leq H(\alpha_0, \beta_1, \dots, \beta_n, \alpha_n) + 1 + \Sigma \alpha_j$$ ☐

and further

Theorem 9: Let P_{BB} be the weighted path length of the tree constructed by construct-tree for distribution $(\alpha_0, \beta_1, \dots, \beta_n, \alpha_n)$ and let P_{opt} be the weighted path length of an optimum tree. Then $(B = \Sigma \beta_i)$

a) $\max \left\{ \dfrac{H-dB}{\log(2+2^{-d})} \; ; \; d \in \mathbb{R} \right\} \leq P_{opt} \leq P_{BB} \leq H + 1 + \Sigma \alpha_j$

b) $P_{BB} \leq P_{opt} + B(\log e + \log(P_{opt}/B)) + 2 \cdot \Sigma \alpha_j$

<u>Proof:</u> a) follows immediately from theorem 5a and 8 and b) follows immediately from theorem 5b and 8.   □

Theorem 9 can be interpreted in two ways. On the one hand it shows that the weighted path length P_{BB} of tree T_{BB} is always very close to the optimum and hence T_{BB} is a good search tree. Essentially, part b) shows

$$P_{BB} - P_{opt} \leq \log P_{opt} \approx \log H$$

On the other hand, it provides us with a small interval containing P_{opt} as well as P_{BB}. This interval is easily computable from the distribution and affords us with a simple a-priori estimate of the behaviour of search trees. This estimate can be used in the decision whether to use weighted trees or not. The bounds given in theorems 5 - 9 are sharp (cf. exercises 18,19).

Let us illustrate our bounds by an example. There is extensive litera-ture about word frequencies in natural languages. In English, the prob-ability of occurrence of the i-th most frequent word (cf. E.S. Schwartz, JACM 1o (1963), 413 - 439) is approximately

$$\beta_i = c/i^{1.12} \quad \text{where} \quad c = 1/\underset{i \geq 1}{\Sigma} (1/i)^{1.12}$$

A simple calculation yields

$$H(\beta_1, \beta_2, \beta_3, \ldots) = -\Sigma \beta_i \log \beta_i \approx 1o.2$$

In the light of theorem 9 we would therefore expect that the weighted path length of an optimum binary search tree for <u>all</u> English words is about 1o.2 and certainly no larger than 11.2. This was also observed in experiments. Gotlieb/Walker took a text of $1o^6$ words and counted word frequencies. Then they constructed (nearly) optimal binary search trees for the N most common words, N = 1o, 1oo, 1 ooo, 1o ooo, 1oo ooo. Let P_N be the weighted path length of the tree constructed for the N most common words. Then $P_N \rightarrow 11$ for $N \rightarrow \infty$ as the figure (due to Gotlieb/ Walker) below suggests. This is in good agreement with theorem 9.

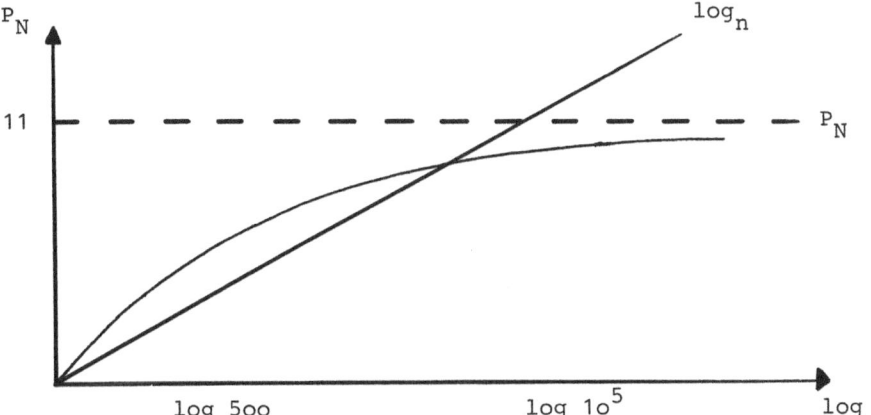

We will now turn to the time complexity of recursive procedure con- struct-tree. Let T(n) be the maximal running time required by construct-tree for a tree with n nodes, i. e. n = j - i. If n = 1, then the body of construct-tree requires constant time. Hence

$$T(1) = c_1$$

for some constant c_1. If n > 1 then k has to be determined and some recursive calls have to be initiated. Let $T_S(n,m)$ be the time required to find k, where m = k - i. We determine $T_S(n,m)$ below when we specify a concrete algorithm for finding k. Construct-tree is called once or twice recursively within the body. In Case D the first call constructs a tree with k - 1 - i = m - 1 nodes and the second call constructs a tree with j - k = n - m nodes. Hence

$$T(n) \leq \max_m [T(m-1) + T(n-m) + T_S(n,m) + c_2]$$

Constant c_2 measures the cost of parameter passing, ... If we define T(0) = 0 then the inequality above also holds true in cases B and C of construct-tree where only one recursive call is started. With the con- vention $T_S(1,m) = 0$ and $c = \max(c_1,c_2)$ we can further simplify our in- equality and obtain

$$T(0) = 0$$

$$T(n) \leq \max_{1 \leq m \leq n} [T(m-1) + T(n-m) + T_s(n,m) + c]$$

We discuss two methods for finding k.

<u>Binary Search</u>: We first try $r = \lfloor (i + 1 + j)/2 \rfloor$. If $s_r \geq cut + 2^{-\ell}$ then $k \leq r$, otherwise $k \geq r$. We iterate as described in III.3.1. and find k in log n steps. Thus $T_s(n,m) \leq d \cdot \log n$ for some constant d, and we obtain

$$T(0) = 0$$

$$T(n) \leq \max_{1 \leq m \leq n} [T(m-1) + T(n-m) + c + d \log n]$$

We infer $T(n) = O(n \log n)$, cf. section II.3.. Conversely,

$$T(n) \geq T(n-1) + d \cdot \log n + c \geq d \cdot \sum_{i=1}^{n} \log i = \Omega(n \log n)$$

<u>Theorem 10</u>: If the search for k in procedure construct-tree is implemented by binary search, then $T(n) = \Theta(n \log n)$.

<u>Exponential and Binary Search</u>: The running time of procedure construct-tree with binary search is $\Omega(n \log n)$ since we use up $\log(j-i)$ time units even if $k \approx i + 1$ or $k \approx j$, i.e. even if the size of the problem to be solved is reduced only by a small amount. If we want to improve upon the $O(n \log n)$ time bound we have to use a search algorithm which finds k fast if k is close to the extremes. A first attempt is to use linear search and to start the search simultaneously at both ends. However, this is not good enough. If $k = (i + 1 + j)/2$ then this method will use $\Theta(j-i)$ steps to find k and again we obtain an $O(n \log n)$ algorithm (exercise 21). So, how can we do better? We should start searching from the end but not in unit steps:

(1) Compare s_r with $cut + 2^{-\ell}$ for $r = \lfloor (i + 1 + j)/2 \rfloor$. If $s_r \geq cut + 2^{-\ell}$ then $k \in \{i + 1, \ldots, r\}$, if $s_r \leq cut + 2^{-\ell}$ then $k \in \{r, \ldots, j\}$. We assume for the sequel that $k \in \{i + 1, \ldots, r\}$. Step 1 has constant cost, say d_1.

(2) Find the smallest t, $t = 0, 1, 2, \ldots$, such that $s_{i+2^t} \geq cut + 2^{-\ell}$.

Let t_0 be that value of t. We can find t_0 in time $d_2(t_0 + 1)$ for some constant d_2. Then $i + 2^{t_0-1} < k \leq i + 2^{t_0}$, i.e. $2^{t_0} \geq k - i = m > 2^{t_0-1}$ and hence $\log m > t_0 - 1$. Thus the cost of step 2 is bounded by $d_2(2 + \log m)$.

(3) Determine the exact value of k by binary search on the interval $i + 2^{t_0-1} + 1, \ldots, i + 2^{t_0}$. This takes $d_3(\log(2^{t_0} - 2^{t_0-1}) + 1)$ $= d_3 t_0 < d_3(1 + \log m)$ time units for some constant d_3.

Exponential (step 2) and binary search (step 3) allows us to find k in $\leq d(1 + \log m)$ time units provided that $i < k \leq \lfloor (i + 1 + j)/2 \rfloor$. Here $m = k - i$ and d is a constant. Similarly, k can be found in $\leq d(1 + \log(n - m + 1))$ time units if $\lfloor (i + 1 + j)/2 \rfloor < k$. Thus $T_s(n,m) = d(1 + \log \min(m, n - m + 1))$ and we obtain the following recurrence relations for the worst case running time of construct-tree.

$$T(0) = 0$$

$$T(n) = \max_{1 \leq m \leq n} \ [T(m-1) + T(n-m) + d(\ 1 + \log \min(m, n-m+1)) + c]$$

Theorem 11: If the search for k in procedure construct-tree is implemented by exponential and binary search, then $T(n) = O(n)$.

Proof: We show by induction on n:

$$T(n) \leq (2d + c)n - d \log(n + 1)$$

This is certainly true for $n = 0$. For $n > 0$ we have

$$T(n) \leq \max_{1 \leq m \leq n} \ [T(m-1) + T(n-m) + d(\log \min(m, n-m+1)) + d + c]$$

$$= \max_{1 \leq m \leq (n+1)/2} \ [T(m-1) + T(n-m) + d \log m + d + c]$$

by the symmetry of the expression in square brackets in $m - 1$ and $n - m$. Next we apply the induction hypothesis and obtain

$$\leq \max_{1\leq m\leq (n+1)/2} [(2d+c)(m-1+n-m)-d(\log m + \log(n-m+1)) + d \log m + (d+c)]$$

$$= (2d+c)n + \max_{1\leq m\leq (n+1)/2} [-d(1 + \log(n-m+1))]$$

The expression in square brackets is always negative and is maximal for $m = (n + 1)/2$. Thus

$$T(n) \leq (2d + c)n - d(1 + \log(n + 1)/2)$$

$$= (2d + c)n - d \log(n + 1) \qquad \qquad \square$$

Let us summarize. Construct-tree constructs trees which are nearly optimal with res pect to average (theorem 9) as well as with respect to single search times (theorems 6 and 7). Construct-tree can be made to run in linear time (theorem 11). We conclude this section by exemplifying theorems 8 to 9 on the example from the beginning of section III.4. We start with theorem 9, which concerns average search times. We have $H \approx 2.27$, $\Sigma \beta_i \lfloor \log 1/\beta_i \rfloor + \Sigma \alpha_j \lfloor \log 1/\alpha_j \rfloor \approx 2.04$, $\Sigma \beta_i \approx 0.29$, $\Sigma \alpha_j \approx 0.71$. $d = 1.05$ maximizes the left hand side of 9a and yields $1.50 \leq P_{opt} \leq 2.0 \leq 2.04 = P_{BB} \leq 3.75$. Of course, the additive constants play an almost dominating role in our bounds for that small value of H. We have seen in the application to an English dictionary that the estimates are much better for large values of H.

We will now turn to theorems 6 and 7 about the behaviour of single searches:

name of node or leaf	depth in T_{opt}	depth in T_{BB}	probability	$-\log p_\perp$	$\bar{\beta}_i, \bar{\alpha}_j$ for $c = 1/2$
x_1	1	2	1/24	4	1/32
x_2	2	1	1/8	3	1/8
x_3	0	0	1/8	3	1/2
x_4	1	1	0	∞	1/8
$(\ ,x_2)$	2	3	1/6	2	1/64
(x_1,x_2)	3	3	0	∞	1/64

(x_2,x_3)	3	2	o	∞	1/16
(x_3,x_4)	2	2	1/8	3	1/16
$(x_4,)$	2	2	5/12	1	1/16

We can see from this table that the upper bounds given by theorem 7
exceed the actual values by 1 or 2. If we apply theorem 6 with c = 1/2
and h = 2 then N_2 = {3,4} and L_2 = {1,2} and

$$\sum_{i \in N_2} \beta_i + \sum_{j \in L_2} \alpha_j = 1/8 \leq 1/4 = 2^{-h}$$

Hence nodes and leaves with total probability $\geq$ 7/8 satisfy
theorem 5a componentwise (cf. the discussion preceding theorem 6).

III. 5. Balanced Trees:

We return to the discussion started in III.3.1.: Realizing operations
Access, Insert and Delete by binary trees. We saw in section III.3.1.
that the height of the tree plays a crucial role.

We consider only unweighted sets in this section, i.e. we are only in-
terested in the size of the sets involved. In other words, if T is a
search tree for set S = $\{x_1 < x_2 < \ldots < x_n\}$ then we assume uniform access
probabilities, i.e. $\beta_i = 1/n$ and $\alpha_j = 0$. As above, we use b_i to denote
the depth of node x_i in T.

$$P = \sum_i (1/n)(b_i + 1)$$

is called the average (internal) path length of T. Theorems 5b and 6 of
the previous section give log n = H $\leq$ P + log P + o.44 and
height(T) $\geq$ log n - 1. The second inequality is obtained by taking the
limit h $\rightarrow$ 0 in theorem 6. Somewhat better bounds can be obtained by
direct computation.

Theorem 1: Let T be a binary search tree for set S = $\{x_1,\ldots,x_n\}$. Then

a) $P \geq \lfloor \log(n+1) \rfloor - 1$

b) $height(T) \geq \lceil \log(n+1) \rceil$

Proof: Since T is a binary tree, there are at most 2^i nodes of depth i
(i $\geq$ 0), and hence at most $\sum_{i=0}^{k} 2^i = 2^{k+1}-1$ nodes of depth $\leq$ k. Thus in a
tree with n nodes there must be at least one node of depth k where
$2^{k+1} - 1 \geq n$. This proves b) since height(T) = max {depth(v) + 1;
v node of T}.

Apparently, a tree T with n nodes has minimal average path length, if
there is 1 node of depth 0, 2 nodes of depth 1,...,2^k nodes of depth k,
and $n - 2^{k+1} + 1$ nodes of depth k + 1. Here k = $\lfloor \log(n+1) \rfloor - 1$. Thus

$$P \geq 1/n(\sum_{i=0}^{k} (i+1)2^i + (k+2)(n-2^{k+1} + 1))$$

$$= 1/n[k \cdot 2^{k+1} + 1 + (k+2)(n-2^{k+1} + 1)]$$

$$\geq \lfloor \log(n+1) \rfloor - 1 \qquad\qquad \Box$$

Theorem 1 shows that logarithmic behaviour is the best we can expect
from binary search trees in the worst case as well as in the average
case. Also, logarithmic behaviour is easy to obtain as long as we restrict ourselves to access operations. This is even true in the case
of weighted sets as we saw in III.4. Insertions and deletions create
new problems; the naive insertion and deletion algorithms of III.3.1
can create extremely unbalanced trees and thus lead to intolerable
search times. Inserting $x_1,...,x_n$ with $x_1 < x_2 <...< x_n$ into an initially empty tree creates a tree with average path length (n+1)/2. Thus
tree search deteriorates to linear search. Extreme deterioration is not

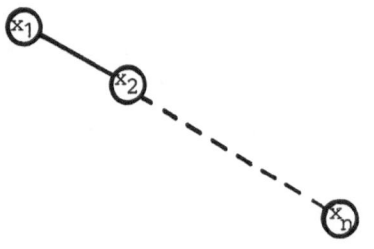

very probable in the case of random
insertions (exercise 9). Deterioration
can be avoided completely if the
tree is rebalanced after every insertion or deletion. We will see
later that rebalancing can be restricted to local changes of the
tree structure along the path from
the root to the inserted or deleted node. In this way, rebalancing time
is at most proportional to search time and hence total cost is still
logarithmic.

All known classes of balanced trees can be divided into two groups:
weight-balanced and height-balanced trees. In weight-balanced trees one
balances the number of nodes in the subtrees, in height-balanced trees
one balances the height of the subtrees. We will discuss one representa-
tive of each group in the text and mention some more in the exercises.

III. 5.1 Weight-Balanced Trees

For this section α is a fixed real, $1/4 < \alpha \le 1 - \sqrt{2}/2$. The bounds on α
will become clear lateron.

Definition: a) Let T be a binary tree with left subtree T_ℓ and right
subtree T_r. Then

$$\rho(T) = |T_\ell|/|T| = 1 - |T_r|/|T|$$

is called the root balance of T. Here $|T|$ denotes the number of leaves
of tree T.

b) Tree T is of bounded balance α, if for every subtree T' of T:

$$\alpha \le \rho(T') \le 1 - \alpha$$

c) BB[α] is the set of all trees of bounded balance α.

In the following tree (leaves are not shown)

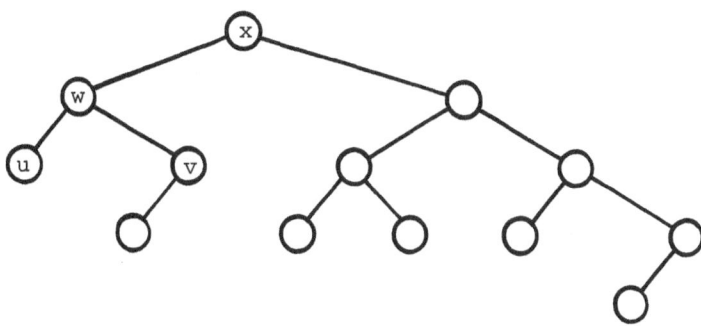

the subtrees with root u (v,w,x) have root balance 1/2 (2/3,2/5,5/14).
The tree is in BB[α] for $\alpha \le 1/3$.

Trees of bounded balance have logarithmic depth and logarithmic average path length.

Theorem 2: Let $T \in BB[\alpha]$ be a tree with n nodes. Then

a) $P \le (1 + 1/n)\log(n + 1)/H(\alpha, 1 - \alpha) - 1$

where $H(\alpha, 1 - \alpha) = -\alpha \log \alpha - (1 - \alpha)\log(1 - \alpha)$

b) $\text{height}(T) \le 1 + (\log(n + 1) - 1)/\log(1/(1 - \alpha))$

Proof: a) For this proof it is easier to work with $\overline{P} = n \cdot P = \Sigma (b_i + 1)$. We show $\overline{P} \le (n + 1)\log(n + 1)/H(\alpha, 1 - \alpha) - n$ by induction on n. $\overline{P}$ is often called total (internal) path length of T. For $n = 1$ we have $\overline{P} = 1$. Since $0 \le H(\alpha, 1 - \alpha) \le 1$ this proves the claim for $n = 1$. So let us assume $n > 1$. T has a left (right) subtree with $\ell(r)$ nodes and path length $\overline{P}_\ell$ ($\overline{P}_r$). Then $n = \ell + r + 1$ and $\overline{P} = \overline{P}_\ell + \overline{P}_r + n$ (cf. the proof of lemma 1 in III.4.1.) and $\alpha \le (\ell + 1)/(n + 1) \le 1 - \alpha$. Applying the induction hypothesis yields

$$\overline{P} = n + \overline{P}_\ell + \overline{P}_r$$

$$\le \frac{1}{H(\alpha, 1-\alpha)}[(\ell+1) \log (\ell+1) + (r+1) \log (r+1)] + 1$$

$$= \frac{n+1}{H(\alpha, 1-\alpha)}[\log (n+1) + \frac{\ell+1}{n+1} \log \frac{\ell+1}{n+1} + \frac{r+1}{n+1} \log \frac{r+1}{n+1}] + 1$$

$$= \frac{(n+1) \log (n+1)}{H(\alpha, 1-\alpha)} + 1 - (n+1) \cdot \frac{H(\frac{\ell+1}{n+1}, \frac{r+1}{n+1})}{H(\alpha, 1-\alpha)}$$

$$\le \frac{1}{H(\alpha, 1-\alpha)} (n+1) \cdot \log (n+1) - n,$$

since $H(x, 1 - x)$ is monotonically increasing in x for $0 \le x \le 1/2$

b) Let $T \in BB[\alpha]$ be a tree with n nodes, let $k = \text{height}(T)$, and let $v_0, v_1, \ldots, v_{k-1}$ be a path from the root to a node v_{k-1} of depth k-1. Let w_i be the number of leaves in the subtree with root v_i, $0 \le i \le k - 1$. Then

$$2 \le w_{k-1} \quad \text{and}$$

$$w_{i+1} \leq (1-\alpha)w_i \quad \text{for } 0 \leq i < k-1$$

since T is of bounded balance α, and therefore

$$2 \leq w_{k-1} \leq (1-\alpha)^{k-1} w_0 = (1-\alpha)^{k-1}(1+n)$$

Taking logarithms finishes the proof. □

For $\alpha \approx 1 - \sqrt{2}/2 \approx 0.2928$ theorem 2 reads

$$P \leq 1.15(1+1/n) \log (n+1) - 1 \qquad \text{and}$$

$$\text{height}(T) \leq 2 \log (n+1) - 1$$

A comparison with theorem 1 shows that the average search time in trees in BB[$1-\sqrt{2}/2$] is at most 15 % and that the maximal search time is at most by a factor of 2 above the optimum.

Operations Access, Insert and Delete are performed as described in III.3.1. However, insertions and deletions can move the root balance of some nodes on the path of search outside the permissible range [$\alpha,1-\alpha$]. There are two transformations for remeding such a situation: rotation and double rotation. In the following figures nodes are drawn as circles and subtrees are drawn as triangles. The root-balances are given beside each node. The figures show transformations "to the left". The symmetrical variants also exist.

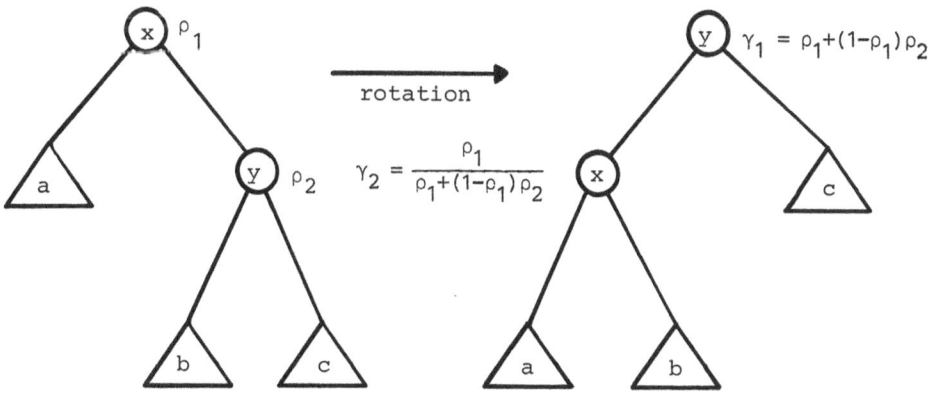

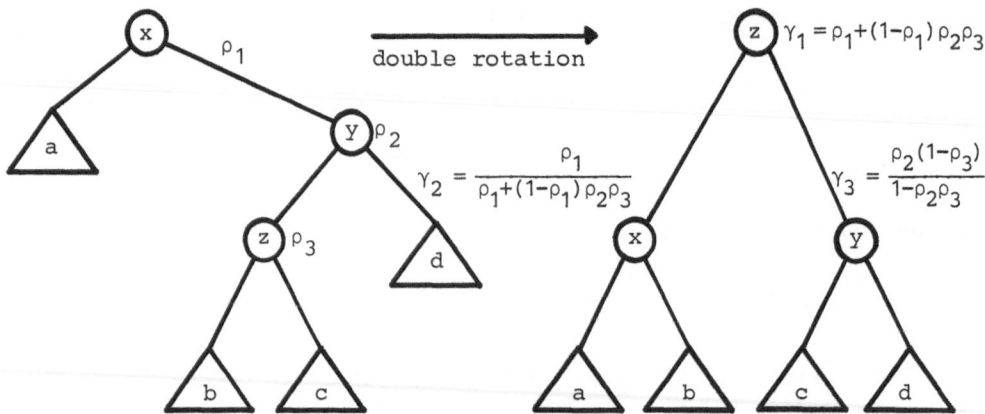

The root balances of the transformed trees can be computed from the old balances ρ_1, ρ_2 (and ρ_3) as given in the figure. We verify this claim for the rotation and leave the double rotation to the reader. Let a,b,c be the number of leaves in the subtrees shown. Then

$$\rho_1 = a/(a+b+c) \text{ and } \rho_2 = b/(b+c)$$

Since

$$a + b = \rho_1 (a+b+c) + \rho_2 (b+c)$$

$$= \rho_1 (a+b+c) + \rho_2((a+b+c) - a))$$

$$= (\rho_1 + \rho_2 (1-\rho_1))(a+b+c)$$

the root-balance of node x after the rotation is given by

$$a/(a+b) = \rho_1/(\rho_1 + \rho_2 (1-\rho_1))$$

and the root-balance of node y is given by

$$(a+b)/(a+b+c) = (\rho_1 + \rho_2 (1-\rho_1)).$$

Let us consider operation Insert first. Suppose that node a is added to the tree. Let $v_0, v_1, \ldots, v_k = a$ be the path from the root to node a. Operation Insert(a) described in III.3.1 creates the following subtree 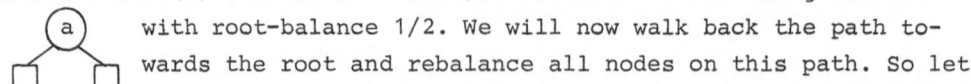 with root-balance 1/2. We will now walk back the path towards the root and rebalance all nodes on this path. So let us assume that we reached node v_i and that the root balances of all proper descendants of v_i are in the range $[\alpha, 1-\alpha]$. Then $0 \le i \le k-1$. If the root-balance of node v_i is still in the range $[\alpha, 1-\alpha]$ then we can move on to node v_{i-1}. If it is outside the range $[\alpha, 1-\alpha]$ we have to rebalance as described in the following lemma.

Lemma 1: For all $\alpha \in (1/4, 1-\sqrt{2}/2]$ there are constants $d \in [\alpha, 1-\alpha]$ and $\delta \ge 0$ (if $\alpha < 1-\sqrt{2}/2$ then $\delta > 0$) such that for T a binary tree with subtrees T_ℓ and T_r and

(1) T_ℓ and T_r are in BB$[\alpha]$
(2) $|T_\ell|/|T| < \alpha$ and either
    (2.1) $|T_\ell|/(|T|-1) \ge \alpha$ (i.e. an insertion into the right subtree of T occured) or
    (2.2) $(|T_\ell|+1)/(|T|+1) \ge \alpha$ (i.e. a deletion from the left subtree occured).
(3) ρ_2 is the root balance of T_r

we have
(i) if $\rho_2 \le d$ then a rotation rebalances the tree, more precisely γ_1, $\gamma_2 \in [(1+\delta)\alpha, 1 - (1+\delta)\alpha]$ where γ_1, γ_2 are as shown in the figure describing rotation.

(ii) if $\rho_2 > d$ then a double rotation rebalances the tree, more precisely $\gamma_1, \gamma_2, \gamma_3 \in [(1+\delta)\alpha, 1-(1+\delta)\alpha]$ where $\gamma_1, \gamma_2, \gamma_3$ are as shown in the figure describing double rotation.

Proof: A complete proof is very tedious and unelegant. It can be found in Blum/Mehlhorn. In that paper one can also find expressions for δ and d as a function of α. In order to give the reader an impression of the proof, we verify some parts of the claim for $\alpha = 3/11$, $d = 6/10$ and $\delta = 0.05$. Let us consider case (i), i.e. $\rho_2 \le 6/10$ and a rotation is applied. We will only verify $\gamma_1 \in [(1+\delta)\alpha, 1 - (1+\delta)\alpha]$ and leave the remaining cases to the reader. Note first that $\gamma_1 = \rho_1 + (1-\rho_1)\rho_2$ is an increasing function of ρ_1 and ρ_2. Hence

$$\gamma_1 \le \alpha + (1-\alpha) \cdot d \qquad \text{since } \rho_1 \le \alpha, \ \rho_2 \le d$$

$$= 78/110 = 1 - (1+1/15)\,3/11 \le 1 - 1.05\,\alpha$$

It remains to prove a lower bound on γ_1. From $|T_\ell|/(|T|-1) \ge \alpha$ or $(|T_\ell|+1)/(|T|+1) \ge \alpha$ and $|T_\ell| \ge 1$ one concludes $\rho_1 = |T_\ell|/|T| \ge \alpha/(2-\alpha)$ and hence

$$\gamma_1 \geq \alpha/(2-\alpha) + (1 - \alpha/(2-\alpha)) \cdot \alpha$$

$$= 81/208 \geq 1.05 \ \alpha \qquad \qquad \square$$

Lemma 1 implies that a BB[α]-tree can be rebalanced after an insertion by means of rotations and double rotations. The transformations are restricted to the nodes on the path from the root to the inserted element. Thus height(T) = O(log $|S|$) transformations suffice; each transformation has a cost of O(1).

We still have to clarify two small points: how to find the path from the inserted element back to the root and how to determine whether a node is out of balance. The path back to the root is easy to find. Note that we traversed that very path when we searched for the leaf where the new element had to be inserted. We only have to store the nodes of this path in a stack; unstacking will lead us back to the root. This solves the first problem. In order to solve the second problem we store in each node v of the tree not only its content, the pointers to the left and right son, but also its size, i.e. the number of leaves in the subtree with root v. So the format of a node is

CONTENT	LSON	RSON	SIZE

The root balance of a node is then easily computed. Also the SIZE field is easily updated when we walk back the path of search to the root.

We summarize: An operation Insert(a,S) takes time O(log $|S|$). This is also true for operation Delete(a,S). Delete(a,S) removes one node and one leaf from the tree as described in III. 3.1. (The node removed is not necessarily the node with content a). Let $v_0, \ldots, v_k$ be the path from the root v_0 to the father v_k of the removed node. We walk back to the root along this path and rebalance the tree as described above.

Theorem 3: Let $\alpha \in (1/4, 1-\sqrt{2}/2]$. Then operations Access(a,S), Insert(a,S), Delete(a,S), Min(S), Deletemin(S) and Ord(k,S) take time O(log $|S|$) in BB[α]-trees. Also operation Sequ(S) takes time O($|S|$).

Proof: The discussion preceding the theorem treats operations Access,

Insert and Delete. The minimum of S can be found by always following
left pointers starting at the root; once found the minimum can also be
deleted in time $O(\log |S|)$. Operation $Ord(k,S)$ is realized as described
in III. 3.1 and $Sequ(S)$ as in I.5.   □

We argued that at most height(T) transformations are required to rebalance a tree in BB[α] after an insertion or deletion. It is easy to find
examples where one actually has to use that many transformations. Take
a tree where all nodes have balance α and perform one insertion (at the
proper place). Then all nodes on the path of search will move out of
the range [α,1-α] and have to be rebalanced. Note however, that this
will move the root balances of all nodes involved in the rebalancing
operations into the interval [(1+δ)α, 1 - (1+δ)α] where δ > 0 if
$\alpha \in (1/4, 1-\sqrt{2}/2)$. Therefore these nodes will not go out of balance for
the near future. This observation leads to

Theorem 4: Let $\alpha \in (1/4, 1-\sqrt{2}/2)$. Then there is a constant c such that
the total number of rotations and double rotations required to process
an arbitrary sequence of m insertions and deletions into the initially
empty BB[α]-tree is ≤ cm.

Proof: Let T_0 be the BB[α]-tree which consists of a single leaf and no
node. The sequence of m insertions and deletions gives rise to a sequence
of trees $T_1,\ldots,T_m$, where T_{j+1} comes from T_j by an insertion or deletion
and subsequent rebalancing. We need some more notation.

A transaction is either an insertion or deletion. A transaction goes
through a node v if v is on the path from the root to the node to be
inserted or deleted. A node v takes part in a single rotation (double
rotation) if it is one of the two (three) nodes explicitly shown in
the figure defining the transformation. Furthermore, nodes retain their
identity as shown in that figure, i.e. if a rotation to the left is
applied to a subtree with root x, then node x has subtrees with weights a
and b respectively after the rotation. Note also that nodes are created
by insertions and then have balance 1/2 and nodes are destroyed by deletions. Finally, a node v causes a single rotation (double rotation)
if v is node x in the figure defining the transformations, i.e. v is a
node which went out of balance.

With every node v we associate accounts: The transaction accounts $TA_i(v)$

and the balancing operation accounts $BO_i(v)$, $0 \leq i < \infty$. All accounts have initial value zero.

The j-th transaction, $1 \leq j \leq m$, has the following effect on the accounts of node v:

a) If the transaction does not go through v then all accounts of v remain unchanged.

b) If the transaction does go through v then let w be the number of leaves in the subtree of T_{j-1} with root v. Let i be such that $(1/(1-\alpha))^i \leq w < (1/(1-\alpha))^{i+1}$. Note that $w \geq 2$ and hence $i \geq 1$. We add one to transaction accounts $TA_{i-1}(v)$, $TA_i(v)$, $TA_{i+1}(v)$. If v causes a rebalancing operation then we also add one to $BO_i(v)$.

Lemma 2: For every node v and every i : $BO_i(v) \leq \dfrac{(1-\alpha)^i}{\delta\alpha} TA_i(v)$ where δ is as in lemma 1.

Proof: We show how to count $\alpha\delta/(1-\alpha)^i$ increments of $TA_i(v)$ for every increment of $BO_i(v)$. Suppose $BO_i(v)$ is increased at the j-th transaction, i.e. the j-th transaction goes through v and moves v out of bounds. Let w be the number of leaves in the subtree of T_{j-1} with root v. Then $1/(1-\alpha)^i \leq w < 1/(1-\alpha)^{i+1}$.

Let $k < j$ be such that: v took part in a rebalancing operation at the k-th transaction or the k-th transaction created v and v did not take part in a rebalancing operation after the k-th and before the j-th transaction. In either case we have $\rho(v) = t'/w' \in [(1+\delta)\alpha, 1 - (1+\delta)\alpha]$ in T_k. Here t' (w') is the number of leaves in the left subtree of v (in the tree with root v) in T_k. Since v causes a rebalancing operation at the j-th transaction we have $\rho(v) = t/w \notin [\alpha, 1-\alpha]$, say $\rho(v) < \alpha$ after the j-th transaction but before rebalancing v. We use t to denote the number of leaves in the left subtree of v in that tree.

Node v did not take part in rebalancing operations between the k-th and the j-th transaction. But its balance changed from t'/w' to t/w and hence many transactions went through v. Suppose that a insertions and b deletions went through v. Then $w = w' + a - b$ and $t \geq t' - b$.

Claim: $a + b \geq \delta\alpha w$

Proof: Assume otherwise, i.e. $a + b < \delta\alpha w$. Then

$$(1+\delta)\alpha \leq t'/w' \leq (t+b)/(w-a+b) \leq \frac{t+b}{w-\delta\alpha w+2b} \leq (t+\delta\alpha w)/(w+\delta\alpha w)$$

$\leq (\alpha w+\delta\alpha w)/(w+\delta\alpha w) < (1+\delta)\alpha$, a contradiction. Note that $\square$

$(t+b)/(w-\delta\alpha w+2b)$ is increasing in b.

We have thus shown that at least $\delta\alpha w \geq \delta\alpha/(1-\alpha)^i$ transactions went through v between the k-th and the j-th transaction. During the last $\delta\alpha w$ of these transactions the weight (number of leaves in the subtree with root v) of v was at least $w - \delta\alpha w \geq 1/(1-\alpha)^{i-1}$ and at most $w + \delta\alpha w < 1/(1-\alpha)^{i+1}$. Hence all these transactions were counted on $TA_i(v)$. $\square$

Lemma 3: For all i : $\sum_v TA_i(v) \leq 3m$

Proof: Let $v_0, \ldots, v_k$ be the rebalancing path for the j-th transaction and let w_ℓ be the weight of node v_ℓ, i.e. the number of leaves in the tree with root v_ℓ. Then $w_{\ell+1} \leq (1-\alpha)w_\ell$ for $\ell \geq 0$. Thus there are at most three nodes on the path with $1/(1-\alpha)^{i-1} \leq w_\ell < 1/(1-\alpha)^{i+1}$. Hence at most three is added to $\sum_v TA_i(v)$ for every transaction. $\square$

It is now easy to complete the proof. $\sum_i \sum_v BO_i(v)$ is the total number of single and double rotations required to process the sequence of m transactions. We estimate this sum in two parts: $i < k$ and $i \geq k$ where k is some integer.

$$\sum_{i \geq k} \sum_v BO_i(v) \leq \sum_{i \geq k} \sum_v ((1-\alpha)^i/\delta\alpha)\, TA_i(v), \text{ by lemma 2}$$

$$\leq \sum_{i \geq k} ((1-\alpha)^i/\delta\alpha)\, 3m \qquad \text{, by lemma 3}$$

$$\leq (1-\alpha)^k\, 3m/\delta\alpha^2$$

and

$$\sum_{i < k} \sum_v BO_i(v) < (k-1)m$$

198

since there is at most one node v for each transaction such that $BO_i(v)$ is increased by that transaction for any fixed i. Hence the total number of single and double rotations is bounded by $[(k-1)+3(1-\alpha)^k/\delta\alpha^2]m$ for any integer k. □

It is worthwhile to compute constant c of theorem 4 for a concrete example. For $\alpha = 3/11$ we have $\delta = 0.05$ (cf. proof of lemma 1). Choosing k = 17 yields c = 19.59. Experiments with random insertions suggest that this is far too crude an estimate; the true value of c is probably close to one. Nevertheless, theorem 4 establishes the fact that the total number of rebalancing operations is linear in the number of insertions and deletions. Furthermore, the proof of theorem 4 also shows that $\sum_v BO_i(v) = O(m (1-\alpha)^i)$; thus rebalancing operations are very rare high up in the tree.

We can use this fact as follows. In chapters VII and VIII we will frequently augment BB[α]-trees by additional information. In these augmented trees the cost of a rotation or double rotation will not be O(1); rather the cost of a rebalancing operation caused by node v will depend on the current "thickness" of node v, i.e. if node v causes a rebalancing operation and the subtree with root v has w leaves then the cost of the rebalancing operation is f(w) time units for some non-decreasing function f. In many applications we will have f(x) = x or f(x) = xlog x.

Theorem 5: Let $\alpha \in (1/4, 1 - \sqrt{2}/2)$ and let f : $\mathbb{R} \to \mathbb{R}$ be a non-decreasing function. Suppose that the cost of performing a rotation or double rotation at node v of a BB[α]-tree is f(th(v)) where th(v) is the number of leaves in the subtree with root v. Then the total cost of the rebalancing operations required for a sequence of m insertions and deletions into an initially empty BB[α]-tree is
$$O(m \cdot \sum_{i=1}^{c\log m} f((1-\alpha)^{-i-1})(1-\alpha)^i) \text{ where } c = 1/\log(1-\alpha)).$$

Proof: If a node v with $(1-\alpha)^{-i} < th(v) \leq (1-\alpha)^{-i-1}$ causes a rebalancing operation then the cost of this operation is at most $f((1-\alpha)^{-i-1})$ time units since f is non-decreasing. Every such rebalancing operation is recorded in account $BO_i(v)$. Hence the total cost of all rebalancing operations is

$$\sum_{v} \sum_{i} BO_i(v) \ f((1-\alpha)^{-i-1})$$

$$\leq \sum_{v} \sum_{i} ((1-\alpha)^i/\delta\alpha) \ TA_i(v) \ f((1-\alpha)^{-i-1}) \text{ by lemma 2}$$

$$\leq (3m/\delta\alpha) \sum_{i=1}^{clog \ m} (1-\alpha)^i \ f((1-\alpha)^{-i-1}) \quad , \text{ by lemma 3}$$

and the observation that $TA_i(v) = 0$ for $i >$ clog m by lemma 1b.   □

Theorem 5 has some interesting consequences. If $f(x) = x^a$ with $a < 1$ then the total rebalancing cost is O(m) and if $f(x) = x(\log x)^a$ for some $a \geq 0$ then the total rebalancing cost is $O(m(\log m)^{a+1})$. Thus even if $f(x)$ is fairly large the amortized rebalancing cost (i.e. rebalancing cost per insertion/deletion) is small. We will use this fact extensively in chapters VII and VIII.

III. 5.2 Height-Balanced Trees

Height-balanced trees are the second basic type of balanced tree. They come in many different kinds: AVL-trees, (2,3)-trees, B-trees, HB-trees, ... and (a,b)-trees which we describe here.

Definition: Let a and b be integers with $a \geq 2$ and $2a-1 \leq b$. A tree T is an (a,b)-tree if

a)   all leaves of T have the same depth
b)   all nodes v of T satisfy $\rho(v) \leq b$
c)   all nodes v except the root satisfy $\rho(v) \geq a$
d)   the root r of T satisfies $\rho(r) \geq 2$.

Here $\rho(v)$ denotes the number of sons of node v.   □

(a,b)-trees are known as B-trees if $b = 2a-1$. In our examples we always use $a = 2$ and $b = 4$. We have to address the following questions: how to store a set in an (a,b)-tree, how to store an (a,b)-tree in a computer, how to search in, insert into and delete from an (a,b)-tree.

Sets are stored in (a,b)-trees in leaf-oriented fashion. This is not

compulsory, but more convenient than node-oriented storage which we
used so far. Let $S = \{x_1 < \ldots < x_n\}$ be a subset of ordered universe U and
let T be an (a,b)-tree with n leaves. We store S in T as follows.

1) The elements of S are assigned to the leaves of T in increasing order from left to right.

2) To every node v of T we assign $\rho(v)-1$ elements $k_1(v), \ldots, k_{\rho(v)-1}(v)$
of U such that for all i $(1 \le i \le \rho(v))$: $k_i(v) < k_{i+1}(v)$ and for all
leaves w in the i-th subtree of v we have $k_{i-1}(v) < CONTENT[w] \le k_i(v)$.

The following figure shows a (2,4)-tree for set $S = \{1,3,7,8,9,10\} \subseteq \mathbb{N}$

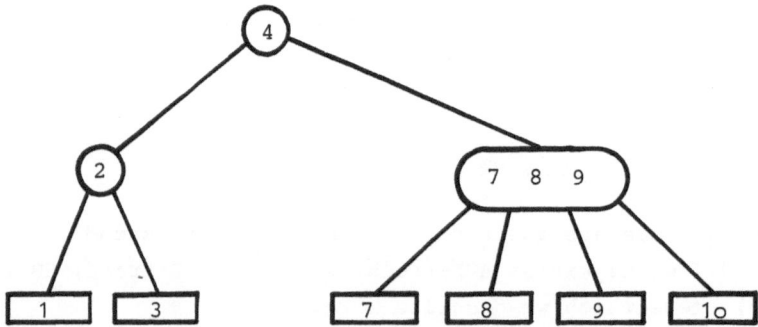

The most simple method for storing an (a,b)-tree in a computer is to
reserve 2b-1 storage locations for each node of the tree, b to contain
the pointers to the sons and b-1 to contain the keys stored in the node.
In general, some of these storage locations are unused, namely, whenever a node has less than b sons. If a node has arity $\rho(v)$ then a fraction $(2\rho(v)-1)/(2b-1)$ of the storage locations will be used. Since
$\rho(v) \ge a$ for all nodes (except the root) at least the fraction
$(2a-1)/(2b-1)$ of the storage locations is used. In (2,4)-trees this
might be as low as 3/7. We will see in section III. 5.3.4 that storage
efficiency is much larger on the average. An alternative implementation
is based on red-black trees and is given at the end of the section.

Searching for an element x in an (a,b)-tree with root r is quite simple.
We search down the tree starting at the root until we reach a leaf. In
each node v, we use the sequence $k_1(v), \ldots, k_{\rho(v)-1}(v)$ in order to guide
the search to the proper subtree. In the following program we assume
that $k_0(v) < x < k_{\rho(v)}(v)$ for every element $x \in U$ and every node v of T.

```
    v ← root of T;
    while v is not a leaf
    do find i, 1 ≤ i ≤ ρ(v)-1,
        such that k_{i-1}(v) < x ≤ k_i(x);
        v ← i-th son of v;
    od;
    if x = CONTENT[v]
    then success else failure fi;
```

The cost of a search in tree T is apparently proportional to
$O(b \cdot height(T))$; there are height(T) iterations of the while-loop and in
each iteration $O(b)$ steps are required to find the proper subtree. Since
b is a constant we have $O(b \cdot height(T)) = O(height(T))$ and again the
height of the tree T plays a crucial role.

Lemma 4: Let T be an (a,b)-tree with n leaves and height h. Then

a) $2 \cdot a^{h-1} \leq n \leq b^h$
b) $\log n / \log b \leq h \leq 1 + \log(n/2)/\log a$

Proof: Since each node has at most b sons there are at most b^h leaves.
Since the root has at least two sons and every other node has at least
a sons there are at least $2 \cdot a^{h-1}$ leaves. This proves a). Part b) follows
from part a) by taking logarithms.   □

We infer from lemma 4 and the discussion preceding it that operation
Access(x,S) takes time $O(\log |S|)$. We will now turn to operation
Insert(x,S).

A search for element x in tree T ends in some leaf w. Let v be the
father of w. If x = CONTENT[w] then we are done. If x ≠ CONTENT[w] then
we proceed as follows:

1) We expand v by giving it an additional son to the right of w (we also
say: we split w), store x and CONTENT[w] in w and the new leaf in appropriate order and store min(x, CONTENT[w]) in v at the appropriate position, i.e. between the pointers to w and the new leaf.

Example: Insertion of 6 into the tree of the previous example yields

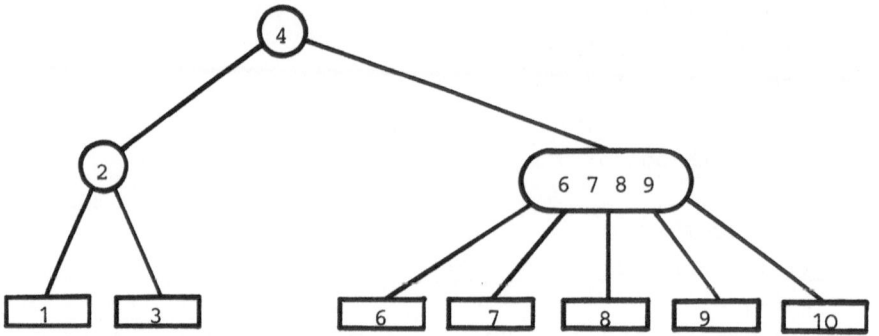

2) Adding a new leaf increases the arity of v by 1. If $\rho(v) \leq b$ after adding the new leaf then we are done. Otherwise we have to split v. Since splitting can propagate we formulate it as a loop.

<u>while</u> $\rho(v) = b+1$
<u>do</u> <u>if</u> v's father exists
  <u>then</u> let y be the father of v
  <u>else</u> let y be a new node and make v the only son of y
  <u>fi</u>;
  let v' be a new node;
  expand y, i.e. make v' an additional son of y immediately to the right of v;
  split v, i.e. take the rightmost $\lceil (b+1)/2 \rceil$ sons and keys $k_{\lfloor (b+1)/2 \rfloor +1}(v),\ldots,k_b(v)$ away from v and incorporate them into v' and move key $k_{\lfloor (b+1)/2 \rfloor}(v)$ from v to y (between the pointers to v and v');
  $v \leftarrow y$
<u>od</u>

<u>Example continued</u>: Splitting v yields

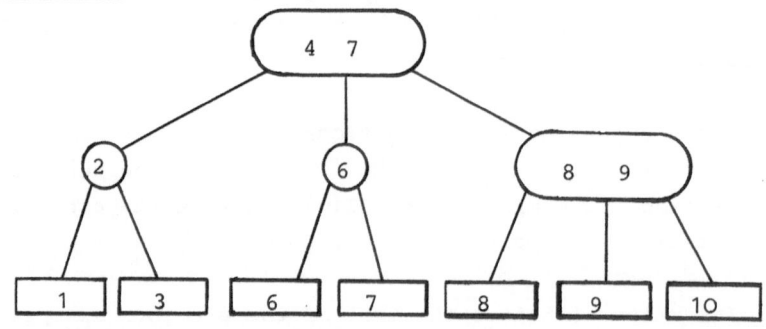

<u>Lemma 5:</u> Let b ≥ 2a-1 and a ≥ 2. Inserting an element x into an (a,b)-tree for set S takes time O(log |S|).

<u>Proof:</u> The search for x takes time O(log |S|). Also we store the path of search in a pushdown store during the search. After adding a new leaf to hold x we walk back to the root using the pushdown store and apply some number of splitting operations. If a node v is split it has b+1 sons. It is split into nodes v and v' with $\lfloor (b+1)/2 \rfloor$ and $\lceil (b+1)/2 \rceil$ sons respectively. Since b ≥ 2a-1 we have $\lfloor (b+1)/2 \rfloor$ ≥ a and since b ≥ 3 we have $\lceil (b+1)/2 \rceil$ ≤ b and thus v and v' satisfy the arity constraint after the split. A split takes time O(b) = O(1) and splits are restricted to (a final segment) of the path of search. This proves lemma 5.   □

Deletions are processed very similarly. Again we search for x, the element to be deleted. The search ends in leaf w with father v.

1) If x ≠ CONTENT[w] then we are done. Otherwise, we shrink v by deleting leaf w and one of the keys in v adjacent to the pointer to w (to be specific, if w is the i-th son of v then we delete $k_i(v)$ if i < ρ(v) and $k_{i-1}(v)$ if i = ρ(v)).

Example continued: Deleting 6 yields

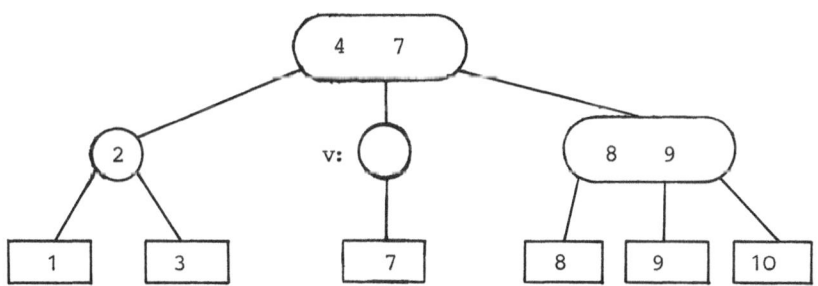

2) Shrinking v decreases ρ(v) by 1. If ρ(v) is still ≥ a then rebalancing is completed. Otherwise v needs to be rebalanced by either fusing or sharing. Let y be any brother of v.

<u>while</u> ρ(v) = a-1 and ρ(y) = a
<u>do</u> let z be the father of v;
    fuse v and y, i.e. make all sons of y to sons of v and move all keys from y to v and delete node y; also move one key (the key

between the pointers to y and v) from z to v; (note that this will
shrink z, i.e. decrease the arity of z by one)
<u>if</u> z is root of T
<u>then</u> <u>if</u> ρ(z) = 1 <u>then</u> delete z <u>fi</u>;
    <u>goto</u> completed
<u>fi</u>;
v ← z;
let y be a brother of v
<u>od</u>;
<u>comment</u> we have either ρ(v) ≥ a and rebalancing is completed or
ρ(v) = a-1 and ρ(y) > a and rebalancing is completed by sharing;
<u>if</u> ρ(v) = a-1
<u>then</u>
    <u>comment</u> we assume that y is the right brother of v;
    take the leftmost son away from y and make it an additional (right-
    most) son of v; also move one key (the key between the pointers to v
    and y) from z down to v and replace it by the leftmost key of y;
<u>fi</u>;
completed:

<u>Example continued:</u> The tree of the previous example can be either re-
balanced by sharing or fusing depending on the choice of y. If y is the
left brother of v then fusing yields

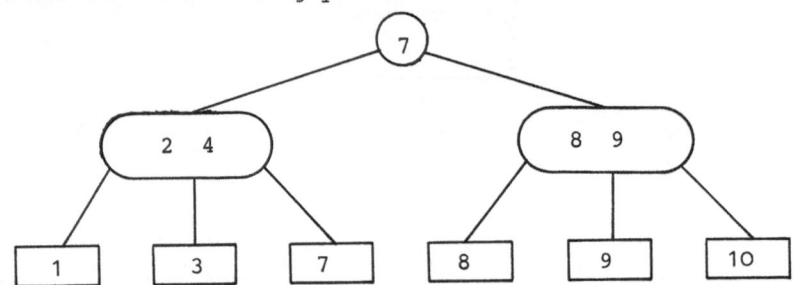

If y is the right brother of v then sharing yields

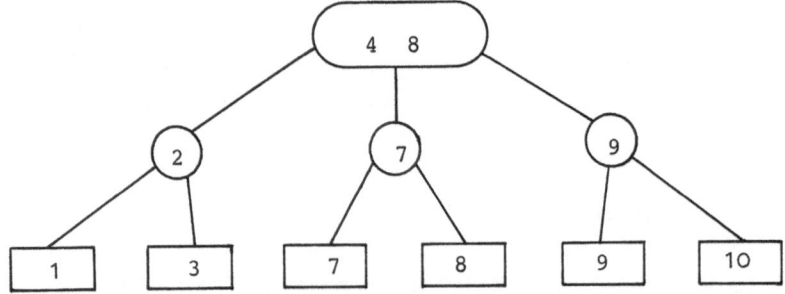

Lemma 6: Let b ≥ 2a-1 and a ≥ 2. Deleting an element from an (a,b)-
tree for set S takes time O(log |S|).

Proof: The search for x takes time O(log |S|). An (a,b)-tree is rebal-
anced after the removal of a leaf by a sequence of fusings followed by
at most one sharing. Each fusing or sharing takes time O(b) = O(1) and
fusings and sharings are restricted to the path of search. Finally note
that a fusing combines a node with a-1 sons with a node with a sons and
yields a node with 2a-1 ≤ b sons.   □

We summarize lemmas 4, 5 and 6 in

Theorem 5: Let b ≥ 2a-1, a ≥ 2. If set S is represented by an (a,b)-
tree then operations Access(x,S), Insert(x,S), Delete(x,S), Min(S),
Deletemin(S) take time O(log |S|).

Proof: For operations Access, Insert and Delete this is immediate from
lemma 4, 5 and 6. For Min and Deletemin one argues as in theorem 3. □

(a,b)-trees provide us with many different balanced tree schemes. For
any choice of a ≥ 2 and b ≥ 2a-1 we get a different class. We will
argue in III.5.3.1 that b ≥ 2a is better than b = 2a-1 (= the smallest
permissible value for b) on the basis that amortized rebalancing cost
is much smaller for b ≥ 2a. So let us assume for the moment that b = 2a.
What is a good value for a? We will see that the choice of a depends
heavily on the intended usage of the tree. Is the tree kept in main
memory, or is the tree stored on secondary memory? In the later case we
assume that it costs $c_1 + c_2 m$ time units to transport a segment of m
contiguous storage locations from secondary to main storage. Here c_1
and c_2 are device dependent constants. We saw in lemma 4 that the
height of an (a,2a)-tree with n leaves is about log n/log a. Let us
take a closer look at the search algorithm in (a,b)-tree. The loop body
which is executed log n/log a times consists of two statements: in the
first statement the proper subtree is determined for a cost of $c_1 + c_2 a$,
in the second statement attention is shifted to the son of the current
node for a cost of $c_1 + c_2 a$. Here $c_2 = 0$ if the tree is in main memory
and $c_1 + c_2 a$ is the cost of moving a node from secondary to main memory
otherwise. Thus total search time is

$$((c_1 + c_2 a) + c_1 + c_2 a) \log n/\log a$$

which is minimal for a such that

$$a \cdot \ln(a-1) = (c_1+C_1)/(c_2+C_2)$$

If the tree is kept in main memory then typical values for the constants are $c_1 \approx c_2 \approx C_1$ and $C_2 = 0$ and we get a = 2 or a = 3. If the tree is kept in secondary storage, say on a disk, then typical values of the constants are $c_1 \approx c_2 \approx C_2$ and $C_1 \approx 1000\, c_1$. Note that C_1 is the latency time and C_2 is the time to move one storage location. In this case we obtain a ≈ 100. From this coarse discussion one sees that in practice one will either use trees with small arity or trees with fairly large arity.

We close this section with the detailed description of an implementation of (2,4)-trees by <u>red-black trees</u>. A tree is colored (with colors red and black) if its edges are colored red and black. If v is a node we use bd(v) to denote the number of black edges on the path from the root to v; bd(v) is the <u>black depth</u> of node v. A <u>red-black tree</u> is a binary, colored tree satisfying the following three structural constraints:

    1) all leaves have the same black depth,
    2) all leaves are attached by black edges,
    3) no path from the root to a leaf contains two consecutive red edges.

In the following diagrams we draw red edges as wiggled lines and black edges as straight lines.

There is a close relationship between (2,4)-trees and red-black trees. Let T be a (2,4)-tree. If we replace nodes with three (four) sons by

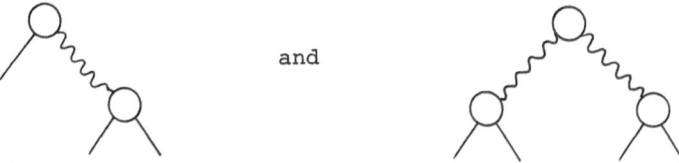

                      and

respectively, then we obtain a red-black tree. In the example from the beginning of the section we obtain:

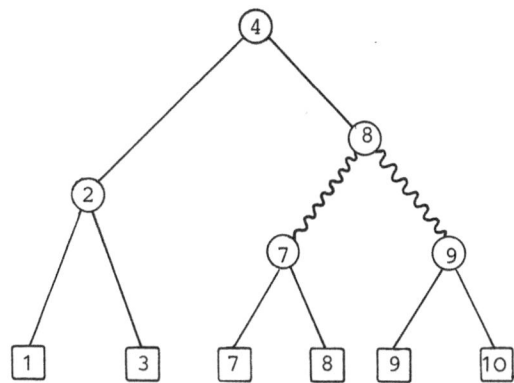

Conversely, if T is a red-black tree and we collapse nodes connected by
red edges then a (2,4)-tree is obtained. Red-black trees allow for a
very efficient and elegant implementation. Each node and leaf is stored
as a record of type node where

    type node = record content : U ;
                        color : (red,black) ;
                        son[0..1] :   ↑node
         end

The field content stores an element of the underlying universe, the
field color contains the color of the incoming edge (the color of the
edge into the root is black by default), and fields son[0] and son[1]
contain the pointers to the left and right son respectively. All son-
pointers of leaves are nil.
In the following programs variables root,p,q,r are of type ↑node, but
we talk simply about nodes instead of pointers to nodes. A node is
called red (black) if its incoming edge is red (black). The program for
operation Access is particularly simple. For later use we store the
path of search in a pushdown store, more precisely we store pairs (z,d)
where z is a pointer to a node and d ∈ {0,1} is the direction out of
node z taken in the search. The following program searches for x ∈ U.

```
(1)     p ← root;
(2)     while  p↑.son[0] ≠ nil                -- a test, whether p is a leaf
(3)     do if  x ≤ p↑.content
(4)        then push (p,0);
(5)             p ← p↑.son[0]
(6)        else push (p,1);
(7)             p ← p↑.son[1]
(8)        fi
(9)     od;
(10)    if p↑.content = x
(11)    then "successful"
(12)    else "unsuccessful"
(13)    fi
```

We will next turn to operation Insert. Suppose that we want to insert
x and also suppose that we executed the program above. It terminates in
line (12) with p pointing to a leaf and with the path of search stacked
in a pushdown store. The leaf p is not stacked. We initialize the
insertion algorithm by replacing leaf p by a red node r with sons p
and a new leaf containing x. This is done in lines

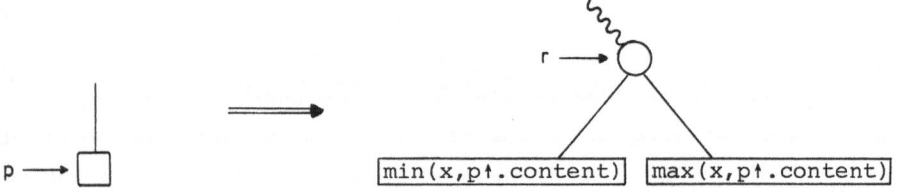

(1) to (15) below. We also redirect the pointer from p's father to the
new node r. If p's father is black this completes the insertion.

```
(1)     new(q);
(2)     q↑.color ← black; q↑.son[0]← q↑.son[1] ← nil;
(3)     q↑.content ← x;
(4)     new(r);
(5)     r↑.content ← min(x,p↑.content);
(6)     r↑.color ← red;
(7)     if  x < p↑.content
(8)     then r↑.son[0] ← q; r↑.son[1] ← p
(9)     else r↑.son[1] ← q; r↑.son 0  ← p
(10)    fi;
```

```
(11)   (q,dir2) ← pop stack;
(12)   q↑.son[dir2] ← r;
(13)   if   q↑.color = black
(14)   then - - "the insertion is completed"
(15)   fi;
```

If node q (as tested in line (13)) is red then we created two
consecutive red edges and therefore destroyed the third structural
constraint. The following program restores the red-black
properties.

```
(16)   (p,dir1) ← pop stack
```

At this point we are in the following situation. Node p is black
(because its son q is red), node q is red and has exactly one red
son, namely r (otherwise, two consecutive red edges would have
existed before the insertion). We will maintain this property as
an invariant of the following loop. In this loop we distinguish
two cases. If both sons of node p are red then we perform a color
flip on the edges incident to p and propagate the "imbalance"
closer to the root. A color flip corresponds to a split in (2,4)-
trees. If p has only one red son then we rebalance the tree by
either a rotation (dir1 = dir2) or a double rotation (dir1 ≠ dir2).
Both subcases correspond to expanding node p in the related (2,4)-
tree and hence terminate the insertion.

```
(17)   while   true
(18)   do   if   p↑.son[1-dir1]↑.color = red
(19)        then   --   p has two red sons and we perform a
                   --   color flip
```

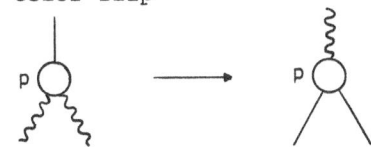

```
(20)            p↑.son[0].color ← p↑.son[1].color ← black;
(21)            p↑.color ← red;
(22)            if   p = root
(23)            then   p↑.color ← black;
(24)                   terminate the insertion algorithm;
```

```
(25)            fi;
(26)            r ← p;
(27)            (q,dir2) ← pop stack;
(28)            if  q↑.color = black
(29)            then  terminate the insertion algorithm
(30)            fi;
(31)            (p,dir1) ← pop stack
(32)     else  if  dir1 = dir2
(33)            then  -- we rebalance the tree by a rotation
```

```
(34)            p↑.son[dir1] ← q↑.son[1-dir1];
(35)            q↑.son[1-dir1] ← p;
(36)            p↑.color ← red; q↑.color ← black;
(37)            if  p = root
(38)            then  root ← q
(39)            else  (r,dir2) ← pop stack;
(40)                   r↑.son[dir2] ← q
(41)            fi
(42)            terminate the insertion algorithm
(43)     else  -- we rebalance the tree by a double rotation
```

```
(44)            p↑.son[dir1] ← r↑.son[dir2];
(45)            q↑.son[dir2] ← r↑.son[dir1];
(46)            r↑.son[dir1] ← q;
(47)            r↑.son[dir2] ← p;
(48)            p↑.color ← red; r↑.color ← black;
(49)            if  p = root
```

```
(50)                  then  root ← r
(51)                  else  (p,dir2) ← pop stack;
(52)                        p↑.son[dir2] ←  r
(53)                  fi;
(54)                        terminate the insertion algorithm
(55)            fi
(56)       fi
(57)  od
```

There are several remarks appropriate at this point. We mentioned already that color flips in red-black trees correspond to splits in (2,4)-tree. What do rotations and double rotations correspond to? They have no equivalent in (2,4)-trees but correspond to the fact that the subtrees shown below are not "legal" realizations of nodes with four

sons. If we would replace the third structural constraint by "red components (=sets of nodes connected by red edges) consist of at most three nodes" then the subtree above were legal and the rotations and double rotations were not required. However, the code which realizes a split would become more cumbersome.

Deletions from red-black trees can be handled by a similar but slightly longer program. The program is longer because more cases have to be distinguished. We leave the details to the reader. There is one important remark to make however. The algorithms for red-black trees as described above simulate (2,4)-trees in the following sense. Let T be a (2,4)-tree and let T' be the red-black tree which corresponds to T as described above. Suppose now that we perform an insertion into (deletion from) T and the same operation on T'. Let T_1 and T_1' be the resulting (2,4)-tree and red-black tree respectively.
Then T_1' corresponds to T_1 in the sense described above. Also, the number of color-flips required to process the the operation on T' is the same as the number of splits required to process the operation on T. We will use this observation frequently in the sequel without explicitly

mentioning it. More precisely, we will derive bounds on the amortized rebalancing cost in (2,4)-trees in the next section. These bounds hold also true for red-black trees (if the programs above are used to re-balance them).

Red-black trees can also be used to implement (a,b)-trees in general. We only have to replace the third structural constraint by: "red components have at least a-1 and at most b-1 nodes" (cf. exercise 27).

Finally, we should mention that there are alternative methods for rebalancing (a,b)-trees, b ≥ 2a, and red-black trees after insertions and deletions. A very useful alternative is top-down rebalancing. Suppose that we want to process an insertion. As usual, we follow a path down the tree. However, we also maintain the invariant now that the current node is not a b-node (a node with b sons). If the current node is a b-node then we immediately split it. Since the father is not a b-node (by the invariant) the splitting does not propagate towards the root. In particular, when the search reaches the leaf level the new leaf can be added without any problem. The reader should observe that b ≥ 2a is required for this strategy to work because we split b-nodes instead of (b+1)-nodes now. The reader should also note that the results presented in section III.5.3.2 below are not true for the top-down rebalancing strategy. However, similar results can be shown provided that b ≥ 2a + 2 (cf. exercises 29 and 32).
Top-down rebalancing of (a,b)-trees is particularly useful in a parallel environment. Suppose that we have several processors working on the same tree. Parallel searches cause no problems but parallel insertions and deletions do. The reason is that while some process modifies a node, e.g. in a split, no other process can use that node. In other words, locking protocols have to be used in order to achieve mutual exclusion. These locking protocols are fairly simple to design if searches and rebalancing operations proceed in the same direction (deadlock in a one-way street is easy to avoid), i.e. if top-down rebalancing is used. The protocols are harder to design and usually have to lock more nodes if searches and rebalancing operations proceed in opposite directions (deadlock in a two-way street is harder to avoid), i.e. if bottom-up rebalancing is used. We return to the discussion of parallel operations on (a,b)-trees at the end of section 5.3.2. In section 5.3.2. we prove a result on the distribution of rebalancing operations on the levels

of the tree. In particular, we will show that rebalancing operations close to the root where locking is particularly harmful are very rare.

III. 5.3 Advanced Topics on (a,b)-Trees

(a,b)-trees are a very versatile data structure as we will see now. We first describe two additional operations on (a,b)-trees, namely Split and Concatenate, and then apply them to priority queues. In the second section we study the amortized rebalancing cost of (a,b)-trees under sequences of insertions and deletions. We use the word _amortized_ to denote the fact that the time bounds derived are valid for sequences of operations. The amortized cost per operation is much smaller than the worst case cost of a single operation. This analysis leads to finger trees in the third section. Finally, we introduce fringe analysis, a method for partially analyzing random (a,b)-trees.

III. 5.3.1 Mergable Priority Queues

We introduce two more operations on sets and show how to implement them efficiently with (a,b)-trees. We then describe the implementation of mergable priority queues based on (a,b)-trees.

Concatenate (S_1,S_2,S_3) $S_3 \leftarrow S_1 \cup S_2$, operation Concatenate is only defined if max $S_1 <$ min S_2.

Split (S_1,y,S_2,S_3) $S_2 \leftarrow \{x \in S_1; \ x \leq y\}$ and
$S_3 \leftarrow \{x \in S_1; \ x > y\}$

Both operations are destructive, i.e. sets S_1 and S_2 (set S_1 respectively) are destroyed by an application of Concatenate (Split).

__Theorem 6:__ Let $a \geq 2$ and $b \geq 2a-1$. If sets S_1 and S_2 are represented by (a,b)-trees then operation Concatenate(S_1,S_2,S_3) takes time $O(\log \max(|S_1|,|S_2|))$ and operation Split(S_1,y,S_4,S_5) takes time $O(\log |S_1|)$.

<u>Proof:</u> We treat Concatenate first. Let S_1 and S_2 be represented by (a,b)-trees T_1 and T_2 of height h_1 and h_2 respectively. We assume that the height of a tree and the maximal element of a tree are both stored in the root. It is easy to see that this assumption does not affect the time complexity of any of the operations considered so far.

Assume w.l.o.g that $h_1 \geq h_2$. Let r_2 be the root of T_2 and let v be the node of depth h_1-h_2 on the right spine of T_1, i.e. v is reached from the root of T_1 by following h_1-h_2 times the pointer to the rightmost son. Fuse v and r_2 and insert the maximal element stored in T_1 as the additional key in the combined node. The combined node has arity at most 2b. If its arity is not larger than b then we are done. Otherwise we split it in the middle and proceed as in the case of an insertion. Splitting may propagate all the way to the root. In any case, the time complexity of the algorithm is $O(|h_1-h_2|+ 1) = O(\max(h_1,h_2)) = O(\log \max(|S_1|,|S_2|))$. Also note that the resulting tree has height $\max(h_1,h_2)$ or $\max(h_1,h_2) + 1$. This finishes description and analysis of Concatenate.

The algorithm for Split $(S_1,y, ,)$ is slightly more complicated. Let T_1 be an (a,b)-tree for S_1. The first thing to do is to search for y and split all nodes on the path of search at the pointer which leads to that successor which is also on the path of search. In the example below splitting along the path to leaf 12 yields:

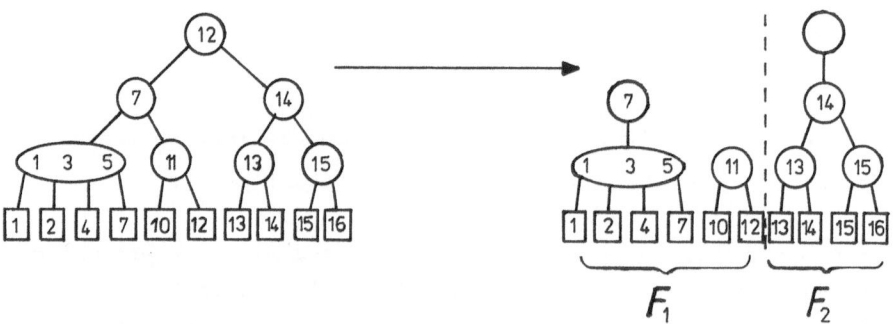

The splitting process yields two forests F_1 and F_2, i.e. two sets of trees. F_1 is the set of trees to the left of the path and F_2 is the set of trees to the right of the path. The union of the leaves of F_1 gives S_4 and the union of the leaves of F_2 gives S_5. We show how to build S_4 in time $O(\log |S_1|)$. The root of each tree in F_1 is a piece of a node on the path of search. Hence F_1 contains at most $h_1 = \text{height}(T_1)$ trees. Let $D_1, \ldots, D_m$, $m \le h_1$, be the trees in F_1 from left to right. Then each D_i is an (a,b)-tree except for the fact that the arity of the root might be only one. Also $\max D_i < \min D_{i+1}$ and $\text{height}(D_i) > \text{height}(D_{i+1})$ for $1 \le i < m$. Hence we can form a tree for set S_4 by executing the following sequence of Concatenates.

$$\text{Concatenate}(D_{m-1}, D_m, D'_{m-1})$$
$$\text{Concatenate}(D_{m-2}, D'_{m-1}, D'_{m-2})$$

.

.

.

$$\text{Concatenate}(D_1, D'_2, D'_1)$$

It is easy to see that applying Concatenate to (a,b)-trees with the possible defect of having a root with arity one yields an (a,b)-tree which might again have that defect. Hence D'_1 is an (a,b)-tree for set S_4 except for that possible defect. If the root of D'_1 has arity 1 then we only have to delete it and obtain an (a,b)-tree for S_4. It remains to analyse the running time of this algorithm. The splitting phase is clearly $O(\log n)$. For the build-up phase let h'_i be the height of D'_i. Then the complexity of the build-up phase is $O(|h_{m-1} - h_m| + \sum_{i=1}^{m-2} |h_i - h'_{i+1}| + m)$.

<u>Claim:</u> $h_{i+1} \le h'_{i+1} \le h_{i+1} + 1 \le h_i$

<u>Proof:</u> Since D_{i+1} is used to form D'_{i+1} we clearly have $h'_{i+1} \ge h_{i+1}$. We show $h'_{i+1} \le h_{i+1} + 1$ by induction on i. For $i = m-2$ we have

$$h'_{m-1} \le \max(h_{m-1}, h_m) + 1 \le h_{m-1} + 1 \le h_{m-2}$$

since $h_m < h_{m-1} < h_{m-2}$ and for $i < m - 2$ we have

$$h'_{i+1} \le \max(h_{i+1}, h'_{i+2}) + 1 \qquad \text{,property of Concatenate}$$

$$\leq h_{i+1} + 1 \qquad\qquad , \; h'_{i+2} \leq h_{i+1} \text{ by I.H.}$$

$$\leq h_i \qquad\qquad , \; \text{since } h_{i+1} < h_i \qquad\qquad \square$$

$$\text{Thus } |h_{m-1} - h_m| + \sum_{i=1}^{m-2} |h_i - h'_{i+1}| + m$$

$$\leq h_{m-1} - h_m + \sum_{i=1}^{m-2} (h_i - h'_{i+1}) + m$$

$$\leq h'_{m-1} - h_m + \sum_{i=1}^{m-2} (h'_i - h'_{i+1}) + m$$

$$\leq m + h'_1 \leq m + h_1 + 1 = O(\log |S_1|). \qquad\qquad \square$$

In our example F_1 consists of two trees. Concatening them yields

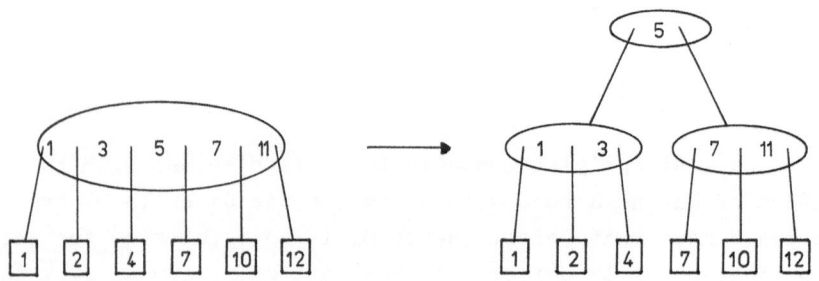

Concatenate is a very restricted form of set union. General set union
of ordered sets is treated in III.5.3.3. below.

However, Concatenate is good enough to handle the union question on <u>un-</u>
<u>ordered</u> lists. A very frequent task is the manipulation of priority
queues; we will see an example in section IV.6 on shortest path
algorithms. The name mergable priority queue represents the problem of
manipulating a set of sets under the operations Insert(x,S), Min(S),
Deletemin(S) and Union(S_1,S_2,S_3). We will add two more operations later.
Note that operation Access is not included in this list. Also note,
that operation Access was the main reason for storing the elements of
a set in sorted order in the leaves of an (a,b)-tree. We give up on that
principle now.

A set S, |S| = n, is represented in an unordered (a,b)-tree T with n
leaves as follows:

1) the leaves of T contain the elements of S in some order
2) each node v of T contains the minimal element in the subtree with
   root v and a pointer to the leaf containing that element.

Operation Min(S) is trivial in this data structure; it takes time O(1).
For Deletemin(S) we follow the pointer from the root to the minimal
element and delete it. Then we walk back to the root, rebalance the tree
by fusing and sharing and update the min values and pointers on the way.
Note that the min value and pointer of a node can be found by looking
at all its sons. Thus Deletemin(S) takes time $O(a \log |S|/\log a)$. We
include factor a because we will see that other operations are propor-
tional to $O(\log |S|/\log a)$ and because we will exploit that fact in
IV.6. Insert(x,S) is a special case of Union where one of the sets is
a singleton. Finally Union(S_1,S_2) reduces to Concatenate and takes
time $O(a \log(\max(|S_1|,|S_2|))/\log a)$. Delete in its pure form cannot be
supported because there is no efficient method for finding an element.
However, a modified form of Delete is still supported. Given a pointer
to a leaf that leaf can be deleted in time $O(a \log|S|/\log a)$ as de-
scribed for Deletemin above. We call this operation Delete*. Finally we
consider operation Demote* which takes a pointer to a leaf and an element x of the universe. Demote* is only applicable if x is smaller than
the element currently stored in the leaf, and changes (demotes) the
content of that leaf to x. Demote* takes time $O(\log |S|/\log a)$ because
one only has to walk back to the root and replace all elements on that
path by x if x is smaller. We summarize in:

<u>Theorem 7</u>: Let $a \geq 2$ and $b \geq 2a - 1$. If sets are represented by unor-
dered (a,b)-trees then operations Min(S), Deletemin(S), Insert(x,S),
Union(S_1,S_2,S_3), Delete*(,S), Demote*(, ,S) take time O(1),
$O(a \log |S|/\log a)$, $O(a \log |S|/\log a)$, $O(a \log(|S_1| + |S_2|)/\log a)$,
$O(a \log |S|/\log a)$ and $O(\log |S|/\log a)$ respectively.

III. 5.3.2 Amortized Rebalancing Cost and Sorting Presorted Files

In this section we study the total cost of sequences of insertions and
deletions into (a,b)-trees under the assumption that we start with an
initially empty tree. We will show that the total cost is linear in the
length of the sequence. The proof follows a general paradigm for analysing the cost of sequences of operations, the bank account paradigm,

which we saw already in the proof of theorem 4 in III. 5.1.. We associate a bank account with the tree ; the balance of that account measures the balance of the tree. We will then show that adding or pruning a leaf corresponds to the withdrawal of a fixed amount from that account and that the rebalancing operations (fusing, sharing and splitting) correspond to deposits. Using finally the obvious bounds for the balance of the account, we obtain the result.

Theorem 8: Let $b \geq 2a$ and a ≥ 2. Consider an arbitrary sequence of i insertions and d deletions (n = i+d) into an initially empty (a,b)-tree. Let SP be the total number of node splittings, F the total number of node fusings and SH be the total number of node sharings. Then

a)　　$SH \leq d \leq n$

b)　　$(2c-1) \cdot SP + c \cdot F \leq n + c + \frac{c}{a+c-1} (i-d-2)$

where $c = \min(\min(2a-1, \lceil (b+1)/2 \rceil)-a, b-\max(2a-1, \lfloor (b+1)/2 \rfloor))$. Note that $c \geq 1$ for $b \geq 2a$ and hence $SP+F \leq n/c + 1 + (n-2)/a$.

Proof:　a) Node sharing is executed at most once for each deletion. Hence $SH \leq d$.

b) We follow the paradigm outline above.

For a node v (unequal the root) of an (a,b)-tree let the balance b(v) of v be

　　　$b(v) = \min(\rho(r)-a, b - \rho(v), c)$

where c is defined as above. Note that $c \geq 1$ for $b \geq 2a$ and a ≥ 2 and that $\rho(v') = \lfloor (b+1)/2 \rfloor$ and $\rho(v'') = \lceil (b+1)/2 \rceil$ implies $b(v') + b(v'') \geq 2c-1$ and that $\rho(v) = 2a-1$ implies $b(v) = c$. For root r (r will always denote the root in the sequel) the balance is defined as

　　　$b^*(r) = \min(\rho(r)-2, b - \rho(r), c)$

Definition: (T,v) is a partially rebalanced (a,b)-tree where v is a node of T if

a) $a-1 \leq \rho(v) \leq b+1$ if $v \neq r$
     $1 \leq \rho(v) \leq b+1$ if $v = r$

b) $a \leq \rho(w) \leq b$ for all $w \neq v,r$

c) $2 \leq \rho(r) \leq b$ if $v \neq r$

Let (T,v) be a partially rebalanced (a,b)-tree. Then the balance of T is defined as the sum of the balance of its nodes

$$b(T) = \sum_{\substack{v \text{ is node of } T \\ v \neq r}} b(v) + b^*(r)$$

Fact 1: Let T be an (a,b)-tree. Let T' be obtained from T by adding a leaf or pruning a leaf. Then $b(T') \geq b(T)-1$.

Proof: obvious.   □

Fact 2: Let (T,v) be a partially rebalanced (a,b)-tree with $\rho(v) = b+1$.

Splitting v and expanding v's father x generates a tree T' with $b(T') \geq b(T) + (2c-1)$.

Proof: Since $\rho(v) = b+1$ we have $b(v) = b^*(v) = -1$

Case 1: v is not the root of T. Let x be the father of v. v is split into nodes, v' and v'' say, of arity $\lfloor (b+1)/2 \rfloor$ and $\lceil (b+1)/2 \rceil$ respectively, and the arity of x is increased by one. Hence the balance of x decreases by at most one and we have

$$b(T') \geq b(T) + b(v') + b(v'') - b(v) - 1$$

Furthermore, $b(v) = -1$ and $b(v') + b(v'') \geq 2c-1$ by the remark above. This shows

$$b(T') \geq b(T) + (2c-1) - (-1) - 1$$
$$\geq b(T) + (2c-1)$$

Case 2: v is the root of T. Then the father x of v is newly created and hence has arity 2 after the splitting of v. Hence

$$b(T') \geq b(T) + b(v') + b(v") - b^*(v) + b^*(x)$$
$$\geq b(T) + (2c-1) - (-1) + 0 \qquad \square$$

Fact 3: Let (T,v) be a partially rebalanced (a,b)-tree with $\rho(v) = a-1$ and $v \neq r$ the root of T. Let y be a brother of v and let x be the father of v.

a) If $\rho(y) = a$ then let T' be the tree obtained by fusing v and y and shrinking x. Furthermore, if x is the root and has degree 1 after the shrinking, then x is deleted. Then $b(T') \geq b(T) + c$.

b) If $\rho(y) > a$ then let T' be the tree obtained by sharing, i.e. by taking 1 son away from y and making it a son of v. Then $b(T') \geq b(T)$.

Proof: a) y and v are fused to a node, say w, of arity $\rho(w) = 2a-1$. Hence $b(w) = b^*(w) = c$.

Case 1: x is not the root of T. Then the arity of x is decreased by one and hence the balance of x is decreased by at most one. Hence

$$b(T') \geq b(T) + (b(w)-b(v)-b(y)) - 1$$
$$\geq b(T) + (c - (-1) - 0) - 1$$
$$\geq b(T) + c$$

Case 2: x is the root of T. If $\rho(x) \geq 3$ before the fusing then the analysis of case 1 applies. Otherwise we have $\rho(x) = 2$ and hence $b^*(x) = 0$ before the fusing, and x is deleted after the fusing and w is the new root. Hence

$$b(T') = b(T) + (b^*(w) - b(v) - b(y)) - b^*(x)$$
$$= b(T) + c - (-1) - 0 - 0$$
$$= b(T) + c + 1$$

·In either case we have shown $b(T') \geq b(T) + c$.

b) Taking one son away from y decreases the balance of y by at most one. Giving v (of arity $a-1$) an additional son increases $b(v)$ by one. Hence $b(T') \geq b(T)$. $\qquad \square$

Fact 4: Let T be an (a,b)-tree with m leaves. Then $0 \leq b(T) \leq$ $c + (m-2) \frac{c}{a+c-1}$

Proof: For $0 \leq j < c$, let m_j be the number of interior nodes unequal the root of degree $a+j$ and let m_c be the number of interior nodes unequal the root of degree at least $a+c$. Then $b(T) \leq c + \sum_{j=0}^{c} m_j \cdot j$ since the balance of the root is at most c.

Furthermore, $2 + \sum_{j=0}^{c} (a+j)m_j \leq m + \sum_{j=0}^{c} m_j$ since the expression on the right side is equal to the number of edges (= number of leaves + non-root nodes) in T and the expression on the left hand side is a lower bound on that number. Hence

$$\sum_{j=0}^{c} (a+j-1)m_j \leq m-2$$

Since

$$j/(a+j-1) \leq c/(a+c-1) \qquad \text{for} \qquad 0 \leq j \leq c$$

we conclude

$$b(T) \leq c + \sum_{j=0}^{c} j \cdot m_j$$

$$\leq c + \sum_{j=0}^{c} \frac{j}{a+j-1} \cdot (a+j-1) \cdot m_j$$

$$\leq c + (c/(a+c-1))(m-2) \qquad\qquad \square$$

In order to finish the banking account paradigm we need to relate deposits, withdrawals and initial and final balance. Since we start with an empty tree T_0, the initial balance $b(T_0)$ is 0. Next we perform i insertions and d deletions and obtain T_n (n=i+d). Since T_n has i-d leaves we conclude $b(T_n) \leq c + (i-d-2)c/(a+c-1)$. Also the total withdrawals are at most n by Fact 1 and the total deposits are at least $(2c-1) \cdot SP + c \cdot F$ by facts 2 and 3. Hence

$$b(T_0) + (2c-1) \cdot SP + c \cdot F - n \leq b(T_n)$$
and thus
$$(2c-1) \cdot SP + c \cdot F \leq n + c + (i-d-2)c/(a+c-1). \qquad\qquad \square$$

Theorem 8 establishes an O(1) bound on the amortized rebalancing cost
in (a,b)-trees for b ≥ 2a. In that respect it is a companion theorem
to theorem 4 on weight-balanced trees. Let us look at some concrete
values of a and b. For a = 2, b = 4 we have c = 1 and hence SP + F ≤ 3n/2.
For (4,13)-trees we have c = 3 and hence SP + F ≤ n/2 + 2/3. We should
also mention that theorem 8 does not hold if b = 2a-1 as can be seen
from the following example; rebalancing always runs all

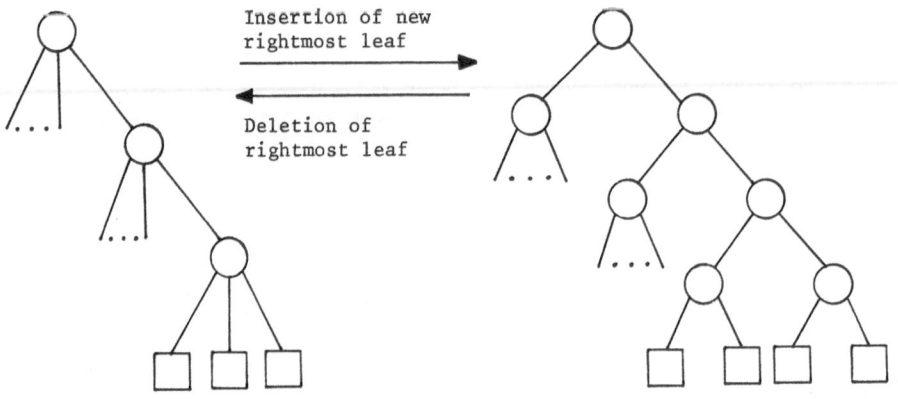

Insertion of new
rightmost leaf

Deletion of
rightmost leaf

the way to the root. However, theorem 8 is true for b = 2a-1 if one
considers insertions only (exercise 30).

Theorem 8 has an interesting application to sorting, more precisely to
sorting presorted files. Let $x_1, \ldots, x_n$ be a sequence which has to be
sorted in increasing order. Suppose, that we know that this sequence
is not random, but rather possesses some degree of sortedness. A good
measure for sortedness is number of inversions. Let

$$f_i = |\{x_j; \ j > i \ \text{and} \ x_j < x_i\}|$$

and $F = \sum_{i=1}^{n} f_i$. Then $0 \le F \le n(n-1)/2$, F is called the number of inversions of the sequence $x_1, \ldots, x_n$. We take F as a measure of sortedness;
F = 0 for a sorted sequence, $F \approx n^2$ for a completely unsorted sequence
and $F \ll n^2$ for a nearly sorted sequence. These remarks are not meant
to be definitions. We can sort sequence $x_1, \ldots, x_n$ by insertion sort,
i.e. we start with the sorted sequence x_n represented by an (a,b)-tree
and then insert $x_{n-1}, x_{n-2}, \ldots, x_1$ in turn. By theorem 5 this will take
total time O(n log n). Note however, when we have sorted $x_{i+1}, \ldots, x_n$
already and next insert x_i, then x_i will be inserted at the f_i-th posi-

tion from the left in that sequence. If $F \ll n^2$, then $f_i \ll n$ for most i and hence most $x_i's$ will be inserted near the beginning of the sequence. What does this mean for the insertion algorithm. It will move down the left spine (the path to the leftmost leaf), for quite a while and only depart from it near the leaf-level. It is then cheaper to search for the point of departure from the left spine by moving the spine upwards from the leftmost leaf. Of course, this requires the existence of son-to-father pointers on the left spine.

Let us consider the insertion of x_i in more detail. We move up the left spine through nodes $v_1, v_2, v_3, \ldots$ (v_1 is the father of the leftmost leaf and v_{j+1} is the father of v_j) until we hit node v_j with $x_i \leq k_1(v_j)$, i.e. x_i has to be inserted into the leftmost subtree of node v_j but not into the leftmost subtree of node v_{j-1}, i.e. either $j = 1$ or $x_i > k_1(v_{j-1})$. In either case we turn around at v_j and proceed as in an ordinary (a,b)-tree search. Note that the search for x_i will cost us $O(height(v_j))$ time units. Since all leaves stored in the subtree rooted at v_{j-2} must have content less than x_i we conclude that $f_i \geq$ number of leaves in subtree rooted at $v_{j-2} \geq 2 \cdot a^{h(v_{j-2})-1}$ by Lemma 4 and hence

$$height(v_j) = O(\log f_i)$$

The actual insertion of x_i costs $O(s_i)$ time units, where s_i is the number of splits required after adding a new leaf for x_i. This gives the following time bound for the insertion sort

$$\sum_{i=1}^{n} [O(\log f_i) + O(s_i)] = O(n + \sum_{i=1}^{n} \log f_i + \sum_{i=1}^{n} s_i)$$

$$= O(n + n \log(F/n))$$

since $\Sigma \log f_i = \log \Pi f_i$ and $(\Pi f_i)^{1/n} \leq (\Sigma f_i)/n$ (the geometric mean is never larger than the arithmetic mean) and since $\Sigma s_i = O(n)$ by theorem 8. We thus have

Theorem 9: A sequence of n elements and F inversions can be sorted in time $O(n + n \log(F/n))$.

<u>Proof:</u> By the preceding discussion.   □

The sorting algorithm (A-sort) of theorem 9 may be called adaptive. The more sorted sequence $x_1, \ldots, x_n$ is, the faster the algorithm. For $F = n \log n$, the running time is $O(n \log \log n)$. This is in marked contrast to all other sorting algorithms, e.g. Heapsort, Quicksort, Mergesort. In particular, it will be faster than all these other algorithms provided that F is not too large. A careful non-asymptotic analysis of A-sort is beyond the scope of this book; it can be found in Mehlhorn/Tsakalidis, where is it shown that A-sort is better than Quicksort for $F \leq 0.02 \cdot n^{1.57}$.

Let us return to theorem 8 and its companion theorem 4 on weight-balanced trees. In the proof of theorem 4 we also established that most rotations and double rotations occur near the leaves. We will now proceed to show a similar theorem for height - balanced trees. We need some more notation.

We say that a splitting (fusing, sharing) operation occurs at height h, if node v which is to be split (which is to be fused with its brother y or shares a son with its brother y) has height h; the height of a leaf being 0. A splitting (fusing) operation at height h expands (shrinks) a node at height h+1. An insertion (deletion) of a leaf expands (shrinks) a node at height 1.

Let (T,v) be a partially rebalanced (a,b)-tree. We define the balance of tree T at height h as:

$$
b_h(T) = \begin{cases} \displaystyle\sum_{\substack{v \text{ node of T of height h}}} b(v) & \text{if h is not the height of the root} \\[2ex] b^*(r) & \text{if h is the height of the root r of T} \end{cases}
$$

where b and b* are defined as in the proof of theorem 8.

<u>Theorem 1o:</u> Let $b \geq 2a$ and $a \geq 2$. Consider an arbitrary sequence of i insertions and d deletions (n = i+d) into an initially empty (a,b)-tree. Let $SP_h(F_h, SH_h)$ be the total number of node splittings (fusings, sharings) at height h. Then

$$SP_h + F_h + SH_h \leq 2(c+2)n/(c+1)^h$$

where c is defined as in theorem 8.

Proof: The first part of the proof parallels the proof of theorem 8.

Fact 1: Let T be an (a,b)-tree. Let T' be obtained from T by adding or pruning a leaf. Then $b_1(T') \geq b_1(T)-1$ and $b_h(T') = b_h(T)$ for h > 1.

Fact 2: Let (T,v) be a partially rebalanced (a,b)-tree with $\rho(v) = b+1$ and height of v equal h. Splitting v generates a tree T' with $b_h(T') \geq b_h(T) + 2 \cdot c$, $b_{h+1}(T') \geq h_{h+1}(T) - 1$ and $b_\ell(T') = b_\ell(T)$ for $\ell \neq h, h+1$.

Fact 3: Let (T,v) be a partially rebalanced (a,b)-tree with $\rho(v) = a-1$, height of v equal h and $v \neq r$ the root of T. Let y be a brother of v and let x be the father of v.

a) if $\rho(y) = a$ then let T' be the tree obtained by fusing v and y and shrinking x. Furthermore, if x is the root of T and has degree 1 after the shrinking, then x is deleted. Then $b_h(T') \geq b_h(T) + c + 1$, $b_{h+1}(T') \geq b_{h+1}(T) - 1$ and $b_\ell(T') = b_\ell(T)$ for $\ell \neq h, h+1$.

b) if $\rho(y) > a$ then let T' be the tree obtained by sharing. Then $b_\ell(T') \geq b_\ell(T)$ for all ℓ.

The proofs of facts 1 to 3 are very similar to the proof of the corresponding facts in theorem 8 and therefore left to the reader.

Fact 4: Let T_n be the tree obtained after i insertions and d deletions from T_0, the initial tree. Let $SP_0 + F_0 := i+d$. Then for all $h \geq 1$

$$b_h(T_n) \geq b_h(T_0) - (SP_{h-1} + F_{h-1}) + (2c \cdot SP_h + (c+1)F_h)$$

Proof: Facts 1-3 imply that splits (fusings) at height h increase the balance at height h by 2c(c+1) and decrease the balance at height h+1 by at most 1. □

Since $b_h(T_0) = 0$ for all h (recall that we start with an empty tree) and $2c \geq c+1$ (recall that $c \geq 1$) we conclude from fact 4

$$SP_h + F_h \leq b_h(T_n)/(c+1) + (SP_{h-1} + F_{h-1})/(c+1)$$

and hence

$$SP_h + F_h \leq \sum_{\ell=0}^{h-1} b_{h-\ell}(T_n)/(c+1)^{\ell+1} + (SP_0 + F_0)/(c+1)^h$$

$$= n/(c+1)^h + \sum_{\ell=1}^{h} b_\ell(T_n)(c+1)^\ell/(c+1)^{h+1}$$

__Fact 5:__ For all $h \geq 1$:

$$\sum_{\ell=1}^{h} b_\ell(T_n)(c+1)^\ell \leq (c+1)(i-d) \leq (c+1) \cdot n$$

__Proof:__ Let $m_j(h)$ be the number of nodes of height h and degree a+j, $0 \leq j < c$, and let $m_c(h)$ be the number of nodes of height h and degree at least a+c. Then

$$(*) \qquad \sum_{j=0}^{c} (a+j)m_j(h) \leq \sum_{j=0}^{c} m_j(h-1)$$

for $h \geq 2$ since the number of edges ending at height h-1 is equal to the number of edges emanating at height h. Setting $\sum_{j=0}^{c} m_j(0) := i-d$ (the number of leaves of T_n) the inequality is true for all $h \geq 1$.

Using $b_\ell(T_n) \leq \sum_{j=0}^{c} j \cdot m_j(\ell)$ and relation (*) we obtain

$$\sum_{\ell=1}^{h} b_\ell(T_n)(c+1)^\ell \leq \sum_{\ell=1}^{h} [(c+1)^\ell \cdot \sum_{j=0}^{c} j \, m_j(\ell)]$$

$$\leq \sum_{\ell=1}^{h} [(c+1)^\ell \cdot \left\{ \sum_{j=0}^{c} m_j(\ell-1) - a \sum_{j=0}^{c} m_j(\ell) \right\}]$$

$$= (c+1) \sum_{j=0}^{c} m_j(0)$$

$$+ \sum_{\ell=1}^{h} (c+1)^\ell [\sum_{j=0}^{c} m_j(\ell-1) - \frac{a}{(c+1)} \sum_{j=0}^{c} m_j(\ell-1)]$$

$$- (c+1)^h \cdot a \cdot \sum_{j=0}^{c} m_j(h)$$

$$\leq (c+1)(i-d)$$

since $a/(c+1) \geq 1$ and $\sum_j m_j(0) = i-d$.   □

Substituting the bound of fact 5 into the bound for $SP_h + F_h$ we obtain

$$SP_h + F_h \leq 2n/(c+1)^h$$

With respect to sharing, note that a fusing at height h-1 either completes rebalancing or is followed by a sharing or fusing at heigth h.

Hence

$$SH_h \leq F_{h-1} - F_h \leq SP_{h-1} + F_{h-1} \leq 2n/(c+1)^{h-1}$$

for $h \geq 2$ and

$$SH_1 \leq SH_1 + F_1 \leq d.$$

Putting everything together we obtain

$$SP_h + F_h + SH_h \leq 2(c+2)n/(c+1)^h$$

for all $h \geq 1$ and theorem 1o is proven.   □

$SP_h + F_h + SH_h$ is the number of insertions and deletions which require rebalancing up to height h or higher. Theorem 1o shows that this number is exponentially decreasing with h (recall $c \geq 1$). This is very similar to lemma 2 of III.5.1. Again note that the proof of theorem 1o relies heavily on the fact that $b \geq 2a$. In fact, theorem 1o is not true for $b = 2a-1$ as the example following the proof of theorem 8 shows. There $SP_h + F_h + SH_h = n$ for all h.

We finish this section with a brief sketch of an application of theorem 1o: (a,b)-trees in a parallel environment. Some applications, in particular real-time data bank applications, call for a very high transaction rate. Very high transaction rates can only be supported by con-

current tree manipulation, i.e. by many processors working on the same
tree. Concurrent searches cause no problem; however, concurrent in-
sertions/deletions do. Note that the rebalancing operations (splitting,
fusing, sharing) require locking of nodes, i.e. whilst node v is rebalanced by one process, the other processes cannot use node v and have
to wait if they want to. Also note, that locking node v will (on the
average) block many other processes if v is close to the root and that
it will block (almost) no other processes if v is close to the leaves.
That's exactly the point where theorem 1o comes in. Theorem 1o guarantees that most rebalancing operations occur close to the leaves and
that therefore blocking of processes is no insurmountable problem. We
refer the reader to Bayer/Schkolnik for a detailed discussion.

III. 5.3.3 Finger Trees

In this section we generalize (a,b)-trees to finger trees. We have seen
in the previous section that it is sometimes better to start searches
in an (a,b)-tree at a leaf. This led to A-sort. Finger trees grow out
of that observation and generalize it. Recall that we used (a,b)-trees
to represent ordered lists. A finger into a list is a pointer to an element of the list. Fingers may be used to indicate areas of high activity
in the list and we aim for efficient searches in the vicinity of fingers. If the list is represented as the leaves of an (a,b)-tree then a
finger is a pointer to a leaf. (a,b)-trees as they stand do not support
efficient search in the vicinity of fingers. This is due to the fact
that neighboring leaves may be connected only by a very long path. Therefore we introduce level-linked (a,b)-trees.

In level linked (a,b)-trees all tree edges are made traversible in both
directions (i.e. there are also pointers from sons to fathers); in addition each node has pointers to the two neighboring nodes on the same
level. The figure on the next page shows a level-linked (2,4)-tree for
list 2, 4, 7, 1o, 11, 15, 17, 21, 22, 24.

A finger tree is a level-linked (a,b)-tree with pointers to some of its
leaves, the fingers. Level-linked (a,b)-trees allow very fast searching
in the vicinity of fingers.

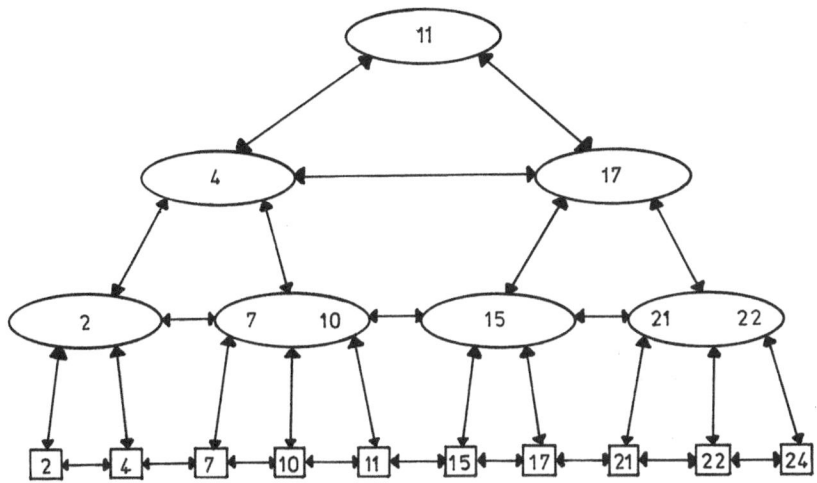

Lemma 7: Let p be a finger in a level-linked (a,b)-tree T. A search for a key k which is d keys away from p takes time $\Theta(1+\log d)$.

Proof: We first check whether k is to the left or right of p, say k is to the right of p. Then we walk towards the root, say we reached node v. We check whether k is a descendant of v or v's right neighbour on the same level. If not, then we proceed to v's father. Otherwise we turn around and search for k in the ordinary way.

Suppose that we turn around at node w of height h. Let u be that son of w which is on the path to the finger p. Then all descendants of u's right neighbour lie between the finger p and key k. Hence the distance d is at least a^{h-1} and at most $2b^h$. The time bound follows. □

Lemma 8: A new leaf can be inserted in a given position of a level-linked (a,b)-tree in time $\Theta(1+s)$, where s is the number of splittings caused by the insertion.

Proof: This is immediate from the description of the insertion algorithm in III.5.2.. Note that it is part of the assumption of lemma 8 that we start with a pointer to the leaf to be split by the insertion. So no search is required, only rebalancing. □

Lemma 9: A given leaf can be deleted from a level-linked (a,b)-tree in time $\Theta(1+f)$, where f is the number of node fusings caused by the deletion.

Proof: Immediate from the description of the deletion algorithm. Again note that it is part of the assumption of lemma 9 that we start with a pointer to the leaf which has to be deleted.   □

Lemma 10: Creation or removal of a finger at a given leaf in a level-linked (a,b)-tree takes time $\Theta(1)$.

Proof: Obvious.   □

We can now appeal to theorem 8 and show that although the search time in level-linked (a,b)-trees can be greatly reduced by maintaining fingers, it still dominates the total execution time, provided that $b \geq 2a$.

Theorem 11: Let $b \geq 2a$ and $a \geq 2$. Then any sequence of searches, finger creations, finger removals, insertions and deletions starting with an empty list takes time

O(total cost of searches)

if a level-linked (a,b)-tree is used to represent the list.

Proof: Let n be the length of the sequence. Since every operation has to be preceded immediately by a search, the total cost for the searches is $\Omega(n)$ by lemma 7. On the other hand the total cost for the finger creations and removals is $O(n)$ by lemma 10 and the total cost of insertions and deletions is $O(n)$ by lemmas 8 and 9 and theorem 8.   □

Theorem 9 on sorting presorted files is a special case of theorem 11. Theorem 11 can be generalized in two directions. We can start with several empty lists and add Concatenate to the set of operations (exercise 33) or we can start with a non-empty list. For the latter generalization we also need a more general version of theorem 8. We need a bound on total rebalancing cost even if we start with a non-empty tree.

Let T be any (a,b)-tree. Suppose now that we execute a sequence of insertions and deletions on T. It is intuitively obvious that only nodes which lie on a path from one of the inserted or deleted leaves to the root are affected (this is made precise in fact 1) below. We will derive a bound on the number of such nodes in fact 5. Of course, only these nodes can change their balance and hence their number gives a bound on the difference of the balance of initial and final tree. An application of the bank account paradigm will then give us a bound on the number of splittings, fusings and sharings (Fact 4).

In order to facilitate the following discussion we introduce the following convention: if a leaf is deleted from an (a,b)-tree, it (conceptually) stays as a phantom. The rebalancing algorithms do not see the phantoms, i.e. the arity of nodes is solely determined by the non-phantom leaves. In the following example phantom leaves are shown as dashed boxes.

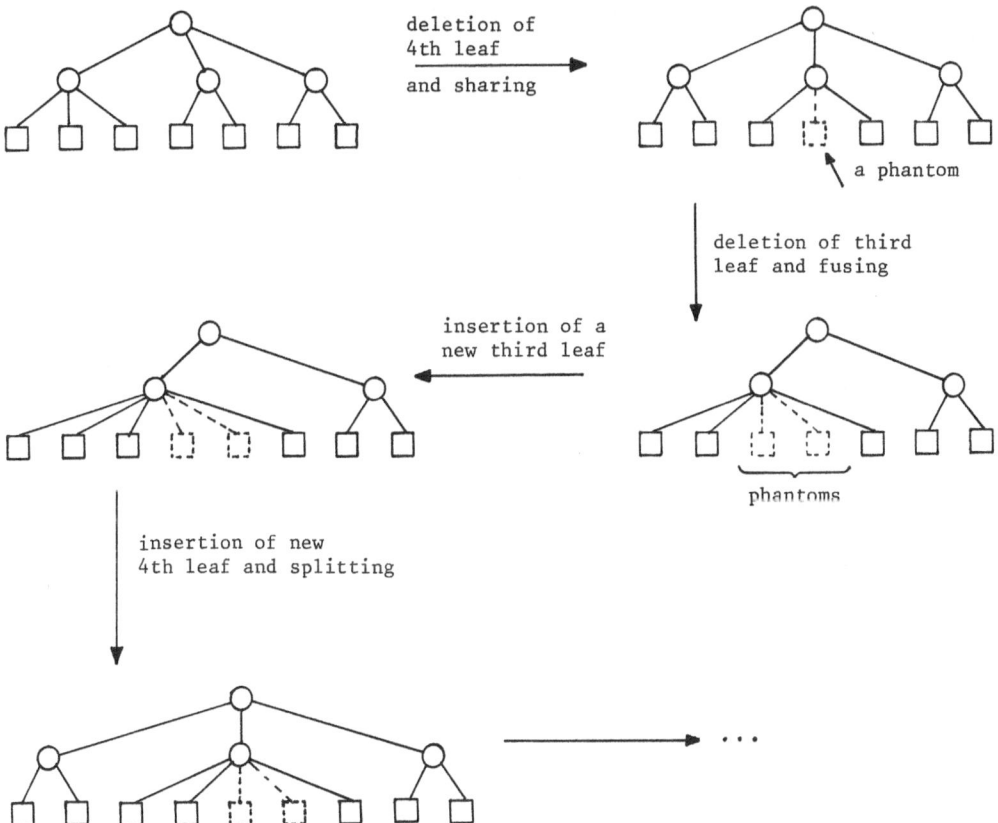

Theorem 12: Let $b \geq 2a$ and $a \geq 2$ and let T be an (a,b)-tree with n leaves. Suppose that a sequence of s insertions and t deletions is performed and tree T' is obtained. Then tree T' has n + s leaves, t of which are phantoms. Number the leaves from 1 to n + s from left to right. Let $p_1, p_2, \ldots, p_{s+t}$ be the positions of the s + t new leaves and phantoms in T', $p_1 \leq p_2 \leq \ldots \leq p_{s+t}$. Let SH(SP,F) be the total number of

sharings (splittings, fusings) required to process this sequence. Then

$$SH + SP + F \leq 9(s+t) + 4(\lfloor \log_a(n+s) \rfloor + \sum_{i=2}^{s+t} \lfloor \log_a(p_i - p_{i-1} + 1) \rfloor)$$

Proof: We first introduce a marking process which (conceptually) marks nodes during the rebalancing process.

Adding a leaf: When a new leaf is added we mark the new leaf and its father.

Splitting a node: Suppose that node v (v will be marked at this point and has a marked son) is split into nodes v' and v". Then v' is marked if it has a marked son, v" is marked if it has a marked son and we mark the father of v' and v".

Pruning a leaf: We mark the phantom and its father.

Fusing: Suppose that node v (v has a marked son at this point) is fused with its brother y. Then we mark v and its father.

Sharing: Suppose that node v (v has a marked son at this point) receives a son from its brother y. Then we mark v and we unmark y (if it was marked).

Fact 1: If interior node v is marked then it has a marked son.

Since the only leaves which are marked are the new leaves and the phantoms we conclude from Fact 1 that all marked nodes lie on paths from the new leaves and the phantoms to the root. In fact 5 we derive an upper bound on the number of such nodes.

Next we need to define some new concepts: critical and noncritical splitting operation and marked balance. A splitting of node v is critical if v's father exists and has arity b. All other splittings are noncritical. Let SPC be the number of critical splittings and let SPNC be the number of noncritical splittings and let SH (F) be the number of sharings (fusings).

Fact 2: SPNC + SH ≤ s+t

Proof: A sharing or noncritical splitting terminates rebalancing.   □

The marked balance of a tree is the sum of the balances of its marked nodes, i.e.

$$mb(T) = \sum_{\substack{w \text{ marked node of } T \\ w \neq \text{ root of } T}} b(w) + \underline{if} \text{ root is marked } \underline{then} \ b^*(r)$$

where the balance of a node is defined as follows.

$$b(w) = \begin{cases} -1 & \text{if } \rho(w) = a-1, \ b+1 \\ 0 & \text{if } \rho(w) = b \\ 2 & \text{if } \rho(w) = 2a-1 \\ 1 & \text{if } a \leq \rho(w) \leq b \text{ and } \rho(w) \neq b, \ 2a-1 \end{cases}$$

and

$$b^*(r) = \begin{cases} -1 & \text{if } \rho(r) = +1, \ b+1 \\ 0 & \text{if } \rho(r) = b \\ 2 & \text{if } \rho(r) = 2a-1 \\ 1 & \text{if } 2 \leq \rho(r) \leq b \text{ and } \rho(r) \neq b, \ 2a-1 \end{cases}$$

Fact 3: Let T' be obtained from T by

a) adding a leaf, then $mb(T') \geq mb(T) - 2$
b) pruning a leaf, then $mb(T') \geq mb(T) - 2$
c) noncritical splitting, then $mb(T') \geq mb(T)$
d) critical splitting, then $mb(T') \geq mb(T) + 1$
e) fusing, then $mb(T') \geq mb(T) + 2$
f) sharing, then $mb(T') \geq mb(T)$

Proof: a) Suppose we add a leaf and expand v. Then v is marked after adding the leaf and may be marked or not before. Hence

$$mb(T') = mb(T) + b(v \text{ after adding leaf}) - [b(v \text{ before adding leaf})]$$

where the expression in square brackets is only present if v is marked before adding the leaf. In either case it is easy to see that $mb(T') \geq mb(T) - 2$.

b) Similar to part a).

c) Suppose we split node v (which is marked at this point) into nodes v' and v" and expand v's father x. Since the splitting is noncritical we have $\rho(x) < b$ before the splitting. Also at least one of v' and v" will be marked after the splitting, x will be marked after the splitting, x may be marked before or not. Hence

$$mb(T') \geq mb(T) + min(b(v'), b(v")) + b(x \text{ after splitting}) - b(v)$$
$$- [b(x \text{ before splitting})]$$

where the expression in square brackets is only present if x was marked before the splitting. Since $min(b(v'), b(v")) \geq 1$ (obviously $\lceil (b+1)/2 \rceil < b$) and since the balance of x can decrease by at most two we conclude

$$mb(T') \geq mb(T) + 1 + 0 - (-1) - 2$$

d) Argue as in case c) but observe that $\rho(x) = b$ before splitting. Therefore

$$mb(T') \geq mb(T) + 1 + (-1) - (-1) - [0]$$
$$\geq mb(T) + 1$$

e) Suppose that we fuse v and its brother y and shrink their common father x. If x is the root and has arity 1 after the fusing then x is deleted. Also v and x are marked after the fusing and at least v is marked before. y and x may be marked before. Hence

$$mb(T') \geq mb(T) + b(v \text{ after fusing})$$
$$+ b(x \text{ after fusing}) - b(v \text{ before fusing})$$
$$- [b(x \text{ before fusing})] - [b(y \text{ before fusing})]$$
$$\geq mb(T) + 2 + (-1) - (-1) - 0$$
$$\geq mb(T) + 2$$

since the balance of x can decrease by at most one.

f) Suppose that v takes away a son from y. Then v is marked before and after the sharing, y is not marked after the sharing and may be marked or not before the sharing. Also the balance of y before the sharing is at most 2.

Hence

$$mb(T') = mb(T) + b(v \text{ after sharing}) -$$
$$b(v \text{ before sharing}) - [b(y \text{ before sharing})]$$
$$\geq mb(T) + 1 - (-1) - 2$$
$$\geq mb(T) \qquad \qquad \square$$

Suppose now that we start with initial tree T (no node marked) and perform s insertions and t deletions and obtain T_n (n = s+t).

Fact 4: a) $mb(T_n) \geq SPC + 2F - 2(s+t)$

b) $mb(T_n) \leq 2 \cdot m$, where m is the number of marked nodes of T_n.

c) All marked nodes lie on a path from a new leaf or phantom to the root.

d) $SPC + F \leq 2(s+t) + 2 \cdot$(number of nodes on the paths from the new leaves and phantoms to the root).

Proof: a) Follows immediately from fact 3, b) is immediate from the definition of marked balance, c) follows from fact 1 and d) is a consequence of a), b) and c). $\qquad \square$

It remains to derive a bound on the number of marked nodes in tree T_n. In Fact 5 we use the name (a,∞)-tree for any tree where each interior node unequal the root has at least a sons and the root has at least 2 sons.

Fact 5: Let T be an (a,∞)-tree with N leaves. Let $1 \leq p_1 \leq p_2 \leq \ldots \leq p_r \leq N$. Let m be the total number of nodes on paths from the root to the leaves with positions p_i, $1 \leq i \leq r$. Then

$$m \leq 3r + 2(\lfloor \log_a N \rfloor + \sum_{i=2}^{r} \lfloor \log_a (p_i - p_{i-1} + 1) \rfloor)$$

Proof: For every node v label the outgoing edges with $0, \ldots, \rho(v)-1$ from left to right.

Then a path from the root to a node corresponds to a word over alphabet $\{0,1,2,\ldots\}$ in a natural way.

Let A_i be the number of edges labelled 0 on the path from the root to leaf p_i, $1 \le i \le r$. Since an (a,∞)-tree of height h has at least $2 \cdot a^{h-1}$ leaves, we conclude $0 \le A_i \le 1 + \lfloor \log_a N/2 \rfloor$. Furthermore, let ℓ_i be the number of interior nodes on the path from leaf p_i to the root which are not on the path from leaf p_{i-1} to the root. Then

$$m \le 1 + \lfloor \log_a N/2 \rfloor + \sum_{i=2}^{r} \ell_i$$

Consider any $i \ge 2$. Let v be the lowest common node on the paths from leaves p_{i-1} and p_i to the root. Then edge k_1 is taken out of v on the path to p_{i-1} and edge $k_2 > k_1$ is taken on the path to p_i. Note that the path from v to leaf p_{i-1} as well as to leaf p_i consists of $\ell_i + 1$ edges.

<u>Claim:</u> $A_i \ge A_{i-1} + \ell_i - 2 \lfloor \log_a (p_i - p_{i-1} + 1) \rfloor - 3$

<u>Proof:</u> The paths from p_{i-1} and p_i to the root differ only below node v. Let s be minimal such that

a) the path from v to p_{i-1} has the form $k_1 \alpha \beta$ with $|\beta| = s$ and α contains no 0.

b) the path from v to p_i has the form $k_2 \, 0^{|\alpha|} \gamma$ for some γ with $|\gamma| = s$.

Note that either β starts with a 0 or γ starts with a non-zero and that $|\alpha| + |\beta| = \ell_i$.

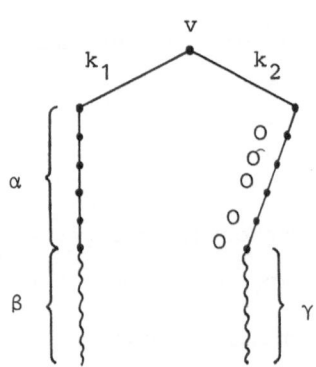

Then $A_i = A_{i-1} + \underline{if}\ k_1 = 0\ \underline{then}\ -1$
$+\ |\alpha|$
$+$ number of zeroes in γ
$-$ number of zeroes in β
$\geq A_{i-1} - 1 + (\ell_i - s) + 0 - s$

It remains to show that $s \leq 1 + \lfloor \log_a(p_i - p_{i-1} + 1) \rfloor$. This is certainly the case if $s = 0$. Suppose now that $s > 0$.

We noted above that either β starts with a zero or γ starts with a non-zero. In the first case consider node w which is reached from v via $k_1\ \alpha\ 1$, in the second case node w which is reached from v via $k_2\ 0^{|\alpha|}0$. All leaf descendants of w lie properly between p_{i-1} and p_i. Furthermore, w has height $s-1$ and hence at least a^{s-1} leaf descendants. This proves

$$a^{s-1} \leq p_i - p_{i-1} - 1$$

and hence

$$s \leq 1 + \lfloor \log_a(p_i - p_{i-1} - 1) \rfloor$$
$$\leq 1 + \lfloor \log_a(p_i - p_{i-1} + 1) \rfloor \qquad \square$$

Using our claim repeatedly, we obtain

$$A_r \geq A_1 + \sum_{i=2}^{r} \ell_i - 2 \sum_{i=2}^{r} \log_a(p_i - p_{i-1} + 1)$$
$$- 3\ (r-1)$$

Since $A_r \leq 1 + \log_a \lfloor N/2 \rfloor$ and $A_1 \geq 0$, this proves

$$\sum_{i=2}^{r} \ell_i \leq 3r - 3 + 1 + \lfloor \log_a N/2 \rfloor + 2 \sum_{i=2}^{r} \lfloor \log_a(p_i - p_{i-1} + 1) \rfloor$$

and hence

$$m \leq 3r - 1 + 2 \lfloor \log_a N/2 \rfloor + 2 \sum_{i=2}^{r} \lfloor \log_a(p_i - p_{i-1} + 1) \rfloor$$

This proves fact 5. $\qquad \square$

At this point, we can put everything together and obtain a bound on the number of rebalancing operations.

$$SH + SP + F \leq SH + SPNC + SPC + F$$
$$\leq s + t + SPC + F \qquad \text{by (Fact 2)}$$
$$\leq 3(s+t) + 2m \qquad \text{by (Fact 4d)}$$

where m is the total number of nodes on the paths from the new leaves and phantoms to the root in the final tree. Since the final tree is an (a,∞)-tree and has n+s leaves and phantom leaves, we conclude from fact5

$$m \leq 3(s+t) + 2(\lfloor \log_a (n+s) \rfloor + \sum_{i=2}^{s+t} \lfloor \log_a (p_i - p_{i-1} + 1) \rfloor)$$

and hence

$$SH + SP + F \leq 9(s+t) + 4(\lfloor \log_a (n+s) \rfloor + \sum_{i=2}^{s+t} \lfloor \log_a (p_i - p_{i-1} + 1) \rfloor)$$

This proves theorem 12.   □

Theorem 12 provides us with a bound on total rebalancing cost if we start with a non-empty (a,b)-tree. We use theorem 12 to generalize theorem 11 to the case where we start with a non-empty list.

Theorem 13: Let $b \geq 2a$ and $a \geq 2$. Let L be a sorted list of n elements represented as a level-linked (a,b)-tree with one finger established. Then in any sequence of searches, finger creations, insertions and deletions, the total cost of the sequence is

O(log n + total cost of searches)

Proof: Let S be any sequence of searches, finger creations, insertions and deletions containing exactly s insertions and t deletions. Let T_{final} be the (a,b)-tree, which represents list L after S is performed. Assume that we keep deleted elements as phantoms. Let the n+s leaves (real leaves and phantoms) of T_{final} be named $1, \ldots, n+s$ from left to right . Assign to each leaf p a label $\ell(p)$, whose value is the number of leaves lying strictly to the left of p which were present initially and which did not become phantoms. These labels lie in the range $0, \ldots, n$.

Consider the searches in S which lead either to the creation of a new finger or to the insertion or deletion of an element. Call an element of L _accessed_ if it is either the source or the destination of such a search (We regard an inserted item as the destination of the search which discovers where to insert it). Let $p_1 < p_2 < \ldots < p_\ell$ be the accessed items.

We shall consider graphs whose vertex set is a subset of $\{p_i | 1 \le i \le \ell\}$. We denote an edge joining $p_i < p_j$ in such a graph by $p_i - p_j$ and we define that cost of this edge to be max $(\lceil \log(\ell(p_j) - \ell(p_i) + 1)\rceil, 1)$. For each item p_i (except the initially fingered item) let q_i be the fingered item from which the search for p_i was made. Each q_i is also in $\{p_i | 1 \le i \le \ell\}$ since each finger except the first must be established by a search. Consider the graph G with vertex set $\{p_i | 1 \le i \le \ell\}$ and edge set $\{(q_i, p_i) | 1 \le i \le \ell$ and p_i is not the originally fingered item$\}$.

Some constant times the sum of edge costs in G is a lower bound on the total search cost, since $|\ell(p_i) - \ell(q_i)| + 1$ can only underestimate the actual distance between q_i and p_i when p_i is accessed. We shall describe a way to modify G, while never increasing its cost, until it becomes

$$r_1 - r_2 - \ldots - r_k,$$

where $r_1 < r_2 < \ldots < r_k$ are the k = s+t inserted or deleted leaves. Since the cost of this graph is $\sum\limits_{1 < i \le k} \max(\lceil \log(\ell(r_i) - \ell(r_{i-1}) + 1)\rceil, 1)$ $\le k + \sum\limits_{1 < i \le k} \log(r_i - r_{i-1} + 1)$, the theorem then follows from theorem 12.

The initial graph G is connected, since every accessed item must be reached from the initially fingered item. We first delete all but $\ell - 1$ edges from G so as to leave a spanning tree; this only decreases the cost of G.

Next, we repeat the following step until it is no longer applicable: let $p_i - p_j$ be an edge of G such that there is an accessed item p_k satisfying $p_i < p_k < p_j$. Removing edge $p_i - p_j$ now divides G into exactly two connected components. If p_k is in the same connected component as p_i, we replace $p_i - p_j$ by $p_k - p_j$; otherwise, we replace $p_i - p_j$ by $p_i - p_k$. The new graph is still a tree spanning $\{p_i | 1 \le i \le \ell\}$ and the cost has not increased.

Finally, we eliminate each item p_j which is not an inserted or deleted leaf by transforming $p_i - p_j - p_k$ to $p_i - p_k$, and by removing edges $p_j - p_k$ where there is no other edge incident to p_j. This does not increase cost, and it results in the tree of inserted or deleted items

$$r_1 - r_2 - \ldots - r_k$$

as desired.   □

Finger trees can be used effectively for many basic set operations such as union, intersection, difference, symmetric difference, ...

__Theorem 14:__ Let A and B be sets represented as level-linked (a,b)-trees, $b \geq 2a$ and $a \geq 2$.

a) Insert(x,A), Access(x,A), Delete(x,A), Concatenate(A,B), Split(x,A) take logarithmic time.

b) Let $n = \max(|A|,|B|)$ and $m = \min(|A|,|B|)$. Then $A \cup B$, $A \otimes B$, $A \cap B$, $A \smallsetminus B$ can be constructed in time $O(\log(\genfrac{}{}{0pt}{}{n+m}{m}))$.

__Proof:__ a) It is easy to see that theorems 5 and 6 are true for level-linked (a,b)-trees.

b) We show how to construct $A \otimes B = (A - B) \cup (B - A)$. Assume w.l.o.g. $|A| \geq |B|$. The algorithm is as follows.

(1) establish a finger at the first element of A;
(2) __while__ B not exhausted
(3) __do__ take the next element, say x, of B and search for it in A starting at the finger;
(4)   insert x into or delete x from A, whatever is appropriate;
(5)   establish a finger at the position of x in A and destroy the old finger
(6) __od__

Let $p_1,\ldots,p_m$, $m = |B|$, be the positions of the elements of B in the set $A \cup B$, let $p_o = 1$. Then the above program   takes time

$$O(m + \log(n+m) + \sum_{i=0}^{m-1} \log(p_{i+1} - p_i + 1))$$

by theorem 13 and the observation that total search time is bounded by

$$\sum_{i=1}^{m-1} \log(p_{i+1} - p_i + 1).$$

This expression is maximized for $p_{i+1} - p_i = (n+m)/m$ for all i, and then has value $O(\log(n+m) + m \log((n+m)/m)) = O(m \log((n+m)/m))$ $= O(\log(\binom{n+m}{m}))$.

In the case of A ∪ B, we only do insertions in line (4). In the case of A ∩ B, we collect the elements of A ∩ B in line (4) (there are at most m of them) and construct a level-linked (a,b)-tree for them afterwards in time O(m).

Finally we have to consider A ∖ B. If |A| ≥ |B|, then we use the program above. If |A| < |B| then we scan through A linearly, search for the elements of A in B as described above (roles of A and B reversed) and delete the appropriate elements from A. Apparently, the same time bound holds.   □

Note that there are $\binom{n+m}{m}$ possibilities for B as a subset of A ∪ B. Hence $\log \binom{n+m}{m}$ is also a lower bound on the complexity of union and symmetric difference.

III. 5.3.4 Fringe Analysis

Fringe analysis is a technique which allows us to treat some aspects of random (a,b)-trees. Let us first make the notion of random (a,b)-tree precise. A random (a,b)-tree is grown by random insertions starting with the empty tree. Let T be an (a,b)-tree with j leaves. An insertion of a new element into T is random if each of the j leaves of T is equally likely to be split by the insertion. This can also be phrased in terms of search trees. Let S be a set with j - 1 elements and let T be a search tree for S ∪ {∞}. Then the elements of S split the universe into j intervals. The insertion of a new element x is random if x has equal probability for being in any one of the j intervals defined above.

We use fringe analysis to derive bounds on $\bar{n}(N)$, the expected number of nodes in a random (a,b)-tree with N leaves, i.e. a tree obtained by N random insertions from an empty tree. Then $\bar{n}(N)(2b-1)$ is the average number of storage locations required for a random (a,b)-tree with N leaves. Since any (a,b)-tree with N leaves has at least $(N-1)/(b-1)$ nodes and hence uses at least $(2b-1)(N-1)/(b-1)$ storage locations we can define $\bar{s}(N) := (N-1)/((b-1)\,\bar{n}(N))$ as the storage utilization of a random (a,b)-tree. We show that $\bar{s}(N) \approx 0.69$ if b = 2a and a is large. This is in marked contrast to worst case storage utilization of $(a-1)/(b-1) \approx 0.5$.

For T an (a,b)-tree let n(T) be the number of nodes of T and let $p_N(T)$ be the probability that T is obtained by N random insertions from the empty tree. Of course, $p_N(T)$ is zero if the number of leaves of T is unequal N. Then

$$\bar{n}(N) = \sum_T p_N(T)\ n(T)$$

Fringe analysis is based on the fact that most nodes of an (a,b)-tree are close to the leaves. Therefore a good estimate of $\bar{n}(N)$ can be obtained by just estimating the number of nodes on the level one above the leaves.

Let $n_i(T)$ be the number of leaves of T which are sons of a node with exactly i sons, $a \le i \le b$. Then $\sum_i n_i(T) = |T|$, the number of leaves of T. Let

$$\bar{n}_i(N) = \sum_T n_i(T)\ p_N(T). \text{ Then } \sum_i \bar{n}_i(N) = N$$

Lemma 9: a) Let T be an (a,b)-tree and let $r = \sum_i n_i(T)/i$. Then

$$- 1/(b-1) + (1 + 1/(b-1))\ r \le n(T) \le 1 + (1 + 1/(a-1))\ r$$

b) Let $\bar{r}(N) = \sum_i \bar{n}_i(N)/i$. Then

$$- 1/(b-1) + (1 + 1/(b-1))\ \bar{r}(N) \le \bar{n}(N) \le 1 + (1 + 1/(a-1))\ \bar{r}(N)$$

Proof: a) Let m be the number of nodes of T of height 2 or more. Then

$n(T) = m + \sum_i n_i(T)/i$ since $n_i(T)/i$ is the number of nodes of arity i and height 1. Also

$$(\sum_i n_i(T)/i - 1)/(b-1) \le m \le (\sum_i n_i(T)/i - 1)/(a-1) + 1$$

since every node of height 2 or more has at most b and at least a sons (except for the root which has at least two sons) and since there are exactly $\sum_i n_i(T)/i$ nodes of height 1 in T. The 1 on the right hand side accounts for the fact that the degree of the root might be as low as 2.

b) immediate from part a) and the definition of $\bar{n}_i(N)$ and $\bar{n}(N)$.   □

We infer from lemma 9 that $\bar{n}(N)$ is essentially $\sum_i \bar{n}_i(N)/i$. We determine this quantity by setting up recursion equations for $\bar{n}_i(N)$ and solving them.

Lemma 1o: Let $b = 2a$ and $a \ge 2$. Then

$$\bar{n}_a(N+1) = \bar{n}_a(N) + a(\bar{n}_b(N) - \bar{n}_a(N))/N$$

$$\bar{n}_{a+1}(N+1) = \bar{n}_{a+1}(N) + (a+1)(\bar{n}_b(N) + \bar{n}_a(N) - \bar{n}_{a+1}(N))/N$$

and

$$\bar{n}_i(N+1) = \bar{n}_i(N) + i(\bar{n}_{i-1}(N) - \bar{n}_i(N))/N \text{ for } a+2 \le i \le b$$

Proof: We prove the second equation and leave the two others to the reader. Let T be an (a,b)-tree with N leaves. Consider a random insertion into T resulting in tree T'. Note that $n_{a+1}(T') - n_{a+1}(T)$ grows by $a + 1$ if the insertion is into a node with either exactly a (probability $n_a(T)/N$) or b (probability $n_b(T)/N$) leaf sons and that $n_{a+1}(T') - n_{a+1}(T)$ goes down by a+1 if the insertion is into a node of height 1 with exactly a+1 sons (probability $n_{a+1}(T)/N$). Thus

$$\bar{n}_{a+1}(N+1) = \sum_T p_N(T)[n_{a+1}(T) + (a+1)(n_b(T)/N + n_a(T)/N - n_{a+1}(T)/N)]$$

$$= \bar{n}_{a+1}(N) + (a+1)(\bar{n}_b(N) + \bar{n}_a(N) - \bar{n}_{a+1}(N))/N \qquad □$$

Let Q(N) be the column-vector $(\bar{n}_a(N), \ldots, \bar{n}_b(N))^T$. Then lemma 1o can be written in matrix form as

$$Q(N+1) = (I + \frac{1}{N} B)Q(N)$$

where

$$B = \begin{pmatrix} -a & & & & & a \\ a+1 & -(a+1) & & & & a+1 \\ & a+2 & -(a+2) & & & \\ & & \ddots & \ddots & & \\ & & & & \ddots & \\ & & & & +b & -b \end{pmatrix}$$

With $q(N) = (1/N) Q(N)$ this can be rewritten as

$$q(N+1) = (I + \frac{1}{N+1} (B-I)) q(N)$$

Note that matrix B-I is singular since each column sums to zero. We show below that $q(N)$ converges to q, a right eigenvector of B-I with respect to eigenvalue 0, as N goes to infinity. Also $|q(N) - q| = O(N^{-c})$ for some $c > 0$. This is shown in theorem 16.

We will next determine $q = (q_a, \ldots, q_b)^T$. From $(B-I)q = 0$ and $\sum_i q_i = \lim_{N \to \infty} \sum_i \bar{n}_i(N)/N = 1$ one concludes

$$q_a = a/((a+1)(b+1)(H_b - H_a))$$

and

$$q_i = 1/((i+1)(H_b - H_a)) \qquad \text{for } a+1 \le i \le b$$

where $H_a = \sum_{i=1}^{a} 1/i$ is the a-th harmonic number.

(The q_i's, $a \le i \le b$, can be found as follows: take q_b as an indeterminate and solve (B-I)q for $q_{b-1}, q_{b-2}, \ldots, q_{a+2}, q_a, q_{a+1}$ in that order. Then use $\sum_i q_i = 1$ to determine q_b). Thus

$$\sum_{i=a}^{b} q_i/i = (\frac{1}{(a+1)(b+1)} + \sum_{i=a+1}^{b} \frac{1}{i(i+1)})/(H_b - H_a)$$

$$= (\frac{1}{(a+1)(b+1)} + \sum_{i=a+1}^{b} (\frac{1}{i} - \frac{1}{i+1}))/(H_b-H_a)$$

$$= (\frac{1}{(a+1)(b+1)} + \frac{1}{a+1} - \frac{1}{b+1})/(H_b-H_a)$$

$$= ((b+1)(H_b-H_a))^{-1} \qquad , \text{ since } b = 2a$$

<u>Theorem 15:</u> Let $b = 2a$ and $a \geq 2$, let $\epsilon > 0$ and let $\bar{s}(N) = (N-1)/((b-1)\bar{n}(N))$ be the storage utilization of a random (a,b)-tree with N leaves. Then

$$|\bar{s}(N) - \ell n2| \leq C/a + \epsilon$$

for some constant C independent of N and a and all sufficiently large N.

<u>Proof:</u> Note first that

$$\frac{N}{(b-1)(1+1/(a-1))\bar{r}(N)} - \epsilon \leq \bar{s}(N) \leq \frac{N}{(b-1)(1+1/(b-1))\bar{r}(N)} + \epsilon$$

for all sufficiently large N by lemma 9b. Here $\bar{r}(N)/N = \sum_i q_i(N)/i =$
$\sum_i q_i/i + O(N^{-c}) = 1/((b+1)(H_b-H_a)) + O(N^{-c})$ for some constant $c > 0$.
Furthermore $H_b-H_a = \sum_{i=a+1}^{b} 1/i = \ell n2 + O(1/a)$ since $\int_{a+1}^{b+1} (1/x)dx \leq$
$\sum_{i=a+1}^{b} 1/i \leq \int_a^b (1/x)dx$.

Thus $|\bar{s}(N) - \ell n2| \leq C/a + \epsilon$ for all sufficiently large N and some constant C. □

Storage utilization of a random $(a,2a)$-tree is thus about $\ell n2 \approx 69\%$. Fringe analysis can also be used to sharpen theorem 8 on the total rebalancing cost. The bound in theorem 8 was derived under the pessimistic assumption that every insertion/deletion decreases the value of the tree by 1. Fringe analysis provides us with a smaller bound at least if we restrict attention to random sequences of insertions. It is not hard to define what we mean by a random deletion; any leaf of the tree is removed with equal probability. However, it seems to be very hard to extend fringe analysis to random insertions and deletions.

We still have to prove convergence of sequence q(N), N = 1,2,... . The answer is provided by the following general theorem which is applicable to fringe analysis problems of other types of trees also.

<u>Theorem 16</u>: Let $H = (h_{ij})_{1 \leq i, j \leq m}$ be a matrix such that

1) all off-diagonal elements are non-negative and each column of H sums to zero and

2) there is an i such that for all j there are $j_0, \ldots, j_k$ with $i = j_0$, $j = j_k$ and $h_{j_\ell, j_{\ell+1}} > 0$ for $0 \leq \ell < k$. Then

a) Let $\lambda_1, \ldots, \lambda_m$ be the eigenvalues of H in decreasing order of real part. Then $\lambda_1 = 0 > \text{Re}(\lambda_2) > \text{Re}(\lambda_3) \geq \ldots \geq \text{Re}(\lambda_m)$

b) Let q(0) be any non-zero m-vector and define $q(N+1) = (I + \frac{1}{N+1} H)q(N)$ for $N \geq 0$. Then q(N) converges to q a right eigenvector of H with respect to eigenvalue 0 and $|q - q(N)| = O(N^{\text{Re } \lambda_2})$.

<u>Proof</u>: a) H is singular since each column of H sums to zero. Thus 0 is an eigenvalue of H. Furthermore, all eigenvalues of H are contained in the union of the disks with center h_{jj} and radius $\sum_{i \neq j} |h_{ij}|$, j = 1,2, ...,m. This is the well-known Gerschgorin criterion (cf. Stoer/ Bulirsch: Numerische Mathematik II, page 77). Thus all eigenvalues of H have non-positive real part.

It remains to show that 0 is an eigenvalue of multiplicity one. This is the case iff the linear term in the characteristic polynomial of H (i.e. det(H-λI)) is non-null. The coefficient of the linear term is $\sum_i \det H_{ii}$, where H_{ii} is obtained from H by deleting the i-th row and column. Application of the Gerschgorin criterion to H_{ii} shows that all eigenvalues of H_{ii} have non-positive real part. Since $\det H_{ii} = \varepsilon_1 \ldots \varepsilon_{m-1}$ where $\varepsilon_1, \ldots, \varepsilon_{m-1}$ are the eigenvalues of H_{ii}, we infer that either $\det(H_{ii}) = 0$ or sign $(\det H_{ii}) = (-1)^{m-1}$. Thus $\sum_i \det H_{ii} = 0$ iff $\det H_{ii} = 0$ for all i.

We will next show that $\det H_{ii} \neq 0$ where i satisfies assumption 2) of the theorem. Assume otherwise. Let $u = (u_1, \ldots, u_{i-1}, u_{i+1}, \ldots, u_m)$ be a left eigenvector of H_{ii} with respect to eigenvalue 0. Let u_t be a component of maximal absolute value in u and let $I = \{j; |u_j| = |u_t|\} \subseteq \{1,\ldots,m\} - \{i\}$. Since $i \notin I$ and $I \neq \emptyset$ there must be $j \in I$, $k \notin I$, such that $h_{kj} > 0$ by assumption 2. We may assume w.l.o.g. that $u_j > 0$. Thus

$$\sum_{\ell \neq i} u_\ell h_{\ell j} \leq u_j \left(\sum_{\ell \in I} h_{\ell j} + \sum_{\ell \notin I} (|u_\ell|/u_j) h_{\ell j} \right)$$

$$\leq u_j \left(\sum_\ell h_{\ell j} + (|u_k|/u_j - 1) h_{kj} \right),$$

$$\text{since } |u_\ell| \leq u_j \text{ and } h_{\ell j} \geq 0 \quad \text{for } \ell \neq j$$

$$< 0$$

since $\sum_\ell h_{\ell j} = 0$, $|u_k|/u_j < 1$ and $h_{kj} > 0$. Hence u is not left eigenvector of H_{ii} with respect to eigenvalue 0.

b) Let $f_n(x) = \prod_{j=1}^{n} (1 + x/j)$ and let $f(x) = \lim_{n \to \infty} f_n(x)$. Then $f(0) = f_n(0) = 1$. Also

Claim: $|f_n(x)| \leq C\, n^{\mathrm{Re}\, x}$ for some C depending on x.

Proof: Note first that $|f_n(x)| = \prod_{j=1}^{n} |1 + x/j| = \exp\left(\sum_{j=1}^{n} \ell n\, |1 + x/j| \right)$. Next note that

$$|1 + x/j|^2 = |1 + \mathrm{Re}(x/j)|^2 + |\mathrm{Im}(x/j)|^2$$

$$\leq |1 + \mathrm{Re}(x/j)|^2 (1 + c\, |\mathrm{Im}(x/j)|^2)$$

for some constant c and all $j \geq j_0$ (c and j_0 depend on x). Taking square roots and substituting into the expression for $|f_n(x)|$ yields

$$|f_n(x)| = \exp\left(\sum_{j \leq j_0} \ell n\, |1 + x/j| + \sum_{j=j_0}^{n} (\ell n(1 + \mathrm{Re}(x/j)) + \right.$$

$$\ell n((1 + c\, |\mathrm{Im}(x/j)|^2)^{1/2})$$

$$\leq C\, n^{\mathrm{Re}\, x}$$

for some constant C depending on x since $\ell n(1 + \mathrm{Re}(x/j)) \leq \mathrm{Re}(x)/j$ and $\ell n((1 + c\, |\mathrm{Im}(x/j)|^2)^{1/2}) \leq (c/2)\, |\mathrm{Im}(x)|^2/j^2$. □

Let q(0) be some m-vector and let $q(N+1) = (I + \frac{1}{n+1} H)q(N)$ for $N \geq 0$.

Then $q(N) = f_n(H)q(0)$ where $f_n(H) = \prod_{1 \leq j \leq n} (I + \frac{1}{j} H)$. We consider matrix

$f_n(H)$ in more detail.

Let $J = THT^{-1} = \begin{pmatrix} J_1 & & 0 \\ & \ddots & \\ 0 & & J_K \end{pmatrix}$ be the Jordan matrix corresponding to H;

$J_1, \ldots, J_K$ are the blocks of the Jordan matrix. We have $J_1 = (0)$, i.e.
J_1 is a one by one matrix whose only entry is zero. Also

$$J_\ell = \begin{pmatrix} \lambda_\ell & 1 & & 0 \\ & \ddots & \ddots & \\ & & \ddots & 1 \\ 0 & & & \lambda_\ell \end{pmatrix} \quad \text{with Re } \lambda_\ell < 0. \text{ Then}$$

$f_n(H) = f_n(T^{-1}JT) = T^{-1} f_n(J)T$ as is easily verified. Also

$$f_n(J) = \begin{pmatrix} f_n(J_1) & & & \\ & f_n(J_2) & & \\ & & \ddots & \\ & & & f_n(J_k) \end{pmatrix}$$

We have (cf. Gantmacher, Matrices, chapter V, example 2)

$$f_n(J_\ell) = \begin{pmatrix} f_n(\lambda_\ell) & \frac{f_n^{(1)}(\lambda_\ell)}{1!} & \frac{f_n^{(2)}(\lambda_\ell)}{2!} & \cdots & \frac{f_n^{(v_\ell-1)}(\lambda_\ell)}{v_\ell!} \\ & \ddots & \ddots & & \vdots \\ & & \ddots & & \\ & & & f_n(\lambda_\ell) & \\ & & & & \end{pmatrix}$$

where v_ℓ is the multiplicity of λ_ℓ and $f_n^{(h)}$ is the h-th derivative of
f_n. The reader can easily verify this identity (for every polynomial f_n)
by induction on the degree. Hence $f_n(J_1) = (1)$, the one by one matrix
whose only entry is one and

$$f_n(J_\ell) = \begin{pmatrix} \varepsilon_{1,1}(n) & \cdots & \varepsilon_{1,v_\ell}(n) \\ & \ddots & \vdots \\ 0 & & \varepsilon_{v_\ell,v_\ell}(n) \end{pmatrix}$$

where $\varepsilon_{i,j} = O(n^{Re\ \lambda}2)$. Thus $q(N)$ converges to $q = T^{-1} f(J)T\ q(0)$ as N goes to infinity. Here $f(J)$ is a matrix with a one in position (1,1) and all other entries equal to zero. Also $H \cdot q = (T^{-1}JT)(T^{-1}f(J)Tq(0)) = T^{-1} J\ f(J)\ T\ q(0) = T^{-1} O\ T\ q(0)$ where O is the all zero matrix. Hence $H\ q = 0$, i.e. q is right eigenvector of H with respect to eigenvalue O. Finally, $|q(N) - q| = O(n^{Re\ \lambda}2)$.

$\square$

III. 6. Dynamic Weighted Trees

In this section we will combine some of the results of section III.4. on weighted trees and section III.5. on dynamic trees and treat <u>dynamic weighted trees</u>. The szenario is as follows: We are given a set $S = \{x_1,\ldots,x_n\}$, $x_1 < x_2 < \ldots < x_n$, of n elements and weights $w_i \in \mathbb{N}$, $1 \le i \le n$. In section 4 we saw how to build good static trees for weighted set S, i.e. we showed how to support operation Access in logarithmic time. More precisely, a search for x_i had essentially cost $O(\log W/w_i)$ where $W = w_1 + w_2 + \ldots + w_n$ is the total weight of set S. Section 5 was devoted to dynamic unweighted sets, i.e. we showed how to realize operations Insert, Delete, Access, Concatenate and Split on unweighted sets in logarithmic time. We will now combine both approaches and show how to do Insert, Delete, Access, Concatenate and Split on weighted sets. What kind of behaviour can we expect in view of the results of section 4? The cost of an Access to an element of weight w in a set of total weight W can certainly be no cheaper than $O(\log W/w)$. Similarly, deleting an element of weight w or splitting at an element of wight w can be no cheaper than accessing and therefore must have cost $\Omega(\log W/w)$. Demotion (decrease the weight by some $\delta > 0$) can be no cheaper than accessing the "demoted element" and therefore must have cost $\Omega(\log W/(w-\delta))$. Promotion (increase the weight by some $\delta > 0$) can be no cheaper than accessing the element in the "promoted" tree and therefore must have cost $\Omega(\log(W+\delta)/w)$. An Insert might have to add a leaf between leaves of minimum weight. It is therefore reasonable to expect that an Insert requires time $\Omega(\log(W+w))$; in fact we will be able to achieve a slightly better bound, namely $O(\log(W+w)/\min(w',w,w''))$ where w' and w" are the weights of the two neighbors of the new node. Finally, a Concatenate operation joins two trees of weight W_1 and W_2 respectively. We might hope to do Concatenates in time $O(\log(W_1+W_2)/\min(W_1,W_2))$. However, we will not be able to achieve that bound (note that even in the unweighted case the cost of a join is related to the height difference of the operand trees which is in general not related to the log of the weight ratio (cf. exercises 28 and 38) and therefore will only show a bound of $O(\log(W_1+W_2)/w)$ where w is the weight of the rightmost element of the first tree.

The main result of this section is that these time bounds are in fact achievable. How can we proceed? How can we generalize weight-balanced or height-balanced trees in order to cope with elements of different weights? A first idea is to balance weights and cardinalities of sets in weight-balanced trees (cf. the generalization of binary search from unweighted to weighted sets in 4.1.) or to let the height of a leaf depend on the weight of the leaf in height-balanced trees, e.g. to set the height of a leaf of weight w to $\lfloor\log w\rfloor$. The following example shows that this idea does not work in its pure form. Consider a set of three elements of weight 1, n, and 1 respectively.

In a weight-balanced binary tree the root will have balance $1/(n+2)$ which can be arbitrarily close to 0. In a height-balanced tree we have three leaves of height log 1, log n and log 1 respectively, i.e. the height of brother nodes can differ by arbitrary amounts.

Three approaches have been considered to the remedy the situation. In the historically first approach one gives up the concept that each element $x \in S$ is represented by a single leaf. Rather, one splits the weight of heavy elements into smaller pieces so as to maintain the balancing criterion. In our example we might represent object $x_2 \in S$ by leaves of weight $2,2,4,\ldots,n/4,n/4,\ldots,4,2,2$ and obtain a balanced tree in this way. Only one of these leaves, namely one of the large pieces of weight

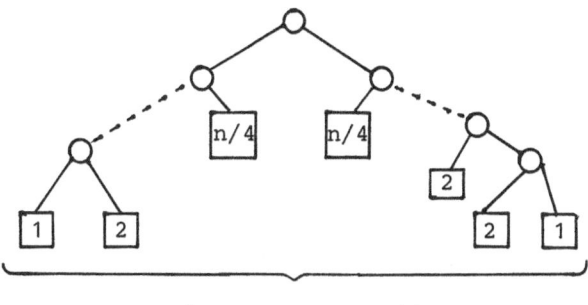

leaves representing

$x_2 \in S$

$n/4$, "really" represents x_2 and searches for x_2 are directed to that
leaf, all other leaves are only there to maintain the fiction of a
fully balanced tree · The details of this approach can be found in
section 6.2.

The historically second approach which can be found in S.W. Bent, D.D.
Sleator, R.E. Tarjan: Biased 2-3 Trees, 21st FOCS, 1980, 248-254,
or H. Güting, H.P. Kriegel: Dynamic k-dimensional search, 5th GI-
Conference on Theoretical Computer Science, LNCS 104,135-145, starts
from the observation that unbalanced nodes need only occur close to
leaves. This can be seen as follows. Suppose that we want to store
elements with weights $w_1, \ldots, w_n$ in the leaves of a binary tree. Let i
be such that $w_1 + \ldots + w_{i-1} \le W/2 \le w_1 + \ldots + w_i$ where $W = w_1 + \ldots +$
w_n. If either $w_1 + \ldots + w_{i-1} > W/3$ or $w_1 + \ldots + w_i \le 2W/3$ then we can
construct a tree with root balance in interval $[1/3, 2/3]$. Otherwise,
we must have $w_i \ge W/3$ and $1 < i < n$ or $w_i \ge 2W/3$ and $i = 1$ or $i = n$.
In either case, one of the following trees is a good search tree; it

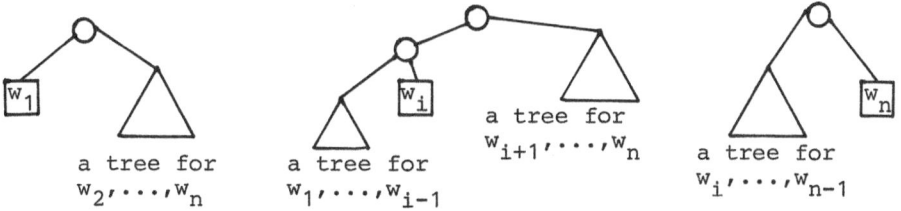

has an unbalanced root and all non-trivial subtrees have weight at most
$W/3$. Thus logarithmic search time is guaranteed and unbalanced nodes
only occur near leaves. A similar statement can be made if we look at
height-balanced trees. In their paper on <u>biased trees</u> Bent/Sleator/
Tarjan show that this property can be maintained dynamically and that
the time bounds stated above can be achieved by biased trees.

The historically third approach is discussed in section 6.1.2. It is based on the idea of self-organizing data structures and definitely the most elegant solution.

This section is organized as follows. In section 6.1. we discuss self-organizing data structures and their amortized and average case behavior. Section 6.1.1. is devoted to self-organizing linear lists and 6.1.2. to self-organizing trees. In section 6.2. we describe D-trees and in section 6.3. we discuss an application of dynamic weighted trees to multi-dimensional searching.

III. 6.1   Self-Organizing Data Structures and their Amortized and
           Average Case Analysis

In this section we discuss self-organizing data structures, more precisely self-organizing linear lists and trees. The idea of self-organization is quite simple. Suppose that we have a data-structure for set $S = \{x_1, \dots, x_n\}$. Whenever we access an element of S, say x_i, then we move x_i closer to the entry point of the data structure. This will make subsequent accesses to x_i cheaper. In this way the elements of S compete for the "good" places in the data structure and high-frequency elements are more likely to be there. Note however, that we do not maintain any explicit frequency counts or weights; rather, we hope that the data structure self-organizes to a good data structure.

Since no global information is kept in a self-organizing data structure the worst case behavior of a single operation can always be horrible. However, the average and the amortized behavior may be good. For an average case analysis we need to have probabilities for the various operations. The data structure then leads to a Markov chain whose states are the different incarnations of the data structure. We can then use probability theory to compute the stationary probabilities of the various states and use these probabilities to derive bounds on the expected behavior of the data structure. In section 6.1.1 we will carry out an average case analysis of self-organizing linear lists.

Amortized analysis is the worst case analysis of an algorithm for a (worst-case) sequence of operations, i.e. the goal of amortized analysis is to derive an upper bound on the cost of a sequence of operations.

We have seen several examples of amortized analysis already, most
notably (a,b)-trees and BB[α]-trees. There are many more examples to
come.

In the analysis of (a,b)-trees we used the <u>bank account paradigm</u>. For
the application of the paradigm in this section we need to discuss its
principles in more detail. Consider a sequence $Op_1, \ldots, Op_m$ of operations
leading us from an initial data structure D_o to a final data structure
D_m.

$$D_o \xrightarrow{\;Op_1\;} D_1 \xrightarrow{\;Op_2\;} \ldots \xrightarrow{\;Op_m\;} D_m$$

Suppose also that we have a function bal: $\{D_o, D_1, \ldots\} \to \mathbb{R}$ from the set
of possible data structures into the set of reals. If D is a data
structure then we call bal(D) the <u>balance</u> of the account of the
structure. A unit of balance represents the ability to pay for O(1)
units of computing time. We <u>define</u> the <u>amortized</u> <u>cost</u> of operation Op_i
by

(x) $a_i := t_i + bal(D_i) - bal(D_{i-1})$

where t_i is the actual execution time of operation Op_i.

<u>Example:</u> In our analysis of (2,4)-trees (section 5.3.2 with a = 2,
b = 4) we used the following account:
     bal(T) = - |{ v; v is a node of T and has exactly three sons}|.
The actual cost of adding a leaf is 1 + s where s is the number of node
splittings caused by adding the leaf. If adding a leaf to tree T causes
s nodes to split and yields tree T' then bal(T') - bal(T) ≤ -(s-1)
since there are at least (s-1) additional nodes in T' with exactly three
sons. Hence the amortized cost of adding a leaf is at most
1 + s - (s-1) = 2.   □

Summing the defining equation of amortized cost over all operations
yields

$$\sum_{i=1}^{m} t_i = \sum_{i=1}^{m} a_i + bal(D_o) - bal(D_m)$$

, i.e. the total actual cost of the sequence of operations is equal to

254

the total amortized cost plus the net decrease in balance between
initial and final configuration. We will mostly use the concept of
amortization as follows. Suppose that we have defined the intended cost
ic_i of operation Op_i by some means; e.g. in dynamic weighted trees the
intended cost of an access operation to an element of weight w in a set
of total weight W is log W/w. We will then try to find an account for
the data structure, i.e. a function bal, such that the amortized cost
of every operation is bounded by the intended cost, i.e.

$$a_i = t_i + bal(D_i) - bal(D_{i-1}) \le ic_i .$$

Then

$$\sum_{i=1}^{m} t_i \le \sum_{i=1}^{m} ic_i + bal(D_o) - bal(D_m),$$

i.e. total actual cost is bounded by total intended cost plus the net
decrease in balance. Amortization is a means of cost sharing between
operations. Operations which do not require their intended cost, i.e.
$t_i \le ic_i$, pay for the cost of operations which exceed their intended
cost, i.e. $t_i > ic_i$. The sharing between the costs is made by the
account associated with the data structure, i.e. an operation deposits
((or withdraws) $ic_i - t_i$ units into (from) the account in order to cover
the cost difference between intended and actual time bound.

In most cases of amortized analysis, we have either bal(D) $\ge$ O
(positive account) or bal(D) $\le$ O (negative account) for all D.

In the case of a positive account we have

$$\sum_{i=1}^{m} t_i \le \sum_{i=1}^{m} ic_i + bal(D_o)$$

,i.e. actual cost is bounded by intended cost plus initial balance. The
interpretation of a positive account is particularly simple. We start
with an initial investment of bal(D_o) units. Using this initial
investment and the units provided by the intended costs of the
operations we can also cover the actual cost. In other words, we use the
account to have operations pay for the cost of later operations which
might overrun their intended cost.

Example: An example of a positive account is provided by our analysis
of BB[α]-trees, cf. theorems 4 and 5 of section 5.1.

Let $1/4 < \alpha < 1 - \sqrt{2}/2$ and let $\delta > 0$ be defined as in lemma 1 of section 5.1. For a binary tree T let

$$\text{bal}(T) = \Sigma \max (0, \alpha + \delta - \rho(v), \rho(v) - (1 - \alpha - \delta))/\delta$$

where $\rho(v)$ is the root balance of node v and the summation is over all nodes of tree T. We claim that the amortized cost of adding or deleting a leaf is O(1) (this follows from the fact that adding a leaf below a node of thickness th(v) can change its root balance by at most 1/th(v) and that the amortized cost of a rotation or double rotation is zero (this follows from the fact that a node v which causes a rebalancing operation, i.e. $\rho(v) < \alpha$ or $\rho(v) > 1-\alpha$, contributes at least one to bal(T) and does not contribute anything after the rotation). Hence the total number of rotations and double rotations is bounded by the order of the number of insertions and deletions; cf. theorem 4 of section 5.1.

□

In the case of a <u>negative account</u> we have

$$\sum_{i=1}^{m} t_i \leq \sum_{i=1}^{m} ic_i - \text{bal}(D_m)$$

, i.e. actual cost is bounded by intended cost plus final debt. In the case of a negative account we use $\text{bal}(D_m)$ to keep track of the cost overrun, i.e. $|\text{bal}(D_m)|$ measures the overrun of actual cost over intended cost. In other words, we use the account to have later operations pay for the cost of preceding operations, and we use $\text{bal}(D_m)$ to keep track of the final dept.

<u>Example:</u> An example of a negative account is provided by our analysis of (a,b)-trees in section 5.3.2. and by the proof of fact 5 in section 5.3.3. which bounds the number of nodes on the paths from the root to the leaves with position p_i, $0 \leq i \leq r$, in an (a,∞)-tree with N leaves, $p_0 \leq p_1 \leq \ldots \leq p_r$. We let D_i be the path from the root to position p_i, $-\text{bal}(D_i)$ to be the number of edges labelled 0 on path D_i ($\text{bal}(D_i)$ is called A_i in the proof of fact 5), t_i to be the number of nodes on path D_i which do not lie on D_{i-1} (called ℓ_i in the proof of fact 5), and $ic_i = 2 \lfloor \log_a(p_i - p_{i-1} + 1) \rfloor + 3$. Then

$$t_i \leq ic_i + \text{bal}(D_{i-1}) - \text{bal}(D_i)$$

as was shown in the proof of fact 5.

□

III. 6.1.1   Self-Organizing Linear Lists

Self-organizing linear search is quite simple. Let $S = \{x_1, \ldots, x_n\}$. We consider operations Access(x), where $x \in S$ is assumed, Insert(x), where $x \notin S$ is assumed, and Delete(x), where $x \in S$ is assumed. We always organize S as a linear list which may be realized as either an array or a linked list. We use pos(i) to denote the position of element x_i in the list. We assume that the cost of operations Access(x_i) and Delete (x_i) is pos(i) and that the cost of operation Insert(x) is $|S| + 1$.

There are many strategies for self-organizing linear search. Two very popular strategies are the Move-to-Front and the Transposition rule.

Move-to-Front Rule (MFR): Operations Access(x) and Insert(x) make x the first element of the list and leave the order of the remaining elements unchanged; operation Delete(x) removes x from the list.

Transposition Rule (TR): Operation Access(x) interchanges x with the element preceding x in the list, Insert(x) makes x the next to last element and Delete(x) removes x from the list.

Example: We give an example for the Move-to-Front Rule.

$$1\ 3\ 4 \xrightarrow{\text{Insert}(2)} 2\ 1\ 3\ 4 \xrightarrow{\text{Access}(3)} 3\ 2\ 1\ 4 \xrightarrow{\text{Delete}(1)} 3\ 2\ 4$$

The cost of this sequence is 4 + 3 + 3 = 10.

Our first goal of this section is to prove that no algorithm can do significantly better that MFR in an amortized sense. We will derive this result in three steps. In the first step we will compare MFR with the frequency decreasing strategy and motivate the account used in the third step. In the second step we define the general concept of an algorithm for maintainig linear lists and its cost and in the third step we will actually derive the result.

For the first step we will restrict ourselves to sequences of access operations only. Let s be such a sequence and let k_i, $1 \le i \le n$ be the number of accesses to element x_i in sequence s. We may assume w.l.o.g. that $k_1 \ge k_2 \ge \ldots \ge k_n$. In the frequency decreasing rule (FDR) we organize S as list $x_1, x_2, \ldots, x_n$ and never change this arrangement. The cost of processing list s under the FD-rule is clearly

$$C_{FDR}(s) = \sum_{i=1}^{n} i k_i.$$ We will show that the cost C_{MFR} is at most twice

that much.

Lemma 1: Let $C_{MFR}(s)$ be the cost of processing sequence s under the MF-rule starting with initial list $x_1, x_2, \ldots, x_n$. Then $C_{MFR}(s) \le 2C_{FDR}(s) - m$ where m is the length of sequence s.

Proof: Let t_j^i, $1 \le j \le k_i$, be the cost of the j-th access to element x_i under the move-to-front rule. We are going to derive a bound on

$$C_{MFR}(s) - C_{FDR}(s) = \sum_{i=1}^{n} \sum_{j=1}^{k_i} t_j^i - \sum_{i=1}^{n} i k_i = \sum_{i=1}^{n} (\sum_{j=1}^{k_i} (t_j^i - i)).$$

Consider an arbitrary pair i,j. If $t_j^i > i$ then there must have been at least $t_j^i - i$ accesses to elements x_h, $h > i$, between the (j-1)-th and the j-th access to element x_i (the o-th access is the initial configuration). Hence

$$\sum_{j=1}^{k_i} (t_j^i - i) \le k_{i+1} + \ldots + k_n$$

for all i, $1 \le i \le n$, and therefore

$$C_{MFR}(s) - C_{FDR}(s) \le \sum_{i=1}^{n} (k_{i+1} + \ldots + k_n)$$

$$= \sum_{i=1}^{n} (i-1) k_i = C_{FDR}(s) - m \qquad \square$$

There is another way of interpreting the proof of lemma 1 which leads to an account to be used later. We argued above that if $t_j^i > i$ then there were at least $t_j^i - i$ accesses... . This suggests to charge the "excess cost" of $t_j^i - i$ of the j-th access to x_i to the accesses to elements x_h, $h > i$, between the (j-1)-th and the j-th access to x_i, i.e.

to charge the excess cost to those x_h, $h > i$, which are in front of x_i when item x_i is accessed for the j-th time. In other words, whenever we access x_h then we charge an extra h-1 time units to this access and use these time units to pay for the excess cost of accesses to elements x_i, $i < h$. In this way, the amortized cost of accessing x_h is 2h - 1.

We can formalize this idea by using an account with balance

$$\sum_{i=1}^{n} |\{ x_h;\ h > i \text{ and } x_h \text{ is in front of } x_i \text{ in the current list }\}|$$

This completes the first step.

In the second step we need to define the general concept of an algorithm for maintaining linear lists and define the running time of such an algorithm. We assume that all algorithms work as follows. To access an element, the list is scanned from the front until the element is located. The cost of accessing element x is the position of x in the list. In order to insert x the element x is added to the rear end of the list, and in order to delete x the element is removed from the list. The cost of an insert is the length of the sequence after the insert and the cost of deleting x is the position of x. Finally, an algorithm has the possibility for rearranging the list at any time. After operations Access(x) and Insert(x) we allow x to be moved closer to the front of the list. Such an exchange is called a <u>free exchange</u> and has no cost. Any other exchange of a pair of consecutive items is called a <u>paid</u> <u>exchange</u> and has a cost of one. Note that the MF-rule and the TR-rule use only free exchanges. We are now ready for the main theorem of this section.

<u>Theorem 1:</u> Let s be an arbitrary sequence of Access, Insert, and Delete operations starting with the empty list and let A be an arbitrary algorithm. Let $C_A(s)$ be the cost of algorithm A on sequence s not counting paid exchanges, let $X_A(s)$ be the number of paid exchanges, and let m be the length of sequence s. Then

$$C_{MFR}(s) \leq 2\ C_A(s) + X_A(s) - F_A(s) - m$$

<u>Proof:</u> We use the bank account paradigm. Let s' be a prefix of s and let L_{MFR} and L_A be the sequences obtained by processing s' under algorithm MFR and A respectively. Assume w.l.o.g. that $L_A = (x_1\ x_2 ... x_n)$. We define our account by

$$\text{bal}(L_{MFR}) = \sum_{i=1}^{n} |\{x_h;\ h > i \text{ and } x_h \text{ is in front of } x_i \text{ in } L_{MFR}\}|$$

$$= \sum_{h=1}^{n} |\{x_i;\ h > i \text{ and } x_i \text{ is behind } x_h \text{ in } L_{MFR}\}|$$

Note that the balance of L_{MFR} is defined with respect to the numbering of elements defined by list L_A. If we want to emphasize this dependency we write $bal(L_{MFR}, L_A)$ instead of $bal(L_{MFR})$.

Let Op be the operation following s' in sequence s. Since an Insert can be viewed as an Access to a fictitious element x_{n+1} we may assume w.l.o.g. that Op is either Access(x_i) for some i, $1 \le i \le n + 1$, or Delete(x_i) for some i. Let t be the position of element x_i in list L_{MFR}. Then the cost of operation Op is t under the MF-rule and i under algorithm A. Note that algorithm A changes list L_A only in a trivial way when processing Op (either by adding x_i at the end or by deleting x_i). We count the effect of the free and paid exchange performed by algorithm A seperately. We have the following claim:

Claim: a) The amortized cost of operation Op is at most $2i - 1$ where i is its cost under algorithm A.

   b) The amortized cost of a free exchange of algorithm A is -1.

   c) The amortized cost of a paid exchange of algorithm A is at most +1.

Proof: a) Let $bal' = bal(L'_{MFR}, L'_A)$ and $bal = bal(L_{MFR}, L_A)$ where the prime denotes the lists after performing operation Op. Since the actual cost of Op is t its amortized cost is $t + bal' - bal$. It therefore suffices to show that $t + bal' - bal \le 2i - 1$.
Let k be the number of items x_h with $h > i$ and x_h is in front of x_i in L_{MFR}. Then $k + (i-1) \ge t - 1$ and hence $k \ge t - i$.

If operation Op accesses element x_i then $bal' - bal \le - k + (i-1)$ since there are k items x_h with $h > i$ and x_h is in front of x_i in L_{MFR} but not in L'_{MFR} and since there are at most $i - 1$ items x_j with $j < i$ and x_i is in front of x_j in L_{MFR} but not in L_{MFR}. This proves $bal' - bal \le - k + (i-1) \le 2i - 1 - t$ if Op accessses element x_i.
If operation Op deletes element x_i then the same argument shows that $bal' - bal = - k \le i - t$.

In either case we conclude that $t + bal' - bal \le 2i - 1$.

b) and c). Note first that the actual cost of a free or paid exchange of algorithm A is zero since no action of algorithm MFR is involved.

Also, a free exchange decreases the balance of list L_{MFR} by one and a paid exchange can increase the balance by at most one.   □

We can now finish the proof by observing that the balance of the initial list is zero, that we deal with a positive account, and by appealing to the bank account paradigm. Hence

$$C_{MFR}(s) \leq 2\, C_A(s) + X_A(s) - F_A(s) - m$$ □

Theorem 1 is a fairly strong statement about the quality of the move-to-front rule: no conceivable algorithm, not even an algorithm which has advance knowledge about the entire sequence of requests, can beat the MF-rule by more than a factor of two. No such result is true for the transposition rule. Consider the following sequence: We first insert $x_1, x_2, \ldots, x_n$ in that order; this generates sequence $x_2 \ldots x_n x_1$ under the transposition rule. We now alternately access x_1 and x_n. The cost of this sequence of requests is $\Omega(n^2 + (m-n)n)$ under the TR-rule. However, the cost under the MF-rule is only $O(n^2 + m)$ which is smaller by an arbitrary factor.

It is also interesting to consider theorem 1 in the case where the initial lists are non-empty. Suppose that we process sequence s and start with initial lists L_{MFR} and L_A of n items each respectively. Then

$$C_{MFR}(s) \leq 2\, C_A(s) + X_A(s) - F_A(s) - m + bal(L_{MFR}, L_A)$$

$$\leq 2\, C_A(s) + X_A(s) - F_A(s) - m + n^2$$

by the proof of theorem 1 and since $bal(L_{MFR}, L_A) \leq n^2$.
This inequality can be interpreted as follows. The MF-rule needs $O(n^2)$ time units in order to make up for the unfavorable initial configuration; after that its cost is at most twice the cost of algorithm A.

For the remainder of this section we turn to expected case behavior. We do so for two reasons:

   - we want to demonstrate the use of Markov chains for the average case analysis of algorithms,
   - we want to show that the MF-rule and the TR-rule have very good expected case behavior. The behavior of the TR-rule is discussed in exercise 44.

For the expected case analysis we consider only sequences of Access operations. Let $S = \{x_1,\ldots,x_n\}$ and let β_i be the probability of an Access to element x_i, $1 \le i \le n$. We assume w.l.o.g. that $\beta_1 \ge \beta_2 \ge \ldots \ge \beta_n$. The frequency decreasing rule arranges S as list $x_1x_2\ldots x_n$ and has expected access time $P_{FDR} = \sum\limits_{i=1}^{n} i\beta_i$. We use the letter P instead of C to emphasize that we discuss expected behavior from now on. The expected access time of the frequency decreasing rule is easily seen to be optimal. Consider a sequence $\ldots x_j x_i \ldots$ in which x_j is directly in front of x_i and $j > i$. Exchanging this pair of elements changes the expected access time by $\beta_j - \beta_i$, a non-positive amount. This shows that the expected access time of the FD-rule is optimal.

For the analysis of the MF and the TR rules we use Markov chains. The following diagram illustrates the transposition rule for a set of three elements. The diagram has $6 = 3!$ states

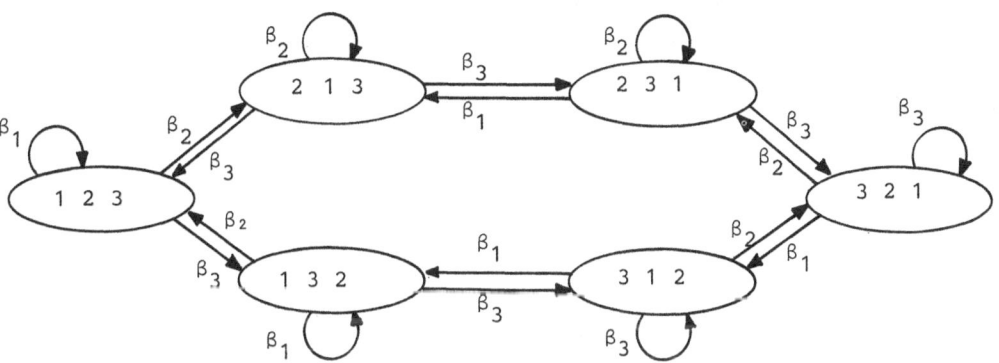

In this diagram 123 denotes linear list $x_1x_2x_3$. If x_3 is accessed (probability β_3) then list $x_1x_2x_3$ is changed into list $x_1x_3x_2$. The transposition rule is analysed in exercise 44.

The move-to-front rule also induces a Markov chain with n! states. The states correspond to the n! linear arrangements of set S, i.e. permutation π represents a linear list where x_i is at position $\pi(i)$. Furthermore, there is a transition from state π to state ρ if there is an i such that $\rho(i) = 1$, $\rho(j) = \pi(j) + 1$ for j such that $\pi(j) < \pi(i)$ and $\rho(j) = \pi(j)$ otherwise. This transition has probability β_i. It is easy to see that this Markov chain is irreducible and aperiodic and therefore stationary probabilities γ_π exist. γ_π is the asymptotic (limiting) probability that the chain is in state π, i.e. that x_i is at position $\pi(i)$ for $1 \le i \le n$. Then

$$P_{MFR} = \sum_{\pi} \gamma_{\pi} \sum_{i} \beta_i \ \pi(i)$$

is the asymptotic expected search time under the move-to-front rule.

<u>Lemma 2:</u> Let $\delta(j,i)$ be the asymptotic probability that x_j is in front of x_i. Then

a) $\quad P_{MFR} = \sum_{i} \beta_i (1 + \sum_{j \neq i} \delta(j,i))$

b) $\quad \delta(j,i) = \beta_j/(\beta_i + \beta_j)$

<u>Proof:</u> a) Let $p_i = \sum_{\pi} \gamma_{\pi} \pi(i)$. Then $P_{MFR} = \sum_{i} \beta_i \cdot p_i$ and p_i is the expected position of element x_i. Furthermore,

$$p_i = \sum_{\pi} \gamma_{\pi} \ \pi(i)$$

$$= \sum_{\pi} \gamma_{\pi} \ (1 + |\{j; \ \pi(j) < \pi(i)\}|)$$

$$= 1 + \sum_{j \neq i} \sum \{\gamma_{\pi}; \ \pi(j) < \pi(i)\}$$

$$= 1 + \sum_{j \neq i} \delta(j,i)$$

since $\sum \{\gamma_{\pi}; \ \pi(j) < \pi(i)\}$ is the asymptotic probability that x_j is in front of x_i.

b) x_j is in front of x_i asymptotically if there is a k such that the last k + 1 accesses are an access to x_j followed by k accesses to elements different than x_j and x_i. Hence

$$\delta(j,i) = \beta_j \sum_{k \geq o} (1 - (\beta_i + \beta_j))^k$$

$$= \beta_j/(1 - (1 - (\beta_i + \beta_j)))$$

$$= \beta_j/(\beta_i + \beta_j)$$

$\square$

__Theorem 2:__ Let $\beta_1 \geq \beta_2 \geq \ldots \geq \beta_n$

a) $P_{MFR} = 1 + 2 \sum\limits_{1 \leq j < i \leq n} \beta_i \beta_j / (\beta_i + \beta_j)$

b) $P_{MFR} \leq 2 \cdot P_{FDR} - 1$

__Proof:__ a) We have

$$P_{MFR} = \sum_i \beta_i (1 + \sum_{j \neq i} \delta(j,i)) \qquad \text{by lemma 2a}$$

$$= \sum_i \beta_i (1 + \sum_{j \neq i} \beta_j / (\beta_i + \beta_j)) \qquad \text{by lemma 2b}$$

$$= 1 + \sum_{j \neq i} \beta_i \beta_j / (\beta_i + \beta_j)$$

$$= 1 + 2 \sum_{j < i} \beta_i \beta_j / (\beta_i + \beta_j)$$

b) Since $\beta_j / (\beta_i + \beta_j) \leq 1$ we infer from part a)

$$P_{MFR} \leq 1 + 2 \sum_i \beta_i (i - 1) = 2 P_{FDR} - 1 \qquad \qquad \square$$

Theorem 2 gives a closed form expression for P_{MFR} which is readily evaluated for particular distributions β (exercise 45) and usually shows that the expected cost of the MF-rule is only a few percent above the optimum. Theorem 2 also shows that P_{MFR} is never more than twice the optimum, a result which can also be obtained as a direct consequence of lemma 1. In exercise 44, the expected behavior of the transposition rule is investigated and it is shown that it is never worse than the expected behavior of the move-to-front rule. Thus the TR-rule exemplifies a drastic difference between expected and amortized behavior. The former is very good the latter is very bad.

III. 6.1.2 Splay Trees

Splay trees are a particular kind of self-organizing tree structure which provide us with a very elegant solution to the weighted dictionary problem.

Let U be an ordered set and let w: U → $\mathbb{N}_0$ be a weight function. We
use splay trees for the representation of subsets of U. More specifi-
cally, splay trees support the following operations. We use x to
denote an arbitrary element of U and T to denote trees. Splay trees use
node-oriented storage organization, i.e. items are stored in all nodes.

Access(x,T): if item x is in tree T then return a pointer to its
location, otherwise return <u>nil</u>

Insert(x,T): insert x into tree T and return the resulting tree (i.e. a
pointer to its root)

Delete(x,T): delete x from tree T and return the resulting tree

Join2(T_1,T_2): return a tree representing the items in T_1 followed by
the items in T_2, destroying T_1 and T_2, (this assumes
that all elements of T_1 are smaller than all elements of
T_2)

Join3(T_1,x,T_3): return a tree representing the items in T_1 followed by
x, followed by the items in T_2, destroying T_1 and T_2
(this assumes that all elements of T_1 are smaller than
x which in turn is smaller than all items in T_2).

Split(x,T)   : returns two trees T_1 and T_2; T_1 contains all items of
T smaller than x and T_2 contains all items of T larger
than x (this assumes that x is in tree T); tree T is
destroyed.

Change Weight(x,T,δ): changes the weight of element x by δ. It is
assumed that x belongs to tree T. The operation returns
a tree representing the same set of elements as tree T.

We will implement all operations listed above by means of the following
operation Splay(x,T), which is unique to splay-trees and gives them
their name.

Splay(x,T) : returns a tree representing the same set of elements as

T. If x is in the tree then x becomes the root. If x is
not in the tree then either the immediate predecessor x^-
of x or the immediate successor x^+ of x in T becomes the
root. This operation destroys T.

We will now show how to reduce all other operations to operation Splay.
In order to do Access(x,T) we do Splay(x,T) and then inspect the root.
Note that x is stored in tree T iff x is stored in the root of the tree
returned by Splay(x,T). To do Insert(x,T) we first do Splay(x,T), then
split the resulting tree into one containing all items less than x
and one containing all items greater than x (this is tantamount to
breaking one of the links leaving the root) and then build a new tree
with the root storing x and the two trees being the left and right
subtree. To do Delete(x,T) we do Splay(x,T), discard the root and
join the two subtrees T_1,T_2 by Join2(T_1,T_2). To do Join2(T_1,T_2) we do
Splay($+\infty,T_1$) where $+\infty$ is assumed to be larger than all elements of U
and then make T_2 the right son of the root of the resulting tree. Note
that Splay($+\infty,T_1$) makes the largest element of T_1 the root and hence
creates a tree with an empty right subtree. To do Join3(T_1,x,T_2) we
make T_1 and T_2 the subtrees of a tree with root x. To do Split(x,T)
we do Splay(x,T) and then break the two links leaving the root. Finally,
to do Change Weight(x,t,δ) we do Splay(x,T).

The following diagram illustrates how all other operations are reduced
to Splay

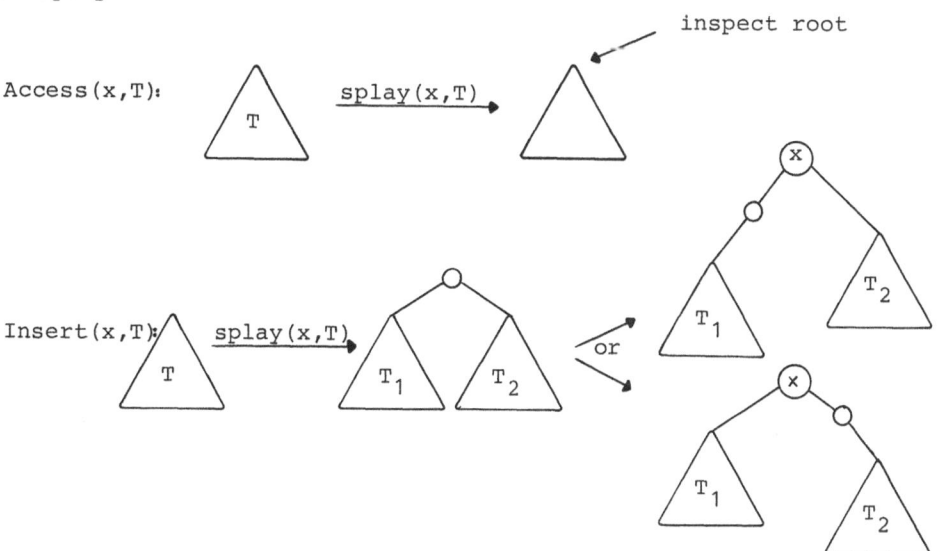

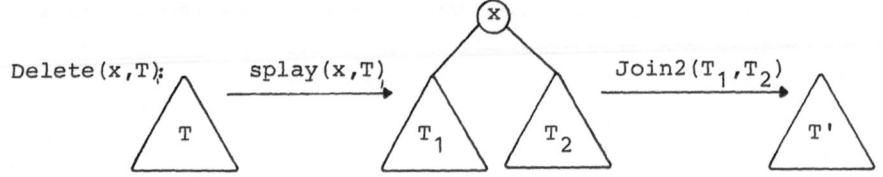

Delete(x,T): $\xrightarrow{\text{splay}(x,T)}$ $\xrightarrow{\text{Join2}(T_1,T_2)}$

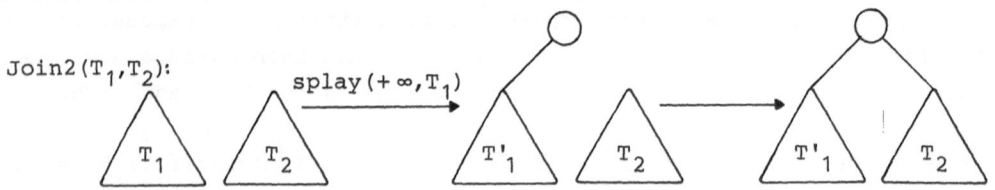

Join2(T_1,T_2): $\xrightarrow{\text{splay}(+\infty,T_1)}$

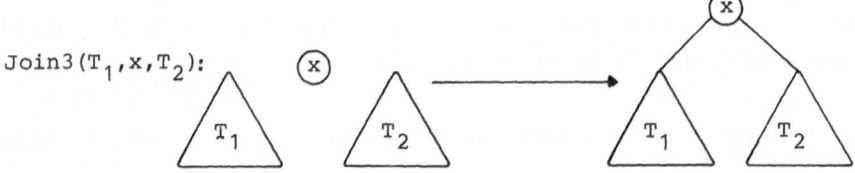

Join3(T_1,x,T_2):

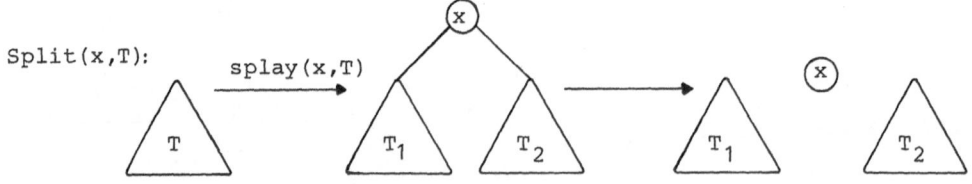

Split(x,T): $\xrightarrow{\text{splay}(x,T)}$

Change Weight(x,T,δ) : Splay(x,T)

It remains to describe the all important operation Splay(x,T). We first
locate the node which is made the root by the splay operation.

```
v ← ↑root;
while  v ≠ nil and v↑.content ≠ x
do  u ← v;
    if  x < v↑.content
    then  v ← v↑.lson  else v ← v↑.rson  fi
od;
if  v ≠ nil  then  u ← v  fi
```

If x is stored in tree T then clearly u points to the node containing x.
If x is not stored in tree T then u points to the last non-nil node on
the search path, i.e. to a node containing either the predecessor or
the successor of x.

We will make node u the root of the tree by a sequence of rotations.
More precisely, we move u to the root by a sequence of splay steps. For
the splay step we distinguish three cases.

Case 1: Node u has a father but no grandfather. Then we perform a
rotation at v = father(u) and terminate the splay operation.

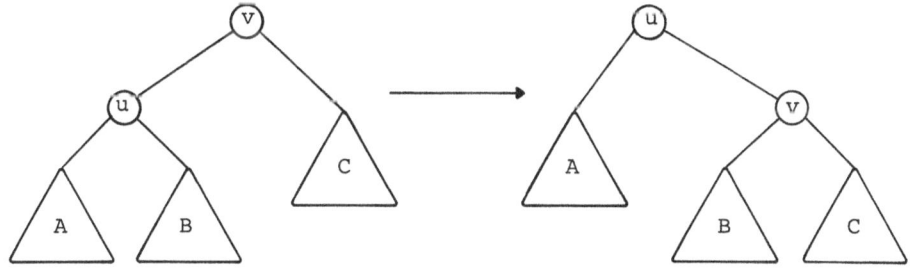

Case 2: Node u has a father v and a grandfather w. Let v the the a-son
of w and let u be the b-son of v, a,b ∈ {left,right}.

Case 2.1. a ≠ b: We perform a rotation at v followed by a rotation at
w. This is tantamount to a double rotation at w.

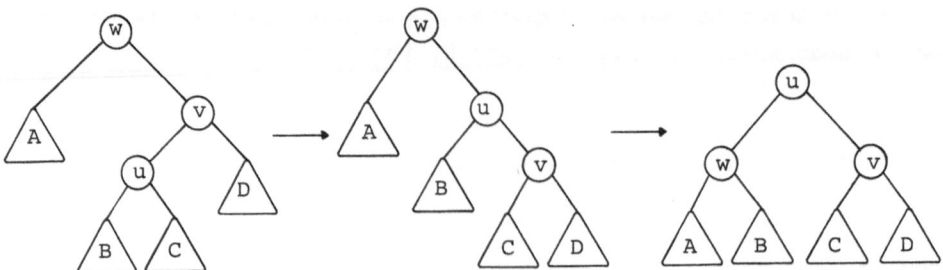

Case 2.2. a = b: We perform a rotation at w followed by a rotation at v.

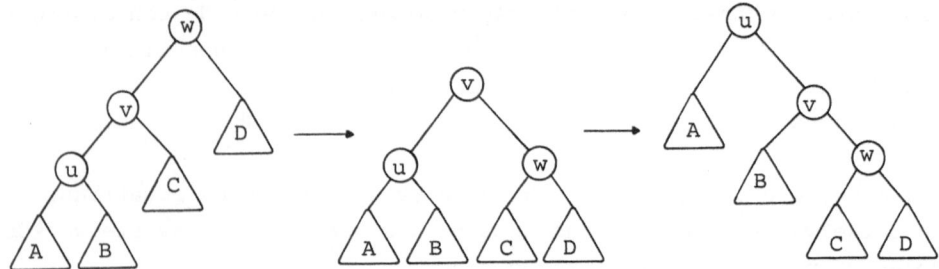

Remark: It is very important that the rotations in case 2.2. are applied in this unconventional order. Note that this order moves node u and its subtrees A and B closer to the root. This is also true for case 2.1. and will be very crucial for the analysis. If the rotations in case 2.2. were performed in the inverse order then the following tree results and this claim were not true.

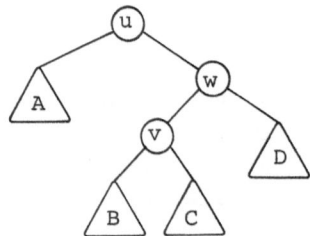

This finishes the description of the splay operation. The following figure shows an example.

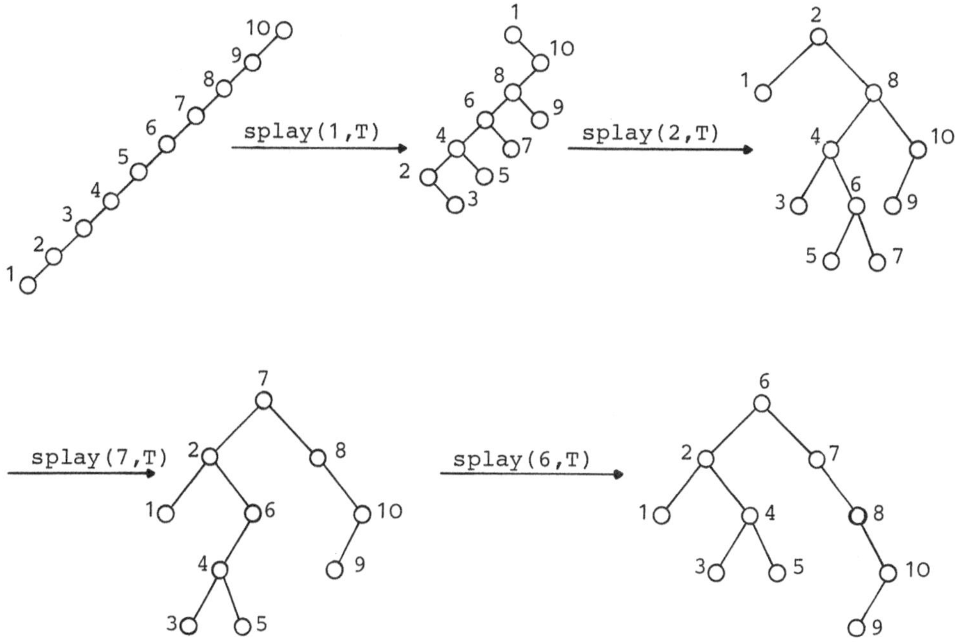

Before we can analyse splay trees we need some more notation. For $x \in U$ we write $w(x)$ to denote the weight of element x. For v a node of a splay tree we write $tw(v)$ to denote the sum of the weights of all elements which are stored in descendants of node v. Note that the total weight of a node changes over time. If T is a splay tree we write $tw(T)$ instead of $tw(root(T))$.

Let u be a node of a splay tree T and let $x \in U$ be the element stored in u. If splay trees are a good implementation of dynamic weighted dictionaries then the (amortized) cost of operation Access(x,T) and hence of operation Splay(x,T) should be $O(\log tw(T)/w(x))$. We aim for the more ambitious bound $O(\log tw(T)/tw(u))$ where u is the node with content x.

What account should we use in order to derive such a bound? Consider a
splay tree T. If T were weight-balanced, i.e. $\alpha \leq tw(lson(v))/tw(v)$
$\leq 1 - \alpha$ for some constant $\alpha > 0$ and every node v then the cost of an access
operation in T would be logarithmic. "Non logarithmic" access time is
therefore related to unbalanced nodes, i.e. nodes v with $tw(lson(v))/$
$tw(v) \approx 1$ or $tw(rson(v))/tw(v) \approx 1$. Let v be an unbalanced node and
consider an access operation which goes through v and proceeds to
$lson(v)$, say. If $tw(rson(v))/tw(v) \approx 1$ and hence $tw(lson(v)/tw(v) \approx 0$
then this search step reduces the total weight of the subproblem more
than we hoped for, i.e. instead of an intended cost of $O(log\ tw(v)/$
$tw(lson(v))$ for reducing the weight from $tw(v)$ to $tw(lson(v))$ the
actual cost is only 1. We should keep the difference between the
intended cost and the actual cost in an account to pay for later cost
overruns. It is natural to conceptually keep the difference between
intended and actual cost on the edge from v to $lson(v)$. Suppose now
that $tw(lson(v))/tw(v) \approx 1$. Then the search step from v to $lson(v)$
brings hardly any progress and therefore we should pay for the search
step out of the account, say by removing one unit from the edge from
v to $rson(v)$. Of course, we should also try to reduce the number of
unbalanced nodes. That is exactly what the splay steps do.

The discussion above suggests that we should use an account of the
form:

$$\sum_{v\ node\ of\ T} log(tw(father(v))/tw(v))$$

$$= \sum_{v\ node\ of\ T} log\ tw(v) - \sum_{v\ leaf\ of\ T} log\ tw(v) + log\ tw(root\ of\ T)$$

If we set the total weights of leaves to 1 (note that leaves do not
contain elements of u), forget about the fact that the root is counted
twice, and for simplicity work with integers instead of reals then we
arrive at

$$bal(T) := \sum_{v\ node\ of\ T} \lfloor log\ tw(v) \rfloor$$

or with the definintion of a rank $r(v) = \lfloor log\ tw(v) \rfloor$ of a node v

$$bal(T) = \sum_{v\ node\ of\ T} r(v).$$

For the following lemma we assume that each splay step takes time 1. We have:

Lemma 3: The amortized cost of operation Splay(x,T) is at most $1 + 3(r(T) - r(u))$ where u is the node of T which is made the root by the splay operation.

Proof: It suffices to prove the following claim.

Claim: Let u,v, and w be as defined in the figures illustrating the three cases of the splay step. The amortized cost of case 1 is at most $1 + 3(r(v) - r(u))$, and of cases 2.1. and 2.2 is at most $3(r(w) - r(u))$.

Proof: In this proof we use $r'(u)$, $r'(v)$, $r'(w)$ to denote the ranks of the various nodes after the splay step. Note that $r'(u) = r(v)$ in case 1 and $r'(u) = r(w)$ in cases 2.1. and 2.2.

We will frequently use the following simple observation about ranks. If z is a node with sons z_1 and z_2 and $r(z_1) = r(z_2)$ then $r(z) \geq r(z_1) + 1$. This follows since $r(z_1) = r(z_2) = k$ implies $2^k \leq tw(z_1), tw(z_2) < 2^{k+1}$ and hence $tw(z) \geq tw(z_1) + tw(z_2) \geq 2^{k+1}$. Thus $r(z) \geq r(z_1) + 1$. Also, $r(father(z)) \geq r(z)$ for all nodes z.

We are now ready to discuss the various cases of the splay step. Note that the actual cost is one in all three cases.

Case 1: The amortized cost of this splay step is
$$1 + r'(v) + r'(u) - r(v) - r(u)$$
$$\leq 1 + r'(v) - r(u) \quad , \text{ since } r'(u) = r(v)$$
$$\leq 1 + r(v) - r(u) \quad , \text{ since } r'(v) \leq r'(u) = r(v)$$
$$\leq 1 + 3(r(v) - r(u)) \quad , \text{ since } r(v) \geq r(u)$$

Case 2.1: The amortized cost of this splay step is
$$1 + r'(u) + r'(v) + r'(w) - r(u) - r(v) - r(w)$$
$$\leq 1 + r'(v) + r'(w) - r(u) - r(v) \quad , \text{ since } r'(u) = r(w)$$
Assume first that $r(w) > r(u)$. Then we conclude further, using $r'(v) \leq r'(u) = r(w)$, $r'(w) \leq r'(u) = r(w)$, $r(v) \geq r(u)$ and $1 \leq r(w)-r(u)$, that the amortized cost is bounded by
$$\leq r(w) - r(u) + r(w) + r(w) - r(u) - r(u)$$
$$= 3(r(w) - r(u))$$

This finishes the proof if $r(w) > r(u)$.

Assume next that $r(w) = r(u)$. Then $r(w) = r(v) = r(u) = r'(u)$.
Also $r'(w) \leq r'(u) = r(u)$ and $r'(v) \leq r'(u) = r(u)$.
If $r'(w) = r'(v)$ then $r'(u) \geq r'(w) + 1$ and hence $r'(w) + r'(v)$
$\leq 2r(u) - 1$. This shows that the amortized cost is bounded above by
zero $(= 3(r(w) - r(u)))$ in this case.

Case 2.2: The amortized cost of this splay step is
$$1 + r'(u) + r'(v) + r'(w) - r(u) - r(v) - r(w)$$
$$\leq 1 + r'(v) + r'(w) - r(u) - r(v) \quad , \text{ since } r'(u) = r(w)$$

Assume first that $r(w) > r(u)$. Then we conclude further, using
$1 \geq r(w) - r(u)$, $r(u) \leq r(v) \leq r(w)$ and $r'(w) \leq r'(v) \leq r'(u) = r(w)$,
that the amortized cost is bounded by
$$\leq r(w) - r(u) + r(w) + r(w) - r(u) - r(u)$$
$$= 3(r(w) - r(u))$$

Assume next that $r(w) = r(u)$. Then $r(w) = r(v) = r(u) = r'(u)$ and
$r'(u) \geq r'(v) \geq r'(w)$. If $r'(u) > r'(w)$ then the amortized cost is
bounded by zero $(= 3(r(w) - r(u))$ and we are done. So assume $r'(u) =$
$r'(w)$. Consider the middle tree in the figure illustrating case 2.2.
We use $F(u), F(v), F(w)$ to denote the ranks in this tree. We have
$F(u) = r(u)$, $F(w) = r'(w)$ and $F(v) = r(w)$. If $r'(w) = r'(u)$ then
$F(w) = r'(w) = r'(u) = r(w) = r(u) = F(u)$ and hence $F(v) > F(w)$ and
therefore $r'(u) > r'(w)$, a contradiction. Hence $r'(u) > r'(w)$ always.
This finishes the proof in case 2.2.   □

The proof of lemma 3 is completed by summing the costs of the individual
splay steps. Note that the sum   telescopes.
The amortized cost of the other operations is now readily computed.
We summarize in

Theorem 3:
The amortized cost of Splay(x,T) is $O(\log tw(T)/tw(x))$.

The amortized cost of Access(x,T) is $O(\log tw(T)/tw(x))$.

The amortized cost of Delete(x,T) is $O(\log \dfrac{tw(T)}{\min(tw(x), tw(x^-))})$

where x^- is the predecessor of x in tree T

The amortized cost of Join2(T_1,T_2) is $O(\log \dfrac{tw(T_1) + tw(T_2)}{tw(x)})$ where

x is the largest element in tree T_1.

The amortized cost of Join3(T_1,x,T_2) is $O(\log \dfrac{tw(T_1) + tw(T_2)}{w(x)})$.

The amortized cost of Insert(x,T) is $O(\log \dfrac{tw'(T)}{\min(tw(x^-),tw(x^+),w(x))})$,

where x^- is the predecessor, x^+ is the successor of x in the final tree
and tw'(T) is the weight of T after the operation.

The amortized cost of Split(x,T) is $O(\log tw(T)/tw(x))$.

The amortized cost of Change Weight(x,T,δ) is $O(\log(tw(T)+\delta)/tw(x))$.

The actual cost of a sequence $Op_1,\ldots,Op_m$ of operations starting with
weight function w: U → IN and a forest of single node trees is bounded
by the sum of the amortized costs of the operations and the initial balance $\sum\limits_{x \in U} \lfloor \log w(x) \rfloor$.

Proof: The bounds on the amortized cost of the various operations
follows from the bound on the amortized cost of the Splay operation and
the realization of the various operations by the Splay operation.
We discuss the various operations briefly.
The bound for the Splay operation was shown in lemma 3. Operation Access
is identical to Splay and the cost of Split(x,T) is the cost of
Splay(x,T) plus 1. The bound on the amortized cost of Join2(T_1,T_2) is
$O(\log tw(T_1)/tw(x) + 1 + (\log (tw(T_1) + tw(T)) - \log tw(T_1)))$
$= O(\log (tw(T_1) + tw(T))/tw(x))$ where x is the largest element in tree
T_1. In this bound, the first term accounts for the cost of Splay$(+\infty,T_1)$
and the second and third term account for the actual cost of making T_2
a son of x and the change in the rank of x caused by making T_2 a son of
x. The cost of Join3(T_1,x,T_2) is $O(1 + (\log (tw(T_1) + w(x) + tw(T_2)) -$
$\log w(x)))$ where the last term accounts for the rank change of x.
The amortized cost of Delete(x,T) is $O(\log tw(T)/tw(x) + \log tw(T)/$
$tw(x^-))$ where the first term accounts for the cost of Splay(x,T) and
the second term accounts for the Join2 operation. The cost of Insert(x,T)
is $O(\log tw(T)/\min(tw(x^-), tw(x^+)) + 1 + (\log (tw(T) + w(x)) -$
$\log w(x)) = O(\log (tw(T) + w(x))/\min(tw(x^-),tw(x^+),w(x)))$ where the
first term accounts for the splay operation and the last term accounts

for the rank change of x. Finally, the cost of Change Weight(x,T,δ)
is $O(\log(tw(T)/tw(x)) + (\log (tw(T) + \delta) - \log tw(T))) =$
$O(\log (tw(T) + \delta)/tw(x))$ where the first term accounts for the Splay
operation and the second term accounts for the rank change of x.
The bound on the cost of a sequence of operations follows from the
observation that the balance of a forest of single node trees is
$\sum_{x \in U} \lfloor \log w(x) \rfloor$ and that the account is positive.   □

Theorem 3 is very remarkable. Note that splay trees have <u>no knowledge</u>
of weights and nevertheless achieve logarithmic behavior. Moreover, the
bounds of theorem 3 are true for <u>all</u> weight functions.

We close this section with a comparison of splay trees and static trees.

<u>Theorem 4:</u> Consider a sequence of Access operations on a set of n
elements. Let t be the number of comparisons needed to process this
sequence in some static binary search tree. Then the cost of processing
this sequence using splay trees is $O(t + n^2)$. This is true for any
initial tree.

<u>Proof:</u> Let U be the set of elements stored in the static tree. Let d be
the depth of the static tree and let d(x) be the depth of element x ∈ U
in the static tree. We use the weight function $w(x) = 3^{d-d(x)}$.

Consider any splay tree T for set U. The balance bal(T) is at most
$\sum_{x \in U} r(x) = \sum_{x \in U} d+1 = O(n^2)$. Also the total weight of T is at most
$\sum_{x \in U} w(x) = \sum_{x \in U} 3^{d-d(x)} \leq \sum_{i=0}^{d} 2^i 3^{d-i} \leq 3^{d+1}$ and therefore the amortized
cost of operation Access(x,T) is $O(\log tw(T)/tw(x)) = O(d(x) + 1)$.
Since d(x) + 1 comparisons are needed to search for x in the static tree
this implies that the amortized cost of the sequence of operations is
$O(t)$. Also the balance of the initial tree is $O(n^2)$. This proves the
bound.   □

We infer from theorem 4 that the cost of a long sequence of Access
operations in a splay tree is of the same order as the cost in the
optimum tree for the sequence. Note, however, that the splay tree
requires some time to "learn" the distribution. This is expressed in
the $O(n^2)$ term.

III. 6.2 D-trees

In this section we describe a second approach to dynamic weighted trees: weighted BB[α]-trees or D-trees. Weighted BB[α]-trees are less elegant than splay trees and in many respects less flexible. In particular, we will not discuss operations Split and Concatenate at all, and restrict Promote and Demote to weight changes by one, i.e. $\delta = 1$, and restrict Deletion to elements of weight one. We leave the more general operations to the exercises. However, weighted BB[α]-trees also have one advantage over splay trees, namely their controlled update cost. This fact will be crucial for the applications of weighted dynamic trees in chapter VIII.

We discussed the amortized rebalancing cost of weight balanced trees and height balanced trees in sections 5.1. and 5.3.2. respectively. In both cases amortized rebalancing cost was constant and rebalancing cost at height h decreased exponentially in h. However, the basis of the exponential function was different. In BB[α] trees, a node of weight w (i.e. w leaf descendants) causes a rebalancing operation only every $\Omega(w)$ transactions which go through the node. No such statement is true for (a,b)-trees. In the applications of chapter VIII, we will augment search trees by additional information. Maintaining the additional information when rotating at a node of weight w will have cost $O(w)$ or even $O(w \log w)$. With the strong bound on the updating cost of BB[α]-trees we will still be able to control the amortized update cost of the augmented trees; with splay trees we cannot control it.

D-trees are an extension of BB[α]-trees. We imagine an object x_i of weight w_i to consist of w_i leaves of weight 1. A D-tree for set S is then a BB[α]-tree T with $W = w_1 + \ldots + w_n$ leaves. The leftmost w_1 leaves are labelled by x_1, the next w_2 leaves are labelled by $x_2, \ldots$.

Definition: a) A leaf labelled by x_j is a j-leaf.

b) A node v of T is a j-node iff all leaves in the subtree with root v are j-leaves and v's father does not have this property.

c) A node v of T is the j-joint iff all j-leaves are descendants of v and neither of v's sons has this property.

d) Consider the j-joint v. w'_j j-leaves are to the left of v and w''_j j-leaves are to the right of v. If $w'_j \geq w''_j$ then the j-node of minimal depth to the left of v is active, otherwise the j-node of minimal depth to the right of v is active.

e) The thickness th(v) of a node v is the number of leaves in the sub-tree with root v.

Only parts of the underlying BB[α]-tree actually need to be stored, in particular all proper descendants of j-nodes can be pruned. Only their number is essential and is stored in the j-node. More precisely, a D-tree is obtained from the BB[α]-tree by

1) pruning all proper descendants of j-nodes

2) storing in each node.
a) a query of the form "if X ≤ x_j then go left else go right"
b) the type of the node: joint node, j-node or neither of above
c) its thickness
d) in the case of the j-joint the number of j-leaves in its left and right subtree.

The queries are assigned in such a way as to direct a search for x_i to the active i-node. More precisely, let v be any interior node of the D-tree and let the active 1-node,...,j-node be to the left of v. Then the query "if X ≤ x_j then go left else go right" is stored in v.

The next figure shows a D-tree for the distribution (w_1, w_2, w_3, w_4) = (2,7,3,4) based on a tree in BB[1/4]. The j-nodes are indicated by squares, active j-nodes by double lines, the thickness of j-nodes is written below them and the distribution of j-leaves with respect to the j-joints is written below the joint nodes.

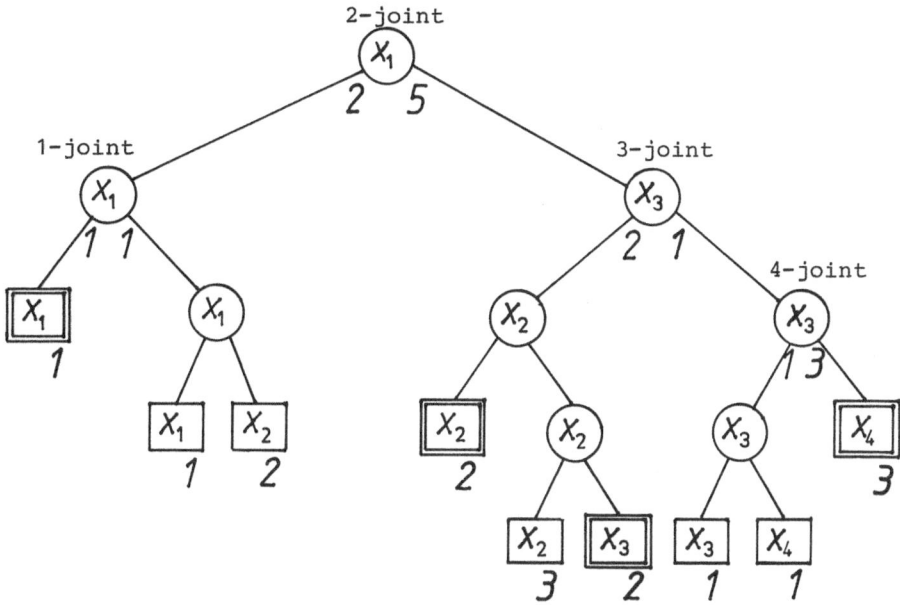

The following Lemma shows that D-trees are good search trees.

Lemma 4: Let b_j be the depth of the active j-node in tree T. Then $b_j \leq c_1 \log W/w_j + c_2$ where $c_1 = 1/\log(1/1-\alpha))$, $c_2 = 1 + c_1$.

Proof: Let v be the father of the active j-node. Then all j-leaves which are on the same side of the j-joint as the active j-node are descendants of v. Hence $th(v) \geq w_j/2$. The argument of theorem 2 of section 5.1. finishes the proof.   □

Next we have to address the question of how to maintain D-trees. The answer is exactly as for BB[α]-trees, but be careful with the additional D-tree information. Suppose we execute an instruction. The search will end in the active j-node. We have to update the thickness of all nodes cn the path of search and the distribution of j-leaves with respect to the j-joint. The j-joint lies on the path of search and so this is easily done. Next we have to ascend the path of search from the active j-node to the root and perform rotations and double-rotations as required. Since a double-rotation is two rotations we only have to treat the case of a rotation. Let us call joint nodes and j-nodes special nodes. If no special node is involved in the rotation

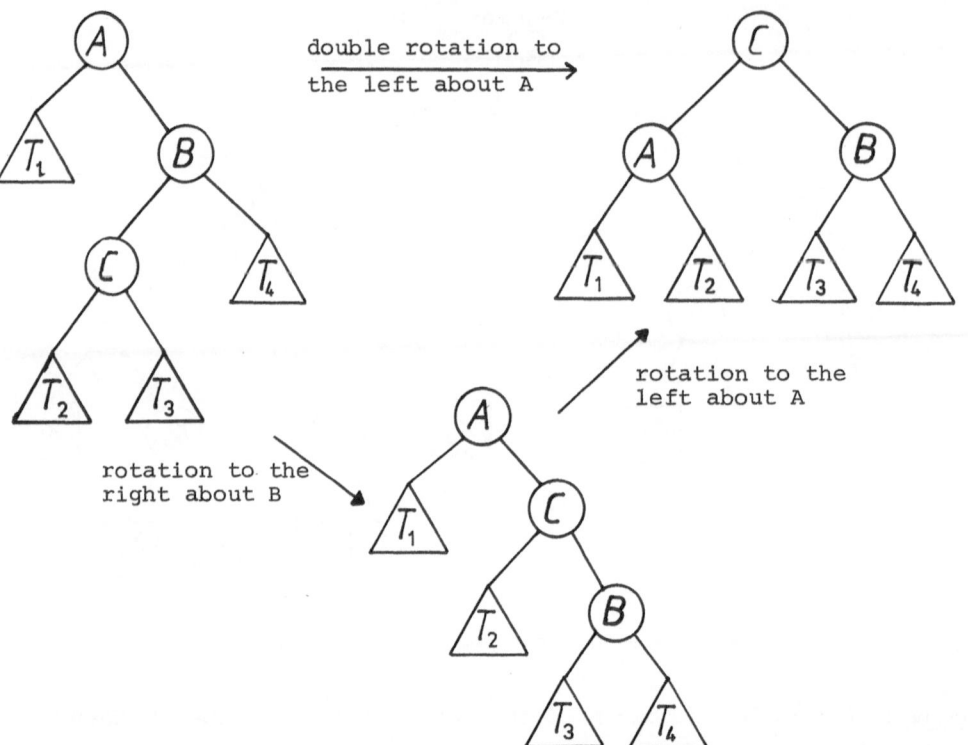

then nc additional actions are required. Suppose now, a special node
is involved in the rotation.

<u>Case 1:</u> A j-node is involved. Then we have the following picture

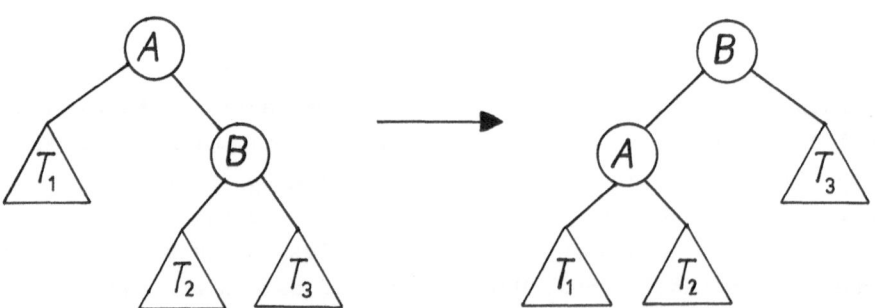

and node B is a j-node before the rotation, i.e. trees T_2 and T_3 do
not exist explicitly. We create them by splitting B into two j-nodes
of thickness $\lfloor th(B)/2 \rfloor$ and $\lceil th(B)/2 \rceil$ respectively. What query should
we assign to B (Note that B is in an interior node now)? Suppose first
that neither A nor B is the j-joint. Then A must be a left descendant
of the j-joint. Otherwise T_1 can only contain j-leaves and hence A

would be a j-node and hence B would not exist. So A must be a left descendant of the j-joint and hence the active j-node lies to the right of A. But then it also lies to the right of B (T₃ could be it) and thus we only have to copy the query from A into B. The discussion above also solves the case where B is the j-joint. Suppose next that A is the j-joint. Then the active j-node will be to the left of B after the split. Let Z be the nearest ancestor of A such that the left link was taken out of Z during the search. Copy Z's query into B. Z can be found as follows: When the nodes on the path of search are stacked during the search, they are also entered into either one of two linear lists: the L-list or the R-list. The L-list contains all nodes which are left via their left links and the R-list contains all nodes which are left via their right links. Then Z is the first node on the L-list. This ends the discussion of B being a j-node.

Example: Rotation to the left about the 4-joint.

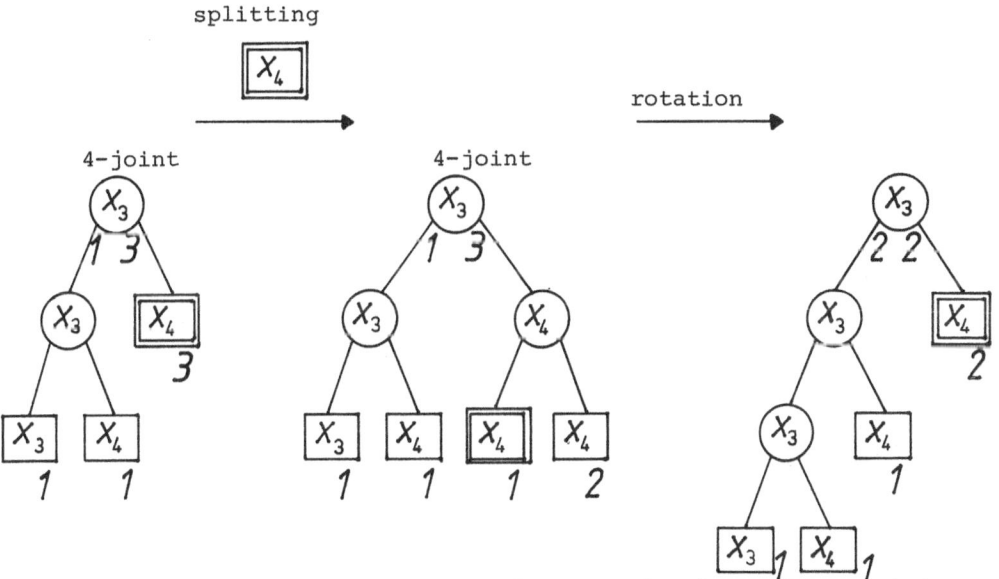

The second possibility is that T_2 and T_3 are j-nodes and hence A is j-node after the rotation. In this case x_1 and x_2 are deleted after the rotation.

Example: Rotation to the left about the father of the active 2-node

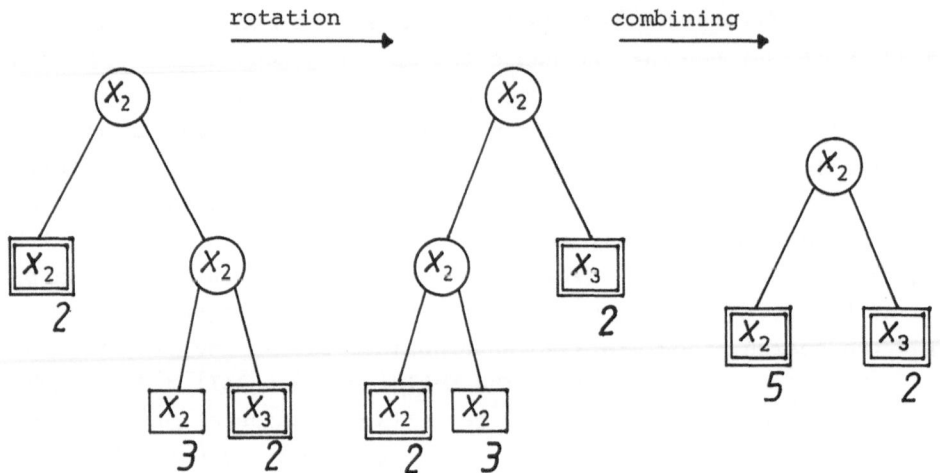

Case 2: A joint node is involved, i.e. either A or B is a joint node or both. If B is a joint node then no additional actions are required. So let us consider the case that A is the j-joint. Let w_j', w_j'' be the distribution of j-leaves with respect to the j-joint A and let s be the thickness of the root of T_2. If $s \geq w_j''$ then T_3 contains no j-leaves and hence A will be the j-joint after the rotation. No action is required in this case.

If $s < w_j''$ then B will be the j-joint after the rotation. The distribution of j-leaves with respect to B is $w_j' + s$, $w_j'' - s$.

Case 2.1.: $w_j' + s \leq w_j'' - s$. Then $w_j' \leq w_j''$ and the active j-node was to the right of A, in fact it was node T_2. Also the active j-node will be to the right of B after the rotation and it still is to the right of A. Hence we only have to copy A's query into B.

Case 2.2.: $w_j' + s > w_j'' - s$. Then the active j-node will be to the left of B after the rotation, and hence it will be node T_2.

Case 2.2.1.: $w_j' \leq w_j''$. Then T_2 also was the active j-node before the rotation. No additional action is required in this case.

<u>Case 2.2.2.:</u> $w_j' > w_j''$. Then the active j-node was to the left of A and hence to the left of B before the rotation. In this case B's query remains unchanged, but A's query has to be changed. Suppose first that A's left son is a j-node. Then A ceases to exist after the rotation and we are done. Suppose next that A's left son is not a j-node. The next figure shows a microscopic view of tree T_1.

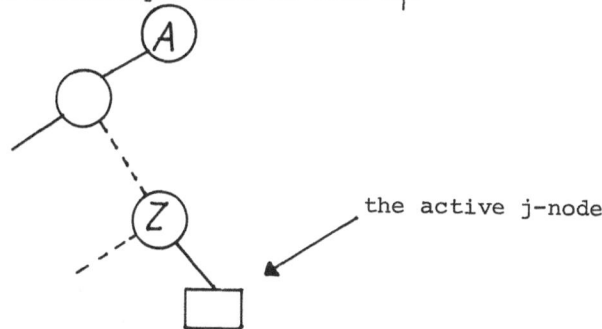

the active j-node

We only have to copy Z's query into A. Z can be found by a brute force search. Note that $th(Z) \geq w_j' \geq w_j/2$. Note also that the thickness s of T_3 is less than $w_j'' \leq w_j/2$. Since $s = th(T_3) \geq \alpha \cdot th(B)$ (the underlying tree is in BB[α]) and $th(B) \geq (1-\alpha)th(A)$ (a rotation to the left about A is performed) we have $s \geq \alpha(1-\alpha)th(A)$ and hence $th(A) \leq w_j/(2 \cdot \alpha(1-\alpha))$. The argument used in the proof of theorem 2 of section 5.1. shows that the depth of Z with respect to A is at most $\log(\alpha(1-\alpha))/\log(1-\alpha)$.

We summarize the discussion in

<u>Theorem 5:</u> Consider a D-tree based on a BB[α]-tree with $1/4 \leq \alpha \leq 1 - \sqrt{2}/2$. Let w_i be the weight of x_i, $1 \leq i \leq n$, and let $W = \sum_i w_i$. Then a search for x_i takes time $c_1 \log W/w_i + c_2$ and a weight change of x_i by ± 1 takes also time $c_1 \log W/w_i + c_2$ for some small constants c_1 and c_2.

<u>Example:</u> We promote x_2 by one in our example. This increases the thickness of the active 2-node from 2 to 3 and moves the balance parameter of the root (the 2-joint) out of the range [1/4,3/4]. A double-rotation (to the left) about the root is required. It is simulated by a rotation to the right about the 3-joint followed by a rotation to the left about the 2-joint. The rotation about the 3-joint requires no special action since $s = th(father of active 3-node) = 5 > 2 =$ number of 3-leaves to the left of 3-joint. We obtain

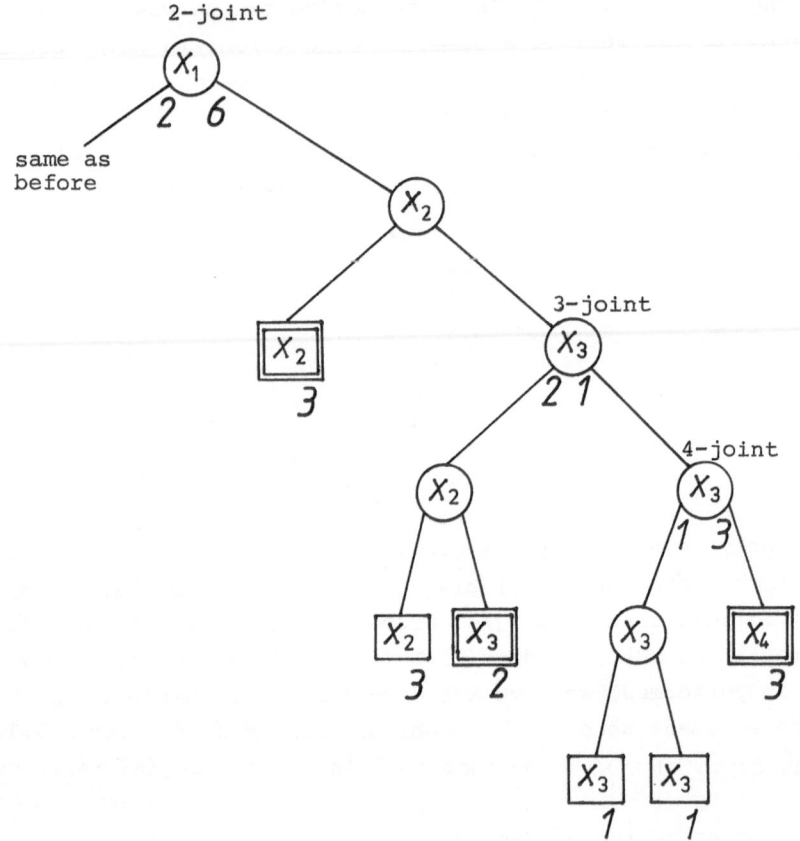

Next we have to rotate about the 2-joint. We have $w_2' = 2$, $w_2'' = 6$ and $s = 3$ and hence case 2.2.1. of the discussion above applies. We obtain

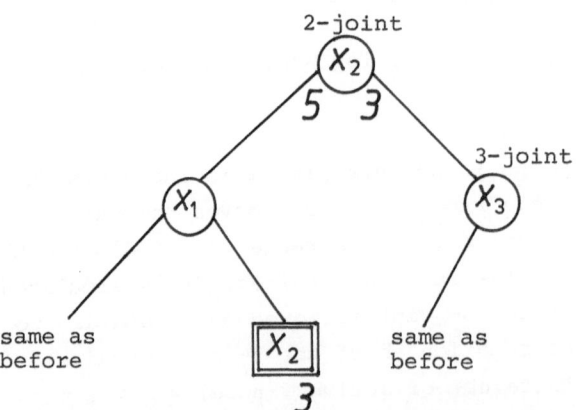

We close this section with a brief discussion of the space requirement and the update behavior of D-trees. The space requirement is clearly O(W) since there are at most W leaves. Since an element x_i can be represented by as many as log w_i i-nodes the space requirement may be non-linear in n. There is a version of D-trees, namely compact D-trees, which overcomes this problem. Also, in the applications in chapter VIII, quantity W and not n will be the relevant parameter.

The basic idea for compact D-trees is to only store special nodes (= active nodes and joints) and nodes having special nodes in both subtrees. Clearly there are only O(n) such nodes. All other nodes are deleted and only some information about their size is kept. The diagram below shows a D-tree for distribution (3,20,4,10) and also its compacted version. In the compacted tree

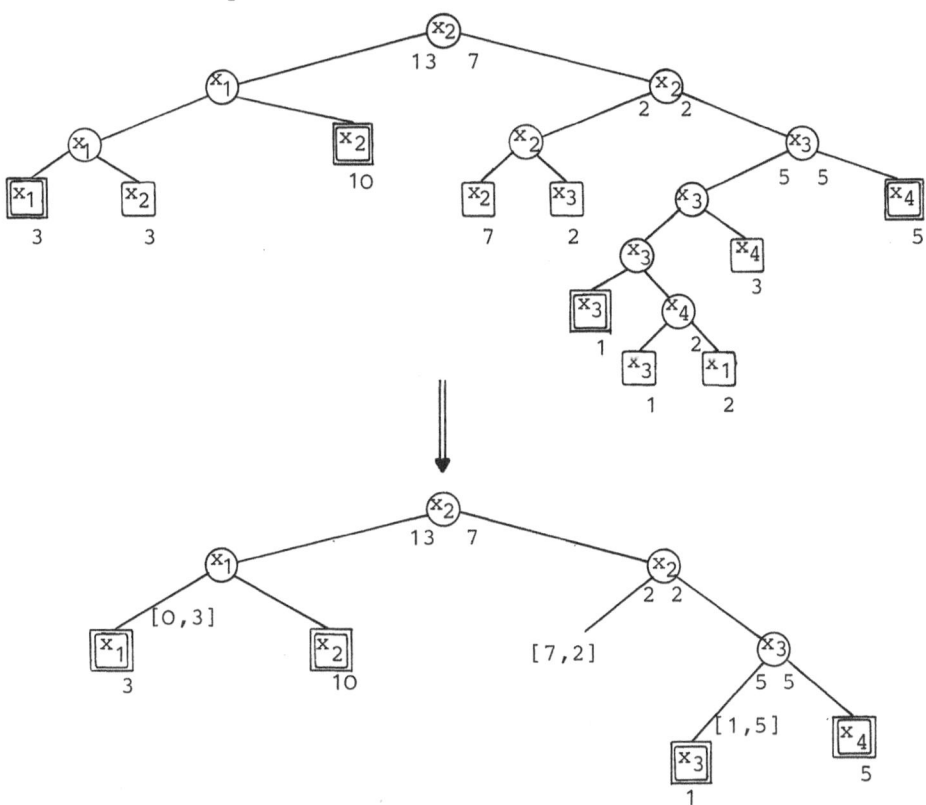

the size of deleted subtrees is recalled in the expressions in square
brackets. For example, the expression [1,5] on the edge from the 4-joint
to the active 3-node represents subtrees emanating to the right from
this edge and having a total of one 3-leaf and five 4-leaves. It can be
shown that compacted D-trees can still be rebalanced efficiently. We
refer the reader to the literature for details.

Let us turn to amortized update cost next. Rotations and double rotations in D-trees are only caused by the underlying BB[α]-tree. Hence
the results of section 5.1. carry over without any change. In particular,
theorem 5 of section 5.1. carries over.

Theorem 6: Let $1/4 \leq \alpha < 1 - \sqrt{2}/2$ and let f: $\mathbb{R} \to \mathbb{R}$ be a non-
decreasing function. Suppose that the cost of performing a rotation or
double rotation at node v of a D-tree based on a BB[α]-tree is f(th(v)).
Then the total cost of the rebalancing operations for a sequence of
m insertions, deletions, promotions, and demotions into an initially
empty D-tree is $O(m \sum_{i=1}^{c\log m} f((1-\alpha)^{-i-1})(1-\alpha)^i)$ where c = 1/log (1/1-α)).

We will use theorem 6 frequently in chapter VIII on algorithmic
geometry.

III. 6.3   An Application to Multidimensional Searching

Dynamic weighted trees have numerous applications. The most obvious one
is the organization of sets under changing or unknown access
probabilities. In this section we describe an application to TRIES and
exact match queries in multi-dimensional spaces. Let U be an ordered
set, d be an integer (=dimension), and let S $\subseteq$ U^d. We want to maintain
set S under searches, insertions and deletions taking comparisons
between elements of U as our basic operation. One solution immediately
comes to mind: Order U^d by lexicographic order, i.e. $(x_1,...,x_d)$
$\leq (y_1,...,y_d)$ if there is an i such that $x_j = y_j$ for j < i and $x_i < y_i$,
and use ordinary balanced trees. This will allow us to perform all
three operations in time O(d·log |S|) since a comparison between two
elements of S takes time O(d). We will show next that this can be
improved to time O(d + log |S|).

<u>Theorem 7:</u> Let $S \subseteq U^d$, $|S| = n$. Then operations Access, Insert and Delete can be supported in (amortized) time $O(d + \log n)$ where a comparison between elements of U is supposed to take one unit of time.

<u>Proof:</u> Let W be the set of all prefixes of elements of S, i.e. $W = \{(x_1, \ldots, x_k); \ 0 \le k \le d \text{ and } (x_1, x_2, \ldots, x_d) \in S\}$. For $w \in W$, $|w| = k$, let $p_w := |\{(x_1, \ldots, x_n) \in S; \ (x_1, \ldots, x_k) = w\}|$. Then $p_\epsilon = |S|$, $\sum_{a \in U} p_{wa} = p_w$ for all w, $|w| < d$, and $p_w = 1$ for $|w| = d$. We represent S by a tree of dynamic weighted trees. More precisely, for every $w \in W$, $|w| < d$, we have a tree T_w for set $\{wa; \ a \in U \text{ and } wa \in U\}$ according to weights p_{wa}. Furthermore, leaf wa of tree T_w points to the root of tree T_{wa} and the root of tree T_ϵ is the entry point of the data structure. An Access for $x = (x_1, \ldots, x_d)$ is performed as follows. We start in tree T_ϵ and search for x_1 in that tree. After locating x_1 in T_ϵ we locate x_2 in T_{x_1}, then x_3 in $T_{x_1 x_2}, \ldots$ until the search is completed by locating x_d in $T_{x_1 x_2 \ldots x_{d-1}}$. The total cost of operation Access is

$$\sum_{i=1}^{d} \text{time needed to locate } x_i \text{ in } T_{x_1 \ldots x_{i-1}}$$

$$= \sum_{i=1}^{d} O(1 + \log(p_{x_1 \ldots x_{i-1}} / p_{x_1 \ldots x_i})) \quad \text{by theorem 3 or 5}$$

$$= O(\sum_{i=1}^{d} 1 + \log p_{x_1 \ldots x_{i-1}} - \log p_{x_1 \ldots x_i})$$

$$= O(d + \log p_\epsilon - \log p_x) = O(d + \log n - \log 1) = O(d + \log n)$$

An Insert of $(x_1, \ldots, x_d)$ in set S is also easily performed. We first do an Access and determine the maximal i such that x_i occurs in $T_{x_1 \ldots x_{i-1}}$. Then we create trivial trees $T_{x_1 \ldots x_{i+1}}, \ldots, T_{x_1 \ldots x_{d-1}}$, insert x_{i+1} into $T_{x_1 \ldots x_i}$ and increase the weight of x_j in $T_{x_1 \ldots x_{j-1}}$ by 1 for $j \le i$.

Thus the cost of an insert is

$$\sum_{j=1}^{i} O(1 + \log((p_{x_1 \ldots x_{j-1}} + 1)/p_{x_1 \ldots x_j})) + O(\log p_{x_1 \ldots x_i}) + O(d-i)$$

$$= O(d + \sum_{j=1}^{i} (\log(2p_{x_1 \cdots x_{j-1}}) - \log p_{x_1 \cdots x_j}) + \log p_{x_1 \cdots x_i})$$

$$= O(d + \log n)$$

A Deletion of $(x_1, \ldots, x_d)$ from set S corresponds to a sequence of Demote operations. It is easily seen that time bound $O(d + \log n)$ also applies to deletions.   □

Theorem 7 is readily extended to weighted multidimensional sets and to operations Concatenate and Split (Exercises 39 and 4o). The data structure used in the proof of theorem 7 is a symbiosis of trees and TRIES. The qlobal data structure is a TRIE. i.e. the "characters" of $x \in U^d$ are determined one after the other. The local data structures are weighted, dynamic trees, i.e. each node of the TRIE is realized by either a splay tree or a D-tree.

III. 7.   A Comparison of Search Structures

In this section we try to summarize the highlights of this chapter and to compare the various data structures presented in the preceding six sections. The following table summarizes the results.

	Unweighted Data	Weighted Data	Access	Insert Delete	Concatenate Split	Secondary Storage	Finger searches	Sequential Access
TRIES	x		$O(\log_k N)$	x		x		x
Hashing	x		$O(\beta)$ expected	x		x		
Perfect Hashing	x		$O(1)$			x		
Interpolation Search	x		$O(\log\log n)$ expected					x
static weighted search trees		x	$O(\log 1/p)$			(x)		x
BB[α]-trees	x		$O(\log n)$	x	x			x
(a,b)-trees	x		$O(\log n)$	x	x	x	x	x
splay trees		x	$O(\log 1/p)$ amortized	x	x			x
D-trees		x	$O(\log 1/p)$	x				x

In the table N denotes the size of the universe, n denotes the size of
the set stored in the data structure, p is the probability of the
element to be accessed, k is the branching factor of the TRIE and β is
the loading factor of the hash table.

There are three data structures which support only operation Access:
Perfect hashing, interpolation search and static weighted search trees.
Perfect hashing guarantees an access time of O(1) and uses about 3n
words of storage for the hash table and essentially n additional words
for the hash program. It can be used for secondary storage and then
requires two accesses to secondary storage, namely one to pick up the
relevant part of the hash program and one to access the actual data.
Perfect hashing (as all hashing methods) does not support sequential
access to the data in its natural order. Note however, that sequential
access in "hashed order" is possible. The other two methods support
sequential access. Interpolation search provides us with O(loglogn)
expected access time and requires no additional storage. Static weighted
trees support weighted data and allow us to access an item with access
probability p in time O(log 1/p). We have seen that expected access time
to a collection of items is O(1) for a variety of frequency distributions. Multi-way weighted trees which were not discussed in the text,
can also be used in secondary storage. TRIES, hashing and balanced trees
(weight-balanced or height-balanced) can be used to handle dynamic
unweighted data. Hashing (with chaining) has an O(β) expected access
time, although worst case access time is Θ(n) and expected worst case
access time is Θ(log n), and supports Access, Insert and Delete.
The expected behavior of hashing with chaining can be turned into
probabilistic behavior by the use of universal hashing. For secondary
storage extendible hashing is particularly appropriate. It requires only
two accesses to secondary storage. Extendible hashing is closely related
to TRIE searching on the hashed keys. TRIES for the unhashed keys
support also sequential access. The branching factor k can be used to
trade between access time and storage requirement.

Balanced trees have logarithmic worst case behavior and also support
additional operations such as split, concatenate and finger searches.
Among the balanced trees, (a,b)-trees are the most flexible and elegant
version. The realization by colored trees is particularly useful.
(a,b)-trees with b ≥ 2a exhibit small amortized rebalancing cost which

we exploit at several occasions, in particular A-sort and finger trees.
Weight-balanced trees are less elegant than (a,b)-trees, require
somewhat more space (an integer has to be stored in each node instead
of a bit as for colored trees), and are usually slower by a constant
factor. However, they also have their merits. Operation Concatenate is
faster (time $O(\log (n_1 + n_2)/\min(n_1,n_2))$ for joining trees of size n_1
and n_2 respectively, instead of time $O(\min(|h_1 - h_2|, h_1,h_2)) =$
$O(\log \max(n_1,n_2))$ as for (a,b)-trees) and more importantly the
amortized number of rotations and double rotations shows a very
controlled behavior. This makes BB[α]-trees the ideal basis for augmented trees in which rotations (and double rotations) have non-
constant cost. For secondary storage, (a,b)-trees with a large value of
a are the preferred choice.

Balanced trees can be extended to weighted data. Splay trees provide us
with a very elegant solution to the weighted dictionary problem and
also show the potential of self-organizing data structures and amortized
analysis. D-trees are less elegant but inherit the strong bounds on
update cost from BB[α]-trees.

III. 8. Subsets of a Small Universe

So far we dealt with subsets S of a very large, basically infinite universe U. In this section we treat the other extreme; set S ⊆ U is about the same size as universe U. Whilst in the former case operation Access is a non-trivial operation and in fact a large part of the preceding sections was devoted to it, operation Access is trivial in the latter case. Direct access by means of arrays is now a possibility. Small universes come up quite frequently. One example is the set of accounts of a bank (accessed via account number), another example are graph algorithms (cf. chapters IV and V).

Throughout this section we assume w.l.o.g. that U = {0,1,...,N-1}.

III. 8.1 The Boolean Array (Bitvector)

Apparently, a set S ⊆ U can be represented by a boolean array BV[0.. N-1]. We have BV[i] = true if i ∈ S and BV[i] = false if i ∉ S. Then operations Access, Insert and Delete take constant time, the best we can hope for.

There is one small drawback of boolean arrays. Initialization takes time O(N). If Ω(N) operations are performed on set S, as it is very often the case in applications, then initialization can be amortized over the sequence of operations.

It is interesting to know that initialization can be avoided altogether by using more space. In addition to array $\overline{BV}$ we use an array A[0.. N-1] and a pushdown store. The stack is realized by array K[0.. N-1] and variable TOP as described in I.4.. Initially TOP = -1. We maintain the following invariant (we assume that BV[i] = 0 for all i is the intended initialization):

   BV[i] = 1   iff $\overline{BV}$[i] = 1 and 0 ≤ A[i] ≤ TOP and K[A[i]] = i

Initially, TOP = -1 and hence BV[i] = 0 for all i as intended. Apparently, the value of BV[i] can still be determined in constant time by using the invariant. Suppose now, that we want to write boolean b into BV[i]. If 0 ≤ A[i] ≤ TOP and K[A[i]] = i then we write b into $\overline{BV}$[i] and are done. Otherwise we execute

```
TOP  ← TOP + 1;
A[i] ← TOP;
K[TOP] ← i;
B̄V[i]  ← b;
```

It is easy to see that this piece of code maintains the invariant. Thus initialization and operations Access, Insert and Delete take time $O(1)$ each.

III. 8.2   The $O(\log \log N)$ Priority Queue

We saw already several methods for maintaining priority queues with running time $O(\log n)$ for operations Insert, Min and Deletemin: Heaps (II.1.2.), balanced trees (III.5.) and unordered (a,b)-trees (III.5.3.1.). Here n denotes the number of elements in the queue. In this section we describe an implementation of priority queues with time $O(\log \log N)$ per operation where N denotes the size of the universe $U = \{0,\ldots,N-1\}$. Thus the data structure described here is faster provided that N is not too large with respect to n, i.e. $N \leq 2^n$.

We use the following notation. For integer $k \geq 2$ we use k' to denote $\lceil k/2 \rceil$ and k" to denote $\lfloor k/2 \rfloor$. For $x \in [0.. 2^k-1]$ we let $x' = x \text{ div } 2^{k"}$ and $x" = x \mod 2^{k"}$. Then $x = x' 2^{k"} + x"$.

Definition: A k-structure T for set $S = \{x_1,\ldots,x_m\} \subseteq [0.. 2^k-1]$ consists of

1) integer T.SIZE = $|\{x_1,\ldots,x_m\}|$.

2) A doubly linked list T.LIST containing $x_1,\ldots,x_m$ in increasing order.

3) A bitvector T.B[0.. 2^k-1] with T.B[x_i] = true for all i and an array T.P[0.. 2^k-1] of pointers. Pointer T.P[x_i] points to element x_i on list T.LIST.

4) A k'-structure T.TOP and an array T.BOTTOM[0...$2^{k'}-1$] of k"-structures. If $m \leq 1$ then structures T.TOP and T.BOTTOM[i], $0 \leq i \leq 2^{k'}-1$, are all empty, i.e. their size fields are 0, the list is

empty and the bitvector is all zero. If m > 1 then T.TOP is a k'-struc-
ture for set $\{x_1',\ldots,x_m'\}$ and for each $x \in [0.. \ 2^{k'}-1]$ T.BOTTOM[x] is a
k"-structure for set $\{x_i''; \ 1 \leq i \leq m \text{ and } x = x_i'\}$.   □

An example is badly needed at this point. Let k = 4 and let S =
{2,3,7,1o,13} be the set stored in 4-structure T. Then T.SIZE = 5 and

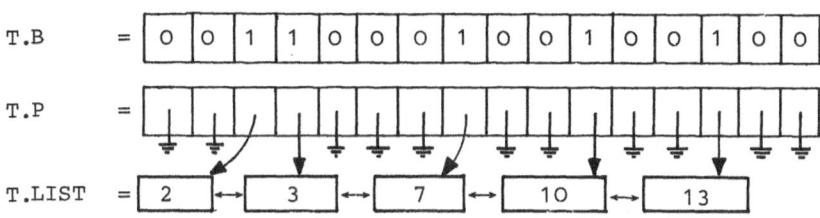

T.TOP is a 2-structure for {0,1,2,3}, T-BOTTOM[0] is a 2-structure for
{2,3}, T.BOTTOM[1] is a 2-structure for {3}, T.BOTTOM[2] is a 2-struc-
ture for {2} and T.BOTTOM[3] is a 2-structure for {1}.   □

The intuition behind this definintion is as follows. In a priority
queue we want to support (at least) operations Insert, Min, and
Deletemin. Operations Insert and Deletemin (once the minimum is known)
are perfectly supported by a bitvector (called T.B) of length $N = 2^k$
and operation Min is supported by an ordered linear list (called
T.LIST). Of course, if we try to combine both data structures by provid-
ing pointers (called T.P) from the array into the linear list we have
a problem with operation Insert. If we want to insert x into the linear
list we need a fast method for locating its successor succ(x) in the
list; the predecessor would also do. The most obvious way of finding
successors is to put a complete binary tree on top of the bitvector
and to use tree search for finding successors. That is the method which
we used in the realization of priority queues by balanced trees. However, there is a major difference which we can use to our advantage:
We are dealing with a fixed complete binary tree. Suppose that we
provide from each leaf, say x, of the tree a pointer to its ancestor,

say x', at depth $\lceil (\log N)/2 \rceil$, i.e. to its ancestor half-way up the tree. In our implementation the nodes at depth $\lceil (\log N/2 \rceil$ are represented by array T.BOTTOM, structure T.TOP represents the top half of the tree and structures T.BOTTOM[i], $0 \le i \le 2^{\lceil (\log N)/2 \rceil} - 1$ represent the bottom half of the tree. The pointers   from leaves x to ancestors x' are not provided explicitly; we simulate them by a simple division by $2^{k''}$. Suppose next that we could decide in time O(1) whether x and succ(x) have the same ancestor at depth $\lceil (\log N/2 \rceil$. In our implementation we can do so by comparing x" with the last element on list T.BOTTOM[x']. LIST. If x and succ(x) have the same ancestor then we can restrict our search to the $O(\sqrt{N})$ descendants of node x', i.e. we only need to find the successor of x" in T.BOTTOM[x']. If x and succ(x) do not have the same ancestor then succ(x) is the first element of the list T.BOTTOM[z'].LIST where z' is the successor of x' in the top half T.TOP of the tree. Thus in either case we can reduce the size of the problem from N to $O(\sqrt{N})$ in time O(1) and hence a time bound of O(loglog N) should result. The details are given below.

Let T be a k-structure for set $S \subseteq [0.. \ 2^k-1]$. Then operations Min S and Member(x,S) take constant time; the minimal element of S is the first element on list T.LIST and $x \in S$ iff T.B[x] = true. For operations Insert and Delete we have to work harder. The algorithms for Insert and Delete use operation Succ(x,S) = min{y $\in$ S; x < y} as a subroutine.

```
(1)   function SUCC(x: [0.. 2^k-1], T: k-structure);
(2)   if k = 1 or T.SIZE ≤ 2
(3)   then search through T.LIST (which is at most 2 elements long)
(4)   else if T.SIZE = 0 or x ≥ max T.LIST
(5)         then SUCC ← "does not exist"
(6)         else x' ← x div 2^⌊k/2⌋; x" ← x mod 2^⌊k/2⌋;
(7)              if T.TOP.B[x'] = 1 and x" ≤ MAX(T.BOTTOM[x'])
(8)              then SUCC ← x' 2^⌊k/2⌋ + SUCC(x", T.BOTTOM[x'])
(9)              else z' ← SUCC(x', T.TOP);
(1o)                  SUCC ← z' 2^⌊k/2⌋ +  MIN(T.BOTTOM[z'])
(11)             fi
(12)        fi
(13) fi
```

Lemma 1: The program above correctly computes SUCC in time $O(\lceil \log k \rceil)$.

Proof: Note first that the successor of x in T does not exist iff either T is empty or x is at least as large as all elements of T. So suppose that T is non-empty and x has a successor and let x', x" be the two parts of x. We have to distinguish two cases; either there is a point in T with first part equal to x' or there is not. If there is a point y in T with y' = x' then we find the successor of x" among the points with first part equal to x'. If the successor exists then we are done (line 8). If it does not exist or if there is no point in T with first part equal to x' then we have to find the successor of x' in the top structure (line 9) and combine it with the first element in the appropriate bottom structure (line 1o). This shows correctness.

Next we analyze the running time of function SUCC. Let R(k) be the maximal running time of SUCC on any k-structure. Then $R(1) = c$ for some constant c. Next note that the running time of SUCC(x,T) is O(1) if x does not have a successor in T. This is true for any k. Thus the time spent in line (7) is O(1) and we obtain the recurrence $R(k) \le c + R(\lceil k/2 \rceil)$ for R where c is some constant. Note that we generate one recursive call on either a $\lfloor k/2 \rfloor$ or a $\lceil k/2 \rceil$-structure and that only a constant amount of time is spent outside the recursive calls. It is now easy to verify by induction on k that $R(k) \le c(1 + \lceil \log k \rceil)$. This is obvious for k = 1. For k > 1 we have

$$R(k) \le c + R(\lceil k/2 \rceil) \qquad \text{, recurrence for R}$$

$$\le c + c(1 + \lceil \log \lceil k/2 \rceil \rceil), \text{ induction hypothesis}$$

$$\le c(1 + \lceil \log k \rceil)$$

For the last step, let ℓ be such that $2^\ell < k \le 2^{\ell+1}$. Then $\lceil \log k \rceil = \ell + 1$ and $2^{\ell-1} < k/2 \le 2^\ell$ and hence $\lceil \log \lceil k/2 \rceil \rceil = \ell$. □

The algorithms for Insert and Delete are now easily derived.

```
(1)  procedure INSERT(x: [0.. 2^k-1], T: k-structure);
(2)  if T.B[x] = false
```

```
(3)    then T.B[x] ← true;
(4)         insert x into T.LIST at the appropriate position (use
            SUCC(x,T) to compute the successor y of x in T. Then insert x
            next to y in T.LIST. The position of y in T.LIST can be
            found via T.P[y]);
(5)         x' ← x div 2^⌊k/2⌋; x" ← x mod 2^⌊k/2⌋;
(6)         case T.SIZE of
(7)         0: do nothing;
(8)         1: let y be the other element of T.LIST and
               let y', y" be the parts of y;
(9)            INSERT(x', T.TOP);
(1o)           INSERT(y', T.TOP);
(11)           INSERT(x", T.BOTTOM[x']);
(12)           INSERT(y", T.BOTTOM[y']);
(13)        2: INSERT(x', T.TOP);
(14)           INSERT(x", T.BOTTOM[x'])
(15)        esac;
(16)        T.SIZE ← T.SIZE + 1
(17) fi
(18) end
```

Lemma 2: The program above inserts an element into a k-structure in
time $O(\lceil \log k \rceil)$.

Proof: The correctness is fairly obvious. There is one subtle point. If
we insert a point x into an empty structure then the parts x' and x" do
not have to be inserted into the top and bottom substructures (line 7).
However, if we insert a second point into a structure then the parts of
the new point x and the old point y have to be inserted (lines 8 - 12).

It remains to determine a bound on the running time of procedure INSERT.
Let R(k) be the maximal running time of INSERT on any k-structure. Then
R(1) = c for some constant c. Next note that INSERT(x,T) takes constant
time if x is already an element of T or if T is empty. This is true for
all k. So suppose that x is not an element of T. Let us concentrate on
the case statement (lines 6 - 15) first. We treat the case that T contains only one element first. Note that the calls in line (9) and (11),
i.e. the calls inserting x' and x", insert points into empty structures
and therefore take time O(1) each. Next note that line (1o) takes constant time if x' = y' and that line (12) takes constant time if x' ≠ y'.
In the former case y' is already in T.TOP and in the latter case y" is

inserted into an empty structure. Thus only one "real" recursive call is initiated. The same statement is true if T has more than one element (lines 13 and 14). Either x' is already an element of T.TOP and then line 13 is trivial or x' is not yet an element of T.TOP and then line 14 is trivial. In either case the cost arising in lines 6 - 15 is bounded by c + R($\lceil k/2 \rceil$) for some c. Line 4 takes time O($\lceil \log k \rceil$). Thus the following recurrence arises for R: R(k) $\leq$ c(1+$\lceil \log k \rceil$) + R($\lceil k/2 \rceil$) which solves for R(k) = O((log k)^2). This is not quite what we wanted.

A simple observation improves the bound to O(log k). We call SUCC in line 4 to find the successor of x. Note that the sequence of recursive calls in SUCC corresponds to the sequence of "non-trivial" recursive calls in INSERT. Thus one call of SUCC computes all successors which we are ever going to need in all calls of INSERT. Thus the total time spent in line 4 summed over all calls of INSERT is O(log k) or O(1) per "non-trivial" call. Thus R(k) $\leq$ 1 + R($\lceil k/2 \rceil$) and hence R(k) = O(log k).

$\square$

```
procedure DELETE(x: [0.. 2^k-1], T: k-structure);
if T.B[x] = 1
then T.B[x] ← 0;
        delete x from T.LIST;
        T.SIZE ← T.SIZE - 1;
        case T.SIZE of
        0:  do nothing;
        1:  DELETE(x', T.TOP);
            DELETE(x", T.BOTTOM[x']);
        ≥2: DELETE(x", T.BOTTOM[x']);
            if T.BOTTOM[x'].SIZE = 0
            then DELETE(x', T.TOP)
            fi
        esac
fi
end
```

Lemma 3: The program above correctly deletes an element from a k-structure in time O(log k).

Proof: Similar to the proof of lemma 2. $\square$

Finally, we have to compute the cost of initializing a k-structure. It is easy to see that the cost of initializing a k-structure is proportional to the space requirement of a k-structure. Let $Sp(k)$ be the space requirement of a k-structure. Then

$$Sp(1) = c$$

$$Sp(k) = c \cdot 2^k + Sp(\lceil k/2 \rceil) + 2^{\lceil k/2 \rceil} Sp(\lfloor k/2 \rfloor) \text{ for } k \geq 2$$

for some constant c.

Lemma 4: $Sp(k) = O(2^k \log k)$.

Proof: A simple induction on k shows that

$$Sp(k) \leq c \cdot 2^k \prod_{\ell=1}^{\lceil \log k \rceil - 1} (1 + 1/2^{2^\ell}) \log(2 \cdot k)$$

The proof is completed by the observation that

$$\prod_{\ell \geq 1} (1 + 1/2^{2^\ell}) = O(1). \qquad \Box$$

We summarize in

Theorem 1: Let $N = 2^k$, let $U = \{0, 1, \ldots, N-1\}$ and let $S \subseteq U$ be represented by a k-structure. Then operations Insert(x,S), Delete(x,S), Min S take time $O(\log \log N)$. Furthermore an empty set can be created in time $O(N \log \log N)$ and the representation takes space $O(N \log \log N)$.

Proof: Immediate from lemmas 1 to 4 above. $\qquad \Box$

The space bound and the time for initialization can be improved to $O(N)$ with a little care without sacrifycing the $O(\log \log N)$ bound for the other operations (cf. exercise 47).

III. 8.3   The Union - Find Problem

The union-find problem is to manipulate a partition of $U = \{0, \ldots, N-1\}$ under the operations $(x \in U,$ A and B are names of blocks of the partition):

Find(x)	output the name of the block containing x
Union(A,B,C)	take blocks named A and B and combine them to a block named C.

We will always assume that we start with the partition consisting on N singleton sets and that the name of set {i} is i initially. The union-find problem has numerous applications, among them handling EQUIVALENCE and COMMON statements in FORTRAN, finding least cost spanning trees, computing dominators in directed graphs, checking flow graphs for re-ducibility, calculating depths in trees, computing least common an-cestors in trees, and solving an off-line minimum problem.

The most obvious solution for the union-find problem is to use an array IS_IN[0.. N-1]. IS_IN[i] contains the name of the set containing i. Then execution of Find(x) reduces to table-lookup and therefore takes constant time. Union(A,B,C) is simple but slow. We scan through array IS_IN and change all A's and B's to C's in time $O(N)$. A small extension of the data structure allows us to reduce the time for the Union operation. We associate with every set name a linear list, the list of its members. Then we only have to step through the elements of A ∪ B in order to process Union(A,B,C). One further extension requires us to only step through either the elements of A or the elements of B; e.g. we might step through the elements of A and change all A's to B's. In addition, we record the fact that the B's in array IS_IN are really C's. This is best done by distinguishing between the internal name (the name appearing in array IS_IN) and the external name (the name appearing in the Union operations) of a set and to provide for two arrays MAPOUT and MAPIN; MAPOUT[i] is the external name of the set with internal name i and MAPIN[A] is the internal name of the set with ex-ternal name A.

We can now introduce an important idea for fast Union-Find algorithms: weighting. When executing Union(A,B,C) step through the smaller of sets A and B.

The complete algorithm for Union(A,B,C) is given below. We use SIZE[A] to store the number of elements in set A.

(1) <u>if</u> SIZE[A] ≤ SIZE[B] <u>then</u> X ← A; Y ← B

                              <u>else</u> X ← B; Y ← A <u>fi</u>;

(2) j ← MAPIN[Y];

(3) <u>for</u> all x ∈ X <u>do</u> IS_IN[x] ← j <u>od</u>;

(4) SIZE[C] ← SIZE[A] + SIZE[B];

(5) concatenate lists MAPIN[X] and j and name it j;

(6) MAPOUT[j] ← C;

(7) MAPIN[C] ← j

<u>Theorem 2:</u> The algorithm above processes a sequence of n - 1 Union operations and m Finds in time O(m + n log n).

<u>Proof:</u> A Find clearly takes time O(1). The cost of an operation Union(A,B,C) is O(min(SIZE[A], SIZE[B])) ≤ c min(SIZE[A], SIZE[B]) for some constant c. Note that lines (1),(2),(4),(5) and (6) take constant time and line (3) takes time proportional to the size of X, which is the smaller of A and B. We use the following accounting technique. The cost of Union(A,B,C) is accounted for by charging c time units to every element of X.

<u>Lemma 5:</u> Let x ∈ U be arbitrary. Then at most c·log n time units are charged to x.

<u>Proof:</u> Whenever x is charged for participating in a Union operation it finds itself in a set after the Union which is at least twice the size of the set containing x before the Union. Since we assumed to start with singleton sets n-1 Union operations can build sets of size at most n. Thus x is charged at most log(n) times.   □

By lemma 5 at most c log n time units are charged to any element of U which ever participates in a Union. Also at most 2(n-1) elements of U participate in the n-1 Unions. Thus the total cost of all Union operations is at most O(n log n).   □

Our first approach to the union-find problem favours Finds. A Find costs O(1) time units, whilst the (amortized) cost of a Union is O(log n) time units. We will next describe a solution which favours Unions. Each set is represented by a tree. The nodes and leaves of the tree are the elements of the set and the root is in addition labelled by the (internal) name of the set. Then Unions are particularly easy. In order to

unite A and B we only have to make the root of the tree labelled A a
son of the root of the tree labelled B, or vice versa. Thus a Union
operation takes constant time. The cost of Find(x) is proportional to
the depth of node x in the tree containing x; access node x (via an
array), traverse the path to the root, and look up the label of the
root. Since the depth of a node is at most n (again assuming that n
Unions are performed) the cost of any Find is at most O(n).

Again the running time can be reduced drastically by applying the idea
of weighting. When executing Union(A,B,C) we make the root of the
smaller set a son of the root of the larger set. Ties are broken arbitrarily. We refer to this rule as the weighted union rule. Before we
can analyse this algorithm we need some notation.

Definition: Suppose that we start with singleton sets and perform n-1
Unions. Let T be the resulting tree. For any x ∈ U let rank(x) be the
height of x in T and let weight(x) be the number of descendants of x
in T.   □

Lemma 6: If the weighted union rule is used then weight(x) $\geq 2^{rank(x)}$
for all x ∈ U. In particular, rank(x) ≤ log n.

Proof: (By induction on rank(x)). If rank(x) = 0 then the claim is obvious because every node is a descendant of itself and therefore
weight(x) ≥ 1 for all x. So let us assume rank(x) ≥ 1. Then there must
be a son y of x with rank(y) = rank(x) - 1. When y was made a son of x
the number of descendants of x was at least the number of descendants
of y (weighted union rule) and hence after the Union which made y a
son of x the number of descendants of x is at least twice the number of
descendants of y. Later unions will not give y any additional descendants, but they might increase the number of descendants of x. Thus

$$\begin{aligned}
\text{weight}(x) &\geq 2 \cdot \text{weight}(y) \\
&\geq 2 \cdot 2^{rank(y)} \qquad \text{, by induction hypothesis} \\
&= 2^{rank(x)}
\end{aligned}$$

Finally, n-1 unions can build sets of size at most n and hence
weight(x) ≤ n for all n.   □

Theorem 3: If the weighted union rule is used then a sequence of n-1
Unions and m Finds takes time $O(n + m \log n)$.

Proof: A Union takes time $O(1)$. Also the maximal height of any tree
built by the unions is log n by lemma 6. Thus a Find takes time at most
$O(\log n)$.   □

A further idea reduces the (amortized) cost of a Find even further:
path compression. Suppose that we execute Find(x). Find(x) requires us
to traverse a path $v_0, v_1, \ldots, v_\ell$ from node $x = v_0$ to the root $r = v_\ell$ of
the tree containing x. We can compress this path by making nodes v_i,
$0 \le i < \ell$, direct descendants of the root $v_\ell = r$. Although this will
not decrease the cost of the present Find, in fact, it will increase
its cost by a constant factor, it will reduce the cost of future finds
for descendants of v_i, $0 \le i < \ell$.

The details of the Find algorithm are given below. In this program we
assume that an array FATHER[0.. N-1] is used to store son-to-father
pointers. More precisely, if FATHER[x] $\ne$ x then FATHER[x] is the
father of x, if FATHER[x] = x then x is a root.

```
procedure Find(x);
r ← x;
while r ≠ FATHER[r] do r ← FATHER[r] od;
while x ≠ r do y ← x; x ← FATHER[x]; FATHER[y] ← r od.
output the label of r
end
```

Path compression by itself produces an efficient union-find algorithm
(cf. exercise 54) even without the weighted union rule. Path compression combined with weighted union provides us with a very efficient
algorithm, an algorithm whose running time is almost but not quite
linear.

Definition: a) Let A: $\mathbb{N}_0 \times \mathbb{N}_0 \to \mathbb{N}_0$ be defined by

$$
\begin{aligned}
A(i,0) &= 0 && \text{for all } i \ge 0 \\
A(0,x) &= 2x && \text{for all } x \ge 0 \\
A(i+1,x+1) &= A(i, A(i+1,x)) && \text{for all } i,x \ge 0
\end{aligned}
$$

b) $\alpha(m,n) = \min\{z \ge 1; A(z, 4\lceil m/n \rceil) > \log n\}$

Theorem 4: If path compression and the weighted union rule is used then a sequence of n-1 Unions and $m \geq n$ Finds takes time $O(m\alpha(m,n))$.

Before we prove theorem 4, it is worthwhile to take a closer look at functions A and α. A is a variant of Ackermann's function. It is not primitive recursive. The table below lists values of $A(i,x)$ for small values of i and x.

x \ i	0	1	2	3	4	5	...	x
0	0	2	4	6	8	10	...	2x
1	0	2	4	8	16	32	...	2^x
2	0	2	4	16	65536	2^{65536}	...	$2^{\cdot^{\cdot^{\cdot 2}}} \}x\text{-times}$
3	0	2	4	65536	$2^{\cdot^{\cdot^{\cdot 2}}} \}65536\text{-times}$			

In particular, if $\log n < A(3,4) = 2^{\cdot^{\cdot^{\cdot 2}}} \}65536\text{-times}$ then $\alpha(m,n) \leq 3$. Thus for all practical purposes, $\alpha(m,n) \leq 3$; the union-find algorithm has practically linear running time.

Proof of theorem 4: It is convenient to slightly reformulate the problem. Let T be any tree which can be formed by n-1 unions using the weighted union rule. We allow to change T by partial finds. A partial find of cost k in some tree is a path $v_0, v_1, \ldots, v_k$ from some node v_0 to some ancestor v_k of v_0, v_k is not necessarily a root. Subsequent path compression makes all v_i's, $0 \leq i < k$, sons of v_k. It is now easy to see that any sequence of n-1 unions intermixed with m finds can be modelled by a sequence of n-1 unions followed by m partial finds of the same cost. The n-1 unions are just the unions in the original sequence. A find is simulated by a partial find with exactly the same starting and end vertex. Thus any sequence of unions and finds can be simulated by a sequence of unions followed by a sequence of partial finds of the same cost. It thus suffices to bound the total cost of sequences of n-1 unions followed by $m \geq n$ partial finds.

Let T be the tree formed by the n-1 unions, let rank(x) be the height of node x in tree T. If (x,y) is an edge of T (in the sequel we will always assume that edges point towards the root) then rank(x) < rank(y). The total cost of all partial finds is proportional to the total number of edges traversed by all partial finds. Let F be that set. We show $|F| = O(m\alpha(m,n))$ by partitioning the edges of F into groups and then bounding the number of edges in each group. Edges are put into groups according to the rank of their endpoints.

For $0 \leq i \leq z$, $0 \leq j$ where z is a parameter to be fixed later, let

$$G_{ij} = \{x; \; A(i,j) \leq \text{rank}(x) < A(i,j+1)\}$$

Set F is partitioned into groups N_k, $0 \leq k \leq z+1$ where

$$N_k = \{(x,y) \in F; \; k = \min\{i; \; \exists j \quad x,y \in G_{ij}\}\}$$

for $0 \leq k \leq z$ and

$$N_{z+1} = F - \bigcup_{0 \leq k \leq z} N_k$$

We also define for $0 \leq k \leq z+1$

$$L_k = \{(x,y) \in N_k; \; \text{of the edges on the partial find containing}$$
$$(x,y), \; (x,y) \text{ is the last edge in } N_k\}.$$

<u>Lemma 7:</u> a) $|L_k| \leq m$ for $0 \leq k \leq z+1$

b) $|N_o - L_o| \leq n$

c) $|N_k - L_k| \leq 5n/8$ for $1 \leq k \leq z$

d) $|N_{z+1} - L_{z+1}| \leq n \cdot a(z,n)$
   where $a(z,n) = \min\{i; \; A(z,i) > \log n\}$

<u>Proof:</u> a) For every partial find there is at most one edge in L_k.

b) Let $(x,y) \in N_o - L_o$. Then there must be a j such that $2j = A(o,j) \leq \text{rank}(x) < \text{rank}(y) < A(o,j+1) = 2(j+1)$. Also there must be an edge $(s,t) \in N_o$ following (x,y) on the same partial find path. Hence $\text{rank}(y) \leq \text{rank}(s) < \text{rank}(t)$. After path compression x's father, say u, is an ancestor of t (maybe t itself) ; in particular $\text{rank}(u) \geq \text{rank}(t) \geq A(o,j+1)$. Thus no later partial find can include an edge $(x,y') \in N_o$. Hence $|N_o - L_o| \leq n$.

c) and d): Consider any node x and let $x \in G_{kj}$, i.e. $A(k,j) \leq \text{rank}(x) < A(k,j+1)$. Suppose that there are q edges $(x,y_1),\ldots,(x,y_q) \in N_k - L_k$

where $\text{rank}(y_1) \le \text{rank}(y_2) \le \ldots \le \text{rank}(x,y_q)$. For all i, $1 \le i < q$, there must be edge $(s_i, t_i) \in N_k$ following (x, y_i) on the same partial find path. Thus $\text{rank}(y_i) \le \text{rank}(s_i) < \text{rank}(t_i)$. Also after path compression, x's father is an ancestor of t_i (maybe t_i itself). In particular, $\text{rank}(t_i) \le \text{rank}(y_{i+1})$.

Also since $(x, y_i) \notin N_{k-1}$, $(s_i, t_i) \notin N_{k-1}$ there must be j', j'' such that

$$\text{rank}(x) < A(k-1,j') \le \text{rank}(y_i) \le \text{rank}(s_i) < A(k-1,j'') \le \text{rank}(t_i)$$

and hence $\text{rank}(y_i) < A(k-1,j'') \le \text{rank}(y_{i+1})$. Thus there exists j''' such that

$$\text{rank}(y_1) < A(k-1,j''') \le A(k-1,j'''+q-1) \le \text{rank}(y_q).$$

At this point the proofs for parts c) and d) split.

c) continued: Since $(x, y_q) \in N_k$ and $x \in G_{k,j}$ we have $y_q \in G_{k,j}$ and hence $\text{rank}(y_q) < A(k,j+1) = A(k-1,A(k,j))$. Thus $A(k-1,j'''+q-1) < A(k-1,A(k,j))$ and hence $j''' + q-1 < A(k,j)$ or $q \le A(k,j)$. Also note that $G_{0,0} = G_{k,0}$ and $G_{0,1} = G_{k,1}$ for all k and hence $j \ge 2$.

We have thus shown that for any $x \in G_{kj}$, $k \ge 1$, $j \ge 2$, there are at most $A(k,j)$ edges $(x,y) \subset N_k - L_k$. Hence

$$|N_k - L_k| \le \sum_{j \ge 2} |G_{kj}| \cdot A(k,j)$$

Lemma 8: $|G_{kj}| \le 2n/2^{A(k,j)}$

Proof: Consider any ℓ with $A(k,j) \le \ell < A(k,j+1)$. We count the number of nodes $x \in G_{kj}$ with $\text{rank}(x) = \ell$. Any two such nodes have disjoint sets of descendants in T. Also any such node has at least 2^ℓ descendants by lemma 6 and hence there are at most $n/2^\ell$ nodes of rank ℓ. Thus

$$|G_{kj}| \le \sum_{A(k,j) \le \ell < A(k,j+1)} n/2^\ell \le 2n/2^{A(k,j)} \qquad \square$$

Substituting into the bound for $|N_k - L_k|$ yields

$$|N_k - L_k| \leq \sum_{j \geq 2} 2n\, A(k,j)/2^{A(k,j)}$$

$$\leq \sum_{j \geq 2} 2n\, 2^j/2^{2^j} \qquad\qquad , \text{ since } A(k,j) \geq 2^j$$

$$\leq 5n/8$$

d) continued: By lemma 6) we have $\text{rank}(y_q) \leq \log n$ and hence $A(z, j''' + q-1) \leq \log n$. Note that $k-1 = z$ in case d). Thus $j''' + q-1 < a(z,n)$, or $q \leq a(z,n)$. Hence there are at most $a(z,n)$ edges $(x,y) \in N_{z+1} - L_{z+1}$ for any x. □

We infer from lemma 7

$$|F| = \sum_{k=o}^{z+1} |L_k| + \sum_{k=o}^{z+1} |N_k - L_k|$$

$$\leq m(z+2) + n + 5n/8z + na(z,n)$$

$$\leq (m + 5n/8)\, \alpha(m,n) + 10m + n$$

, by choosing $z = \min\{i \geq 1; A(i, 4\lceil m/n \rceil) > \log n\} = \alpha(m,n)$ and observing that $a(z,n) = a(\alpha(m,n),n) = \min\{x; A(\alpha(m,n),x) > \log n\} \leq 4\lceil m/n \rceil \leq 8m/n$

$$= O(m\, \alpha(m,n))$$

since $m \geq n$. □

The running time of the union-find algorithm with path compression and weighted union is almost linear. However, it is not linear. Tarjan has shown that almost any conceivable union-find algorithm requires time $\Omega(m\, \alpha(m,n))$ to process a sequence of $n-1$ Unions and $m \geq n$ Finds. Applications of the Union-Find problem are discussed in exercises 48 to 52.

III.9. Exercises

1) Write programs for operations Access, Delete and Insert in compressed tries.

2) Write a program for operation Access in TRIES which are compressed
according to the overlay technique discussed in III.1.2.. Make sure
that your program works correctly for unsuccessful searches.

3) Show that the expected worst case cost of hashing with chaining is
$\Theta((\log n)/\log \log n)$ provided that $0.5 \le \beta \le 1$. Note that theorem 3 of
section 2.1. only states an upper bound.

4) In section 2.4. we developed universal hashing for hashing with
chaining. Can we also apply the concept of universal hashing to hashing with open addressing?

5) Let $m = 10$ and $S = \{2,19,31,64,93,103,111,115,7,9\}$. Construct a
perfect hash function. Repeat for $m = 15$.

6) Let $H \subseteq \{h;\ h: [0..\ N-1] \rightarrow [0..\ m-1]\}$ be c-universal. Then $c \ge 1 - m/N$.
Hint: Show $\sum\limits_{x,y \in U} \delta_h(x,y) \ge N(N-1)/m$ for every function h:
$[0..\ N-1] \rightarrow [0..\ m-1]$.

7) For $s \in \mathbb{N}$ let $rep_s : \{0,1\}^s \rightarrow [0...2^s-1]$ be defined by
$rep_s(a_{s-1},...,a_0) = \sum\limits_{i=0}^{s-1} a_i 2^i$ where $a_i \in \{0,1\}$. Let $N = 2^r$, $m = 2^g$
and let B be the set of s by r matrices over $\{0,1\}$. Let $H = \{h_A; A \in B\}$,
where $h_A : [0..\ N-1] \rightarrow [0..\ m-1]$ is defined as $h_A(x) = rep_s(A \cdot rep_r^{-1}(x))$.
Here, matrix multiplication $A \cdot rep_r^{-1}(x)$ is over $\mathbb{Z}_2$, the field of two
elements.

a) Show that H is 1-universal. Hint : Let $x,y \in [0..\ N-1]$, $x \ne y$. Then
$h_A(x) = h_A(y)$ iff $A(\vec{x} - \vec{y}) = 0$ where $\vec{x} = rep_r^{-1}(x)$ and $\vec{y} = rep_r^{-1}(y)$.
Since the set of vectors of dimension r form a vector space over $\mathbb{Z}_2$,
we conclude from $A(\vec{x} - \vec{y}) = 0$ that all rows of A are orthogonal to
$\vec{x} - \vec{y}$.

b) Let $S \subseteq [0..\ N-1]$, $|S| = n$ and let $x \in [0..\ N-1]$. Use part a) to compute $\mu = [\sum_{h \in H} \delta_h(x,S)]/|H|$.

c) Compute variance $\sigma^2 = (\sum_{h \in H} \delta_h(x,S)^2)/|H| + \mu^2$ of random variable $\delta_h(x,S)$.

d) Use part c) and Chebychev's inequality to show $\text{prob}(\delta_h(x,S) \geq t \cdot \mu) \leq (2 + m/n)/(t - 1)^2$.

8) Let U be the set of real numbers between O and 1. Discuss the use of hash function $h : x \rightarrow \lfloor xm \rfloor$ where m is the size of the hash table.

9) Let π be a permutation of $1,2,\ldots,n$. Let $T[\pi]$ be the tree obtained by inserting $\pi(1),\ldots,\pi(n)$ in that order into an initially empty tree. Insertion is done as described in section 3.1..

a) Let $P(T[\pi])$ be the external path length of $T[\pi]$, i.e. $P(T[\pi]) = \sum\{d(v); v \text{ leaf of } T[\pi]\}$ where $d(v)$ is the depth of leaf v. Show that $\sum_\pi P(T[\pi])/n! = O(n \log n)$, i.e. the expected external path length of a randomly grown tree is $O(n \log n)$. Hint : compare the analysis of Quicksort.

b) Let $d(T[\pi])$ be the depth of $T[\pi]$. Show that $\sum_\pi d(T[\pi])/n! = O(\log n)$, i.e. the expected depth of a randomly grown tree is $O(\log n)$. Note that part b) does not follow from part a).

1o) Let A_i, $1 \leq i \leq n$, be an n_i by n_{i+1} matrix. We want to compute matrix product $A_1 A_2 \ldots A_n$. We assume that it costs $O(pqr)$ time units to multiply an p by q with an q by r matrix. Use dynamic programming to find an optimal evaluation order. Note that $(A_1 A_2)A_3$ has cost $n_1 n_2 n_3 + n_1 n_3 n_4$ and that $A_1(A_2 A_3)$ has cost $n_1 n_2 n_4 + n_2 n_3 n_4$.

11) Let $L_1,\ldots,L_n$ be the set of words. We want to compute the product (catenation) $L_1 L_2 \ldots L_n$. Assume that it costs $p \cdot q$ time units to multiply a set of size p with a set of size q and that the resulting set has size pq. Find the optimal evaluation order.

12) Given $a_1, a_2, \ldots, a_n \in \mathbb{N}$ find $S \subseteq \{1,2,\ldots,n\}$ such that $\max(\sum_{i \in S} a_i, \sum_{i \notin S} a_i)$ is minimal. Use dynamic programming.

13) Design a 2DPDA which runs for an exponential number of steps on some inputs.

14) Let $L = \{a_1 \ldots a_n; a_i \in \{0,1\}$ and there is $j \geq 2$ such that $a_1 \ldots a_j = a_j a_{j-1} \ldots a_1\}$, i.e. L consists of all strings which start with a non-trivial palindrom. Show that L can be recognized by a 2DPDA.

15) Given strings $a_0 \ldots a_{n-1}$ and $b_0 \ldots b_{n-1}$, find an O(n) algorithm to determine whether there exists an k, $0 \leq k \leq n-1$, such that $a_i = b_{(k+i) \bmod n}$ for $0 \leq i < n$.

16) Let $S = \{p_1, \ldots, p_m\}$ be a set of patterns. Design an algorithm to determine all occurrences of strings in S in some text x. Running time?

17) A string $x = a_1 \ldots a_n$ is a subsequence of string $y = b_1 \ldots b_m$ if there are $i_1 < i_2 < \ldots < i_n$ such that $a_j = b_{i_j}$ for $1 \leq i \leq n$. Design an O(nm) algorithm to decide whether x is a subsequence of y.

18) In III.4.1., lemma 6 we start with a binary tree T and derive a probability distribution from it. Show that T is optimal for this dis-tribution. (Hint : Construct-tree of section 4.2. constructs T when applied to the derived distribution). Conclude that the lower bound given in theorem 5 is existentially sharp.

19) Show that the upper bounds given in theorems 7 and 8 are existen-tially sharp.

2o) Analyse method 1 for constructing nearly optimal binary search trees. Method 1 is described at the beginning of section 4.2.. What is the quality of the trees produced? What is the running time of the algorithm?

21) Analyse the time complexity of construct-tree (section 4.2.) when k is determined by linear search starting at both ends simultaneously. Answer: O(n log n).

22) Design a balanced tree scheme where the worst case rebalancing cost after an insertion or deletion is O(log log n). Hint : Use-weight balanced trees. If n elements are stored then rebalance up to height

O(log log n) as described in the text. With every node v of height log log n associate a pointer which points to an ancestor p(v) of v in the tree. If a transaction goes through v then we also rebalance p(v), if necessary, and advance p one step towards the root. Show that the root balance of nodes of height log log n or more cannot deteriorate too much.

23) Let L be a sequence of n elements. If x and y are pointers into list L then Insert(x) inserts a new element immediately to the right of x, Delete(x) deletes the element to which x points and Order(x,y) returns true if x is before y in the list.

a) Show how to implement all three operations with worst case time O(log n).

b) A labelling Num : L → [1.. n^k] for some small k is a good labelling if Order(x,y) iff Num(x) < Num(y). Show that a good labelling can be maintained in amortized time O(log n) per insertion/deletion, i.e. the total cost of a sequence of n insertions/deletions is O(n log n). (Hint : use Lemma 2 of section 5.1.).

c) Divide L into n/log n pieces of length log n each. Realize each piece as an ordinary linked list and keep the pieces in a balanced tree as in part b). Design an algorithm which realizes all three operations with amortized cost O(1).

24) Consider the following operations on trees. Insert(x) gives node x an additional (rightmost) son, Delete(x) deletes node x and makes all sons of x to direct sons of father(x). Ancestor(x,y) returns true iff x is an ancestor of y.

a) Associate with every node x of the tree labels x_1 and x_2. For tree T with root x and subtrees $T_1, \ldots, T_k$ let Pre(T) = x_1 Pre(T_1)...Pre(T_k) x_2 and let Post(T) = x_1 Post(T_k)...Post(T_1) x_2. Show: x is an ancestor of y in T iff x_1 precedes y_1 in Pre(T) and Post(T).

b) Use a) and exercise 23 to design a data structure which supports Insert, Delete and Ancestor in amortized time O(1).

25) Let T be a binary tree. The height h(v) of node v is the longest path from v to a leaf. The height balance hb(v) of v is the height dif-ference of the two sons of v, i.e. hb(v) = h(x) - h(y) where x(y) is the left (right) son of x. Tree T is an <u>AVL-tree</u> if hb(v) $\in$ {-1,0,+1} for all nodes of T.

a) Are the following trees AVL-trees?

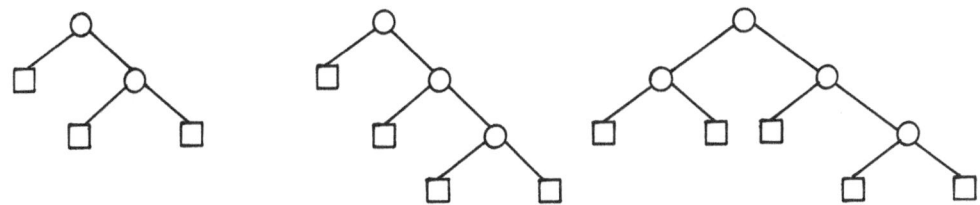

b) Let T be an AVL-tree of height h and n leaves. Then log n $\leq$ h $\leq$ 1.44 log(n+1). (Hint: Show n $\leq$ 2^h and n $\geq$ Fib(h+1) where Fib(0) = Fib(1) = 1 and Fib(h+2) = Fib(h+1) + Fib(h) for h $\geq$ 0 by induction on h; Fib is the sequence of Fibonacci numbers).

c) Show how to rebalance AVL-trees after insertions and deletions (Hint: Adding or deleting a leaf may change the height balance of some nodes to ± 2. Use rotations and double rotations to remedy the situa-tion. One operation suffices in the case of insertions, many rotations/ double rotations might be required in the case of deletions.

26) Let T be a binary tree and v a node of T. Let s(v) be the lenght of a shortest path from v to a leaf and let h(v) be the length of a longest path to a leaf; h(v) is the height of v. T is <u>half-balanced</u> if h(v) $\leq$ 2 s(v) for every node v of T.

a) Let T be a half-balanced tree with height h and n leaves. Then h $\leq$ 2 log(n+2) + 2. (Hint: show

$$n \geq \begin{cases} 2^{h/2+1} - 2 & \text{if h is even} \\ 3 \cdot 2^{(h-1)/2} - 2 & \text{if h is odd} \end{cases}$$

by induction on h).

b) Show how to rebalance half-balanced trees after insertions and dele-

tions. (Hint: Use rotations, double rotations and triple rotations).
Show that at most <u>one</u> single, double, triple rotation is required to
rebalance the tree after an insertion or deletion.

27) This exercise treats <u>red-black</u> trees in more details (cf. end
of section III.4)

    a) Design an algorithm for deleting a leaf from a red-black tree.

    b) In the text, we used red-black trees with leaf-oriented
storage organization, i.e. set S was stored in the leaves and internal
nodes are only used as a directory. Develop the algorithms for node-
oriented storage organization, i.e. set S is stored in the internal
nodes and leaves have empty content. In order to improve storage
utilization use a <u>single</u> record of type node to represent <u>all</u> leaves.
The diagram below shows a node-oriented red-black tree for set
S = {2,4,7,8}.
Use the "single leaf" as a sentinel in searches, i.e. if you search
for x then store x in the sentinel first so as to make every search
successful.

    c) Discuss operations Split and Concatenate for red-black trees.
Use both storage organizations.

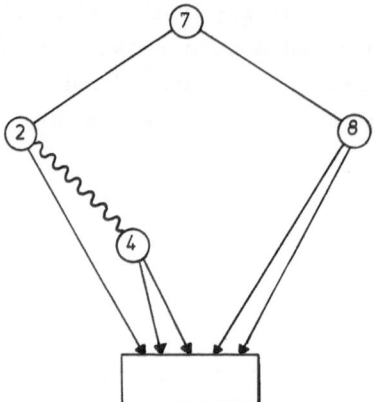

d) Show how to implement (a,b)-trees for arbitrary a and b, b ≥ 2a-1,
by colored trees (Hint: All leaves have identical black depth and are
attached via black edges. Moreover, if we delete all black edges then all
components (which are now kept together by red edges), except the component containing the root, have at least a-1 and at most b-1 nodes).

28) Show that the following statement is false: There is c > 1 such that for every (2,4)-tree with n leaves and node v of depth d we have: the number of leaves below v is bounded by n/c^d. Note that the statement is true for BB[α]-trees.

29) Show how to rebalance (a,b)-trees top-down; b ≥ 2a, a ≥ 2. (Hint: Follow a path down the tree as usual. Make sure that the father of the current node has arity ≤ b-1 (≥ a+1) in the case of an insertion (deletion). This allows us to split (fuse, share) the current node if its arity is b (a) without having to back up.

3o) Formulate and prove an analogon to theorem 8 (section 5.3.1.) for (a,2a-1)-trees and sequences of insertions only (Hint: Use the account b(v) = 2a - 1 - ρ(v) where ρ is the arity of v).

31) Same as exercise 3o) but for theorem 1o instead of theorem 8.

32) In exercise 29) we outlined how to rebalance (a,b)-tree top-down. Formulate and prove an analogon to theorem 8 (of section 5.3.1.) for sequences of insertions and deletions provided that b ≥ 2a + 2. Is a similar theorem true if b = 2a or b = 2a + 1?

33) Operation Concatenate was defined in section 5.3.1.. We assume for this exercise that Concatenate is implemented as follows. If trees T_1 and T_2 are concatenated then we walk up the left spine of T_1 and the right spine of T_2 simultaneously until one of the roots is met. Then we proceed as described in section 5.3.1..

a) Show that the cost of concatenating T_1 and T_2 is O(s + min(h_1,h_2)) where s is the number of splittings required and h_i is the height of T_i.

b) Start with n (a,b)-trees with one leaf each: Perform a sequence of n Concatenate operations. Show that the total cost is O(n). (Hint: In addition to the account used to prove theorem 8 (of 5.3.2.) use the following account: the sum of the heights of all trees. Note that this quality is n initially and is decreased by at least min(h_1,h_2) - 1 by concatenating T_1 and T_2).

c) Use part b) to extend theorem 11 (of 5.3.3.) to also allow Concatenate.

34) Show that theorem 14 (of 5.3.3.) stays true if ordinary (2,4)-trees are used instead of level-linked (2,4)-trees.

35) Start with n singleton sets and perform an arbitrary sequence of set unions to build up a single ordered set of n elements. Show that the total cost is O(n log n) if sets are represented as level-linked (2,4)-trees (Hint: Use theorem 14, b of 5.3.3.).

36) Use fringe analysis to improve upon theorem 8 of 5.3.2. for sequences of random insertions. (Hint: Use it to improve upon fact 4 in the proof of theorem 8).

37) Use fringe analysis to approximate the expected number of balanced (hb(v) = 0) nodes in a random AVL-tree (cf. exercise 25 for a definition of AVL-trees).

38) Show how to do operations Concatenate and Split on BB[α]-trees. Show that the cost of Concatenate is O(log ((n+m)/min(n,m))) if the trees to be concatenated have n and m leaves respectively. Compare this bound to the bound derived for (a,b)-trees in 5.3.1.. Observe exercise 28.

39) Extend theorem 6 of III.6. to weighted sets.

4o) Extend theorem 6 of III.6. to operations Concatenate and Split, i.e. show how to do these operations in time O(d+log |S|).

41) Discuss the amortized behavior of the following variant of the move-to-front-rule (section 6.1.1). Whenever an element is accessed it is moved half-way to the front of the list. Show that
$C_{HWR}(s) \le 4C_A(s) + 2X_A(s)$ for any algorithm A and any sequence s.

42) Write a RAM program for the move to front rule realizing the linear list a) as an array and b) as a linked list. If the linear list is realized as an array then moving an element from the i-th position to the front also requires to physically move elements in positions 1,...,i - 1 one position to the rear. This can be done simultaneously with the search. Compute expected running time and compare with the running time for the optimal arrangement.

43) Let $S = \{x_1, \ldots, x_n\}$, let β_i be the probability of accessing x_i and let L_i be the cost of comparing with x_i. If the x_i's are stored on magnetic tape then L_i may be the length of x_i. The expected search cost is $\sum_i L_i \sum \{\beta_j; \pi(j) \geq \pi(i)\}$ when x is stored in the $\pi(i)$-th position show that expected search cost is minimized if $\beta_i/L_i < \beta_j/L_j$ implies $\pi(i) < \pi(j)$. Can you generalize self-organizing linear search to this situation?

44) Set $S = \{x_1, \ldots, x_n\}$ and let β_i be the probability of accessing x_i. Assume $\beta_1 \geq \beta_2 \geq \ldots \geq \beta_n$.

a) Show that the stationary probability of arrangement π is $\gamma_\pi = c \cdot \prod_{i=1}^{n} \beta_i^{n-\pi(i)}$ under the transposition rule where c is such that $\sum_\pi \gamma_\pi = 1$.

b) Let π be an arrangement where x_i is in front of x_j and let $\bar{\pi}$ be the arrangement obtained by interchanging x_j and x_i. Then $\gamma_{\bar{\pi}} \leq (\beta_j/\beta_i)\gamma_\pi$. Conclude from this that $\delta_{TR}(j,i) \leq (\beta_j/\beta_i)(1-\delta_{TR}(j,i))$ where $\delta_{TR}(j,i)$ is the asymptotic probability that x_j is in front of x_i and $j > i$. Conclude further that $\delta_{TR}(j,i) \leq \gamma_j/(\gamma_i + \gamma_j) = \delta_{MFR}(j,i)$ for $j > i$.

c) Use b) to show that $P_{TR} \leq P_{MFR}$ for all distributions $(\beta_1, \ldots, \beta_n)$. Hint: Use lemma 1, a to express P_{XYZ} in terms of $\delta_{XYZ}(j,i)$ where $XYZ \in \{TR, MFR\}$.

45) Use the explicite expression given for P_{MFR} in theorem 1 to compute P_{MFR} and P_{MFR}/P_{opt} for the following distributions.

a) Zipf's law: $\beta_i = 1/(iH_n)$ where $H_n = \sum_{1 \leq i \leq n} 1/i$.

b) Exponential distribution: $\beta_i = ca^i$ where $c = 1/\sum_{1 \leq i \leq n} a^i$.

c) Lotka's law: $\beta_i = c/i^2$ where $c = 1/\sum_{1 \leq i \leq n} i^{-2}$.

46) Let $k \geq 1$ be an integer. Batch accesses into groups of k. Invoke the move to front (transposition) rule only if all k requests in a group are to the same element. Compute $P_{MFR}(k)$, the expected search cost under the move to front rule if requests are batched into groups

of k requests.

47) Let $S \subseteq [0 .. N-1]$, $N = 2^k (\log k)$ for some k. Let $S_i = \{x \in S; (\log k) \leq x < (i+1)\log k\}$ for $0 \leq i < 2^k$. Represent S as follows. Store $\{i; S; \neq \emptyset\}$ in a priority queue as described in section 8.2. and store each non-empty S_i in a linear list. Show that the data structure requires linear space $O(N)$, can be created in time $O(N)$ and supports Insert, Delete, Min in time $O(\log \log N)$.

48) Let N be an integer. Consider operations Insert(x,S) and Delete-min(S) where $x \in [0 \ldots N-1]$ and $S \subseteq [0 \ldots N-1]$. Consider a sequence $Op_1, \ldots, Op_m$ and discuss the following variants of the problem.

a) On-line: The answer to operation Op_i must be given before operation Op_{i+1} is known. (Hint: Use the $O(\log \log N)$ priority queue).

b) Off-line: $Op_1, \ldots, Op_m$ are known, before any answer must be given. (Hint: Reduce to Union-Find. Let $Op_1, \ldots, Op_m = \alpha_1 D \alpha_2 D \alpha_3 \ldots \alpha_m D$ where α_i is a sequence of Insert instructions and D represents a Deletemin instruction. Create m disjoint sets $A_1, \ldots, A_m$ with $i \in A_j$ if Insert(i) occurs in α_j. Observe, if $1 \in A_j$ then 1 is the output of the j-th Deletemin instruction, ...).

49) Discuss the following weighted union rule for the Union-Find problem: If trees T_1 and T_2 are to be united then make the tree of smaller height a subtree of the tree of larger height. Ties are broken arbitrarily. Show that the cost of a sequence of n unions and m finds is $O(n + m \log n)$.

50) Show that theorem 2 of section 8.3. is best possible, i.e. describe a sequence of n unions and m finds which force the algorithm to run for $\Omega(m \log n + n)$ steps.

51) Consider a forest of disjoint trees over node set $0, \ldots, n-1$. Link(r,v) makes r, the root of one of the trees, a son of v, a node in another tree. Depth(v) outputs the current depth of node v. Show how to use the union-find data structure to solve this problem. (Hint: If T is one of the trees in the forest then the nodes of T form one of the sets in the union find problem. Recall that these sets are stored as trees.

Maintain function help on the nodes of the union-find trees such that
Depth(v) = Σ help(w) where the summation is over all ancestors of v in
the union-find tree containing v).

52) Design a Union-Find algorithm with worst case complexity O(log n).
Can you do better?

53) Analyse the following Union-Find algorithm: Path compression is
used but the weighted union rule is not used.

III.10 Bibliographic Notes: TRIES were introduced by Fredkin(60). The compression technique for sparse tables is due to Ziegler, the analysis
(theorems 3, 4 and 5) is taken from Tarjan/Yao (79).

A very detailed account of hashing can be found in Knuth (73). The
analysis of the expected worst case cost of hashing is due to Gonnet
(81) and the analysis of open addressing is due to Peterson (57).
Perfect hashing was first discussed by Sprugnoli (77); he describes
heuristic methods for constructing perfect hash functions. Section 2.3.
on perfect hashing is based on Fredman/Komlos/Szemeredi (82), lemma 1,
theorems 1o, 11, 12, and Mehlhorn (82), theorems 6,7,8,12. Theorem 13
has not appeared before. Universal hashing was first described by
Carter/Wegman and theorems 14, 15 and 16 are taken from Carter/Wegman
(77). Exercise 7 is taken from Markowsky, Carter and Wegman (78).
Theorem 17 is taken from Mehlhorn (82). Extendible Hashing is discussed in
Larson (78), Litwin (78), Fagin et al. (79), A. Yao (8o), Flajolet/
Steyaert (82).

A detailed analysis of interpolation search can be found in Perl/Itai/
Avni (78). The discussion in the text is due to Perl/Reingold (77).
Willard (to appear) extended interpolation search to non-uniform prob-
ability distributions.

The $O(n^2)$ dynamic programming algorithm for optimum binary search trees
is due to Knuth (71); theorem 2 on quadrangle inequalities is due to
F. Yao (8o). If β_i = O for all i then an optimum tree can be constructed
in time O(n log n), cf. Hu/Tucker (71) or Garsia/Wachs (77). The linear
time simulation of 2 DPDA's on RAMs is by Cook (71); the proof given in
text follows Jones (77). The linear time pattern matching algorithm

is from Knuth/Morris/Pratt (74). A general discussion of tabulation can
be found in Bird (80).

The section of nearly optimal trees is based on P. Bayer (77) (theorem
5), Güttler/Mehlhorn/Schneider (8o)(theorem 6), Fredman (75) (theorem
11), Mehlhorn (75) (exercise 21) and Mehlhorn (77) (theorem 7 and 8).
Extensions to multiway trees can be found in Altenkamp/Mehlhorn (8o)
and Mehlhorn (8o).

Weight-balanced trees (theorems 2 and 3) were introduced by Nievergelt/
Reingold (73); lemma 1 and theorem 4 are taken from Blum/Mehlhorn (8o);
(a,b)-trees were introduced by Bayer/Mc Creight (72); theorem 5 comes
from their paper. The extensions to mergable priority queues is by
Hopcroft (7o). Theorems 8, 1o, 11, 12, 13 and 14 are from Huddleston/
Mehlhorn (82), extending work of Brown/Tarjan (8o). Theorem 9 was first
shown by Guibas et al (77); the proof given here is due to Brown/
Tarjan (8o) and Mehlhorn (79). Fringe analysis was introduced by A. Yao
(78) and theorem 15 comes from that paper. Theorem 16 is taken from
Eisenbarth/ et. al. (82). An analysis of (a,b)-trees under random insertions and deletions can be found in Mehlhorn (82). AVL-trees
(exercise 25) were introduced by Adel'son-Velskii (62), half-balanced
tree (exercise 26) by Olivié (82), and red-black trees (exercise 27) by
Guibas/Sedgewick. Exercises 23 and 24 are taken from A. Tsakalidis (83).

The move to front rule for self-organizing linear search was first
analysed by Mc Cabe(65). Exercises 44, 45 and 46 are taken from Rivest
(76), Hendricks (76), and Gonnet/Munro/Suwanda (79). The amortized
analysis of the move to front rule was started by Bentley/Mc Geoch (82)
and then refined by Sleator/Tarjan (83).

Splay trees were introduced by Sleator/Tarjan (83). D-trees were introduced by Mehlhorn (81). The application of weighted dynamic trees to
multi-dimensional searching is taken from Mehlhorn (79). Other solutions
to the weighted dictionary problem can be found in Bent/Sleator/Tarjan
80) and Gutting/Kriegel (82).

The O(log log N) priority queue is by v. Emde Boas/Kaas/Zijlstra (77)
and v. Emde Boas (77). The analysis of the union-find algorithm with
path compression and weighted union is due to R.E. Tarjan (75). Exercises 48 and 51 are taken from Aho/Hopcroft/Ullman (73).

IX. Algorithmic Paradigms

There are basically two ways for structuring a book on data structures
and algorithms: problem or paradigm oriented. We have mostly followed
the first alternative because it allows for a more concise treatment.
However, at certain occassions (e.g. section VIII.4 on the sweep paradigm in computational geometry) we have also followed the second approach. In this last chapter of the book we attempt to review the entire book from the paradigm oriented point of view.

Solving an algorithmic problem means to search for a solution to the
problem within a set of possible candidates (= search space, state
space).

Exhaustive search, i. e. a complete scan of the state space, is the
most obvious searching method. Pure exhaustive search is rarely efficient and should only be used for small state spaces. We found several
ways of improving upon exhaustive search, most notably branch and bound,
tabulation, and dynamic programming. In the branch and bound approach
(VI.6.2) to optimization problems one explores the state space in the
order of decreasing promise, i. e. one has the means of estimating the
quality of partial solutions and always works on the partial solution
with maximal promise. The precision of the search depends on the quality of the estimates. It is usually quite difficult (or even impossible)
to analyse the complexity of branch and bound algorithms in a satisfying
way.

In more structured state spaces one can use dynamic programming and
tabulation (III.4.1, IV.7.3, and VI.6.1). Dynamic programming is particularly useful when the problem space ist structured by size in a
natural way and when solutions to larger problems are easily obtained
from solutions to (all, sufficiently many) smaller problems. In this
situation it is natural to solve all conceivable subproblems in order
of increasing size in a systematic way. The efficiency of dynamic programming is directly related to the size of the state space. We en-
countered a large state space in the application to the travelling
salesman problem (VI.6.1) and a fairly small state space in the application to optimum search trees (III.4.1) and least cost paths (IV.7.3).
In some occassions, e. g. III.4.1, the search could be restricted to a
suitably chosen subset of the state space.

<u>Tabulation</u> (III.4.1) is a general method of obtaining dynamic programming algorithms from top-down exhaustive search algorithms. The idea is to store the solutions to all solved subproblems in a table for latter look-up. We have used this idea for converting a backtracking algorithm for optimum search trees into the dynamic programming algorithm and for simulating 2-way deterministic pushdown automata in linear time on a RAM. The latter simulation led to the linear time pattern matching algorithm.

The <u>divide - and - conquer</u> paradigm is also applied to problem spaces which are structured by size. A problem instance is solved by generating several subproblems (<u>divide</u>), solving the subproblems (<u>conquer</u>), and combining the answer to the subproblems to an answer for the original problem instance (<u>merge</u>). The efficiency of the method is determined by the cost of generating the subproblems, the number and the size of the subproblems, and the cost of merging the answers. Divide - and - conquer algorithms lead to recursive programs and their analysis leads to recursion equations. We discussed recursion equations in sections II.1.3 and VII.2.2. The paradigm of divide - and - conquer was used very frequently in this book: in sorting and selection algorithms (II.1.2, II.1.3, and II.4), in all data-structures based upon trees (III.3 to III.7, VII.2.1 and VII.2.2, and VIII.5.1), in the planar separator theorem and its applications (IV.10), in the matrix multiplication algorithms (V.4), and in the divide - and conquer algorithms for computational geometry (VIII.5.2). Finally, the treatment of decomposable searching problems and dynamization (VII.1) has a very close relationship to the divide - and - conquer paradigm. In most applications of the paradigm a natural structure of the problem instances was used for the division step. For example, if the problem instance is a tuple then we can split the tuple into its first and its second half (merge sort, binary search, matrix multiplication,...) and if the problem instance is a set of objects from an ordered set then we can split the set into its lower and its upper half (the linear time selection algorithm, applications in geometry,...). The situation was slightly different in multidimensional divide - and - conquer (VII.2.2). There we frequently solved an instance of size n in d-dimensional space by generating two d-dimensional subproblems of size about n/2 and one (d-1)-dimensional subproblem of size n. Another interesting application of the paradigm is to planar graphs. We have seen two strategies. The first strategy is given by the planar separator theorem of section IV.10.2. It allows us to

split a planar graph of n nodes into two subgraphs of about half the
size by the removal of only $O(\sqrt{n})$ nodes. Moreover, the separating set
can be determined in linear time. We used the planar separator theorem
in several efficient algorithms on planar graphs, e. g. least cost path,
chromatic number, ... The second strategy is given by the fact that a
planar graph always contains a large set of independent nodes of small
degree. We used this fact in searching planar subdivisions (VIII.3.2.1)
and in the hierarchical representation of convex polyhedra (VIII,
exercise 2).

Trees are a prime example for the divide - and - conquer paradigm. In
trees one either organizes the universe (section III.1 on TRIES) or one
organizes the set to be stored in the tree. The latter approach was
used in sections III.3 to III.7 and leads to balanced trees. In these
trees one chooses an element of the set for the root which balances the
subproblems. In balanced trees for unweighted data balancing is done
either according to the cardinality of the subproblems (weight - balanced trees) or according to the height of the subtrees (height - balanced trees). In trees for weighted data balancing is done according to
the probability of the subproblems. We have also seen on two occassions
(III.6.1 on weighted dynamic trees for multidimensional searching and
VIII.5.1.3 on segment trees) that search structures for unweighted complex data can sometimes be constructed from trees for simpler but weighted data. The former approach, i. e. organizing the universe, was used
in section III.1 on TRIES and in the static version of interval, priority search, and segment trees (VIII.5.1). The organization of the universe gives rise to particularly simple tree structures.

Closely related to trees which organize the universe are key transformation (=hashing) and direct access(II.2, III.2 and III.8). In these
methods one uses the key or a transformed key in order to directly
access data. This immediately implies small running times. Another
application of the very same idea is presorting, i. e. transforming a
problem on an arbitrary set into a problem on a sorted set by sorting.
It is then often possible to identify the objects with an initial
segment of the integers which opens up all methods of direct access. We
used presorting in sections VII.2.2 on multi-dimensional divide - and -
conquer and in section VIII.5 on orthogonal objects in computational
geometry.

In graphs we studied two methods for their systematic exploration: breadth - first and depth - first search. Breadth - first search is particularly useful for distance type problems and was therefore used intensively in least cost path computations (IV.7). Depth - first search has the important property that components are explored one by one and is therefore the natural method of exploration in connectivity problems. We used DFS to determine biconnected and strongly connected components and to test planarity.

Frequently, solutions to problem instances can be found iteratively or in a step by step fashion. Examples are the construction of optimal merging patterns (II.1.4), network flow and matching problems (IV.9), the construction of least cost spanning trees (IV.8), and the construction of convex hulls (VIII.2). In some of these examples (e. g. least cost spanning trees or optimal merging patterns) each step performs an action which is locally optimal. This variant of iteration is sometimes called the greedy approach. In other applications of this paradigm (e. g. network flow) a solution is improved iteratively. Frequently, the concept of augmentation applies to these situations.

In the chapter on algorithmic geometry we discussed the sweep paradigm at length (VIII.4, VIII,5.1). Its power stems from the fact that it reduces the dimension of geometric problems for the cost of turning static into dynamic problems. In particular, two-dimensional static problems can often be reduced to one-dimensional dynamic problems which can then be solved using some sort of balanced tree.

The method of reduction also played a major role in other parts of the book. The entire chapter on NP - completeness is centered around the notion of reduction or transformation. We used reductions to structure the world of problems, to define and explore classes of equivalent problems (VI.1 to VI.5), to transfer algorithms (from network flow to matching in IV.9, from matrix product over the integers to matrix product over the set of booleans in V.5, from iso - oriented objects to general objects in VIII.5.2, and from straight-line to circular objects in VIII.6), and to transfer lower bounds (from sorting to element uniqueness in II.6, from decision trees to RAMs in II.3 and from boolean matrix product to matrix product over semi-rings of characteristic zero in V.7).

Balancing is also an important concept. In least cost path computations (IV.7) we balanced the cost.of various priority queue operations
by a careful choice of the data structure, in multi - dimensional trees
(VII.2.1) we balanced the power of the coordinates by using them in the
split fields in cyclic order, and in divide - and - conquer algorithms
we always tried to balance the size of the subproblems. It is important
to observe that perfect balancing is usually not required in order to
obtain efficient solutions; approximate balancing will also do. In fact,
approximate balancing is called for in order to cope with dynamic behavior.
A typical example are balanced trees. In BB[α]-trees (VIII.5.1) we do
not require each node to have root balance in the range [1/3,2/3] although such a tree always exists but leave more leeway and in height-
balanced trees (VIII.5.2) we allow nodes to have between a and b sons.
Introducing an amount of freedom beyond the necessary amount often has
dramatic effects on the (amortized) behavior of these schemes. Again,
balanced trees are typical examples but so are the dynamization methods
of VII.1. For example, BB[α]-trees work for $\alpha \leq 1-\sqrt{2}/2$, but $\alpha < 1-\sqrt{2}/2$
improves the amortized rebalancing cost dramatically. Similary (a,b)-
trees work for b $\geq$ 2a-1 but choosing b $\geq$ 2a improves the behavior considerably (III.5.2 and III.5.3).

Another way of interpreting approximate rebalancing is redundancy, i.e.
to allow additional freedom in representation. The concept of redundancy can also be applied to storage space. We saw at several occassions,
most notably range trees (VII.2.2) and dd-trees (VII.2.1), that storing
objects several times can reduce search time considerably. In dd-trees
multi-dimensional objects are stored without redundancy; they provide
us with rootic search time and it was shown in VII.2.3.1. that this is
optimal. Range trees store data in a hightly redundant fashion: they
use non-linear storage space and provide us with polylogarithmic
search time. In fact, the slack parameter of range trees allows us to
trade between time and space.

Redundant structures frequently show good amortized behavior because
rebalancing a node of a redundant structure moves the node away from
the critical situations. Amortized analysis was used in the sections
on dynamization and weighting (VII.1), range trees (VII.2.2), (dynamic)
interval (VIII.5.1.1) and segment trees (VIII.5.1.3), BB[α]-trees
(III.5.1), (a,b)-trees (III.5.3) and the union-find problem (III.8).
A general discussion of the bank account paradigm for amortized
analysis can be found in section III.6.1.

Worst case analysis (and amortized analysis which is the worst case
analysis of sequences of operations) is the dominant method of analysis
used throughout this book. Expected case analysis was done in only a few
places; e. g. quicksort (II.3), selection (II.4), TRIES (III.1.1),
hashing (III.2), interpolation search (III.3.2), weighted trees (III.4),
self-organizing linear search (III.6.1.1),and transitive closure (IV.3).
Expected case analysis rests upon an a-priori probability distribution
on problem instances and therefore its predictions should be interpreted
with care. In particular, it should always be checked whether reality
conforms with the probability assumptions. Note however, that the expected running of many algorithms is fairly robust with respect to
changes in the distribution. For example, a near-optimal search tree
for distribution ß ist also a near-optimal search tree for distribution
ß' provided that ß and ß' do not differ too much. Furthermore, a careful analysis of algorithms with small expected running time sometimes
leads to fast algorithms with small wort case running time (e.g. selection) or to fast probabilistic algorithms (e.g. quicksort and hashing).

Self-organization is another important principle. In self-organizing
data structures the items compete for the good places in the structure
and high-frequency elements are more likely to be there. This results
in good expected and sometimes also amortized behavior.

Generalization was the central theme of chapter V and also section
VII.1. In chapter V we dealt with path problems over closed semi-rings,
a generalization of least cost paths, transitive closure, maximal cost
paths, and many other path problems. In section VII.1 we derived general methods for dynamizing static data structures for decomposable and
order decomposable searching problems. Numerous applications of these
general methods can be found in chapters VII and VIII.

The last two principles which we are going to discuss are approximation
algorithms and probabilistic algorithms. These paradigms suggest to
either change the problem to be solved (solve a simpler problem) or to
change our notion of computation (use a more powerful computing machine).
We observed at several places that a "slight" change in the formulation
of a problem can have a drastic effect on its complexity: The satis-
fiability problem with three literals per clause is NP-complete but

with two literals per clause it becomes fairly simple, the precedence constrained scheduling problem is NP-complete but if the precedence relation is a tree or there are only two machines then the problem is in P. Similarly, the computation of the convex hull of a point set takes time $\theta(n \log n)$ but if the points are sorted by x-coordinate then time $O(n)$ suffices. For optimization problems there is a standard method for simplifying the problem; instead of asking for an optimal solution we are content with a nearly optimal solution. This approach is particularly important when the optimization problem is NP-complete and therefore we devoted the entire section V.7 to <u>approximation algorithms</u> for NP-complete problems. We saw that some NP-complete problems resist even approximate solution but many others have good or even very good approximation algorithms. Even inside P approximation algorithms are important. A good example are the weighted trees of section III.4. The best algorithm for constructing optimum weighted trees has running time $\theta(n^2)$ and there is an $O(n)$ algorithm which constructs nearly optimal trees. Already for moderate size n, say $n = 10^4$, the difference between n^2 and n is substantial.

<u>Probabilistic algorithms</u> are based on a more flexible notion of computation, i. e. it is postulated that a perfect coin is available to the machine. (Less than perfect coins will also do for fast probabilistic algorithms as we saw in section I.2). We encountered probabilistic algorithms in many different contexts, e. g. the construction of perfect hash functions (III.2.3), universal hashing (III.2.4), probabilistic quicksort (II.1.3), graph connectivity (IV.9.2) and primality testing (VI.8). These applications may be grouped into two classes. In the first class coin tosses are used to randomize inputs (probabilistic quicksort, universal hashing). Typically, a random transformation is applied to the input and then a standard deterministic algorithm with small expected running time is used. The expected running time of the probabilistic algorithm on a <u>fixed</u> input then matches the expected running of the deterministic algorithm. The important difference is that the randomized algorithm controls the dices but a deterministic algorithm does not; the latter is at the mercy of its user who generates the problem instances. In the second class (construction of perfect hash functions, graph connectivity, primality testing) coin tosses are used to randomize the search for an element of some set with a desirable property. Typically, the property is easily checked and the elements having the property are abundant. However, no intimate knowledge about their location is available.

The design of an efficient algorithm is particularly satisfying if its performance matches a <u>lower bound</u> and hence the algorithm is optimal. Unfortunately, only a few algorithms have been shown to be optimal. We saw three approaches to proving lower bounds in this book. The first approach is the <u>information-theoretic</u> one and the typical argument goes as follows: In order to distinguish between N possibilities any algorithm requires log N steps. Of course in order to make this argument sound one has to define and study the primitive operations, the set of possible outcomes, and how the primitives operate on the set of possible outcomes. We used the information-theoretic approach in sections II.1.6 and II.3 on lower bounds for sorting and related problems, in section III.4 on searching in weighted sets, and in a modified form also in section VII.3.1 on lower bounds for partial match retrieval in minimum space. The second approach is by <u>simplification</u> which we used to prove the lower bound on the complexity of matrix multiplication (V.7). In this approach one designs transformation rules which allow to simplify an optimal program without increasing cost. The final product of the simplification process is then amenable to direct attack. The third approach uses <u>combinatorial methods</u> and was used in the sections on dynamization (VII.1.1) and the spanning bound (VII.3.2). In this approach one relates the complexity of an algorithm to a combinatorial quantity (the spanning complexity of a family of sets in VII.3.2 and various path lengths of binary trees in VII.1.1) and then analyses the combinatorial quantity.

Appendix

The appendix contains some frequently used equalities and inequalities. It is divided into three parts. The first part lists some facts about the entropy function, the second part gives some summation formulae and the third part lists a few inequalities.

Let $\gamma_1, \ldots, \gamma_n$ be a probability distribution, i.e. $\gamma_i \in \mathbb{R}, \gamma_i \geq 0$, and $\sum_i \gamma_i = 1$. The entropy of this distribution is defined as

$$H(\gamma_1, \ldots, \gamma_n) = - \sum_{i=1}^{n} \gamma_i \log \gamma_i$$

where $0 \cdot \log 0 = 0$. □

E1) Let $\delta_1, \ldots, \delta_n$ be another distribution. Then $H(\gamma_1, \ldots, \gamma_n) \leq$

$$- \sum_{i=1}^{n} \gamma_i \log \delta_i \text{ with equality iff } \gamma_i = \delta_i \text{ for all i.}$$

Proof: From $\log x = (\ln x)/\ln 2$ and $\ln x \leq x-1$ we infer

$$H(\gamma_1, \ldots, \gamma_n) + \sum_{i=1}^{n} \gamma_i \log \delta_i = (1/\ln 2) \cdot \sum_{i=1}^{n} \gamma_i \ln(\delta_i/\gamma_i)$$

$$\leq (1/\ln 2) \sum_{i=1}^{n} \gamma_i (\delta_i/\gamma_i - 1)$$

$$= 0 . \qquad □$$

E2) $0 \leq H(\gamma_1, \ldots, \gamma_n) \leq \log n$

Proof: $0 \leq \gamma_i \leq 1$ implies $-\gamma_i \log \gamma_i \geq 0$ and hence $H(\gamma_1, \ldots, \gamma_n) \geq 0$. The second inequality follows from E1) with $\delta_i = 1/n$, $1 \leq i \leq n$.

E3) (grouping property):

$$H(\gamma_1, \ldots, \gamma_n) = H(\gamma_1 + \gamma_2, \gamma_3, \ldots, \gamma_n) + (\gamma_1 + \gamma_2) H(\frac{\gamma_1}{\gamma_1 + \gamma_2}, \frac{\gamma_2}{\gamma_1 + \gamma_2}) .$$

Proof: By substituting the definition of H and simple calculation. □

In the second group we list some frequently used sums and integrals,

S1) $\sum_{i=1}^{k} i \, 2^i = (k-1) 2^{k+1} + 2$ for $k \geq 1$

Proof: An elementary proof uses induction on k. More generally, we can proceed as follows. Consider

$$f(x) = \sum_{i=1}^{k} i \, x^i = x \sum_{i=1}^{k} i \, x^{i-1} = x \cdot \sum_{i=1}^{k} \frac{d}{dx} x^i$$

$$= x \frac{d}{dx} (\sum_{i=1}^{k} x^i) = x \frac{d}{dx} (\sum_{i=o}^{k} x^i - 1)$$

$$= x \frac{d}{dx} ((x^{k+1}-1)/(x-1)) = (x + x^{k+1}(kx-k-1))/(x-1)^2 \quad .$$

Hence $f(2) = 2 + (k-1) 2^{k+1}$ □

S2) $H_k = \sum\limits_{i=1}^{k} 1/i$ is the k-th harmonic number. We have

$$\ln k \leq H_k \leq 1 + \ln k \; .$$

Proof: From $\int\limits_{k}^{k+1} (1/x)\,dx \leq 1/k \leq \int\limits_{k-1}^{k} dx$

we infer $H_k \geq \int\limits_{1}^{k+1} (1/x)\,dx = \ln(k+1)$ and

$$H_k = 1 + \sum_{i=2}^{k} 1/i \leq 1 + \int_{1}^{k} (1/x)\,dx = 1 + \ln k \; . \qquad \square$$

S3) $\sum\limits_{i=1}^{n} H_k = (n+1) H_n - n$ for $n \geq 1$.

Proof: $\sum\limits_{k=1}^{n} H_k = \sum\limits_{k=1}^{n} \sum\limits_{i=1}^{k} 1/i = \sum\limits_{i=1}^{n} (n-i+1)/i = (n+1) H_n - n$. □

In the third group we list some frequently used inequalities.

I1) $\ln(1+x) \leq x$

I2) $\ln(1+x) \geq x/(1+x)$ for $x \leq 0$

Proof: Consider the line through point $(1,0)$ with slope $\frac{d}{dy} \ln(1+y)\big|_{y=x} = \frac{1}{1+x}$. This line is below $\ln(1+x)$ at point x. □

I3) $\ln(1+x) \geq x/(1-\delta)$ for $-\delta \leq x \leq 0$

    Proof: immediate from I2) .

I4) $e^x \geq 1+x$

I5) $e^x - 1 \leq x \cdot e^{x_0}$ for $0 \leq x \leq x_0$.

Bibliography

We use the following abbreviations for journals and proceedings:

ACTA   Acta Informatica
CACM   Communications of the ACM
EIK   Elektronische Informationsverarbeitung und Kybernetik
FCT   Foundations of Computing Theory
FOCS   IEEE Symposium on Foundations of Computer Science
ICALP   International Colloquium on Automata, Languages and
                Programming
Inf & Control   Information and Control
IPL   Information Processing Letters
JACM   Journal of the ACM
JCSS   Journal of Computer and System Sciences
LNCS   Springer Lecture Notes in Computer Science
MFCS   Mathematical Foundations of Computer Science
SICOMP   SIAM Journal of Computing
STOC   ACM Symposium on Theory of Computing
TCS   Theoretical Computer Science

Adel'son-Velskii, G.M., Landis, Y.M. (1962): An algorithm for the
    organization of information, Soviet Math. Dokl. 3, 1259-1262

Adleman, L. (1978): Two Theorems of random polynomial Time, 19th
    FOCS, 75-83

Aho, A.V., Hopcroft, J.E., Ullman, J.D. (1974): The Design and Analysis
    of Computer Algorithms, Addison Wesley

Altenkamp, D., Mehlhorn, K. (1980): Codes: Unequal Letter Costs,
    Unequal Probabilities, JACM 27, 412-427

Bayer, P.J. (1975): Improved Bounds on the Cost of Optimal and Balanced
    Binary Search Trees, Technical Report, Dept. of Computer Science,
    MIT

Bayer, R., McCreight, E. (1972): Organization and Maintenance of Large
    Ordered Indizes, ACTA INFORMATICA 1, 173-189

Bayer, R., Schkolnik, M. (1977): Concurrency of Operations on B-Trees,
    ACTA INFORMATICA 9, 1-22

Ben-Or, M. (1983): Lower Bounds for Algebraic Decision Trees,
    15th STOC, 80-86

Bent, S.W., Sleator, D.D., Tarjan, R.E. (1980): Biased 2-3 Trees,
    21st FOCS, 248-254

Bentley, J.L., Haken, D., Saxe, J.B. (1980): A General Method for
    Solving Divide-and-Conquer Recurrences, SIGACT Newsletter 12, 36-44

Bentley, J.L., McGeoch, C. (1982): Worst-case analysis of self-
    organizing sequential search heuristics, Proc. of the 20th
    Allerton Conference on Communication, Control, and Computing

Bird, R.S. (1980): Tabulation Techniques for Recursive Programs, ACM
    Computing Surveys 12, 403-417

Blum, N., Mehlhorn, K. (1980): On the Average Number of Rebalancing
    Operations in Weight-Balanced Trees, Theoretical Computer
    Science 11, 303-320

Blum, M., Floyd, R.W., Pratt, V.R., Rivest, R.L., Tarjan, R.E. (1972):
    Time Bounds for Selection, JCSS 7, 448-461

Brown, M.R., Tarjan, R.E. (1978): A Representation for Linear Lists
    with Movable Fingers, 10th STOC, 19-29

Carter, J.L., Wegman, M.N. (1977): Universal Classes of Hash Functions,
    9th STOC, 106-112

Cook, S.A., (1971): Linear Time Simulation of two-way deterministic
    pushdown automata, IFIP Congress, 172-179

Cook, S.A., Reckhow, R.A. (1973): Time bounded random access machines,
    JCSS 7

Eisenbarth, B., Ziviani, N., Gonnet, G.H., Mehlhorn, K., Wood, D. (1982):
    The Theory of Fringe Analysis and its Application to 2-3 Trees and
    B-trees, Inform. & Control 55, 125-174

Elgot, C.C., Robinson, A. (1964): Random Access Stored Program Machines,
    JACM 11, 365-399

Emde Boas, P.v. (1977): Preserving order in a forest in less than loga-
    rithmic time and linear space, IPL 6, 80-82

Emde Boas, P.v., Kaas, R., Zijlstra, E. (1977): Design and Implementa-
    tion of an efficient priority queue, Math. Systems Theory 10,
    99-127

Fagin, R., Nievergelt, J., Pippenger, N., Strong, H.R. (1979):
    Extendible Hashing - A Fast Access Method for Dynamic Files,
    ACM Trans. of Database Systems 4, 315-344

Flajolet , Ph., Steyaert, J.M. (1982): A branching process arising in
    dynamic hashing, trie searching and polynomial factorization, 9th
    JCALP, LNCS 140, 239-251

Floyd, F.W. (1964): Algorithm 245: treesort 3, CACM 7, 701

Fredkin, E. (1960): Trie Memory, CACM 3, 490-499

Fredman, M.L. (1975): Two Applications of a Probabilistic Search Tech-
    nique: Sorting X+Y and Building Balanced Search Trees, 7th STOC,
    240-244

Fredman, M.L., Komlós, J., Szemeredi, E. (1982): Storing a Sparse Table
    with O(1) Worst Case Access Time, 23rd FOCS, 165-169

Garsia, A.M., Wachs, M.L. (1977): A new algorithm for minimum cost
    binary trees, SICOMP 4, 622-642

Gonnet, G.H. (1981): Expected Length of the longest probe sequence in
    hash code searching, JACM 28, 289-304

Gonnet, G.H., Munro, J.I., Suwanda, H. (1979): Toward Self-Organizing
    Linear Search, 20th FOCS, 169-174

Gotlieb, C.C., Walker, W.A. (1972): A Top-Down Algorithm for Construc-
    ting Nearly Optimal Lexicographical Trees, Graph Theory and Com-
    puting, Academic Press

Gries, D. (1971): Compiler Construction for digital computers, John
    Wiley & Sons, New York

Guibas, L.J., McCreight, E.M., Plass, M.F., Roberts, J.R. (1977):
    A new representation for linear lists, 9th STOC, 49-60

Guibas, L.J., Sedgewick, R. (1978): A dichromatic framework for balanced trees, 19th FOCS, 8-21

Güttler, R., Mehlhorn, K., Schneider, W. (1980): Binary Search Trees: Average and Worst Case Behavior, EIK 16, 41-61

Hendricks, W.J. (1976): An Account of Self-Organizing Systems, SICOMP 5, 715-723

Hoare, C.A.R. (1962): Quicksort, Computer Journal 5, 10-15

Hong, J.W. (1979): On Lower Bounds on Time Complexity of Some Algorithms, Scientia Sinica 22, 890-900

Hotz, G. (1972): Rechenanlagen, Teubner-Studienbücher, Teubner-Verlag, Stuttgart

Hu, T.C., Tucker, A. (1971): Optimum Computer Search Trees, SIAM J. of Applied Math. 21, 514-532

Huddleston, S., Mehlhorn, K. (1982): A new data structure for representing sorted lists, ACTA INFORMATICA 17, 157-184

Huffman, D.A. (1952): A method for the construction of minimum-redundancy codes, Proc. I.R.E. 40, 1098-1101

Jones, N.D. (1977): A note on linear time simulation of deterministic two-way pushdown automata, IPL 6, 110-112

Knuth, D.E. (1968): The Art of Computer Programming, Vol. 1: Fundamental Algorithms, Addison-Wesley

Knuth, D.E. (1971): Optimum Binary Search Trees, ACTA INFORMATICA 1, 14-25, 270

Knuth, D.E. (1973): The Art of Computer Programming, Vol. 3: Sorting and Searching, Addison Wesley

Knuth, D.E., Morris, J., Pratt, V. (1974): Fast Pattern Matching in Strings, Stanford Technical Report, 74-440

Larson, P.A. (1978): Dynamic Hashing, BIT 18, 184-201

Litwin, W. (1978): Virtual Hashing: A Dynamically Changing Hashing, Proc. Very Large Data Base Conf., 517-523

Lum, V.Y., Yuen, P.S.T., Dodd, M. (1971): Key to address transformation techniques, CACM 14, 228-239

Markowsky, G., Carter, J.L., Wegman, M. (1978): Analysis of a universal class of hash functions, MFCS 78, LNCS 64, 345-354

Martin, T.H. (1971): Sorting, ACM Computing Surveys 3, 147-173

McCabe, J. (1965): On Serial Files with Relocatable Records, Operations Research 12, 609-618

Mehlhorn, K. (1975): Nearly Optimum Binary Search Trees, ACTA INFOR-MATICA 5, 287-295

Mehlhorn, K. (1977): Best Possible Bounds on the Weighted Path Length of Optimum Binary Search Trees, SICOMP 6, 235-239

Mehlhorn, K. (1979): Dynamic Binary Search, SICOMP 8, 175-198

Mehlhorn, K. (1979): Sorting Presorted Files, 4th GI-Conference on Theoretical Computer Science, LNCS 67, 199-212

Mehlhorn, K. (1980): An Efficient Algorithm for the Construction of Nearly Optimal Prefix Codes, IEEE Transactions on Information Theory, IT-26, 513-517

Mehlhorn, K. (1981): Arbitrary Weight Changes in Dynamic Trees, RAIRO Theoretical Informatics 15, 183-211

Mehlhorn, K. (1982): On the Program Size of Perfect and Universal Hash Functions, 23rd FOCS, 170-175

Mehlhorn, K. (1982): A partial analysis of height-balanced trees under random insertions and deletions, SICOMP 11, 748-760

Meijer, H., Akl, S.G. (1980): The Design and Analysis of a New Hybrid Sorting Algorithm, IPL 10, 213-218

Nievergelt, I., Reingold, E.M. (1973): Binary Search Trees of Bounded Balance, SICOMP 2, 33-43

Olivié, H.J. (1982): Half-balanced binary search trees, RAIRO Theoreti-cal Informatics 16, 1, 51-71

Paul, W.J., Simon, J. (1980): Decision Trees and Random Access Machines, Symposium über Logik und Algorithmik, Zürich

Perl, Y., Itai, A., Avni, H. (1978): Interpolation Search - A Log Log N Search, CACM 21, 550-553

Perl, Y., Reingold, E. (1977): Understanding the Complexity of Interpolation Search, IPL 6, 219-222

Peterson, W.W. (1957): Uniform Hashing, IBM J. of Research and Development 1, 135-136

Reif, J.W. (1982): On the Power of Probabilistic choice in synchronous parallel computation, 9th JCALP, LNCS 140, 442-450

Rivest, R.L. (1976): On Self-Organizing Sequential Search Heuristics, CACM 19, 63-68

Rivest, R.L., Knuth, D.E. (1972): Computer Sorting, Computing Reviews 13, 283-289

Schmidt, A. (1981): On the Number of relational operators necessary to compute certain functions of real variables, Int. Report, TU Karlsruhe

Sedgewick, R. (1977): The Analysis of Quicksort Programs, ACTA INFORMATICA 7, 327-355

Shepherson, J.C., Sturgis, H.E. (1963): Computability of Recursive Functions, JACM 10, 217-255

Sleator, D.D., Tarjan, R.E. (1983): Self-Adjusting Binary Trees, 15th STOC, 235-245

Sleator, D.D., Tarjan, R.E. (1983): Amortized Efficiency of List Update and Paging Rules, Bell Laboratories, Intern. Report

Sprugnoli, R. (1977): Perfect Hash Functions: A single probe retrieval method for static sets, CACM 20, 841-850

Strassen, V. (1973): Die Berechnungskomplexität von elementarsymmetrischen Funktionen und von Interpolationskoeffizienten, Num. Math. 20, 238-251

Tarjan, R.E. (1975): Efficiency of a good but not linear set union
    algorithm, JACM 22, 215-225

Tarjan, R.E., Yao, A.C.-C. (1979): Storing a Sparse Table, CACM 22,
    606-611

Tsakalidis, A. (1983): Einige Resultate für das Wörterbuchproblem,
    Ph.D. thesis, Univ. des Saarlandes

van Leeuwen, J. (1976): On the construction of Huffmann Trees, 3rd
    ICALP, 382-410, Edinburgh University Press

Williams, J.W.J. (1964): Algorithm 232: Heapsort, CACM 7, 347-348

Willard, D.E. (1983): Searching Nonuniformly Generated Files in log
    log n runtime, to appear SICOMP

Yao, A.C. (1977): Probabilistic Computation - Toward a Unified Measure
    of Complexity, 18th FOCS, 222-227

Yao, A.C.-C. (1978): On Random 2-3 Trees, ACTA INFORMATICA 9, 159-170

Yao, A.C.-C. (1980): A note on the Analysis of Extendible Hashing,
    IPL 11, 84-86

Yao, A.C.-C. (1981): A Lower Bound to Finding Convex Hulls, JACM 28,
    780-787

Yao, A.C.-C. (1982): Theory and Applications of Trapdoor Functions,
    23rd FOCS, 80-91

Yao, F.F. (1980): Efficient Dynamic Programming Using Quadrangle Ine-
    qualities, 12th STOC, 429-435

Subject Index

W. M. Waite, G. Goos

Compiler Construction

1984. 196 figures. XIV, 446 pages
(Texts and Monographs in Computer Science)
ISBN 3-540-90821-8

This text, written by two leaders in the field of
compiler construction, explains to the reader how
compilers for programming languages are built. Describing the necessary tools (and how to create and use
them), the authors break the task into modules,
placing equal emphasis on the action and data aspects
of compilation. Attribute grammars are used extensively to provide a uniform treatment of semantic
analysis, competent code generation and assembly.
The authors also show how intermediate representations can be chosen automatically on the basis of attribute dependence. Thus semantic analysis, code generation and assembly no longer appear idiosyncratic, but
are discussed in terms of a uniform model subject to
automation. This will improve the reader's understanding of the compilation process and of the
decisions that must be made when designing a
compiler.

Springer-Verlag
Berlin
Heidelberg
New York
Tokyo

D. Gries

The Science of Programming

2nd printing. 1983. XV, 366 pages
(Texts and Monographs in Computer Science)
ISBN 3-540-90641-X

Contents: Why Use Logic? Why Prove
Programs Correct? – Propositions and Predica-
tes. – The Semantics of a Small Language. – The
Development of Programs. – Appendices 1–4. –
Answers to Exercises. – References. – Index.

This is the first text to discuss the theory and
principles of computer programming on the basis
of the idea that a proof of correctness and a program should be developed hand in hand. It is
built around the method first proposed by Edsger
W. Dijkstra in his monograph **The discipline of
Programming** (1976), involving a "calculus for
the derivation of programs." Directing his mate-
rials to the computer programmer with at least
one year of experience, Gries presents explicit
principles behind program development, and
then leads the reader through programs using
those principles. Propositions and predicate calculus are presented as a tool for the programmer,
rather than simply an object of study. The reader
should come away with a fresh outlook on programming theory and practice, and assurance to
develop correct programs effectively.

Springer-Verlag
Berlin
Heidelberg
New York
Tokyo